Muslim Medical Ethics

Studies in Comparative Religion
Frederick M. Denny, Series Editor

MUSLIM MEDICAL ETHICS

From Theory to Practice

Edited by
JONATHAN E. BROCKOPP *and* THOMAS EICH

The University of South Carolina Press

A slightly different version of "Enduring the Plague" appeared in *Islamic Law and Society* 14 (2007): 109–29; permission for reprinting this article was granted by Brill Academic Publishers and supported by a grant from the Rock Ethics Institute of Pennsylvania State University. "Competing Needs and Pragmatic Decision-Making" is a revised version of an article that appeared in *Social Science and Medicine* 63, no. 2 (2006): 418–29, under the title "'Women Do What They Want': Islam and Permanent Contraception in Northern Tanzania"; used with permission from the publisher, Elsevier Limited.

Published by the University of South Carolina Press
Columbia, South Carolina 29208

www.sc.edu/uscpress

Manufactured in the United States of America

17 16 15 14 13 12 11 10 09 08 10 9 8 7 6 5 4 3 2 1

Library of Congress Cataloging-in-Publication Data

Muslim medical ethics : from theory to practice / edited by Jonathan E. Brockopp and Thomas Eich.
p. cm. — (Studies in comparative religion)
Includes bibliographical references and index.
ISBN 978-1-57003-753-5 (pbk : alk. paper)
1. Medical ethics—Religious aspects—Islam. 2. Islamic ethics. I. Brockopp, Jonathan E., 1962– II. Eich, Thomas. III. Series: Studies in comparative religion (Columbia, S.C.)
[DNLM: 1. Ethics, Medical. 2. Bioethical Issues. 3. Islam. 4. Religion and Medicine. W 50 M987 2008]
R725.59.M87 2008
297.5—dc22 2008018611

This book was printed on Glatfelter Natures, a recycled paper with 30 percent postconsumer waste content.

CONTENTS

SERIES EDITOR'S PREFACE

The Muslim world in its golden age was a principal global context for development of advanced medical knowledge and practices, including remarkable surgical techniques and diagnostic procedures, that were incorporated in many regions of the African-Eurasian world, including Christian Europe down to as recently as the eighteenth century. The ethical dimensions of medical and healing practices were always of particular importance to Muslims.

The world of modern medical science has witnessed the invention and development of radically new possibilities, practices, and procedures, some of which may challenge traditional religious values. This book is made up of a clearly organized collection of contributions from specialists in a wide and richly diverse range of areas, from the humanities to medicine and the social sciences. The essays address medical and bioethics in relation to such challenging contemporary issues as decisions regarding surplus embryos; fetal gene therapy; the permissibility of organ donation, end-of-life care, and autopsy; women's reproductive rights and contraception from Muslim perspectives; transplants and Muslim ethics in Egypt (and beyond); organ trafficking; negotiating/balancing personal autonomy and religion in clinical settings; teaching Islamic medical ethics (in both traditional Muslim and Western contexts), and more.

There is as yet only a relatively small corpus of published work on Muslim medical ethics. The interdisciplinary balance and diversity of this volume provide a clear and cogent sampling of some significant topics and of regions where Muslim medical, cultural, religious, legal, and ethical principles and practices are developing both in relation to fundamental Islamic teachings and contemporary developments. The book's position is that there is not now nor has there ever been either a "monolithic Islam" or an essential "Islamic position" on medical matters. The editors and contributors provide a balanced discourse about the "theoretical underpinnings of Muslim medical ethics and application of theory in everyday life."

Frederick Mathewson Denny

PREFACE

This book takes advantage of several academic disciplines, from history to anthropology, to examine both the theoretical underpinnings of Muslim medical ethics and the application of that theory in everyday life. It does not provide a set of guidelines for dealing with Muslim patients; nor does it seek to establish the Muslim view on any particular issue. Rather, in considering theory and practice together, it aims to discover something about how Muslims use their rich cultural heritage to respond to the challenges of modern medical technology.

Each of the five sections is preceded by a brief overview that describes the purpose and scope of the section. Although the book is meant to be read as a whole, with historical and theoretical sections providing essential background for the discussion of applied ethics, these divisions also facilitate use of the book in the bioethics, religious studies, or medical anthropology classrooms. In all the essays the authors challenge common assumptions about Islam and Islamic ethical discourse. Like adherents of other faiths, Muslims are deeply engaged by the technological challenges of modern biomedicine, and they respond to those challenges with enormous creativity, whether as patients, doctors, or religious scholars. In aggregate this book demonstrates that religiously based normative statements and medical practice are informed by each other in an ongoing, productive discourse. The breadth and boundaries of this discourse are clarified in discussions of specific issues on the cutting edge of ethical debates: for example, fertilized eggs, patient autonomy, and organ trafficking.

Given the interdisciplinary nature of the book, technical terms have been kept to a minimum, and transliteration of Arabic and other foreign terms has been simplified. Along these lines, dates are given according to the Common Era, not according to the Muslim calendar. For those who know Arabic, technical terms are fully transliterated in the extensive glossary.

This project has been several years in the making and is the result of an unprecedented collaborative effort, beginning with the first International Conference on Medical Law and Ethics in Islam held at the University of Haifa, Israel, in March 2001, continuing through the publication of *Islamic Ethics of Life: Abortion, War, and Euthanasia* (Columbia: University of South Carolina Press, 2003), and culminating in another international conference, "Islam and Bioethics," at Pennsylvania State University in 2006. We would like to acknowledge the efforts of Ersilia Francesca, Sherine Hamdy, Ilhan Ilkilic, Birgit Krawietz, Farhat Moazam,

Ebrahim Moosa, and Vardit Rispler-Chaim, who devoted many hours to the success of this project. Because of a grant from the Institute for Asian and African Studies at Humboldt University, most of these scholars were able to meet for three days of intense, engaged discussion in Berlin, which laid the intellectual foundation for this book; we are especially grateful to the director of the institute, Prof. Dr. Peter Heine, for his support.

At the Pennsylvania State University our efforts were supported by generous grants from the College of Liberal Arts, the Department of History, and the Institute for the Arts and Humanities. We also thank our many colleagues and friends who have supported this project both directly and indirectly, especially Malika Ajouaou, David Atwill, Björn Bentlage, Paula Droege, Gerhard Endress, Johannes Grundmann, David Hufford, Ray Lombra, Sally McMurry, the late Bill Petersen, Nina Safran, Marica Tacconi, and Susan Welch. At the University of South Carolina Press we thank Fred Denny for his early advice on this volume and his commitment to this project, and Linda Haines Fogle for efficiently guiding us through the editorial process. Our students at the Pennsylvania State University and Bochum University deserve thanks for sharpening our wits and keeping us focused on real-life situations.

Above all this book would not have come into being without the generous support of the Rock Ethics Institute of the Pennsylvania State University. The institute provided funds for the hiring of research assistants Sandhya Bhattacharya and Kristen Petersen and devoted both funds and the services of its expert office staff, Kathy Rumbaugh and Barb Edwards. In addition the institute underwrote permission costs for reprinting Justin Stearns's article in this volume.

In gratitude for her vision, dedication, and unflagging support, we dedicate this book to Nancy Tuana, DuPont/Class of 1949 Professor of Philosophy and Director of the Rock Ethics Institute.

THOMAS EICH *and* JONATHAN E. BROCKOPP

Introduction

Medical Ethics and Muslim Perspectives

Both in Europe and in North America, citizens and politicians are becoming keenly aware of their Muslim minority populations, sometimes courting their interests and sometimes discriminating against them. The small town of Lewiston, Maine, for example, has been welcoming immigrants from war-torn Somalia for years. As this Muslim population has increased, certain accommodations have been made, such as the designing of new hospital gowns to conform to their standards of modesty.[1] Interestingly, the staff discovered that many non-Muslim patients also preferred the new, more modest gowns.

There are several points worth noting in this story. First, our globalized world is becoming increasingly intertwined. Muslims in Maine, Catholics in Cairo, and atheists in India force us to reconsider any claim to universal ethical norms. Where those norms do seem universal, such as a prohibition on killing the innocent, they may be interpreted and applied in very different ways. Second, we must resist the temptation to simplify these complex cultures, to reduce them to a single set of guidelines. While it is nice to be offered a choice of hospital gowns, it would be patronizing to say to a patient, "Oh, you're Muslim; you need to wear this gown." The fact is, standards of modesty vary significantly across Muslim cultures, reminding us that in any religious tradition as old and complex as Islam, the relation between theoretical norms and their application in daily life can be quite complex.

The subtitle of this volume, *From Theory to Practice,* highlights our collective engagement with this nexus and our conviction that attention to one without the other is inadequate to the task of describing and understanding Muslim medical ethics. What is at stake here is a conversation between the therapeutic world of body, mind, and healer and the religious world of divine sources and their interpretation. So, while both Muslims and non-Muslims might agree on the Hippocratic dictum that the physician should, above all, "do no harm," they would likely disagree as to why this is so. Our interest here, therefore, is as much in the theoretical underpinnings of such a rule as in the application of that rule to specific circumstances, and in the analysis of those underpinnings, we hope to understand something of the religion of Islam.

The religion of Islam, however, is not nearly so simple as it might first appear; in fact, what counts as a "divine source" can vary significantly. While some Muslim ethicists emphasize the legal tradition as the heart and soul of ethical understanding, others look to spiritual masters, literary texts, or the lived practice of a particular area as more authoritative. Indeed one of the most interesting discussions at the 2006 Pennsylvania State University conference, "Islam and Bioethics," centered on the importance of *adab* as a basis for medical ethics. *Adab,* usually translated as "etiquette," has a broad range of meaning and reflects local usage, though it may make reference to the practice of the Prophet Muhammad (sometimes referred to as "the Prophet") and other paradigmatic figures. It certainly includes what might be called "bedside manner," such as how (or even whether) to tell a patient that he/she is dying of cancer. In recognition of these locally determined perceptions of Islam, we have chosen to call this book *Muslim Medical Ethics,* rather than the more common "Islamic Medical Ethics." Doing so downplays any perception that one person, or one source, can encompass the highly contextualized space of the ethical encounter.

From Theory to Practice also suggests a hierarchy of sorts: theory comes first, and then practice. Indeed, this is precisely the way that many scholars describe medical ethics, especially those ethical systems that depend on reasoned application of principles. It is doubtful, however, that things ever work out this neatly in the world of medical practice. As techniques change or as new diseases appear, the principles must be revisited and adjusted, and so practice affects and sometimes changes theory. In the modern world, consultative bodies try to stay on top of these changes, offering advice to physicians and other health-care practitioners. However, as several contributors to this volume demonstrate, it is ultimately the individual physician and patient who must choose how to interpret and enforce those decisions in everyday life. Therefore the movement "from theory to practice" is also meant to highlight the question: What happens to theoretical ideals when they hit the ground of medical practice?

The Sources for Theory

While medical encounters are almost infinitely variable, the story of Islam is fairly easy to outline. According to Muslim belief, Muhammad had started receiving God's Revelation some fourteen hundred years ago, the year 610 of the Common Era, in Mecca (modern-day Saudi Arabia). This process continued until Muhammad's death in 632. Later these revelations, understood to be the words of God, were collected in the Qur'an that people now possess. However, Muhammad was more than God's mouthpiece. In the year 622 he emigrated from Mecca to a city called Yathrib, which became known as Medina, the city of the Prophet. There the Muslims constituted a distinct sociopolitical group with Muhammad as its leader. Consequently Muhammad filled several social roles at Medina, such as judging in disputes, determining political policy, and even serving as healer. The sayings and deeds of Muhammad during these years were recorded by later generations in a literary form known as hadith. These, in turn, formed the core of a second source of authority for later generations, the so-called Sunna, the way that Muhammad, God's chosen Prophet, did things. Eventually the Sunna was elevated to a position almost equaling that of the Qur'an in Muslim theological, legal, and moral discourse.

At the beginning of this period theological and legal debates had been closely intertwined. However, in the course of the first five hundred years of Islamic history, they were channeled into different disciplines, *kalam* (speculative theology) and *fiqh* (jurisprudence), with specific methods, assumptions, and goals.[2] *Fiqh* actually means "insight" in the sense of a process rather than a fixed result, and it is one of several subdisciplines in a system called Sharia (literally "the way"). Often, Sharia is rendered as "Islamic law," and it does, in fact, include the sort of rules organizing human life, such as regulations for correct economic transactions or criminal law, that are expected from law. Yet, until the modern era, Islamic law was never codified; nor was it ever the exclusive system of law in any culture. Moreover the religious experts (*'ulama'*) consider theological issues and questions of moral conduct to be an integrated part of the Sharia.

This last point can be briefly illustrated with the discussion of elective abortion for the purpose of determining the sex of the child.[3] Does the Sharia allow the abortion of an embryo after its sex has been established by prenatal diagnosis just because the parents would prefer to have a child of the other sex? The *'ulama'* unanimously answer this legal question in the negative.[4] However, then they join this legal judgment with a lengthy discussion of its theological impact within the framework of the Sharia: Does the ability to establish the sex of the unborn by modern technologies infringe on one of God's essential prerogatives? After all, the Qur'an states: "Knowledge of the Hour is with God. He sends down rain, and knows what is in the wombs. No one can tell what tomorrow will bring, nor in what land they are to die" (Q 31:34).

The very fact that this question is asked points to an overlap of legal and theological discussions that is typical for Sharia texts. The authorities cited here are openly worrying about the implications, and sheer power, of modern medicine, pointing to the fact that the premodern sources of law, the Qur'an and the Sunna, did not conceive of a world in which physicians could gain this sort of knowledge or exercise this sort of power over life and death.

The juxtaposition of divine, immutable texts with a rapidly changing therapeutic environment also serves to highlight the role of the *'ulama'* as interpreters of the law. Literally defined as "the people of knowledge," the *'ulama'* hold a revered place in Islamic history. Highly trained in the Qur'an and Sunna, as well as in the arts of interpretation and commentary, these scholars form one vital link between contemporary issues and the divine sources. It follows then that their writings represent Islamic law not as a static, immutable entity but rather as a discursive tradition that seeks to apply God's unchanging law to the ever-changing world in which we live.

Shiites also recognize the authoritative position of the *'ulama';* yet their account of divine sources and the role of scholarly interpretation is slightly different, ultimately stemming from their account of the succession to Muhammad's political and religious leadership by his cousin and son-in-law 'Ali b. Abi Talib. Eventually 'Ali lost his political and military struggle, dying in 661 at Karbala in Iraq.[5] Those who had favored 'Ali over his political opponent Mu'awiya were called the "Party of 'Ali," *shi'atu 'Ali* in Arabic, from which we get the word *Shiite.* During the first centuries following 'Ali's death they developed into a distinct group with its own concepts of political and religious authority. Pivotal was the idea that legitimate political power could be in the hands of only one of 'Ali's progeny, the so-called imams. The sixth of these imams, Ja'far al-Sadiq (d. 765), became one of the most important sources for the development of Shiite *fiqh,* which differed from Sunni *fiqh* in preferring hadith reports passed down through the imams, along with the Sunna of the Imams. Sunnis and Shiites therefore diverge in terms of which hadith collections they deem authoritative, which is one of the reasons for differing developments in Shiite and Sunni statements on bioethical issues.

A second, important difference lies in the structure of contemporary religious authority, which is more hierarchical and more clearly defined among Shiite than among Sunni Muslims. According to the doctrine of the Twelver Shiites, the largest group of Shiites today, the line of 'Ali's successor broke off with the Twelfth Imam. It is believed that he did not die but vanished and waits at a hidden place until the end of the world in order to return. In the absence of the Twelfth Imam, no political authority can be fully legitimate. When Iran was transformed into a Shiite country in the sixteenth century, the *'ulama*'s relation to political power changed, culminating in the nineteenth-century doctrine of the *marja' al-taqlid* (example for emulation). According to this doctrine, religious learning legitimizes interventions of the scholars into worldly affairs. In a hierarchical peer system a student of religion can climb several steps, each of which signifies a new level of religious learning. Few manage to get to the highest level of *marja' al-taqlid.* A *marja'* is considered learned enough by his peers, as well as a substantial number of Shiite Muslims, to be declared their ultimate authority in worldly affairs. This means that the followers of a particular *marja'* must live exclusively according to his rulings. They cannot change their *marja'* as long as he is alive. Since choosing a particular *marja'* is a deeply individual affair, *marja's* can have followers all over the world, who also support them financially. Therefore the spiritual as well as political role of the Shiite *'ulama'* differs significantly from the situation of their

Sunni colleagues, who cannot claim exclusive followership; nor do Sunni *'ulama'* have significant resources of income that are not controlled by the state.[6]

As pointed out above, the *fiqh* is highly dynamic and constantly reacts to social change. Recent research in Sunni *fiqh* has shown that this process of adaptation took the way of several textual genres, primarily commentaries and fatwas.[7] A fatwa is a nonbinding legal opinion issued by a religious scholar in response to a request (in Shiism, however, a fatwa by a *marja'* is considered binding to those who have given allegiance to that *marja'*). Fatwas on the same issue can differ depending on time, space, or author, thus producing a remarkable pluralism in opinion. Eventually certain opinions started dominating the scholarly discourse and historically were integrated into the standard reference works of *fiqh*, whereas others were forgotten and are now lost to us. Today fatwas are given in any imaginable form of human communication: by telephone, on the Internet, on television or radio, and by the classical handwritten form.

In their assessments or rulings, the *'ulama'* are guided by certain principles such as public benefit (*maslaha*), and changing circumstances mean that the application of the same principle might produce different results. For example, the *'ulama'* were, at first, reluctant to allow organ transplantation in the late 1960s and early 1970s. On the one hand, they argued, there is the harm done to the donor's body by removing its organs and thus violating its corporal integrity, which has to be respected during life as well as after death. Against this the possible benefit has to be weighed: the improved health conditions of the organ recipient and her ability to survive her disease. This changed significantly in the mid-1980s as transplants became more common and more effective, tipping the balance of harm and benefit.[8] Thus apparently contradictory rulings relying on similar principles can be explained by changed historical circumstances.

The Practice of Muslim Medical Ethics

Muslim approaches toward bioethical questions were first discussed in Western languages in the 1960s with several extensive articles about the treatment of contraception and abortion in Islamic law.[9] These studies were linked to the attempted introduction of population-control programs in Middle Eastern countries, and they relied primarily on Arabic texts of classical Islamic jurisprudence (*fiqh*). Primary reliance on Arabic sources is somewhat reasonable in terms of the theory of Islamic ethics, but in terms of practice, it overemphasizes the importance of the Arabic-speaking world (fewer than one-fifth of Muslims today). Nonetheless dependence on Arabic sources continues to characterize the study of Muslim bioethics even in the early twenty-first century.

After little interest in Muslim bioethics in Western academia and only a few publications in the field by Muslim scholars in the 1970s, the 1980s saw the start of bioethical debates in recently created institutions, such as the Majma' al-fiqh al-islami of the Organization of Islamic Conferences (Jedda) and the al-Majmaʿ al-fiqhi al-islami of the Muslim World League (Mecca); both are usually translated as the Islamic Fiqh Academy. The bioethical debates at these institutions are linked to the introduction of modern medical technologies such as in vitro fertilization (IVF) or respiratory machines into Middle Eastern countries during the 1980s. Wherever these new technologies were introduced in the world, they produced significant legal and ethical debates. Not surprisingly then, Muslim religious scholars entered sometimes heated discussions about, for example, the permissibility of switching off respiratory machines in the case of a brain-death diagnosis or gamete donation in procedures of artificial inseminations. The different stances taken in these religious debates were analyzed in several groundbreaking studies published in the 1980s and early 1990s, which can partly be viewed as contributions to these very debates in their own right.[10]

The time since the early 1990s has seen three key developments both in the field of Muslim bioethics and in its study. The first was a rising awareness of bioethical issues on a global level, manifested in the creation of a special committee at UNESCO to follow progress in the life sciences and their applications, the International Bioethics Committee (IBC), in 1993. After its inception, countries of predominantly Muslim populations were well represented at this institution.[11] This institutionalized representation of Muslim approaches to bioethical concerns on an international level has been followed by the creation of national bioethics committees in several countries, such as Tunisia, Egypt, and Saudi Arabia, since the second half of the 1990s.

The rising awareness of the increasingly globalized nature of bioethical issues led to a second important development, an increasing interest in Muslim bioethics among bioethicists publishing in Western languages.[12] This trend was manifested in the political arena in the context of the stem cell debate, in which national bioethics committees of countries where Muslims are a small minority (for example, Israel, Germany, and the United States) consulted Muslim religious scholars' opinions on this issue.[13] The turn of the millennium has continued to see an increasing interest in Muslim ethics, although still insufficient,[14] in publications relating to the clinical setting.[15]

The third and perhaps most important development in the study of Muslim bioethics since the 1990s is the increasing interest of medical anthropologists in the Muslim world.[16] Their studies focus on the application of legal, moral, or ethical norms in the medical sector, thus addressing, among other things, the decisive question of what statements by Muslim religious experts actually mean to Muslim patients. The anthropological focus on categories such as class and gender, as well as the comparison of cases from the whole of the Muslim world, has therefore broadened the field significantly. The fundamental importance of these studies lies in their actor-oriented approach, showing that the acts of Muslim patients are influenced by a wide variety of factors; religious norms expounded by the *'ulama'* form one of the factors, but perhaps not the most important one. These studies are therefore instrumental in forcing researchers to abandon mono-causal and monolithic explanations of Muslim behavior. The case orientation of many of these studies can also be used to contextualize rulings and discussions by the *'ulama'*.

Anthropologists may also be credited with significantly expanding the scope of research to non-Arab countries such as Iran, Tajikistan, or Pakistan and also to the situation of Muslim migrants in Western countries.[17] However, the effect of this increase in scope, as well as the inclusion of non-Arab Muslims in international bodies such as the IBC of UNESCO, is to question the traditional authority of Arab *'ulama'*. Moreover the social science focus on descriptive ethics over normative ethics also tends to displace the traditional role of legal authorities in determining "Islamic" bioethics. For many Muslims, bioethical issues are resolved on the basis of economic or family concerns as much as specifically religious concerns. Moreover, where religion is invoked, it may well be in the guise of Sufi precepts or the words of a popular preacher, rather than an official fatwa.[18] At the 2006 Pennsylvania State University conference, no single issue was more contentious than the debate between those who invoked traditional Islamic authorities and those who appealed to the "lived experience" of Islam. By including all of these voices here, alongside those of physicians, historians, and others, this volume seeks to enrich the debate while also encouraging a broad view of this emerging field. At the same time, however, we recognize that taking this broad view of the field can have the effect of de-legitimizing traditional centers of authority.

Among the current developments in the field of Muslim bioethics, two seem particularly noteworthy. First, the literature thus far has primarily addressed Sunni sources almost exclusively. Recently the urgent need to study discussions among Shiite *'ulama'* has been recognized especially because of remarkable developments in Iran concerning birth control, IVF, and organ transplantation, affecting Shiite populations in other countries as well.[19] Second, the question of how to integrate Muslim bioethics into the education of medical practitioners is only now being asked,[20] as a logical extension of new interest in clinical issues in Muslim bioethics. Therefore scholars involved in the academic study of Muslim bioethics must now keep in mind new sets of questions such as pedagogy, accessibility of original sources, and specific situations in the daily life of medical practice.

This Volume

The above discussion demonstrates that the field of Muslim medical ethics has been gradually moving away from a static approach that downplays the variety of Muslims' contributions to bioethical debates. Both the inherent dynamics of the

Sharia and the lived experiences of over a billion Muslims suggest that a discursive, interdisciplinary approach is warranted. We argue that combining several approaches, methodologies, and disciplines facilitates a more thorough understanding of these contributions and their different layers of meaning. The disciplines brought together in this volume—humanities, medicine, and social science—all depend on the theoretical framework of the Sharia, and yet they also demonstrate the contingent nature of Islamic law in the context of Muslims' lives.

To highlight the possibilities of this approach, this book has been organized thematically, working from historical and theoretical foundations, through application of norms in various local and clinical settings, to the questions of teaching bioethics. The attentive reader will note, however, that some topics are treated rather extensively (for example, assisted reproductive technologies and organ transplantation), while others are completely absent (for example, gene therapy and cloning). We have made no attempt to cover all major bioethical issues, and this uneven treatment should not be seen as reflective of Muslim interests in any particular issue. It is, however, an indication of the great need for more work in this emerging field.

This book begins with a look back through history. Samar Farage and Justin Stearns provide insights into how ethical points of view on medical issues are shaped by scientific assumptions, which vary according to historical circumstances. Farage traces the history of the pulse as a major tool of diagnosis in Galeno-Islamic medicine. The conceptualization of the pulse was linked to an integrated understanding of the human body as a combination of matter and spirit, thus forming a stark contrast to the objectified human body in the contemporary clinical setting of Western medicine. Stearns's analysis of debates on the bubonic plague likewise demonstrates that different scientific assumptions led to different conclusions among Spanish *'ulama'* of the fourteenth century. Moreover these scientific assumptions, particularly the issue of whether or not the plague was contagious, had important theological implications, not unlike today's debates on abortion and euthanasia.

The next section, comprising essays by Thomas Eich and Sherine Hamdy, brings us into the modern era, analyzing bioethical issues in the Sharia on the normative level. Eich addresses the possible use of frozen embryos for research, while Hamdy looks at organ transplantation. The primary interest of these authors, however, is in the way that authoritative ethical statements are constructed in the contemporary Islamic world. For example, Eich discovers that two leading ethics committees produced contradictory statements on the use of frozen embryos for research. Through a detailed analysis of the deliberative records from those committees, he traces the political and structural differences that led to these differing positions. Hamdy is concerned with another form of authority, the relationship between the *fuqaha'* (jurists; those trained in the discipline of *fiqh*) and the public media in Egypt. She shows that opposing fatwas issued in this context can be explained by differing views on the technology of organ transplantation and its benefits for society rather than by diverging approaches to Qur'an, Sunna, or Sharia principles.

Contributions to the next section scrutinize the ways in which accepted religious norms are applied to specific medical challenges in African and Middle Eastern societies. Susi Krehbiel Keefe describes Tanzanian Muslim women's attitudes toward sterilization, a practice that is commonly regarded as forbidden by the *'ulama'*. Krehbiel Keefe shows the many different considerations that play into individual decisions, arguing that they are shaped pragmatically and not simply determined by religious teachings. In her contribution on infertility in Mali, Viola Hörbst describes the different layers of interaction between a husband and his wife in the case of male-factor infertility, arguing that it severely impacts on gender relations within the marriage because of society's stigmatization of male infertility. Like Krehbiel Keefe, she also argues that religion is only one among several other factors shaping decisions. Debra Budiani and Othman Shibly describe the buying and selling of human organs in Egypt, showing how these practices are justified by the organ vendors as well as organ buyers. Interestingly the organ vendors refer, among other things, to a religious obligation to provide their children with means for proper living and education as justification for selling one of their kidneys. Hamza Eskandarani traces the standards in the assisted reproductive technology sector in countries of the Gulf Cooperative Council (Bahrain, Kuwait, Oman, Qatar, Saudi Arabia, and the United Arab Emirates). He demonstrates that despite the existence of ethical guidelines issued by the *'ulama'* for this sector, no common standards are applied in the laboratories on a national or an international level.

The three studies of the next section address the experiences of Muslim minority populations in Europe and North America, specifically regarding care at the end of life. Iqbal Jaffer (a medical student) and Shabbir Alibhai (a practicing physician) draw on their experience with the Shiite communities of Toronto, Canada, to point out key issues that differentiate this community from those of other Muslims. As mentioned above, Shiism has received little discussion in the literature on Muslim medical ethics, and their extensive interview with a leading Shiite cleric demonstrates the ways that religious authorities depend on the clinical experience of physicians. In the following essay Shabbir Alibhai joins Michael Gordon to compare Shiite end-of-life-ethics with the views of Orthodox Judaism. Discussing a series of hypothetical cases, they show that in both traditions concerns for a patient's autonomy can be outweighed by family or community considerations. Such an attitude presents a stark contrast to the dominant approach to bioethics in North America, based on the school of Beauchamp and Childress, which has little place for family concerns.[21] The final contribution to this section, by Stef Van den Branden and Bert Broeckaert, moves us to European Muslim communities. In their extensive interviews with elderly Moroccan migrants in Belgium, they discovered a set of attitudes toward palliative care and euthanasia quite different from that of most Belgians. For these Muslims, pain and the process of dying are seen as entirely within the context of God's decree. Therefore pain-control measures, even if taken to extreme limits, are considered to be unproblematic. However, euthanasia is rejected as an unwarranted intervention into God's will. In all three of these studies, the authors share a deep concern that health-care workers in North America and Europe develop some familiarity with these important minority populations.

The fifth and final section of this book takes this concern one step further by addressing issues related to the teaching of Muslim medical ethics. Hasan Shanawani and Mohammad Hassan Khalil open up this section by examining one of the key tools used by medical and bioethics researchers worldwide. In their review of articles on Muslim medical ethics in major medical journals, they point out the paucity of articles overall. Their review also suggests that authors, and perhaps journal editors, tend to avoid in-depth or complex discussions and that as a result, the diversity of the Muslim world is poorly represented in the literature most commonly used by medical practitioners. Given the general lack of knowledge about the Muslim world in the West, these findings may not be surprising, but in the following essay Hassan Bella finds a similar situation in Saudi Arabia, his country of residence. To find out what his colleagues in the medical profession think, he engaged in a creative "Delphi process" with medical personnel in Saudi Arabia to consider both the content of Islamic medical ethics (IME) and how to teach this subject. The initial response was quite mixed, but the Delphi process is a controlled conversation that can move the participants toward consensus on these key questions. In the final contribution to this section, Abdulaziz Sachedina draws on his experience in teaching about Islamic bioethics both in Iran and in North America, arguing that a comparative approach is essential in both environments, but for very different reasons. His sample syllabus offers a template for those interested in teaching a course in a university setting, but his overall reflections on the field form a fitting final essay for the book.

The last word, however, is left for Marcia Inhorn, one of the most important scholars in this field. After critically assessing the contributions of this book, she issues a significant challenge, one that we share. Inhorn points out that focusing on individual ethical issues, such as stem cells, euthanasia, or cloning, can be problematic insofar as it prevents scholars from connecting to other bioethical concerns. One might even identify a canon of key issues that form the content of many courses in bioethics at colleges and universities. While such a focus has the virtue of bringing a nascent field such as Muslim medical ethics into the heart of bioethical debates in the West, Inhorn points out that it runs the risk of diverting us from reflecting on HIV/AIDS, immunizations, drug trials, and the health effects of war, violence, and environmental degradation.

To return to the Somali immigrants in Maine, accommodating the needs of these Muslim patients is an important task. Redesigning hospital gowns can be a way of humanizing the clinical encounter. However, incorporating such changes into our presumptions of health, medicine, and ethics should mark the beginning of this ethical encounter, not its culmination. If done well, learning about Muslim medical ethics ought to challenge our very perception of the categories and content of ethics. In the case of these Somali immigrants, hearing about the war and famine that have caused them to flee to Maine should provoke us to broaden bioethics to include the health effects of warfare and environmental devastation. It may also lead us to consider the causes of that war and the many ties, both positive and negative, that bind us to the peoples of East Africa, South Asia, the Middle East, and the rest of the world. In this way Muslim medical ethics can form an integral part of the ethical reflection of all peoples, encouraging us to reflect critically on our own values.

NOTES

1. Cathryn Domrose, "I-See-U: Nurses, Hospitals Getting to Bottom of Johnny Coat Alternatives for Modest Patients," *NurseWeek,* March 14, 2005, www.nurseweek.com/news/Features/05–03/JohnnyCoat.asp.

2. Baber Johansen, *Contingency in a Sacred Law: Legal and Ethical Norms in the Muslim* Fiqh (Leiden: Brill, 1999), 19–40.

3. See, for example, Shukrī Sālih Ibrāhīm al-Sa‘īdī, "Al-Tahakkum fī nau‘ al-janīn," *al-Sharī‘a wa-l-qānūn: Majallat Kullīyat al-sharī‘a wa-l-qānūn bi-Jāmi‘at al-Azhar bi-l-Qāhira* 23, no. 2 (2001): 329–91.

4. This consensus has not, however, prevented Muslims from seeking to determine the sex of a fetus in other ways. See Vardit Rispler-Chaim, "Contemporary Muftis between Bioethics and Social Reality: Pre-selection of the Sex of a Fetus as a Paradigm," *Journal of Religious Ethics* 38 (March 2008): 53–76.

5. For a useful overview of Shiism, see Moojan Momen, *An Introduction to Shi`i Islam: The History and Doctrines of Twelver Shi`ism* (New Haven, Conn.: Yale University Press, 1985). For a more detailed discussion of debates over authoritative leadership, see Asma Afsaruddin, *Excellence and Precedence: Medieval Islamic Discourse on Legitimate Leadership* (Leiden: Brill, 2002).

6. There are, of course, exceptions. Masters of Sufi orders, such as the Tijanis or the Mourids, can serve in much the same capacity and are also supported by a worldwide network of followers. See Leonardo Villalón, *Islamic Society and State Power in Senegal* (Cambridge: Cambridge University Press, 1995).

7. Wael Hallaq, *Authority, Continuity and Change in Islamic Law* (Cambridge: Cambridge University Press, 2001); Baber Johansen, "Legal Literature and the Problem of Change: The Case of the Land Rent," in *Islam and Public Law: Classical and Contemporary Studies,* ed. Chibli Mallat (London: Graham and Trotman, 1993), 29–47.

8. Ebrahim Moosa, "Languages of Change in Islamic Law: Redefining Death in Modernity," *Islamic Studies* 38, no. 3 (1999): 305–42; Johannes Grundmann, "Scharia, Hirntod und Organtransplantation: Kontext und Wirkung zweier islamischer Rechtsentscheidungen im Nahen und Mittleren Osten," *Orient* 45 (2004): 27–46.

9. Omaia Elwan, "Empfängnisregelung und Abtreibung im Islam," in *Rechtsvergleichung und Rechtsvereinheitlichung,* ed. Eduard Wahl and others (Heidelberg: Winter, 1967), 439–70; Elwan, "Das Problem der Empfängnisregelung und Abtreibung: Die herrschende Auffassung des Staates und der religiösen Kreise in islamischen Ländern," *Zeitschrift für vergleichende Rechtswissenschaft* 10 (1968): 25–80; Erwin Gräf, "Die Stellungnahme des islamischen Rechts zu Geburtenregelung (tanẓīm al-nasl) und Geburtenbeschränkung (taḥdīd al-nasl)," in *Der Orient in der Forschung,* ed. Wilhelm Hoenerbach (Wiesbaden: Harrassowitz, 1967), 209–32; W. DeJong, "Abortion and Islam (in Dutch)," *Tijdschrift voor ziekenverpleging* 21, no. 16 (1968): 666; DeJong, "Islam and Medical Ethics (in Dutch)," *Tijdschrift voor ziekenverpleging* 23, no. 2 (1970): 63–65, and 23, no. 7 (1970): 359–61. Several articles on abortion, family planning, and contraception appeared in English in *Birthright,* the journal of the Family Planning Association of Pakistan, in the early 1970s. In addition Hassan Hathout began publishing in the 1970s on issues of abortion and contraception, in English, in Middle Eastern medical journals.

10. Abul Fadl Mohsin Ebrahim, "Islamic Ethics and the Implications of Modern Biomedical Technology: An Analysis of Some Issues Pertaining to Reproductive Control, Biotechnical Parenting and Abortion" (Ph.D. diss., Temple University, 1986); Fazlur Rahman, *Health and Medicine in the Islamic Tradition: Change and Identity* (New York: Crossroad, 1987); Birgit Krawietz, *Die Hurma: Schariatrechtlicher Schutz vor Eingriffen in die körperliche Unversehrtheit nach arabischen Fatwas des 20. Jahrhunderts* (Berlin: Duncker & Humblot, 1991); Vardit Rispler-Chaim, *Islamic Medical Ethics in the Twentieth Century* (Leiden: Brill, 1993).

11. For a documentation of the work of IBC, see its home page at http://portal.unesco.org/shs/en/ev.php-URL_ID=1879&URL_DO=DO_TOPIC&URL_SECTION=201.html.

12. See, for example, Hassan Hathout, "Islamic Basis for Biomedical Ethics," in *Transcultural Dimensions in Medical Ethics,* ed. Edmund Pellegrino and others (Frederick, Md.: University Publishing Group, 1992), 57–72; Hassan Hathout and B. Andrew Lustig, "Bioethical Developments in Islam," in *Theological Developments in Bioethics: 1990–92* (Dordrecht: Kluwer, 1993), 133–47; Gamal I. Serour, "Islam and the Four Principles," in *Principles of Health Care Ethics,* ed. Raanan Gillon (Chichester: John Wiley and Sons, 1994), 75–91.

13. See, for example, Abdulaziz Sachedina, "Human Clones: An Islamic View," in *The Human Cloning Debate,* ed. Glenn McGee (Berkeley, Calif.: Berkeley Hills Books, 1998), 231–44; Report of the Bioethics Advisory Committee of the Israel Academy of Sciences and Humanities on the Use of Embryonic Stem Cells for Therapeutic Research, August 2001, http://www.academy.ac.il/bioethics/English/main-e.html, accessed April 3, 2007; Wortprotokoll der Jahrestagung des Nationalen Ethikrats 23. Oktober 2003 Der Umgang mit vorgeburtlichem Leben in anderen Kulturen, http://www.ethikrat.org/veranstaltungen/jahrestagungen.html, accessed April 3, 2007.

14. In this book Hasan Shanawani and Mohammad Khalil describe the relevant articles in some detail in "Reporting on 'Islamic Bioethics' in the Medical Literature: Where Are the Experts?" Abdulaziz Sachedina offers an explanation for the lack of critical engagement in "Defining the Pedagogical Parameters of Islamic Bioethics."

15. See, for example, A. S. Daar and B. al-Khitamy, "Bioethics for Clinicians: 21. Islamic Bioethics," *Canadian Medical Association Journal* 164, no. 1 (2001): 60–63; A. R. Gatrad and A. Sheikh, "Medical Ethics and Islam: Principles and Practice," *Archives of Disease in Childhood* 84, no. 1 (January 2001): 72–75; Ilhan Ilkilic, *Begegnung und Umgang mit muslimischen Patienten: Eine Handreichung für die Gesundheitsberufe* (Tübingen: Interfak. Zentrum für Ethik in den Wissenschaften, Eberhard-Karls-Universität Tübingen, 2003).

16. To name only two, see, for example, Sandra D. Lane, "Gender and Health: Abortion in Urban Egypt," in *Population, Poverty and Politics in Middle East Cities,* ed. Michael E. Bonine (Gainesville: University of Florida Press, 1997), 208–34; and Marcia C. Inhorn, *Local Babies, Global Science: Gender, Religion, and In Vitro Fertilization in Egypt* (New York: Routledge, 2003).

17. Diane M. Tober, Mohammad-Hossein Taghdisi, and Mohammad Jalali, "'Fewer Children, Better Life' or'As Many as God Wants,'" *Medical Anthropology Quarterly* 20, no. 1 (2006): 50–71 (for Iran); Farhat Moazam, *Bioethics and Organ Transplantation in a Muslim Society: A Study in Culture, Ethnography, and Religion* (Bloomington: Indiana University Press, 2006) (for Pakistan); Salmaan Keshavjee, "Bleeding Babies in Badakhshan Symbolism, Materialism, and the Political Economy of Traditional Medicine in Post-Soviet Tajikistan," *Medical Anthropology Quarterly* 20, no. 1 (2006): 72–93; Carolyn F. Sargent, "Reproductive Strategies and Islamic Discourse: Malian Migrants Negotiate Everyday Life in Paris, France," *Medical Anthropology Quarterly* 20, no. 1 (2006): 31–49.

18. Compare the essays by Sherine Hamdy and Hassan Bella in this volume.

19. Marcia C. Inhorn, "Making Muslim Babies: IVF and Gamete Donation in Sunni versus Shi'a Islam," *Culture, Medicine and Psychiatry* 30 (2006): 427–50; Homa Hoodfar and Samad Assadpour, "The Politics of Population Policy in the Islamic Republic of Iran," *Studies in Family Planning* 31 (2000): 19–34; Behrouz Broumand, "Transplantation Activities in Iran," *Experimental and Clinical Transplantation* 3, no. 1 (2005): 333–37. One of the few scholars to have included Shiite discussions into his analysis of Islamic bioethics from the start is Abdulaziz Sachedina.

20. P. R. Del Pozo and J. J. Fins, "The Globalization of Education in Medical Ethics and Humanities: Evolving Pedagogy at Weill Cornell Medical College in Qatar," *Academic Medicine: Journal of the Association of American Medical Colleges* 80, no. 2 (2005): 135–40; K. U. al-Umran and others, "Medical Ethics and Tomorrow's Physicians: An Aspect of Coverage in the Formal Curriculum," *Medical Teacher* 28/29 (March 2006): 182–84.

21. T. L. Beauchamp and J. F. Childress, *Principles of Biomedical Ethics* (Oxford: Oxford University Press, 2001).

ONE

Before the Biomedical Paradigm

Overview

One striking aspect of debates among contemporary Muslim scholars is the use of historical references: the Qur'an, the practices of the Prophet Muhammad, and also the great physicians of Islamic history. These paradigms are held to be true in an ultimate sense, relevant for Muslims today and in the future; they provide formative concepts for modern Muslim medical ethics. However, they need careful reading and are not always easy to interpret. In the two studies of this section, Samar Farage and Justin Stearns provide insights into a world before the biomedical paradigm, that is, a world in which fundamental assumptions about medicine and its boundaries differed radically from those of today.

The first essay, by Samar Farage, takes up the unlikely topic of the pulse. In our world of PET scans and MRIs, taking a patient's pulse is an expected, though hardly necessary, part of the physician's office ritual; it is rarely seen as a diagnostic tool. In contrast Farage finds that the pulse was of central importance to traditional Islamic medicine, not merely because premodern physicians did not have the benefit of modern technology, but because the whole paradigm of medicine and healing was different.

Premodern Islamic medicine drew much of its inspiration from ancient Greece, so much so that Farage calls it the "Galeno-Islamic" tradition, after the Greek physician Galen (d. circa 200). She shows that illness in this world was not the attack of a foreign entity (germ or virus), but rather the result of some form of imbalance. This imbalance could have several causes, some of which today could be called "physical," others "psychological." Further, since the human being was viewed as intimately connected to the rest of the universe, indeed a microcosm reflecting and relating to the macrocosm, disturbances in this relationship were seen as possible causes of sickness. In this context the pulse was not seen as a mere beat, which could easily be measured by counting; it was seen as the core expression of the multifaceted web of different relations in which the patient was entangled. It was "rhythmic," "qualitative," and "ensouled," as Farage puts it. Therefore the pulse had to be "read"; it had to be "understood."

To read a pulse required a perception of the doctor-patient relationship entirely different from that of today. The doctor had to get in touch with the sick person directly, without the use of instruments. The relationship between doctor and patient was "mimetic": they mirrored one another and affected one another. The doctor's physical touch when reading the pulse was part of a routine that could include sniffing urine, tasting perspiration, and interviewing family members.

In the modern world, this intimate relationship has been transformed into a diagnostic one, but Farage argues that this is the result of a whole shift in perception, one that is not entirely desirable. Early modern concepts of "mind-body dualism," for example, split the "self" off from the body, which was seen as mere matter. The heart became a pump, no longer the seat of love, anger, and perception; physicians were separated from their patients by instruments, such as the stethoscope, and the pulse lost its music. The history of the pulse then serves as a stark reminder of the changes that have taken place in the world of medicine over the past several hundred years. These changes demand that students of ethics pay close attention to historical arguments, and that we consider the contexts within which these premodern physicians operated. As Farage points out, contemporary Muslim medical ethics should not focus exclusively on texts from the legal tradition, but should also consider historical, medical, and philosophical texts as part of a more comprehensive discussion of ethical issues in medicine.

The second essay in this section, by Justin Stearns, focuses more narrowly on two authors from fourteenth-century Muslim Spain. In this study of the concept of contagion, Stearns compares two legal scholars (Ibn Lubb and Ibn al-Khatib) who held opposite views about the right behavior when facing the plague. Should one flee from an area affected by the plague or not? The answer to this question was not as obvious as it might seem. First, according to Ibn Lubb, fleeing from the plague could be interpreted as an attempt to flee from God's will. Here, Ibn Lubb is making reference to a fundamental premise of Islamic theology, that God is the source of all things, both good and bad. If the plague strikes your town by God's leave, the proper role of the human creature is to accept God's will. While this may seem odd, a similar argument lies at the heart of the way many religious people face death and dying.

The second problem with this behavior is the more subtle issue of contagion, which seems to suggest that a disease such as the plague has a mind of its own. In other words it spreads of its own will, in contradiction of the will of God. The argument that a disease is contagious, then, could be regarded as denying God's omnipotence and therefore tantamount to blasphemy. Ibn al-Khatib's main counterargument was empiricism: observation would prove that the plague was spread via contagion. As Stearns unfolds this story, however, it is not entirely clear that Ibn Lubb was simply an antiempiricist. More is going on here than first appears.

This discussion about proper ethical behavior in times of medical crisis from the fourteenth century serves as an example of how profoundly ethical discussions are shaped by cultural assumptions. Even empiricism cannot escape the limitations of what we "know" to be true. The examples of Ibn Lubb and Ibn al-Khatib may seem quaint, even silly, from our perspective. Yet, as Stearns points out, we would be foolish to believe that our own views of science and medicine are any less determined by similar assumptions. Perhaps even more important, however, is the discursive quality of this old ethical debate that remains a hallmark of bioethics, in both the Islamic and non-Islamic worlds. Both Ibn Lubb and Ibn al-Khatib are struggling to balance empirical evidence against the time-tested knowledge of sacred texts; they disagree, it is true, but it is also worth noting that our historical sources preserve both sides of the argument, demonstrating that the debate is just as valuable as the correct solution.

SAMAR FARAGE

The Ethics of the Physician in the Galeno-Islamic Tradition

From Baghdad to Cordoba, medical thinking for more than fourteen hundred years was dominated by the writings of the preeminent second-century Greek physician and philosopher Galen of Pergamum. Muslim translations of Galen had begun by the eighth century, first into Syriac and later into Arabic. By the ninth century 129 works of Galen had been translated into Arabic and were distributed for study and commentary all over the expanding Islamic world. Consequently Muslim medical knowledge and practice were deeply colored not only by Galen's classification of diseases and therapies but equally by his understanding of physiology, psychology, and the nature of the human body. Centuries later the rediscovery of the Greek heritage in the Latin West was in no small measure because of the retranslations from Arabic into Latin of ancient Greek texts. The eleventh-century School of Salerno, where many of these retranslations were conducted, and forgotten medical practices were revived, remains a potent reminder and exemplar of the manifold cross-currents in the formation and reformation of medical knowledge in the Muslim world.

Studying the history of pulse diagnosis in the Galeno-Islamic medical tradition sheds light on the medical encounters between patients and physicians throughout this tradition. Use of the phrase "Galeno-Islamic" emphasizes the fact that the medical writings of all the major Muslim *hakims* (physicians) since the ninth century, from Hunayn Ibn Ishaq (d. 873) and al-Razi (Razes, d. 925) to al-Majusi (d. 994) and Ibn Sina (Avicenna, d. 1037), were fundamentally indebted to the translation and transmission of Greek medical learning and knowledge.[1]

The rise of scientific medicine around the seventeenth century marked the twilight of Galenic medicine in the West.[2] Nevertheless the practice of Galeno-Islamic medicine still flourished as late as the mid-nineteenth century across the Near East and South Asia. However, the colonial rule of eighteenth- and nineteenth-century Europe was decisive in shifting the cultural soil in which these indigenous and traditional medical practices were nurtured.[3] Yet even today, though thoroughly eclipsed by modern medicine, Galeno-Islamic medicine continues to be practiced, particularly in parts of Pakistan and India. There it is called *Unani* (Greek) medicine, which clearly reveals its historical roots.[4]

The Nature of the Pulse

In the Galeno-Islamic medical tradition, the pulse was a keystone of the medical arts since it revealed the condition of health, disease, and the states in between. As such, the pulse was a fundamental diagnostic, prognostic, and therapeutic aid to the physician. Its importance is underscored by the fact that Galen wrote eighteen books and eighty-nine small treatises on the causes of pulses, the distinctions between pulses, and the art of prognosis from listening to pulses. Unsurprisingly all Muslim medical works started with or contained several chapters on the pulses.[5] Indeed, a well-told tale of Ibn Sina suggests that competent pulse listening decisively distinguished a physician from a charlatan: "Avicenna had just successfully treated the sovereign's wife. When Avicenna boasted that his fingers were so sensitive as to feel the rhythms of the pulse even through a string attached to a patient's wrist, the King decided to teach him a lesson. He said, 'an individual will be hidden behind a curtain with a string connected around the wrist. You may only touch the string and if you are successful in your diagnosis you will be rewarded richly. However, if you are wrong you will be banished and all your possessions will be confiscated.' Avicenna agreed to the challenge. Behind the curtain a string was attached to the tibial pulse of a cow. Avicenna placed his fingers on the string, listening carefully, and then announced, 'All this patient needs is grass.'"[6]

Galeno-Islamic sphygmology was fundamentally distinct from modern-day conceptions of the pulse. Galen defined the pulse as "the peculiar action initiated of the heart, hence of the arteries, which are moved in systole [contraction of the heart] and diastole [relaxing of the heart] by which a balance of the innate heat is maintained and animal spirits generated in the brain."[7] By Galen's time it was well accepted that the pulse was the simultaneous movement of the arteries and the heart. The heart was not yet the *pump* of William Harvey. The heart was thought of in analogy to a furnace and therefore as the seat of innate heat.[8] The arteries, like bellows that draw in air to blow away furnace soot and conserve a healthy fire, breathed and regulated the innate heat. The arteries also carried the *psyche zootikon,* or vital spirits, thereby moving *both* blood and spirits.[9] Hence, pulsation carried the animal (vital) spirits responsible for sensation and movement throughout the body and generated the rational (psychic) spirits that were the sources of human action, will, and choice.[10] These spirits were instruments (*organa*) through which the soul exercised its capacities in the body: those of generation, growth, sensation, and thought.[11]

The pulse was differentiated by ten categories, some of which are size, quickness, frequency, regularity, and rhythm.[12] Each category comprised between three and four dimensions, each of which was further divided into three states: of excess, of deficiency, and of the mean. For example, in the category of size, the artery was characterized by breadth, length, and height. For each of these dimensions the three divisions of excess, deficiency, and the mean were potentially present, but only one set of three was in accordance with nature. Hence, twenty-seven varieties of the pulse were recognized for a single beat or movement, whether diastole or systole. In addition pulses responded to and changed in accord with a) the natural causes including age, sex, humors, elements, and temperaments; b) unnatural causes such as food, exercise, evacuation, bathing, sleep, and emotional state; and c) the preternatural (contranatural) causes consisting of the various diseases and their symptoms.[13] Evidently, pulse listening was an art that demanded much learning and many years.

The names of the pulses bespoke their qualitative nature. The "worming pulses" were those that resembled a "worm winding its way through the artery, surging in the manner of a wave," whereby the entire artery did not undergo diastole at the same time. If the diastole was large, it was simply referred to as "wave-like pulses." There were "ant-like pulses" that were small, frequent, and faint. If these pulses were uneven in interruption, they became "gazelle-like pulses." If uneven with a recurrence, they were called "double-hammer pulses." The keen physician could differentiate "saw-edged pulses" from "hectic pulses," "undulating pulses" from "twisted pulses," "chord-like pulses" from "beat-dropping pulses," and so on.[14] A physician familiar with this enormous variety of pulses could thus detect and name the most subtle imbalance in a patient's natural constitution.

The Pulse as Messenger

To the trained physician's discriminating touch, the pulse sounded imbalances in both body and soul. Hence, physical ailments, inflammations, fevers, and even the onset of death, no less than secret loves, hidden pregnancies, festering angers, and debilitating melancholia, were narrated by the pulse. The *hakim* aimed to cure not only ailments of the body but also disorders of the soul. Thus, for example, in *Adab al-tabib,*[15] one of the most exhaustive works of the medical arts in the tradition, al-Ruhawi says that "the philosophers can improve the soul whereas the virtuous physician can improve both soul and body."[16] In contrast to the mind-body dualism of contemporary medicine, body and soul were interrelated as matter and form in the Galeno-Islamic tradition, which was rooted in a humoral understanding of the body.[17] The mixture or balance of bodily humors affected the soul, and as stated by Galen, "the faculties of the soul depend on the mixtures of the body and we derive a good mixture from our food and drink and other daily activities and this mixture is the basis on which we build the virtue of the soul." The soul was affected not only by the humoral balances in the body but also by imbalances in its bodily seats, since the soul had corporeal localizations. The rational or psychic soul resided in the brain, the natural soul resided in the liver, and the vital or animal soul in the heart. The residue of this Galeno-Islamic tradition resonates still in *Unani* medicine, where the word *mizaj* refers simultaneously to a state of the soul and bodily disposition.

This union of body and soul explains the importance of what came to be called "spiritual medicine" in the tradition. Several works on spiritual medicine were included as compendiums to works on bodily medicine and focused on temperance and the superiority of reason as a guide to the passions.[18] Thus, when a physician heard the pulse, he not only heard the material flows of the humors but also touched the soul and its passions. For this reason we find, throughout the Galeno-Islamic tradition, a description of the pulse as "a messenger that does not lie, a mute announcer that tells of secret things by its movements."[19] Stories abound of effective cures for disorders of the soul through an acute perception of pulsations. For instance, Avicenna's preeminence in such matters is widely noted:

> A relative of the sovereign of Jourgan [Gorgan] was sick. He was complaining of an illness which the efforts of all the physicians of the country could not relive. Avicenna was invited for advice. After examining the patient, he requested the help of someone who knew the names of all the districts and streets of the province. He made him repeat these names while he himself had his finger on the pulse of the patient. Upon the pronunciation of the name of a certain town, Avicenna noticed a trouble in the pulsation. Now, he said, I need a person acquainted with all the quarters, streets and houses of the town. The same phenomenon was noticed upon the pronunciation of the name of a certain street and again upon listing the names of the members of a certain family. Avicenna concluded: "this boy is in love with the girl living in that particular house in the specified street of the subject town. The face of that girl is the remedy which can cure the patient." Marriage was thus celebrated at the proper time as indicated by Avicenna. This ensured a perfect cure.[20]

Nature: In the Concrete and the Cosmic

In the Galeno-Islamic tradition, philosophy and medicine were wedded, as suggested by the word *hakim,* which means both "doctor" and "wise man." The physician was trained in the three parts of philosophy: logic, so as to speak and judge better; ethics, so as to act appropriately; and physics, so as to understand one's place in the cosmos. Both philosophy and medicine were "practical arts of living" that entailed detailed rules of conduct and thought aimed at a conversion and transformation of oneself toward the good through daily practice.[21] One strove toward the good by cultivating both health and virtue. In medicine the excellence that was health was expressed by the proper blending and balancing (Greek: *krasis,* Arabic: *mizaj*) of the four humors. The balance of the humors was particular to each person and influenced his/her constitution or temperament. There were choleric, sanguine, phlegmatic, and melancholic temperaments according to the particular mixture of humors and qualities. Similarly, in philosophy, virtue was cultivated action rooted in the knowledge of what was moderate and intermediate between excess and deficiency (*i'tidal bayna al-ifrat wa-l-taqsir*). Thus the healthy and virtuous life was one lived in accordance with the mean according to nature.

Further, medical practice, aimed at cures of the body and the soul, was embedded within a cosmological order. The proportions of the humors reflected correspondences in the macrocosm. Each humor was analogously tied to its planet, season, and element. The bodily basis of the soul implied therefore that personal changes mirrored cosmic movements. Thus, for example, melancholia was influenced by the presence of Saturn no less than by the seasons.

The pulse uniquely embodied this intimate correspondence between microcosm and macrocosm. By virtue of its rhythmic quality, numerical proportions, and circular regularity, the pulse was inherently musical.[22] In evaluations of a patient, musical harmonies of the pulse pointed to health and illness, as suggested by Avicenna in the first book of the *Canon:*

> You should know that there is in the pulse a musical nature, for as the art of music is realized in the melody (composition of sounds) according to the relation between them as to high pitch and low, and in the rhythmical recurrence of time intervals between the striking of strings, so it is with the pulse: its temporal relation in respect to swiftness (duration of movements) and frequency (duration of pauses) is a rhythmical relation; and its qualitative relation as to strength and weakness (of the impact on the finger) and size of dilation is a relation like that of melody. And as the time units of rhythm and the duration of notes may be concordant or discordant, so the variations of the pulse may be orderly and may be disordered and the qualitative relation of the pulse as to strength and weakness and size may be concordant or discordant, indeed uneven. . . . Now Galen holds that the observed values of metrical proportion are in accordance with one of these musical relations mentioned: either in the relation of the octave and fifth which is triple (3:1), in the relation of the octave which is the double (2:1) or in the relation of the fifth which is that which adds a half (3:2), etc. . . . I am amazed that these relations should be detected by touch; but it is easier for one who executes the progression of rhythm and the proportion of sounds in practicing the art and then has the opportunity to become acquainted with musical theory, so as to correlate the art with the discipline. Such a man, when he turns his attention to the pulse, would be enabled to identify these relations by touch.[23]

Moreover, the musical harmonies of the octave, quinte, and quart not only were expressed in the harmonies of the body and soul but also were linked to the harmonies of the spheres.[24] These ideas were so engrained in the tradition that by the Middle Ages and the Renaissance several physicians dispensed altogether with words and expressed their knowledge of the pulse simply in musical scales.[25] Music brought the heavens to men and altered their dispositions; hence the important link between the curative and ethical effects of music and medicine in the Galeno-Islamic tradition.[26]

The union of philosophy and medicine was founded on the norms of a teleological nature that aimed toward balance and harmony of all its parts and functions.[27] For this reason the Hippocratic maxim was widely repeated all through the Galeno-Islamic tradition: "Nature is the first healer that does nothing in vain." Illness resulted from a disturbance in the natural balance. Accordingly, all a physician could do was to understand nature in order to assist and conform to its tendencies. Therefore the medical art was practiced within the bounds of a natural order that tended toward health and virtue as the right balance of the humors and the passions. Thus the physician-philosopher was a guide to living according to the mean as proportion. This mean was not an abstract norm but what was fitting to a particular person in a particular place and time.[28]

The Ethics of the Physician

When facing his patient, a *hakim* was obliged to discover and encourage the three proportions (balance of the humors, temperance of the passions, and the relation between microcosm and macrocosm) that defined health and virtue. Since the physician could not assist nature without hearing its voice, in the Galeno-Islamic tradition it was the pulse that revealed the proportions in health and virtue and their imbalances in diseases and vices.[29] The pulse was thus the privileged site for grasping nature as both concrete and cosmic. Pulse-taking was like the anamnesis of a patient, except that it was nature here that narrated his/her history. The pulse revealed the bios of the patient, his/her habits of soul and body, and his/her stance in the world. Fundamental to the medical art, the pulse helped in all three phases: diagnosis, prognosis, and therapy. These three aspects of medicine were not separate since each required knowledge of the past, present, and future of the patient. The pulse not only revealed specific illnesses but also allowed the physician to determine their stage of development and evaluate whether therapy or cures were effective. "Diagnosis" was not a technical term but referred to differentiating knowledge (Greek: *diagnosis*). Such differentiation relied on the ability to observe and detect signs (Greek: *semeion,* Arabic: *dala'il*) and symptoms (Greek: *sumptoma,* Arabic: *a'rad*). Differential diagnosis (Arabic: *tashkhis muqaran*) was thus a semiological exercise anchored in observation and reasoning.[30]

For this reason, the instructions on pulse-taking were elaborate. They included instructions about the choice of wrist depending on the gender of the patient; the position of the patient's palm; the position and spacing of the physician's fingers; and the appropriate mental and physical conditions of both patient and doctor. Thus, for example, the pulse is best taken at rest, but neither after a long period of idleness nor violent exercise nor after a heavy meal or fast. The person must be free of emotional discomfort and in a calm state of mind.[31] By skillful touch, the physician would inspect the impact of the arteries against the finger and the ratio between diastole and systole as well as the pauses that separated them. Knowing the intricate varieties of the pulse required the sharpening of all the senses and a keen intellect. Because touch was the only sense without intermediary and responded immediately to all kinds of changes in the pulse, it was preeminent among the senses to be cultivated by the physician.[32] However, to pronounce his verdict on the condition of the patient, the *hakim* required an elaborate consultation which in all its aspects centered on a relation of trust and compassion. His success thus depended on an intimate knowledge of the particular nature of the patient and an understanding of cosmic forces.

The medical encounter in the Galeno-Islamic tradition involved three stages: direct sense perception (*aesthesis*), an extensive questioning of the patient and deduction through keen reasoning.[33] The physician had to first feel the patient, which is why, for instance, physicians sniffed the breath, feces and urine of patients, tasted the seven flavors of their sweat and examined their skin, nails, pupils, and tongue. The patient's room, habits, clothing and even her relatives were subject to the physicians' purposeful curiosity. This intense and intimate examination occurred over time not only because the physician had to grasp the difference between health and illness for each patient but also to determine the stage of the illness itself.

Second, the physician questioned the patient as to his ills and pains, way of life and even dreams. The importance of the patient's word made clear that a relation of mutual confidence was crucial to a successful treatment. Finally the physician reasoned through logical demonstrations and proofs to classify the particular nature of the patient and his afflictions.[34] The supreme act of the physician was to judge the appropriate cause and treatment of the imbalances. Medical judgment relied crucially on the common sense which was the site for commingling (*synaesthesis)* of the givens of the external senses.[35] In the tradition, the common sense was physically located in the brain and served to link the internal and the external senses and hence, allowed the physician to judge what was fitting and proper for the particular patient's well-being.[36]

The shared experience of both patient and doctor of flowing humors, as expressed in the pulse, permitted the physician to empathize with the patient. In Islamic ethics, *rifq,* and in Greek ethics, *philanthropia,* reflected this relation of empathy and compassion.[37] As the physician had to reckon with tragic events, dramas and struggles, the relation between physician and patient was best described as mimetic, agonal, and philanthropic. The medical encounter involved three sets of ethical duties: one for the patient, one for the physician and one for the relation between them. Both physician and patient had to follow elaborate regimens aimed at cultivating certain dispositions and habits of body and soul.[38] The physician had to follow a set of duties that included being learned, well mannered, properly attired and moderate in behavior. The patient was required to be truthful and obedient. These virtues exhibited by both physician and patient hastened the healing powers of nature by forging a relationship of trust, confidence and compassion. Interestingly the root of the term *akhlaq* in Arabic as well as *ethos* in Greek points not only to innate disposition but also to the cultivation of a second nature through habitual practices. We can see from this that Ethics was understood in the Galeno-Islamic tradition as relational. It aimed at the formation of good character and the cultivation of virtue in both physician and patient. Ethics was thus a lived practice that centered on personal conduct in a relation.

The Mechanical Pulse

I have suggested that the pulse in the Galeno-Islamic tradition was proportionate, rhythmic, qualitative and ensouled. I now briefly describe the rupture in medical history that is the rise of scientific medicine through the prism of the pulse. In comparison to the pulse of the tradition, the pulse today is mute, soulless, insensible and quantifiable. Such a pulse also reveals some dimensions of the modern day relationship between physician and patient.

Since the early Enlightenment, the scientific ethos driven to objectivity, precision, standardization and comparability found too many imprecisions in the qualitative pulse.[39] Despite many prior attempts at reducing quality to quantity by instrumentation, from Herophilus's rudimentary water clock and Galileo's "pulsilogium" based on string and weight, to Hérisson's sphygmometer that visually portrayed the pulse on a mercury column, it was only with the Galenic physician Sir John Floyer's *The Physician's Pulse Watch*, that the pulse truly became quantifiable and mechanical.[40] From these measurements, he established a quantitative universal measure of the pulse for the best constitution—at 70–75 beats per minute. It took one hundred years and countless experiments to develop Laennec's stethoscope which permitted the modern diagnosis based on reading an instrument that stood between the physician and the patient. He justified such instrumentation by his distrust of the patient's narrative and by his belief that "morbid sounds elicited by the body are more reliable and dependable indices of nature." The visualization of the pulse was not complete until Etienne Jules Marey invented the sphygmograph in 1860. It had one lever attached to the artery and the other one to a pen that recorded on a sheet pulse motions. The sphygmograph totally transformed the subjective character of pulse-feeling into an objective graphic representation that permanently recorded a fleeting moment. It was the first of many instruments that attempted to capture such transient movements of the body (from breath to blood and later to brain waves). The sphygmograph would lead to the electrocardiogram and to the definitions in the 20th century of the pulse as an electrical wave. It allowed for the visualization of what once only could be felt. Today, the latest technique in pulse measurement does away with sense of touch entirely. A pulse monitor attached to the body simply measures electrical discharges to gauge the rate of pulse waves. The pulse as an electric wave cannot be felt, only measured, recorded and displayed.

The measurable graphic pulse implies that the pulse can no longer be sensed. Instrumentation changed the face of medicine and the relation between sense perception and understanding. The validity of reason was based on the validity of sense perception and the validity of sensation was ultimately contingent on the logical inexorability of the natural order expressed in analogical metaphors. Modern science allowed things to be known from the inside out and no longer from the outside in through the senses. The modern doctor stands outside the world in order to comprehend it.[41]

More crucial, the modern pulse is also soulless. The heart, Harvey thought, is a mechanical pump or a piece of machinery and the arteries as a conduit for blood alone. Both heart and arteries were emptied of vital spirits. Descartes was instrumental in cementing the modern mind-body dualism. The body as *res extensa* and the soul as *res cogitans,* gained different functions and belonged to different orders. Since the soul was excluded from the study of nature, it also implied that philosophy and medicine parted ways and that health and virtue no longer had anything to do with one another. The science of medicine became possible as human physiology could follow the laws of mechanics.

The soulless measurable pulse is also severed from any connection to the world soul and world harmony. The link between the macrocosm and microcosm was thus broken. The four corners of *homo quadratus* of the Middle Ages comprising sky, earth, man and soul was flattened to a line on an EKG. Where once the world was man writ large and man the world writ small, from now on, both man and world were disconnected and matter made lifeless.

The Silence of Nature

The unheard pulse of modernity is coeval with at least three fundamental changes in medicine. First, the haptic sense was atrophied by the visual sense. Cold vision came to dominate warm touch partly because it was thought to allow for a universality that transcended the confusion of tongues. The words of the patient as well as the pulse as storyteller were now reduced to a babble of voices that had to be silenced. The "objective physician" of Laennec was made deaf to the dramatic stories told by both patient and pulse and therefore could no longer empathize with the sick person. Indeed, the once mimetic relation between patient and physician was thereby transformed into a diagnostic one. Sensual perception that intimately linked doctor and patient formed the basis for the ethical encounter in the Galeno-Islamic tradition. Such an ethical relation is made difficult when instruments are trusted more than people. Second, a new notion of disease as entitative emerged in the late Renaissance.[42] Disease as entities that attacked the body from the outside and left their footprints on different loci, placed the body at war. Disease was no longer an imbalance and the pulse could no more express proportions of the humors, much less reveal states of health and disease. Thus, third, the humoral body gave way to a solid clinical entity called "The Body." Humoral fluids were alive; embodied histories of health and disease as dispositions that narrated both the *bios* and second nature of the patient. The clinical body of scientific medicine, drawn from the dissection of corpses, has no stories to tell and could find no ear to hear them. It is on the ruins of the soul and on a new conception of nature as dead matter that the history of the body as an object of a medical gaze becomes possible. Only the body that has a history independent of its cosmological underpinnings can be objectified, constructed, deconstructed. Only on such a lifeless object can the modern doctor intervene: to prod, poke and manipulate through instruments, to subject to destructive experimental drugs and procedures, to regulate and monitor on life-support systems.

Conclusion

This brief historical excursion into the world of the pulse sheds light on the gulf between the Galeno-Islamic medical tradition and modern medical practice and thought. In my opinion the transformation of the pulse from the breath of life into a vital sign of a standardized and universal body is also indicative of a fundamental shift from the ethics of the physician to medical ethics and bio-ethics more recently. The *hakim* is morally bound by the limits of nature and the underpinnings of a cosmological order that color every aspect of both patient and physician's lives. The *hakim* does not intervene when he knows he should not, but he alleviates suffering, assisting the patient to withstand the agony of illness and to find the right balance of health and virtue. He encourages the patient to live virtuously and to endure his or her mortal condition. In contrast to the ethics of a physician, which has always been concrete and relational and directed at a particular person, contemporary professional ethics, whether of medicine or business, refers to rules and regulations that aim to minimize the possible damage caused by technoscientific interventions.

Furthermore, if there is a distinction between ethical practice on the one hand and juridical prescriptions on the other, then it is difficult to read bioethics back into the ethics of a physician. The cross-fertilization of medical ideas and practices continues as before between Muslim lands and the "West" particularly in the context of the spread of bio-medicine. However, it seems to me that seeking ethical precedent or justification for bio-medicine in Muslim texts will necessarily narrow the focus of historical studies onto religious/legal texts. I suspect that a dispassionate survey of "medical ethics" in the Galeno-Islamic tradition would reveal that it is in medical and philosophical texts that the subject is discussed most comprehensively. Therefore it seems to me necessary that research be conducted on uncovering this rich vein of medical thought and practice in the Muslim world. I suggest that a fuller grasp of the Galeno-Islamic medical tradition is crucial to a fuller understanding of the issues that face students of "Islamic bioethics."

NOTES

1. Among the major medical compendia were Ḥunayn Ibn Isḥāq's *Masā'il* fi-*l-ṭibb* (Cairo: Al Ahram Center, 1980); al-Rāzī 's encyclopedia, *Al-Hāwī fī-l-ṭibb* (Hayderabad: Dā'irat al-ma'ārif al-'uthmāniyya, 1955); al-Majūsī 's monumental work, *Kāmil al-ṣinā'a fī-l-ṭibb* (Frankfurt: Ma'had Ta'rīkh al-'Ulūm al-'Arabiyah, 1985); and Ibn Sīnā's *Al-Qānūn fī-l-ṭibb* (New Delhi: Jamia Hamdard, 1993). The *Canon* of Ibn Sīnā, who is known in the West as Avicenna, remained the undisputed medical authority in the Latin West until the sixteenth century and in the Muslim world until the nineteenth century. The apogee of Arabic translations occurred during the Abbasid period under al-Ma'mun and al-Mansur in Baghdad. Soon after, however, centers of learning in Kairouan, Cordoba, Gurganj, and Damascus continued this monumental effort. On the construction of what I have named "the Galeno-Islamic medical tradition" forged from the transmission and preservation of Galenic texts in the Islamic world, consult the following: Cyril Elgood, *Medical History of Persia and the Eastern Caliphate* (London: Cambridge, 1951); E. G. Browne, *Arabian Medicine* (Westport, Conn.: Hyperion, 1921); Manfred Ullmann, *Islamic Medicine* (Edinburgh: Edinburgh University Press, 1978); Fazlur Rahman, *Health and Medicine in the Islamic Tradition: Change and Identity* (New York: Crossroad, 1987). See also Lucien Leclerc, *Histoire de la medecine arabe,* 2 vols. (Paris: Ernest Leroux, 1876); and Danielle Jacquart and F. Micheaux, eds., *La medecine arabe et l'occident medieval* (Paris: Maisonneuve, 1990).

2. For an overview of the rise and eclipse of Galenism in the West, consult Oswei Temkin, *Galenism: Rise and Decline of a Medical Philosophy* (Ithaca, N.Y.: Cornell University Press, 1973); Ludwig Edelstein, *Ancient Medicine* (Baltimore: Johns Hopkins University Press, 1967). For a short introduction, see Samar Farage, "Galenic Medicine," in *Encyclopedia of Science, Technology and Ethics,* ed. Carl Mitcham (New York: Macmillan, 2005), 2:812–13.

3. For regional variations, see Nancy Gallagher, *Medicine and Power in Tunisia 1780–1900* (London: Cambridge University Press, 1983); Elgood, *Medical History;* Khaled Fahmy, "Women, Medicine and Power," in *Remaking Women: Feminism and Modernity in the Middle East,* ed. L. Abu Lughod (Princeton, N.J.: Princeton University Press, 1998). See also Mervat Hatem, "The Professionalization of Health and the Control of Women's Bodies as Modern Governmentalities in 19th century Egypt," in *Women in the Ottoman Empire,* ed. M. Zilfi (Leiden: Brill, 1997), 66–80; Naghib Mahfouz, *The History of Medical Education in Egypt* (Cairo: Government Press, 1935).

4. For a good summary, see Helen Sheehan and S. J. Hussain, "Unani Tibb: History, Theory and Contemporary Practice in South Asia," *Annals of the American Academy of Political and Social Science* 583 (2002): 122–35. See also J. C. Bürgel, "Secular and Religious Features of Medieval Arabic Medicine," *Asian Medical Systems: A Comparative Study,* ed. Charles M. Leslie (Berkeley: University of California Press, 1976), 44–62; N. Izhar, "The

Unani Traditional Medical System in India: A Case Study in Health Behavior," *Geographica Medica* 19 (1989): 163–85; M. Z. Siddiqi, "The Unanī Ṭibb (Greek Medicine) in India," *Islamic Culture* 42 (1968): 161–72; C. Liebeskind, "Unani Medicine and the Subcontinent," in *Oriental Medicine: An Illustrated Guide to the Asian Arts of Healing*, ed. J. Van Alphen and A. Aris (Boston: Shambala, 1996), 39–66.

5. See the ninth- and tenth-century compendia mentioned by Ibn Abī Usayba in *'Uyūn al-Anbā' fī -ṭabaqāt al-aṭibba* (Beirut: Dār Maktabat al-Ḥayāt, 1965). Ibn al-Nadīm's *The Fihrist of Ibn al-Nadīm*, trans. Bayard Dodge (New York: Columbia University Press, 1985), commenting on the medical books required for all medical students, mention the "Alexandrian Curriculum" comprising sixteen books of Galen, which included his "The Book of the Pulse for Learned Men," translated into Latin as *De Pulsibus ad Tirones.* See Leclerc, *Histoire de la medecine arabe*, 1:244–50.

6. B. Kapki, "Deep Listening: Revealing the Pulse," *Massage and Body Work* (April/May 2002): 22.

7. Avicenna's *Canon* defined the pulse in similar terms, as did al-Majūsī in *Kāmil al-Ṣinā'a* and Ḥunayn Ibn Isḥāq in *Masā'il fī-l-ṭibb.* For a historical survey, see Sir Clifford Allbutt, *Greek Medicine in Rome* (London: Macmillan, 1921). The only work that touches superficially on the pulse in Islamic or Arabian medicine is R. B. Ambers and A. M. Babey Brooke, *The Pulse in Occident and Orient* (New York: Santa Barbara Press, 1966).

8. See Rudolph Siegel, *Galen's System of Physiology and Medicine* (Basel and New York: S. Karger, 1968); C. R. S. Harris, *The Heart and Cardio-vascular System in Ancient Greek Medicine* (Oxford: Oxford University Press, 1973); Shigehisa Kuriyama, *The Expressiveness of the Body and the Divergence of Greek and Chinese Medicine* (New York: Zone Books, 1999).

9. Consider, for example, Avicenna's definition: "pulsation pneumatizes the blood and cools the innate heat as well as generates psychic pneuma." Al-Majusi explains that the arteries carry blood and spirits as follows: "when the heart expands, creating a vacuum, the closely connected arteries draw from it air and light blood. Upon contraction, these arteries empty the air and blood into the lungs to fill again from the heart's next expansion" (*Kāmil*, 1).

10. Detailed explanations can be found in Galen, *On Medical Experience*, trans. H. A. R. Gibb (London: Oxford University Press, 1944). See also Rupert Hall's "Studies in the History of the Cardio-vascular System," *Bulletin of the History of Medicine* (1960): 391–413; Harris, *Heart and Cardio-vascular System;* Siegel, *Galen's System.*

11. See Avicenna, *Kitāb al-shifā'* (Cairo: al-Hay'a al-Miṣriyya, 1983).

12. The ten varieties are consistently present in all Arabic works on the pulse from Tabari to Avicenna. For a good description of the pulse and its variations, see Emmet Horine, "An Epitome of Ancient Pulse Lore," *Bulletin of the History of Medicine* 10 (1941): 209–49; R. Vance, "The Doctrine of the Pulse—An Analysis of Its Character and Summary of Its Indications," *Cincinnati Lancet* 26 (1878).

13. Succinct explanations of the three causes can be found in J. Rather, "The Things Non-natural," *Clio Medica* 3 (1968): 337–47; Jerome Bylebyl, "Galen and the Non-natural Causes of the Variations of the Pulse," *Bulletin of the History of Medicine* 45 (1971): 482–85; and Peter Niebyl, "The Non Naturals," *Bulletin of the History of Medicine* 45 (1971): 486–92. For a lengthy explanation, consult Ḥunayn Ibn Isḥāq's *Masā'il fī -l-ṭibb* and al-Majūsī's

Kāmil al-ṣināʿa. For instance, it is well known that the pulses of men and women differ: men in general have a much larger pulse than women; it is also much more vigorous, slightly slower, and considerably sparser. Pulses can also vary by age: the pulse of the newborn is comparatively frequent, while that of an old man sparser. Temperament and body shape can also affect the pulse, so that slender people have a larger pulse but much slower and only a little stronger. Naturally hot people have a larger, quicker, and more frequent pulse. The pulse undulates by day and night—in the course of the night it becomes more faint and small. As regards the acquired states of the body, the pulse of a naturally thin person who becomes fat will acquire the same qualities as that of a naturally fat person. The same applies to acquired mixtures as a result of habits.

14. See Galen's "Distinctions in the Pulses," in *Galen Opera Omnia,* ed. C. G. Kuhn (Leipzig: C. Knoblochii, 1892), 4:94–107, 120–29. This qualitative understanding of the pulse was standard in all major works in the Galeno-Islamic tradition.

15. An excellent translation of this book is Martin Levey's "Medical Ethics of Medieval Islam with Special Reference to al-Ruhawi 'Practical Ethics of the Physician,'" *Transactions of the American Philosophical Society* 57 (1967): 1–100.

16. This definition of *falsafa* was quite dominant in Islamic medicine following Galen and Plato: see Abū Bakr Muḥammad b. Zakariyya al-Rāzī 's *Al-Sīra al-falsafiyya or The Spiritual Physick of Rhazes,* trans. A. Arberry (London: Luzac and Co., 1950); and Yaʿqub b. Isḥāq al-Kīndī 's *Al-Falsafa al-ūlā* (Damascus: Dār Maʿād, 1977). On reason as the vehicle to decipher signs of God, see Seyyed Hossein Nasr, "The Meaning and Role of Philosophy in Islam," *Studia Islamica* 37 (1973): 57–80. See also G. E. Von Grunebaum, "Concept and Function of Reason in Islamic Ethics," *Oriens* 15 (1962): 1–17.

17. The four humors are black bile, yellow bile, blood, and phlegm. These are fluid entities that course through the arteries and veins while also constituting the material basis and affecting the condition of organs.

18. Modeled on Galen's "On the Passions and Errors of the Soul in Galen," in *Galen: Selected Writings,* ed. Peter Singer (London: Oxford, 1997), 100–149. He prescribed cures for psychic diseases such as anger, conceit, envy, lust, and lying. Al-Kindī seems to have written a book on spiritual medicine, but it was lost, making al-Rāzī the first Muslim writer in the tradition of medicines for disorders of the soul. His discussion appears in a book that was a compendium to his medical work, *Al-Manṣūrī,* so-called because it was commissioned by al-Manṣūr, ruler of the province of Rayy, who asked him to write on the reformation of character and good conduct. After al-Rāzī, several physicians, such al-Jurjānī and al-Jawzī, wrote books with the same title. Avicenna's treatments on the disorders of the soul appear in his *Kitāb al-Shifāʾ,* one of the greatest works on the soul and its cures.

19. Both al-Majūsī and Ḥunayn Ibn Isḥāq have identical descriptions of the pulse. This seems one of the most repeated descriptions throughout the European Middle Ages.

20. From Browne, *Arabian Medicine,* 86.

21. Every great Islamic physician was also a noted philosopher—for example, al-Rāzī, al-Kindī, Ibn Sīnā, and Ibn Rushd. Al-Rāzī 's *Al-Sīra al-falsafiyya* is a good illustration of this link between philosophy and medicine. Galen wrote a revealing text with the pointed title *Why the Best Physician Is Also a Philosopher,* in *Galen: Selected Writings. 3–34.* For a general survey of philosophy as a practical art in antiquity, consult Pierre Hadot, *Philosophy as a Way of Life* (London: Blackwell, 1995).

22. When evaluating a patient, a physician employed the musical analogy to hear the rhythm of the pulse as good (*eurhythmic*) or bad (*arrhythmia*). Consonance was related to the rhythmical regularity of the pulse, and *arrhythmia,* or discordance, meant that the pulse could be unharmonious in itself or because it was disproportionate to age, constitution, and so on. A great change in meter implied a great change in bodily states, so the pulse was not only a static aid but also was taken to measure the transformation of the condition of the patient from one state to another.

23. Avicenna, *The Canon of Medicine,* ed. L. Bakhtiar (Chicago: Kazi, 1999), lecture 12, p. 291. Evidence of such musical conceptions of the pulse can be found in medical writings from Avicenna's *Qānūn* to Averroes's *Kitāb al-Kulliyat,* from Ibn Dawūd's *Al-Antākī* up to al-Nuzha's *Al-Mubhija* in the sixteenth century.

24. From Plato through Augustine—who in his book *On Music* states: "the rhythms of the pulse and breathing are produced by the operations of the soul, in which number and rhythm were inherent"—to Boethius, body and soul were united in music. The pulse was part of *musica humana,* which mirrored the *musica mundana.* According to Boethius, in his book *Fundamentals of Music,* ed. C. Palisca (New Haven, Conn.: Yale University Press, 1989), *musica humana* consisted of three elements: a) the fit proportion or *temperatio* of soul and body; b) *temperatio* among the rational soul and the irrational parts; and c) the proper mixing of elements and proportions in the body.

25. See Nancy Siraisi, "The Music of the Pulse in the Writings of Italian Academic Physicians of the 14th/15th Century," *Speculum* 50 (1975): 689–710; S. K. Henninger, *Touches of Sweet Harmony* (Berkeley, Calif.: Huntington Library, 1974); Leofranc Holford-Strevens, "The Harmonious Pulse," *Classical Quarterly* 43 (1993): 475–79.

26. See H. G. Farmer, *History of Arabian Music to the 13th Century* (London: Luzac and Co, 1929); Amnon Shiloah, *The Dimension of Music in Islamic and Jewish Culture* (London: Variorum, 1993). In this historical light, contemporary musical therapy in medicine appears as a tinny copy of the original.

27. Nature was a philosophical concept as well as a moral limit. It was the limit of becoming for each being, limit that could not be transcended or transgressed without damage to the integrity of the thing itself—outside "nature" there was monstrosity in the biological order, things out of proportion or artifice in the human order. Nature was the expression of what was appropriate to a particular individual constitution, his complexion and reactions to outside factors. For a brief introduction to ideas of nature in the Galeno-Islamic tradition, consult F. Somlsen, "Nature as Craftsman in Greek Thought," *Journal of the History of Ideas* 24 (1963): 473–96; Max Neuburger, "An Historical Survey of the Concept of Nature from a Medical Viewpoint," *Isis* 35 (1944): 16–38; Stanley G. Whitby, "Nature and Morality," *Ethics* 51 (1940): 49–65; Sachiko Murata, *The Tao of Islam* (New York: State University of New York Press, 1992); Sayyed Hossein Nasr, *An Introduction to Islamic Cosmological Doctrines* (New York: State University of New York Press, 1993). See especially P. Moraux, "Galien comme philosophe de la Nature," in *Galen: Problems and Prospects,* ed. V. Nutton (London: Wellcome Institute for the History of Medicine, 1981), 87–116; Neuburger, "Historical Survey"; Whitby, "Nature and Morality"; and Louis Massignon, "La Nature dans la pensée islamique," *Eranos Jahrbuch* 14 (1946): 145–48.

28. See Edelstein, *Ancient Medicine;* Ionnis Evrigenis, "Doctrine of the Mean in Aristotle's Ethical and Political Theory," *History of Political Thought* 20 (1999): 393–416; T. Tracy,

Physiological Theory and the Doctrine of the Mean in Plato and Aristotle (Chicago: Loyola University Press, 1969); W. Oates, "The Doctrine of the Mean," *Philosophical Review* 45 (1936): 382–98; F. Rosenthal, "The Physician in Medieval Muslim Society," *Bulletin of the History of Medicine* 52 (1979): 475–91; E. Pellegrino, *Medicine and Philosophy* (London: Oxford, 1981).

29. As recently as 1820 the physician Julius Rocco stated that "it is impossible to second or assist nature if the physician refuses to listen to her voice by making a regular clinical examination of the patient's pulse." These words, still rooted in the Galenic tradition of the West, emphasize not only the centrality of the pulse to the medical art but also the natural limits of medicine. In *Méthode très facile pour developer les secrets de la nature dans le corps humain par l'exploration du Pouls* (Paris, 1821), 33, Jean Lavy writes: "le sphygmique nous permet de connaitre si les dispositions de la nature sont bonnes ou mauvaises, afin de les seconder, ou de les contenir, ou du moins les diriger vers les organes moins importants. . . . L'obligation du médecin est de seconder la nature le médecin est le ministre de la nature car c'est elle qui guérite les maladies. . . . La douleur c'est les cris de la nature" (pulse taking allows us to know whether the dispositions of nature are good or bad, in order to assist them, or contain them, or at least to guide them toward less important organs. . . . The obligation of the physician is to assist nature for the physician is the minister of nature, but it is nature that cures the ill). See also Kuriyama, *Expressiveness of the Body.*

30. On the distinction between signs and symptoms, consult Danielle Jacquart and G. Troupeau, "La Consultation Médicale de l'observation du malade à la prescription," in *A l'ombre d'Avicenne: La Médecine au temps des Califes,* ed. Jeanne Mouliérac (Paris: Institute du Monde Arabe, 1997), 77–81. Most Islamic physicians reaffirmed the distinction. See, for example, Ibn Sīnā's *Qānūn.*

31. Thus, in the *Pulse for Beginners,* Galen states that "all changes come about in relation to differences in nature; for the arteries move differently in different individuals. These differences must be understood by one hoping to recognize the cause and the extent of the pulse's change; and such individual differences may be precisely learned by examination. The artery must be observed on a number of occasions, most particularly when the patient is in perfect health and resting from all vigorous activity. If that was not possible, the physician used his intellectual faculties to infer what the moderate pulse was from a general knowledge of nature (common nature of man). And there is a common nature of people whose mixture is on the hot side, and another of those on the cold side" (*Galen Opera Omnia,* ed. Kuhn, 8:504–6, quotation at p. 504).

32. In *Pulse for Beginners,* Galen urges "the student to train both his intellectual faculties and his sense of touch, in order that he may be able to recognize pulses in practice, not just to distinguish them in theory" (*Galen Opera Omnia,* ed. Kuhn, 8:504–6, quotation at p. 504).

33. For a good discussion of Galenic diagnosis, see Luis Garcia Ballaster, "Problems in Diagnosis," *Galen: Problems and Prospects,* ed. Vivian Nutton. London: Wellcome Institute for the History of Medicine, 1981, 13–46. Also consult Vivian Nutton, "Galen at the Bedside: Methods of a Medical Detective," *Medicine and the Five Senses,* eds. Roy Porter and W. F. Bynum (London: Cambridge, 1987), 7–16; Walter Rises, "The Structure of Galen's Diagnostic Reasoning," *Bulletin of the New York Academy of Science* 44 (1968): 778–91; and Iago

Gladstone, "Diagnosis in Historical Perspective," *Bulletin of the History of Medicine* 9 (1941): 367–84.

34. J. Barnes, "Galen on Logic and Therapy," *Galen's Method of Healing,* eds. Fridolf Kudlien and R. Durling (Leiden: Brill, 1991), 50–101; G. E. R. Lloyd, "Theories and Practices of Demonstration in Galen," in *Rationality in Greek Thought,* eds. M. Frede and G. Stryker (Oxford: Clarendon, 1996), 255–77; R.J. Hankinson, *Cause and Explanation in Ancient Greek Thought* (Oxford: Clarendon, 1998).

35. H. Olmsted "The Moral Sense: Aspects of Aristotle's Ethical Theory," *American Journal of Philology* 69 (1948): 42–61. Also, D. K. Modrak, *Aristotle: Power of Perception* (Chicago: University of Chicago Press, 1987) and S. Everson, *Aristotle on Perception* (Oxford: Clarendon, 1997). For Islamic philosophy, see Harry A. Wolfson, "The Internal Senses in Latin, Arabic and Hebrew Philosophical Texts," *Harvard Theological Review* 28 (1935): 69–133; Avicenna Latinus, *Liber de Anima* (Louvain, Belgium: Peters Pub., 1968). A good summary of this is in F. Rahman, *Avicenna's Psychology* (London: Oxford, 1952). See also Avicenna, *Livre des directives et remarques,* ed. A. M. Goichon (Paris: Vrin, 1972).

36. According to ʿAlī Ibn Riḍwān (d. 1067): "For your diagnosis and the indications that you observe, you should always choose things that are extremely powerful and easy to recognize and these are what can be perceived by sight, touch, hearing, taste and smell and by the intellect. When these are properly grasped, they show the nature of the disease. Nature in fact has given us these faculties in order that by them we may recognize the true character of things and the faculty of sense perception has organs that are natural to man and can be used for testing." Cited by Nutton, "Galen at bedside," 103.

37. See Lain Entralgo, *Doctor and Patient* (New York: Macmillan, 1967).

38. See Martin Levey, "Medical Ethics of Medieval Islam with Special Reference to al-Ruhawi." See also Abū Bakr al-Rāzī, *Akhlāq al-ṭabīb,* annotated by A. M. Soubhi (Cairo: Dār al-Turāth, 1977).

39. The article from Diderot's *Encyclopédie* devotes sixty-seven pages to the study of the pulse in the Galenic, Chinese and Mechanical tradition. After a lengthy description of diagnosis by the pulse in the Galenic world, the author says that the mechanical pulse came into existence because physicians who were unable to cope with varieties of pulses, rejected what they could feel for the relatively simpler comforts of counting numbers. www.lib.uchicago.edu/efts/ARTFL/projects/encyc, accessed 2/26/2008.

40. John Floyer, *The Physician's Pulse Watch: or An Essay to Explain the Old Art of Feeling the Pulse* (London: Sam Smith, 1707). See J. Duffin, "The Cardiology of R. T. H. Laennec," *Medical History* 33 (1989): 42–71; and Peter Kandela, "The Stethoscope," *Lancet* 352 (1998): 997. For a more general history, see Stanley Joel Reiser, "The Science of Diagnosis: Diagnostic Technology," in *Companion Encyclopedia of Medicine,* eds. Roy Porter and William F. Bynum (London: Routledge, 1993), 826–51; Merriley Borrell, "Training the Senses, Training the Mind," in *Medicine and the Five Senses,* eds. William F. Bynum and Roy Porter (London: Cambridge, 1993), 244–321; and S. Joel Reiser, *Medicine and the Reign of Technology* (London: Cambridge, 1968).

41. See A. Mark Smith, "Knowing Things Inside Out: The Scientific Revolution from a Medieval Perspective," *American Historical Review* 35 (2000): 726–44; A. Koyre, *From the Closed World to the Infinite Universe* (Baltimore: Johns Hopkins University Press, 1968); Steven Shapin, "The Philosopher and the Chicken: On the Dietetics of Disembodied

Knowledge," in *Science Incarnate: Historical Embodiments of Natural Knowledge,* eds. C. Lawrence and S. Shapin (Chicago: University of Chicago Press, 1996), 21–50; M. Nicolson, *The Breaking of the Circle* (New York: Columbia, 1960).

42. The landmark work of M. Foucault, *The Birth of the Clinic* (New York: Vintage, 1973), began a now burgeoning field in the history of medicine. The shift into modern medicine has now been related back to Paracelsus, who was the first to define disease as an ontological entity. Paracelsus (Phillip von Hohenheim) identified diseases as real entities different in material and composition, which arose from specific causes. Jan Baptista van Helmont, Sydenham and others elaborated complex systems of classifications. Vesalius' anatomical dissection could infer the illnesses of the living from the pathology of the cadavers. Morgagni stated that diseases had seats in the body. They leave footprints on the tissues of the body, or as Von Helmont expressed it, diseases were "spina in fixa" that had to be removed.

JUSTIN STEARNS

Enduring the Plague

Ethical Behavior in the Fatwas of a Fourteenth-Century Mufti and Theologian

In the second half of the fourteenth century, plague (*Yersinia pestis*) swept repeatedly through the Mediterranean, devastating both the Christian and Muslims worlds.[1] Much has been written about the effects of the plague on the economic and intellectual foundations of those societies it struck, and some scholars have offered initial comparisons of how Muslims and Christians responded to the natural disaster.[2] Two renowned and respected scholars of Nasrid Granada addressed the ethical and social challenges posed by the plague, and their writings can offer deeper insight into the nature of law, medicine, and theology in the post-formative period of Muslim thought. Whereas it has often been assumed that both Islamic law and theology functioned to hamper the practice of science and medicine, an argument can be made that ethical concerns regarding the community's welfare as well as critical evaluations of empirical evidence were expressed through legal and theological vocabularies. Medicine and law, theology and ethics influenced each other on this issue in an ongoing conversation.

Ibn al-Khatib (d. 1374) and Ibn Lubb (d. 1381) played important roles in the political and intellectual life of Granada during the fourteenth century. Ibn al-Khatib was the most prominent historian in al-Andalus of his time and was best known as Granada's most powerful political figure, serving twice as vizier. Known for his learning as well as his political acumen, Ibn al-Khatib ultimately fell victim to court intrigue and, after accusations of heresy were leveled against him, was summarily murdered in Fez in 1374.[3] The Granadan vizier was a prolific author, and his works ranged far beyond history, including poetry, mysticism, geography, and medicine. In the wake of the Black Death of 1349, Ibn al-Khatib wrote a treatise entitled *The Satisfaction of the Questioner Regarding the Appalling Illness* (*Muqniʿat al-sāʾil ʿan al-maraḍ al-hāʾil*). This work dealt chiefly with the medical aspects of the plague, but included in its strong defense of the need to flee the plague was an unabashed attack on those legal scholars who denied the principle of contagion.[4] For Ibn al-Khatib, any Prophetic traditions and prior legal arguments that denied contagion had to yield before the empirical evidence that supported the contagious nature of the plague. To think otherwise would be to expose the Muslim community to needless danger and would go against the underlying principles of the Sharia.

One of Ibn al-Khatib's teachers, and the most prominent Granadan legal authority of his day, Ibn Lubb, has received considerably less attention in modern scholarship than his student has.[5] He was the author of several short works but is chiefly known for his legal decisions (known as fatwas), many of which were gathered by al-Wansharisi at the end of the fifteenth century and included in his famous compendium, *al-Mi'yar.* From the scant evidence available, it would appear that Ibn Lubb and Ibn al-Khatib enjoyed friendly relations, and it is possible that Ibn Lubb made an attempt to intercede for his former student after the latter's fall from grace.[6] In *al-Mi'yar* we find two fatwas by Ibn Lubb on the subject of the plague.[7] In both of these he denies the phenomenon of contagion and argues for the importance of tending to the sick. While Ibn al-Khatib's views on the plague were, it seems, universally ignored by subsequent generations, Ibn Lubb's fatwas were favorably cited into the nineteenth century.[8] Unfortunately, it is not possible to date the writings of Ibn al-Khatib and Ibn Lubb any more precisely than to note that Ibn al-Khatib wrote his plague treatise soon after the initial outbreak of the Black Death in 1349, and Ibn Lubb gave his two fatwas between that time and his death in 1381.[9] Neither scholar referred to the other's views, and we do not know which of the two sources preceded the other.

Both Ibn al-Khatib and Ibn Lubb formulated their opinions from within a legal framework at a time when the social fabric of the *umma* (Muslim community) was coming under extraordinary pressure. Despite this, they came to diametrically opposite points of view. Examining how these two scholars arrived at their conclusions shows how they justified the behavior they advocated within an ethical framework.[10] Based on how current historiography has employed their opposing arguments, broad points can be made concerning the nature of Islamic law in the premodern period.

The Ethics of Empirical Evidence

Toward the end of Ibn al-Khatib's plague treatise we read:

> One principle that cannot be ignored is that if the senses and observation (*al-mushāhada*) oppose traditional evidence (*al-dalīl al-sam'ī*), the latter needs to be interpreted, and the correct course in this case is to interpret it according to what a group of those who affirm contagion say (*bi-mā dhahaba ilayhi ṭā'ifatun mimman athbata al-qawl bi-l-'adwā*). In the Law there are many texts that support this, such as [the Prophet's] saying may God pray for him and grant him peace: "The sick should not be watered with the healthy," and the saying of the Companion: "I flee from the will of God to His will." This is not the place for prolixity on this subject. The discussion, based on the Law, regarding the existence

> or non-existence of contagion, is not among the duties of medicine (*hādhā al-fann*), but instead it arises only parenthetically and by way of example, and this is analyzed in its place.
>
> To sum up, to play deaf to such an inference is to be malicious (*za'ārah*), it is blasphemy (*taṣāqur*) against God, and holding the lives of Muslims to be cheap. A group of pious people in the Maghrib (*al-'idwa*) have renounced [their previous view] to the people, bearing witness against themselves that they no longer give fatwas to this effect [that is, not believing in contagion], in order to avoid being in the position of declaring it permissible for people to engage in suicidal behavior (*mustaqillīn mushhidīn 'alā anfusihim bi-l-rujū' 'an al-fatāwā bi-dhālik taḥarrujan min taswīgh al-ilqā' bi-l-yad ilā-l-tahlukah*) [a reference to Q 2:195]. God protect us from nonsense (*al-khaṭal*) and grant us success in both speech and action.[11]

For a full understanding of Ibn al-Khatib's argument, it is necessary to refer to the legal debate that existed around the issue of contagion. In a series of traditions found in the six canonical collections of hadith, the Prophet Muhammad offered seemingly contradictory opinions on whether or not a disease can pass between healthy and sick animals and people. The Prophet, on the one hand, denied the existence of contagion along with other pre-Islamic misconceptions, such as the belief in evil omens, ghouls, owls that perch on graves of the dead and call for the revenge of the slain, and certain possibly infectious stomach worms.[12] On the other hand, as Ibn al-Khatib notes, he also advised against mixing healthy animals with sick animals, adding that one should flee from lepers as though they were lions.[13] The tension between these two groups of traditions is addressed on at least two occasions in the hadith. In the first case, the famed traditionist Abu Hurayra (d. circa 678) relates both that there is no contagion and that healthy and sick animals should not be watered together. Abu Hurayra is then confronted by his nephew, and flustered, he denies ever having related that the Prophet had denied contagion.[14] Subsequently, opponents of contagion would note that other reliable chains of transmitters may be cited to support the "no contagion" tradition and that Abu Hurayra's denial was in no way proof for its existence.[15]

The second case is found in a tradition stating that after the Prophet publicly pronounced that there is no contagion, a Bedouin stood up and asked him about a case in which a mangy camel entered a group of healthy camels, after which they too became mangy. The Prophet retorted: "And who infected the first?"[16] Later commentators inferred from the Prophet's statement that since God caused the first camel to become mangy, it was likewise divine action that caused the others to become mangy.[17]

These two traditions suggest that it is possible that as early as the Prophet's lifetime in the seventh century there was substantial confusion among Muslims regarding the existence or nonexistence of contagion.[18] A marker of the prominence of the debate and its relevance to the larger question of the reliability of Prophetic tradition is the fact that Ibn Qutayba (d. 889), the famous polymath and defender of Prophetic tradition, took up the matter in his *Reconciliation of Contradictions in Prophetic Tradition (Ta'wīl mukhtalif al-ḥadīth)* at the time when the six canonical collections of Prophetic tradition were being compiled.[19] Ibn Qutayba took a more nuanced, if perhaps confused, stance on the question than many of his successors would, arguing that while there is no contagion, certain diseases such as scabies and leprosy can be transmitted through contact.[20] That plague did not make the list of transmittable diseases can in part be explained by an episode in early Islamic history that was later documented at length in collections of Prophetic tradition. In the fourteenth century Ibn al-Khatib would also reference this episode in his plague treatise.

The conquest of Syria took place during the caliphate of 'Umar b. al-Khattab (634–44). Plague broke out in the town of 'Amwās. When Umar heard of this, he was on his way to Syria with a large retinue, and he asked his companions whether or not they should continue toward the plague-struck area. In the ensuing debate, the Prophetic companion 'Abd al-Rahman b. 'Awf (d. 652) recounted a tradition in which the Prophet had affirmed that one should neither enter nor exit from a plague-struck area. Relying on this tradition, and seemingly reluctant to approach the plague, 'Umar ordered his party to return to the *Ḥijāz.* He was immediately challenged by another companion of the Prophet, Abu 'Ubayda (d. 640), who accused him of fleeing from the will of God. The caliph's retort, cited by Ibn al-Khatib and Ibn Lubb, was that he was fleeing from the will of God to the will of God.[21] The debate around the existence and possible nature of contagion continued in the genre of commentaries on Prophetic tradition from the time of Ibn Qutayba in the ninth century to that of Ibn al-Khatib and beyond, with the majority of authors arguing that contagion does not exist. In part these scholars were able to reconcile the problematic traditions by citing the legal principle of *sadd al-dhari'a,* or forbidding a nominally permissible course of action because it would lead to a prohibited action.[22] Following this logic, it was not because of contagion that the Prophet forbade approaching the plague and mixing healthy with sick animals, but because credulous and uneducated Muslims might be fooled by the apparent existence of contagion to believe that diseases have the ability to transmit themselves, and thus—by positing the existence of a causative agent other than God—they would slip into believing in polytheism.[23] It is important to note that in their efforts to refute the existence of contagion, hadith commentators invoked what were principally legal arguments (for example, *sadd al-dhari'a*), not theological ones, although they laid the groundwork for later jurists and theologians such as Ibn Lubb.[24]

Despite Ibn al-Khatib's claim that his plague treatise was not the place to expand on legal rationales for permitting Muslims to flee from the plague, he presented his reader with a dual-faceted legal argument in favor of the efficacy of contagion. The first aspect can be found in his selective citation of Prophetic tradition: he chose to mention two traditions that, when combined, strongly suggested the validity of contagion and the acceptance of this fact by the Prophet's companions. The second aspect of his compressed argument can be found in his blanket refutation of legal arguments and Prophetic traditions that were detrimental to the Muslim community. In taking this step, he arguably chose to present his reader with a rationale implicitly based on the good of the Muslim community (*maslaha*). In doing so, he may have been drawing on a legal principle that, while controversial, had gained prominence by the eleventh century.[25] It is worth remembering that it was in Ibn al-Khatib's lifetime that the doctrine of *maslaha* was given its most comprehensive reformulation since al-Ghazali (d. 1111) as *maqasid al-shari'a* by Ibn Lubb's most famous student, al-Shatibi (d. 1388).[26] Generally defined as the preservation of religion, life, reason, progeny, and property, the *maqasid* of the law provided jurists with a method to privilege general objectives over specific injunctions. In this respect they overlap in scope with *maslaha,* and at issue here is the degree of importance given to *maslaha* as a legal principle. While al-Ghazali acknowledged *maslaha,* he treated it as a type of *qiyas,* refusing to see in it an independent source of legal reasoning.[27] Al-Shatibi's innovation lay in being able to separate *maslaha* from the classical theory of law possessing four sources (Qur'an, Sunna, *ijma'*, and *qiyas*) and relate it directly to Qur'an and Sunna.[28] Yet, while al-Shatibi's discussion of *maslaha* would have ramifications for later generations, Ibn al-Khatib, who never mentions *maslaha* explicitly, makes no reference to them.

Of central importance to Ibn al-Khatib is the question of what the appropriate ethical behavior is in a time of plague. Basing his thoughts on empirical evidence, Ibn al-Khatib can see no benefit to staying in a plague-struck area. Indeed, he goes so far as to equate a decision to do so with endangering oneself.[29] He bitterly attacks those legal scholars who have advocated placing oneself in danger, noting that some of them have in fact recanted their former views. For Ibn al-Khatib, the only proper response to the plague is to advise all Muslims to avoid persons who have been infected and to flee from an area in which the plague is found.

Framing Ethical Choices with Theology

Unlike Ibn al-Khatib, Ibn Lubb drew heavily on previous legal and religious works that had addressed the issue of contagion. Not surprisingly, Ibn Lubb cites earlier authorities who had argued against contagion and who referred to the principle of *sadd al-dhari'a* to explain those traditions that suggested its existence. However, Ibn Lubb brought new life to the argument denying contagion by introducing the theological language of Ash'arism. By the eleventh century, Ash'arism, named after the prominent Iraqi theologian Abu Hasan al-Ash'ari (d. circa 941), had spread to the Maghrib and al-Andalus, where it continued to flourish through the Almoravid and Almohad periods.[30] Less attention has been paid to the presence of Ashʿarism in Nasrid Granada. Similarly scholars have largely neglected studying whether and how Ashʿarism influenced legal discourse.[31] It can be argued that Ibn Lubb, while choosing to support a majority legal opinion—the denial of contagion—did so with arguments drawn from Ashʿarism, thus giving his fatwas additional theoretical support and continuing relevance to later scholars. Early in his first legal opinion, Ibn Lubb attacks those who base their belief in contagion on empirical evidence:

> Consider the fact that the strong gale of wind in summer on the [otherwise] still sea in the evening is often of this type. It is not right that you say that the evening caused [the wind] to move or to appear, nor that the early morning caused [the wind] to be still. They are only events associated with specific moments and are the continuation of the norm and the prevailing condition. This [association] does not necessarily contradict [the idea that these things occur without earthly causation] nor does it detract [from the validity of this view,] since the association of one thing with another does not mean that [the first] is [the second's] cause, nor that [the former] has influence on [the latter] or connection with [its] existence. The belief in contagion, according to this view, becomes an aspect (*shai'*) of the sicknesses of which nothing is known and which has no proven existence (*rajman bi'l-ghayb wa hawā bi-lā dalāl*) [a possible allusion to Q 18:22]. This is especially the case when Prophetic tradition has informed differently from this [a belief in contagion] concerning these [sicknesses].[32]

It is striking that Ibn Lubb cites Prophetic tradition here as a secondary form of authority, which supports the primary authority of the central theological argument of occasionalism. Occasionalism, the belief that God causes each and every action to occur and that two moments have no causal relation to each other, is a central tenet of Ashʿarism, which serves in part to deny causal efficacy to anything but God.[33] It can be understood in relation to Ashʿarism's solution to the problem of free will, the doctrine of acquisition (*kasb*), in which man acquires responsibility for actions that God creates for him. Implicit in occasionalism is that no thing possesses a nature or essence that is independent of God and which could thus cause anything on its own. This is not to say that Ashʿaris deny the regular occurrence of one event after another: it can be expected, for example, that cotton, when brought into contact with fire, will burn. The burning, however, is not considered to be caused by a property of the fire itself, but because it is God's habit (*ʿada,* less frequently *sunna*) to cause cotton to burn when it encounters fire. Initially it would seem that followers of Ashʿarism would have no problem with the phenomenon of disease being transmitted as long as it was acknowledged that it was God and not the disease itself that effected the transfer from one person to another. Still there were two possible problems. The first was that the concept of contagion could and often was interpreted to imply that diseases have natures that allow them to pass from one human or animal to another. In the eyes of Ash'ari theology, support of this "Naturalism," as heresiographers came to call it by the tenth century at the latest, is tantamount to polytheism and is clearly heretical.[34] Admittedly the issue could be resolved by introducing the concept of secondary causation, in which God gives entities a limited ability of causation.[35] Although such a possibility is not explicitly ruled out by Ibn Lubb, he chooses to emphasize that diseases themselves do not function as agents of disease transmission. Rejecting secondary causation is, in fact, vital for Ibn Lubb's argument, as it would not be ethical for him to advocate that Muslims remain close to a source of danger without cause. Instead, he cites the Prophet's response to the above-mentioned observant Bedouin in order to emphasize his own point that temporal association between events in no way implies causation:

> . . . that is to say, the one [God] who did this the first time without contagion is also the one who did it to the second when you say it was through contagion. The Prophet, Peace be Upon Him, did not deny the presence of that which infects (*yata'addī*) in a place or through association or close relations (*mulābasa*). Yes, the Prophet decreed the belief that this is one of the creations of God the Most High who creates what He wishes and how He wishes. The Prophet denied the belief in the existence of a sickness that acts on another (*fī ghayr maḥallihi*) through its nature (*bi-ṭib'ihi*) according to the belief of ignorant times. As for it [the sickness] being a cause, God the Most High created similar ones other than this and it did not benefit him. He did not wish for it [the transmission of disease] to be called 'contagion' but instead 'its passing' (*jawzuhu*). Therefore God ordered the distancing from the leper, as one flees from something harmful (*al-ḍarar*), dangerous places (*al-mahālik*) and calamities (*wujūh al-ma'āṭib*), fleeing from the decree of God to the decree of God (*min qadar Allāh ilā qadar Allāh*).[36]

Not unlike Ibn Qutayba, Ibn Lubb admits here that sickness may pass between people, but he strongly denies that this could happen through its own nature and that the sickness may be considered to be a cause.

The second possible objection to plague being contagious, also taken up in this passage by Ibn Lubb, was to acknowledge that God had created proximity to some diseases—such as leprosy—as a condition for the transmission of disease, but that this was not the case with plague. For Ibn Lubb, it follows that when a believer is confronted by the plague, he should not fear the possibility of infection, but should rather trust in God and consider his responsibilities as a Muslim. Ibn Lubb is quite clear on the nature of these responsibilities: in a time of sickness, as confirmed in Prophetic tradition, it is the duty of Muslims to take care of the sick and to look after them. The extraordinary nature of plague—what differentiated it from other diseases and also strongly suggested that it was not in fact contagious—was that dying from it resulted in martyrdom. At the end of his first fatwa, Ibn Lubb argues, based on Prophetic tradition and episodes from early Islamic history, that the plague should be considered a blessing for the Muslim *umma,* and that, as the Prophet had stated, if a Muslim dies of the plague, he will receive the reward of martyrdom.[37] It is precisely this line of argument that the famous scholar of Prophetic tradition, Ibn Hajar al-Asqalani (d. 1449), would follow half a century later in his book-length treatise on the virtues of dying of the plague.[38] What is striking about the structure of Ibn Lubb's legal opinions is precisely that he does not give place of preference to the Prophetic traditions that promise heaven to those who die of plague, and that instead he stresses the communal responsibilities of Muslims in this world. Like Ibn al-Khatib, but based on a different comprehension of plague etiology, Ibn Lubb argued implicitly for an understanding of the law that is based on the importance of communal welfare. Unlike Ibn al-Khatib, who held that the lives of Muslims are threatened by the plague, Ibn Lubb saw the plague as principally endangering the social fabric of the Muslim *umma* and formulated his legal opinions accordingly. And, unlike Ibn al-Khatib, Ibn Lubb did not place his response to the legal and social challenge posed by the plague within a medical treatise, but in a pair of fatwas that attracted enough attention to be collected by al-Wansharisi over a century later.[39]

Empiricism, Historiography, and Ethics

It is not surprising that Ibn al-Khatib's strident defense of empiricism and his harsh words for narrow-minded jurists have been widely acclaimed in western scholarship. They support too well the conventional view that Muslim jurists were (and are) obsessed with Prophetic tradition and distanced from reality. Within this framework, Ibn al-Khatib is seen as a lone voice of reason in an age when few others had the courage to stand up to a religious establishment that, it is assumed, was oppressive and censorious.[40] I would to like to propose a different interpretation.

Both Ibn al-Khatib and Ibn Lubb strove to find an ethical answer to the challenge posed by epidemic disease. They differed on whether or not plague is contagious. It is worth recalling that Muslim physicians from the time of al-Razi in the ninth century had long considered plague, along with numerous other diseases, including leprosy, to be contagious.[41] Muslim jurists, with some exceptions, had since the time of Ibn Qutayba, similarly supported the belief that some diseases can be transmitted, although for theological reasons they avoided calling this transmission "contagion." The jurists differed with the physicians solely on the subject of the plague, and they did so for two reasons: first, a substantial body of Prophetic traditions supported the notion that dying of the plague is a good thing; and, second, and this was in my opinion the more important factor, many jurists were not convinced by the empirical evidence that the plague was contagious, or that it could be transmitted between individuals.

With some notable exceptions, plague is *not* contagious.[42] For both Ibn al-Khatib and Ibn Lubb, the concept of contagion implied that a disease is able to transmit itself *directly* from one person or animal to another.[43] In the case of plague, direct transmission occurs only in pneumonic and septicemic cases, when the plague bacteria find their way into the lungs or blood stream, respectively. Once this happens, the bacteria can easily be passed to others through coughing or the exchange of blood. The vast majority of plague victims that Ibn al-Khatib and Ibn Lubb would have seen, however, would have been struck by bubonic plague, in which the bacteria infect the lymph nodes and produce painful, swollen buboes.[44] In bubonic plague, the plague bacteria are not transmitted directly from one victim to another; instead, the victims are infected independently by fleas. In the majority of the cases, the fleas are rat fleas (*Xenopsylla cheopis*), which have acquired the plague bacteria from their hosts. In some cases plague bacteria can be transmitted by human fleas (*Pulex irritans*), but this is rare.

In Europe the debate over whether or not plague was contagious raged until the end of the nineteenth century. Only in 1894 did the French doctor Alexandre Yersin (d. 1943) identify the plague bacteria in Hong Kong.[45] At the time, alternate hypotheses for the source of plague included miasma, a medical theory popular in the Middle Ages, in which sickness is produced by the inhaling of bad air. Along with contagion, miasma had been popular among both Christian and Muslim doctors in the pre-modern period as the cause of plague.[46] Returning to fourteenth-century Granada, it would seem rather forced to continue to see Ibn al-Khatib as a lone voice of reason and Ibn Lubb as a blind slave to tradition. Both men were attempting to address an overwhelming situation with insufficient knowledge, and both came to the task with specific preconceptions. Whereas Ibn al-Khatib believed that empirical evidence supported the existence of contagion, if he had looked closer, he might have noticed that the facts did not fit his understanding as neatly as he would have liked. Ibn Lubb, on the other hand, would not have found anything in the consequences of bubonic plague that would have shaken his belief in occasionalism: sometimes proximity to a plague victim would result in the transmission of the disease, sometimes not. In addition the empirical evidence was not sufficiently compelling to force him to include plague among those diseases that God customarily caused to be transmitted to others when they were in proximity to the afflicted.[47]

Conclusion

In a short article published in 1971, Fazlur Rahman argued that the theoretical presuppositions of Ashʿari theology, specifically the concepts of occasionalism and *kasb*—the human acquisition of acts created by God—conflicted with the notion of legal obligation at the heart of Islamic legal theory. In addition he noted that this conflict had been discussed by the Damascene scholar Ibn Taymiyya (d. 1328), although this criticism had been largely ignored by subsequent generations.[48] In the above discussion, I have shown that this was, at the very least, not always the case. Instead, we find the Granadan mufti Ibn Lubb invoking Ash'ari theology in order to strengthen a legal argument that was well established in the Maliki school of law and advocating what he saw to be the requisite ethical and legal action to be taken in the time of plague. Yet, in the centuries following the Black Death, the subject of contagion was revisited numerous times, as the theological arguments advanced by Ibn Lubb were repeatedly juxtaposed with the type of empirical observations made by Ibn al-Khatib.[49] Clearly, while theological reasoning could be employed to strengthen a legal argument, it brought its own problems with it. How theology influenced the practice and theorization of law from the fourteenth to the nineteenth centuries—the era in question—is a question that is much larger than the subject considered here, and one that, regrettably, has received little attention. What is clear, however, is that with regard to the subject of contagion, jurists wrestling with the problem of finding an ethical solution to the plague were influenced not only by medicine and theology, but—in later centuries—by Sufism as well with its emphasis on the concept of *tawakkul* (reliance upon God).[50] Indeed, the difficulty inherent in the attempt to separate the discourses of medicine, legal theory, theology and Sufism can be clearly seen well beyond the fourteenth century in such texts as Ahmad b. Ajiba's (d. 1809) *Sulūk al-durar fī dhikr al-qaḍā' wa-l-qadar,* which combines Ash'ari arguments and a refutation of empirical observation with a description of the meritorious deeds of those who trust in God and undertook the washing of the bodies of those who had died of the plague.[51] If nothing else, we learn from such texts, as from those of Ibn al-Khatib and Ibn Lubb, that the practice of Islamic law in the fourteenth century was seldom carried out in a theoretical vacuum, and that jurisprudents who were also doctors, theologians and Sufis, drew upon these discourses in the framing of the legal decisions.

Both Ibn al-Khatib and Ibn Lubb strove to find an ethical solution to an impossible situation. Both scholars proceeded from the assumption that the good of the community played an important role in the formulation of positive law, even if their varying understandings of plague etiology generated disparate outcomes. The larger implication of this observation for Islamic Law is perhaps unsurprising: as the facts available to jurists change, so will their views on specific subjects. In the case of plague, the legal position has changed along with the facts. In a recent collection of essays on the interaction between medicine and faith, the former Grand Mufti of Tunis, Muhammad al-Mukhtar al-Salami, addresses the issue of contagion in the light of current medical knowledge.[52] After reviewing all relevant Prophetic traditions, he explains that a belief in contagion is permissible as long as it is based on an understanding of contagion as a product of secondary causation and not as the result of the disease's own nature. As mentioned above, such a position was refuted by prominent proponents of Ashʿarism as heretical, and would have been difficult to accept on theological grounds.[53] In part, however, the mufti is able to unite the conflicting views of Ibn al-Khatib and Ibn Lubb, for while supporting the phenomenon of contagion, he also stresses the importance of visiting and consoling the sick. Strikingly he emphasizes that there is an escape from contagion: it is, after all, God who controls all things, and it is in God that man should trust.[54] This argument shows how for al-Salami, as for many other Muslim jurists in both the pre-modern and modern periods, the articulation of substantive law involves the consideration of disciplines such as medicine, theology and Sufism in the careful balancing of the community's spiritual and social needs.

As suggested by the above discussion, the facts on which legal decisions are based are often unclear or contested, and social and political forces often impede legal change.[55] In contemporary bioethical debates, for example, the social and political construction of what are designated as facts has been richly documented.[56] In decisions handed down in recent decades by both Egypt's Dar al-Ifta' and the Muslim World League, any mention of the Prophet's denial of contagion is studiously avoided while Qur'anic verses, Prophetic traditions and legal principles that support isolation of the sick are emphasized.[57] If we are to achieve a deeper understanding of contemporary, as well as premodern ethical positions in Islam, we must examine not only the conclusions individual scholars arrived at, but also the manner in which these conclusions were reached and the construction of the facts upon which they were based.

NOTES

1. I would like to thank David Powers, Michael Cook, and Nathalie Peutz for their comments and suggestions on various drafts of this essay. In addition I am grateful to James Davis for a conversation we had on ethics and its relation to law. I am indebted to Jonathan Brockopp and Thomas Eich for their advice and support.

2. See Michael Dols, "The Comparative Communal Responses to the Black Death in Muslim and Christian Societies," *Viator* 5 (1974): 269–87; and Marie-Hélène Congourdeau and Mohamed Melhaoui, "La peception de la peste en pays Chrétien Byzantine et Musulman," *Revue des Études Byzantines* 59 (2001): 95–124. For a recent, insightful study of the effects of the Black Death on Egypt and England, see Stuart J. Borsch, *The Black Death in Egypt and England: A Comparative Study* (Austin: University of Texas Press, 2005).

3. On the trial of Ibn al-Khatib, see the excellent article of M. Isabel Calero Secall, "El Proceso de Ibn al-Jaṭib," *Al-Qanṭara* 22 (2001): 421–61.

4. See the discussion below.

5. On the life of Ibn Lubb, see *Biblioteca de al-Andalus* (Almería: Fundación Ibn Tuyafl, 2006), 4:24–28, for the entry by Amalía Zomeño, to whom I am grateful for providing me

with an advance copy. Ibn al-Khatib wrote respectfully of Ibn Lubb in *Al-Iḥāṭa fī akhbār al-Gharnāṭa* (Cairo: Dār al-Khanjī, 2001), 4:253–55.

6. Calero Secall, "El Proceso de Ibn al-Jaṭīb," 428–29. In an episode recounted by Ibn Lubb's famous student al-Shatibi (d. 1387), we find Ibn Lubb and Ibn al-Khatib taking part in a *majlis* assembled by Abu 'Abdallah al-Maqqari, the great-grandfather of the famous Moroccan historian of al-Andalus. The episode is found in Ibrāhīm b. Mūsā al-Shāṭibī, *Al-Ifādāt wa-l-inshādāt* (Beirut: Mu'assisat al-Rasūl, 1983), 126–27; and is quoted in Abū l-'Abbās Aḥmad b. Muḥammad al-Maqqarī, *Nafḥ al-Ṭīb* (Beirut: Dār Ṣādir, 1988), 5:265–66.

7. Abū l-'Abbās Aḥmad Ibn Yaḥyā al-Wansharīsī, *Al-Mi'yār al-mu'rib* (Rabat: Dār al-Gharb al-Islāmī, 1990), 11:352–60.

8. See Muḥammad b. Aḥmad al-Rahūnī (d. 1814), *Jawāb fī aḥkām al-ṭā'ūn*, manuscript found in al-Khizāna al-'Amma, Rabat, in the collection D 2251, 1–48. Al-Rahuni's treatise was partially included (from page 17 onward) in Abū 'Īsā Sīdī al-Mahdī al-Wazzānī (d. 1923), *Al-Mi'yār al-jadīd al-jāmi' al-mu'rib 'an fatāwa al-muta'akhkhirīn min 'ulamā' al-maghrib*, ed. 'Umar b. 'Attād (Morocco: Wizārat al-Awqāf wa-l-Shu'ūn al-Islāmiyya, 1996), 3: 241–56 (rather obscurely, in the chapter on *ḥajj*). For an earlier reliance in the genre of plague treatises on Ibn Lubb's fatwas, see Muḥammad b. Aḥmad al-Ḥājj (d. after 1715), *Mas'ala fi ḥukm al-'adwa*, manuscript found in al-Khizāna al-Mālikiyya, Rabat, call number Za 12369, folios 79–95, 90r–v.

9. As the plague struck al-Andalus repeatedly during the second half of the fourteenth century, Ibn Lubb's fatwas do not necessarily date from the plague's initial outbreak in 1349.

10. On the possibilities of studying ethics through law in an Islamic context, see Kevin Reinhart, "Islamic Law as Islamic Ethics," *Journal of Religious Ethics* 11, no. 2 (1983): 186–203.

11. Muḥammad al-'Arabī al-Khaṭṭābī, *Al-Ṭibb wa-l-aṭibbā' fī -l-Andalus al-islāmiyya* (Beirut: Dār al-Gharb al-Islāmī, 1988), 2:188. This passage is difficult at times. Compare the text and translation given in M. J. Mueller, "Ibnulkhatîbs Bericht über die Pest," *Sitzungsberichte der königliche bayerische Akademie der Wissenschaften zu München* 2 (1863): 6–8, 18–21; as well as the English translation (based on Mueller's edition) given in John Aberth, *The Black Death: The Great Mortality of 1348–1350* (Boston: Bedford/St. Martins, 2005), 114–16. Ildefonso Garijo Galán, Jorge Lirola Delgado, and Pilar Lirola Delgado are currently preparing a scholarly edition of all three Andalusian plague treatises, and once it appears, this edition will greatly facilitate research into the Muslim response to the plague in al-Andalus.

12. Given here is a composite version of the relevant traditions that contains all the elements whose existence was denied. Individual traditions contain various constellations of these elements. See Aḥmad Ibn Ḥanbal, *Al-Musnad* (Cairo: Dār al-Ḥadīth, 1995), 9:124 (*musnad* Abī Hurayra), 9:359 and 423–24 (*musnad* Jābir); Bukhārī, *Ṣaḥīḥ* (Cairo, 1898), 7:256 (related from Abū Hurayra); Muslim, *Ṣaḥīḥ* (Cairo: Dār al-Ḥadīth, 1991), 4:1744 (variants from Abū Hurayra and Jābir); Muḥammad b. Yazīd Ibn Māja, *Sunan* (Beirut: Dār Iḥyā' al-Turāth, 1975), 2:1170–71 (related by Ibn'Abbās).

13. For the tradition on healthy and sick animals, see Mālik b. Anas, *Al-Muwaṭṭa'* (Beirut: Dār al-Gharb al-Islāmī, 1994), 476; Ibn Ḥanbal, *Al-Musnad,* 9:124, 260 (musnad

Abī Hurayra); Ibn Māja, *Sunan,* 2:1171. See also al-Bukhārī, *Ṣaḥīḥ,* vols. 3–4, 15–16, where, after being informed that he was sold camels that are *huyyām*—afflicted with a sickness of constant thirst—Ibn 'Umar notes that the camels should drink but that he does not need to return them, for the Prophet had said that there is no contagion. For the tradition equating lepers with lions, see 'Abd al-Razzāq Ibn Hammām al-Ṣan'ānī, *Al-Muṣannaf* (Beirut: Dā r al-Kutub al-'Ilmiyya, 2000), 10:25; Ibn Ḥanbal, *Al-Musnad,* 9:292 (the editor notes that the *isnād* is weak but the tradition sound); al-Bukhārī, *Ṣaḥīḥ,* vols. 7–8, 17.

14. Muslim, *Ṣaḥīḥ Muslim* (Beirut: Dār IbnḤazm, 1995), 4:1390–92; al-Bukhārī *Ṣaḥīḥ,* vols. 7–8, 31. This is the most detailed version of the tradition. Note that in Ibn Ḥanbal's *Al-Musnad,* 9:260, Abu Hurayra does in fact relate as one tradition both the denial of contagion and the admonition not to water sick and healthy animals together. Other versions of the confrontation, in which, notably, the challenger is not identified as Abu Hurayra's nephew and in which Abu Salama (d. 712) does not mention the possibility of abrogation to explain the apparent contradiction (as he does in the above examples), can be found in 'Abd al-Razzāq, *Al-Muṣannaf,* 10:24; and Sulaimān Ibn al-Ash'ath Abū Dāwūd, *Sunan Abī Dāwūd* (Beirut: Dār al-Kutub al-'Ilmiyya, 1996), 3:16.

15. An example of Abu Hurayra's denial of having related the "no contagion" tradition being discounted can be found in Muḥammad b. 'Alī al-Shawkānī's (d. 1834) treatise on the plague, *Itḥāf al-mahra bi-l-kalām 'alā ḥadīth lā 'adwā wa-lā ṭiyarata;* see *Kitāb al-fatḥ al-rabbānī min fatāwa al-Imam al-Shawkānī,* ed. Abū Muṣ'ab Muḥammad Ṣubḥī b. Ḥasan Ḥallāq (San'a: Maktabat al-Jīl al-Jadīd, 2002), 4:1944.

16. 'Abd al-Razzāq, *Al-Muṣannaf,* 10:24; Ibn Ḥanbal, *Al-Musnad* (Beirut: Dār al-Fikr, 1991), 1:444 (camels and mange), 539–40 (sheep and scabies), both the *musnad* of Ibn 'Abbās; ibid., 2:523 (*musnad* Abī Hurayra); Muslim, *Ṣaḥīḥ Muslim* (1995), 4:1390; al-Bukhārī, *Ṣaḥīḥ,* vols. 7–8, 31.

17. See especially Aḥmad Ibn 'Umar al-Qurṭubī, *Al-Mufhim li-mā ashkala min talkhīṣ kitāb Muslim* (Damascus: Dār Ibn Kathīr, 1996), 5:621–22; and Aḥmad b. 'Alī Ibn Ḥajar al-'Asqalānī, *Fatḥ al-bārī bi-sharḥ al-Bukhārī.* (Cairo: Maktabat al-Kulliya al-Azhariyya, 1978), 21:377. Ibn Ḥajar alters and abbreviates the passage slightly.

18. This is not the place to enter into the ongoing debate regarding the dating of traditions attributed to the Prophet. Nevertheless there seems to be no immediate reason why the Prophet could not have expressed himself on the issue of contagion. For the experiences with the plague of the first generation after the Prophet, see the works by Conrad and Van Ess mentioned below in note 21.

19. 'Abdallāh b. Muslim Ibn Qutayba, *Ta'wīl mukhtalif al-ḥadīth,* ed. Riḍā Faraj al-Hamāmī (Beirut: al-Maktaba al-'Aṣriyya, 2003), 98. On this passage, see Lawrence Conrad, "A Ninth-Century Muslim Scholar's Discussion of Contagion," in *Contagion: Perspectives from Pre-modern Societies,* ed. Lawrence Conrad and Dominik Wujastyk (Burlington, Vt.: Ashgate, 2000), 163–77.

20. It is unclear why Ibn Qutabya differentiated between leprosy and plague, describing the former as transmissible and the latter as not. See Conrad, "Ninth-Century Muslim Scholar's Discussion of Contagion," 173. There are at least two ways in which he could have justified such a differentiation: either by invoking the concept of God's custom (*'āda*), which, in its Ash'ari form had not yet been formulated, or by commenting on the tradition that stated that dying of the plague led to the status of a martyr. He did neither.

21. Lawrence I. Conrad, "'Umar at Sargh: The Evolution of an Umayyad Tradition on Flight from the Plague," in *Story-Telling in the Framework of Non-fictional Arabic Literature,* ed. Stefan Leder (Wiesbaden: Harrossowitz, 1998), 488–528. See also Josef Van Ess, *Der Fehltritt des Gelehrten* (Heidelberg: Universitätsverlag C. Winter, 2001), esp. 38–41 and 244–50. Van Ess disagrees with Conrad on many matters, including the dating of the final version of the tradition. There are methodological differences as well. Conrad regards the mixed reception received by 'Abd al-Raḥman b. 'Awf's citing of the Prophetic tradition against fleeing the plague as a reason for thinking that Prophetic tradition had not achieved the importance it would subsequently hold, whereas Van Ess holds that those versions that include the citation must be later ones, for the citation of a Prophetic tradition should have settled the matter immediately. Compare Conrad, "'Umar at Sargh," 498–99; with Van Ess, *Der Fehltritt des Gelehrten,* 38–41.

22. On *sadd al-dharī 'a* in general, see Mohammad Hashim Kamali, *Principles of Islamic Jurisprudence,* 2nd ed. (Cambridge: Islamic Texts Society, 1991), 310–20. An overview of the place of *sadd al-dharī 'a* in the Māliki school can be found in 'Umar al-Jīdī 's *Al-Tashrī 'al-Islāmī* (Morocco: Manshūrāt 'Akāẓ, 1987), 118–19. See also Maribel Fierro, "El principio mālikī *'sadd al-dharā'ī* '' en el *Kitāb al-ḥawādith wa-l-bida'* de Abū Bakr al-Turtūshī ," *al-Qanṭara* 2 (1981): 69–87. Ibrāhīm b. Mūsā al-Shāṭibī discusses it in his *Al-Muwāfaqāt fī uṣūl al-aḥkām* (Beirut: Dār al-Ma'rifa, 1994), 2:556–58.

23. Ibn Qutayba rejected this argument in *Ta'wīl mukhtalif al-ḥadīth,* 98. Supporters of this view can be found in Yusuf b. 'Abdallāh Ibn 'Abd al-Barr, *Al-Tamhīd fī-mā fī l-Muwaṭṭa' min al-ma'ānī wa l-asānīd* (Beirut: Dar al-Kutub al-'Ilmiya, 1992), 24:197–98; Muḥammad b. 'Alī al-Māzarī, *Al-Mu'lim bi-fawā'id Muslim* (Beirut: Dār al-Gharb al-Islāmī, 1992), 3:102–3; 'Iyāḍ b. Mūsā, *Ikmāl al-mu'lim bi-fawā'id Muslim,* 9 vols. (Mansurah: Dar al-Wafa' li-l-Tiba'a wa-l-Nashr, 1998), 9:142; al-Qurṭubī, *Al-Mufhim,* 5:620–26. In Yaḥyā Ibn Sharaf al-Nawawī, *Sharḥ Ṣaḥīḥ Muslim* (Beirut: Dār al-Qalam, 1987), 468, the author notes that believing in contagion may lead to apostasy.

24. This is not to say, of course, that such legal arguments could not have theological implications. It is precisely such examples that show how interlinked theological and legal discourses were. Another possible source for the debate around God's commands is the commentators who interpreted the Prophet saying, for example, "Flee the leper as you do the lion" as not referring to contagion but merely as a recommendation for those who preferred not to look at the disfigured bodies of lepers. Faced with a wide variety of imperatives in both Qur'an and Sunna, legal theorists argued that not every imperative necessarily carried the same force. See Wael Hallaq, *A History of Islamic Legal Theories* (Cambridge: Cambridge University Press, 1997), 48.

25. Hallaq, *History of Islamic Legal Theories,* 132. On the importance of *maslaha* in the Mālikī madhhab and the relationship of *maṣlaḥa* to *maqāṣid al-sharī 'a,* see Ahmad al-Raysūnī, *Naẓariyyat al-maqāṣid 'inda al-Imām al-Shāṭibī* (Rabat: Dār al-Amān, 1991), 25–87; and Muhammad Khalid Masud, *Shatibi's Philosophy of Islamic Law* (New Delhi: Kitab Bhaven, 1997), 127–68.

26. Masud, *Shatibi's Philosophy of Islamic Law,* 119–20, 151. Compare with Hallaq, *History of Islamic Legal Theories,* 166–67, 182–83. Masud's work was first published in 1977, and while Hallaq refers briefly to Masud's book on 162–63, he chooses not to engage its argument. This is regrettable for many reasons, one being that while both authors characterize

Shatibi's legal theory as, in part, a reaction to certain arguments made by Sufis in al-Andalus in the fourteenth century, only Masud mentions that al-Shatibi was a Sufi himself. In Masud's analysis, then, al-Shatibi's legal theory reflects not a disagreement between jurists and mystics so much as the concern of a jurist for the correct practice of mysticism. See Masud, *Shatibi's Philosophy of Islamic Law,* 70. For discussions of *maslaha* in the twentieth century, see Hallaq, *History of Islamic Legal Theories,* 207–55; and Felicitas Opwis, "*Maṣlaḥa* in Contemporary Islamic Legal Theory," *Islamic Law and Society* 12 (2005): 182–223. Yasir Ibrahim's recent dissertation on *maqāṣid al-sharī 'a* is also useful: "The Spirit of Islamic Law and Modern Religious Reform: *Maqāṣid al-sharī 'a* in Muḥammad 'Abduh and Rashī d Riḍā's Legal Thought" (Ph.D. diss., Princeton University, 2003).

27. Masud, *Shatibi's Philosophy of Islamic Law,* 142.

28. Ibid., 161. See also Hallaq, *History of Islamic Legal Theories,* 166–67, 205–6.

29. It is difficult to know to what degree Ibn al-Khatib's interpretation of Q 2:195 was shared by his contemporaries ("Spend in God's cause: do not contribute to your destruction with your own hands, but do good, for God loves those who do good." I cite the recent translation of M. A. S. Abdel Haleem, *The Qur'an* [New York: Oxford University Press, 2004], 22). Many commentators seem to have understood the verse to refer to the (spiritual) danger one placed oneself in by *not* taking part in the *jihād* against the enemies of God. While Tabarī mentions the prohibition of suicide as one of the many interpretations given to the verse, other commentators such as Ibn Kathīr and al-Qurṭubi interpret the verse as primarily emphasizing the importance of carrying out and supporting *jihād.* See Ahmet Kuramustafa, "Suicide," in *Encyclopedia of the Qur'ān* (Leiden: Brill, 2005–6), 5:159–62; Ismā'īl b. 'Umar Ibn Kathīr, *Tafsīr al-Qur'ān al-'Aẓīm* (Beirut: al-Maktaba al-'Aṣriyya, 1998), 1:200–201; and Aisha Bewley, trans., *Tafsir al-Qurtubi* (London: Dar al-Taqwa, 2003), 1:499–501.

30. Delfina Serrano Ruano has argued for the prevalence and importance of Ash'arism during the Almoravid and Almohad periods in "Los Almorávides y la Teología Ash'arí: Contestación o Legitimación de una Disciplina Marginal?," in *Identidades Marginales,* ed. Cristina de la Puente (Madrid: Consejo Superior de Investigaciones Científicas, 2003), 461–516; and in "Por qué llamaron los almohades antropomorfistas a los almorávides?," in *Los almohades: Problemas y perspectives,* ed. Patrice Cressier, Maribel Fierro, and Luis Molina (Madrid: Consejo Superior de Investigaciones Científicas, 2005), 2:815–52.

31. The following exceptions, while suggestive, indicate how much work has yet to be done in this area: Fazlur Rahman, "Functional Interdependence of Law and Theology," in *Theology and Law in Islam,* ed. G. E. Grunebaum (Wiesbaden: Otto Harrassowitz, 1971), 89–97; Masud, *Shatibi's Philosophy of Islamic Law,* 40; Hallaq, *History of Islamic Legal Theories,* 136, 207–8.

32. *Al-Mi'yār,* 11:353.

33. A useful recent study on occasionalism is Dominik Perler and Ulrich Rudolph, *Occasionalismus: Theorien der Kausalität im arabisch-islamischen und im europäischen Denken* (Göttingen: Vendenhoeck & Ruprecht, 2000).

34. On the underlying logic of the argument, see Marie Bernard, "La critique de la notion de nature (*ṭab'*) par le kalām," *Studia Islamica,* 51 (1980): 59–107.

35. One such example can be found in the work of al-Ḥasan b. Mas'ūd al-Yūsī (d. 1102/1691), *al-Muḥāḍarāt,* ed. Muḥammad Ḥajjī (Ribat: Dār al-Maghrib, 1976), 96–98.

36. Al-Wansharīsī, *al-Mi'yār,* 11:355–56. Ibn Lubb here cites the same episode referred to by Ibn al-Khatib—that of 'Umar at Sargh—and provides the reader with the contrary interpretation that 'Umar avoiding the plague was a case of *sadd al-dharī 'a* in order to prevent Muslims mistakenly believing that disease had causative power in and of itself.

37. Al-Wansharīsī, *Al-Mi'yār,* 11:357. The tradition "The plague-struck is a martyr" (*al-maṭ'ūn shahīd*) is found in Bukhārī (ṭibb, 3), Abū Dāwud (Janā'iz, 11), al-Nisā'ī (Jihād, 36; Janā'iz, 14), Ibn Māja (Jihād, 17), and the *Muwaṭṭa'* (Janā'iz, 36). On the weakness of this tradition, see Van Ess, *Der Fehltritt des Gelehrten,* 43.

38. Aḥmad b. 'Alī Ibn Ḥajar al-'Asqalānī, *Badhl al-ma¯'ūn fī faḍl al-ṭā'ūn,* ed. Aḥmad 'Iṣṣām 'Abd al-Qādir al-Kātib, (Riyadh: Dār al-'Āṣima, 1990).

39. My point here is not so much that the genre of a fatwa guaranteed a wider reading audience than that of a medical treatise, but that Ibn Lubb's elaboration of a response to the plague was more amenable and compelling to later scholars than that of Ibn al-Khatib.

40. Michael Dols, *The Black Death in the Middle East* (Princeton: Princeton University Press, 1977), 93–94, and Manfred Ullmann, *Die Medizin im Islam* (Leiden: Brill, 1970), 246–47. Ullmann glosses Ibn al-Khatib in a slightly different fashion in his more popular *Islamic Medicine* (Edinburgh: Edinburgh University Press, 1978), 95–96. There he notes that Ibn al-Khatib's belief in contagion was extraordinary only because of the strength of the conviction with which it was professed, and that his true contribution lay in distinguishing the plague from other epidemic diseases. For another analysis of Ibn al-Khatib as a lone voice of reason, see Marie-Hélène Congourdeau and Mohamed Melhaoui, "La peception de la peste en pays Chrétien Byzantine et Musulman," *Revue des Études Byzantines* 59 (2001): 95–124; 110.

41. Zakariyyā al-Rāzī, *al-Ḥāwī fī l-ṭibb.* (Beirut: Dar al-Kutub al-'Ilmiyya, 2000), 8:3823–24.

42. For a brief overview of the biology of plague see Ole Benedictow, *The Black Death 1346–1353: The Complete History* (Rochester, NY: The Boydell Press, 2004), 7–24.

43. As Michael Dols has noted, in the pre-modern period no clear differentiation was made between contagion and infection. See Dols, *The Black Death in the Middle East,* 74.

44. On the Black Death not being a case of primarily pneumonic plague, see Benedictow, *The Black Death 1346–1353,* 27–31.

45. For an account of his discovery and that of Kitasato Shibasaburo, see Edward Marriott's *Plague: A Story of Science, Rivalry and the Scourge That Won't Go Away* (New York, N.Y.: Metropolitan Books, 2002).

46. See Vivian Nutton "The Reception of Fracastoro's Theory of Contagion: The Seed That Fell among Thorns?" *Osiris,* 6 (1990): 196–234, at 198.

47. In the 15th century, Ibn Ḥajar al-'Asqalānī argued that the plague is not contagious because he had seen cases in Egypt in which, in a family living together in close quarters, some would be stricken by the plague and others would not. See *Badhl al-mā'ūn,* 104–5.

48. Rahman, "Functional Interdependence of Law and Theology," 94–97. Rahman addressed the same subject in his *Islam* (Chicago: University of Chicago Press, 1979), 114–15.

49. My study of plague treatises and fatwas from the 14th-19th centuries deals with this issue (Stearns, Ph.D. diss., Princeton University, 2007).

50. A central theoretical problem posed to the jurisprudents by some Sufis was the degree to which there was inherent in legal obligation (*taklīf*) the need to expose oneself to hardship (*mashaqqa*). The relevance of this question as to whether one should remain in a plague struck area is clear: depending on one's understanding of plague's etiology and the existence of secondary causation, tending to the plague-sick could be seen as either a laudatory example of trusting in God or needlessly exposing oneself to danger. Al-Shatibi noted that Sufis might well set themselves higher standards for the degree of hardship that they expose themselves to, but that these standards should be applied to all Muslims. See Masud, *Shatibi's Philosophy of Islamic Law,* 191. Al-Shatibi was clear that not every hardship was to be endured by the believer, and that it was in fact the believer's duty to protect himself from hardship and sickness if these had not occurred because of something he had done. See *al-Muwāfaqāt,* 1: 452–54.

51. Ibn 'Ajība, *Sulūk al-durar fī dhikr al-qaḍā' wa-l-qadar,* manuscript in Rabat, al-Khizāna al-'Amma, D 2589, 1–22. On Ibn 'Ajība, an exegete and Sufi from Fes, see 'Umar Riḍā Kaḥḥāla, *Mu'jam al-Mu'allifīn,* (Beirut: Mu'assasat al-Risālah, 1993), 1: 300.

52. Muḥammad al-Mukhtār al-Salāmī, *al-Ṭibb fī ḍaw' al-īmān,* (Beirut: Dār al-Gharb al-Islāmī, 2001), 28–32.

53. For al-Bāqillanī 's (d. 1012) refutation of secondary causation, see Marie Bernard, "La critique de la notion de nature (*ṭab'*) par le *kalām,*" 75–78. For supporters of secondary causation being characterized as unbelievers see Muḥammad b. Yūsuf al-Sanūsī (d. 1490), *Les Prolégomènes Théologiques de Senoussi,* (Algiers: Imprimerie Orientale Pierre Fontana, 1908), 108–9. Compare, however, with the case of al-Yūsī (footnote 35), whose views on the ṣubject of secondary causation were exceptional.

54. Al-Salāmī, *al-ṭibb fī ḍaw' al-īmān,* 31–32.

55. For an example of how European business interests impeded the implementation of quarantines in 19th century Tunis, see Nancy Gallagher, *Medicine and power in Tunisia 1780–1900* (Cambridge: Cambridge University Press, 1983), 40–45.

56. See, *inter alia,* Sarah Franklin, "Science as Culture, Cultures of Science," *Annual Review of Anthropology* 24 (1995): 163–84, and more specifically on the ways in which one's choice and definition of facts can define a bio-ethical debate see Thomas Banchoff, "Path Dependence and Value-Driven issues: The Comparative Politics of Stem Cell Research," *World Politics* 57 (2005): 200–230. As Franklin observes (with relevance to the differences in approach of Ibn al-Khatib and Ibn Lubb) in "Science as Culture, Cultures of Science," 166: "The claim, for example, that empiricism can be unmarked, that is, can provide an evidentiary basis that "speaks for itself," is after all a point of view, and one that may be held by science studies scholars as well as by scientists themselves. Moreover it is a point of view with a history that establishes a cultural tradition: the tradition of "value-neutrality" or transparency. To distinguish between pure and applied knowledge, between hard and soft sciences invokes not only this value system, but the hierarchical nature of it, thus exemplifying the kind of cultural fact at issue here."

57. For a relevant decisions from Egypt's Dār al-Iftā' see the fatwa of the Mufti Ḥassanayn Muḥammad Makhlūf from 1947 (http://www.dar-alifta.org/ViewFatwa.aspx?ID=3257, accessed September 22, 2006). Like Ibn al-Khatib the Mufti interprets Q 2:195 to signify a Muslim's responsibility not to put himself in danger. For the Muslim World League's explanation of how the Prophet foresaw the danger of contagious disease, see http://www.nooran.org/Q/24.htm, accessed September 22, 2006.

TWO

Normative Muslim Medical Discourses

Overview

Ethics must have normative statements. Whether generalized rules, such as "Do unto others as you would have them do unto you," or specific guidelines on the permissibility of abortion or euthanasia, normative statements are central to the ethicist's task. Religious ethicists have the particular burden of applying the normative statements already recognized by that religious tradition. As Thomas Eich and Sherine Hamdy demonstrate in the essays of this section, there is no straight line from norm to application. To take one example, everyone agrees that the Qur'an opposes murder and promotes the saving of lives, but now that scientists can extract a single human egg cell (an oocyte) and join it with a single sperm cell, is the result a human life such that killing it is murder? Is it a crime to destroy something that cannot even be seen by the unaided eye?

The fundamental questions at play here are: What does a certain normative statement actually mean and who has the authority to decide? These essays focus on these questions by analyzing two very different issues, frozen embryos and organ transplantation. Both issues are very much products of the modern world, involving procedures that would have been the stuff of science fiction a century ago. Frozen embryos are a by-product of assisted reproductive technologies (ARTs) that take individual egg and sperm cells, join them outside the womb, and then implant them. The procedure is difficult and uncomfortable, so more eggs are extracted, and embryos made, than are usually necessary; remaining embryos are either discarded or frozen to be used later. Organ transplantation seems almost routine in Europe and North America, though the immunosuppressant drugs that make it practical were developed only in the 1980s. In addition to major organs (heart, kidney, liver), tissues, such as tendons, are now also harvested and transplanted on a regular basis.

Muslim ethicists have been engaged in debates on both these issues; to see how normative statements are produced and interpreted, Eich and Hamdy analyze a variety of statements by contemporary Muslim religious scholars (*'ulama'*). Thomas Eich compares recommendations (*tawsiyat*) issued by committees of *'ulama'* on the possible use of frozen embryos. In particular, he looks at contradictory *tawsiyat* published by similar committees at about the same time; these committees were almost identical in composition and relied largely on the same body of expert studies. The creation of committees to decide ethical issues is an innovative development in the Islamic world. As Eich explains, these committees were formed as part of a modern reaction against the traditional form of ethical debate examined above by Justin Stearns. Their purpose, in part, was to develop ethical guidelines that would transcend local and regional differences. To some extent, they are successful in this endeavor, and their recommendations are commonly cited in Western publications on bioethics.

In unpacking the language utilized by these committees on the issue of frozen embryos, Eich delves into what he calls "Islamic embryology." He finds that members of these committees employ terms that come straight out of the Qur'an, but in so doing, they conceal some rather significant developments in the meanings of these terms since the 1980s. As a result, he argues, terminological clarity was never achieved, and various members end up using the same key terms to refer to quite different things.

In her essay Hamdy introduces us to several Egyptian scholars who have weighed in on the issue of organ transplantation. Currently Egypt allows transplants only from living donors, effectively limiting the procedure to kidney transplants, since a person can survive with only one kidney. Further, Egyptian law is highly restrictive of the procedure. The actual experiences of individual Egyptians working around these restrictions are the focus of Debra Budiani and Othman Shibly's research, presented in the next section. Hamdy focuses on the production of norms, particular the notion popularized by Shaykh Muhammad Mutwalli Sha'rawi (d. 1998) that "the body belongs to God."

Hamdy compares Sha'rawi's arguments against organ transplantation with those of Shaykh Muhammad Sayyid Tantawi, who came down in favor of it. The comparison is particularly interesting as these two figures, both classically trained scholars, gained their authoritative status from very different quarters. Tantawi is the rector of al-Azhar University, one of the oldest and most venerable institutions in the Islamic world. In contrast, Sha'rawi was a popular preacher, with a television show that continutes to be broadcast in Egypt years after his death.

Hamdy finds that the two do not differ in their approaches to Islamic scripture or legal tenets but that they do differ in their assessments of the use and implications of the technology in question. While both scholars argue that human beings do not have full power of disposal over their bodies (because "the body belongs to God"), they disagree whether organ transplantation is a safe and helpful technology. In his argumentation Sha'rawi focuses on the technology's flaws and uses these to bolster his conviction that transplanting organs infringes on general rules laid down by God in several ways. Consequently he considered organ transplantation to be an unjustified practice. In contrast, Tantawi does not consider it his task to assess the medical aspects of organ transplantation, stating that this question has to be left to the medical experts. With this move, he arrives at significantly different conclusions while drawing on the same textual sources used by Sha'rawi. Sha'rawi viewed all kinds of organ transplantation critically, but Tantawi considers only organ trade to be reprehensible.

Drawing on this example, Hamdy explains the casuistic approach of the *'ulama'*: something that might be strictly forbidden under some circumstances might be allowed in other situations. Against this background she questions the assumption that there could be a single Islamic response to issues such as organ transplantation. She argues that in Islamic legal ethics, questions such as financial costs or graft survival are integrated into the process of a religious scholar's ethical thinking and consequently have an impact on it. Therefore differing statements of the *'ulama'* are often caused not by different readings of the religious texts but by differing assessments of the technology in question.

Both Eich and Hamdy make it abundantly clear that normative declarations of contemporary *'ulama'*, whether speaking as members of committees or as individuals, should not be regarded as absolute statements derived directly from religious texts. Rather, they have always to be contextualized for their actual meaning to be understood. In the case of transnational committees, Eich finds that such groups are no less subject to the very dissent and disagreement that they were supposed to obviate. Moreover their very structure opens the door to several new techniques to organize, direct, or even manipulate ethical debates.

THOMAS EICH

Decision-Making Processes among Contemporary 'Ulama'

Islamic Embryology and the Discussion of Frozen Embryos

Since the early 1980s techniques of reproductive medicine have spread all over the world, including to countries of predominantly Muslim populations. During a first, short phase, infertile couples traveled to Australia, the United States, or European countries to receive in vitro fertilization (IVF) treatments. From the second half of the 1980s onward, these techniques were introduced into Middle Eastern countries.[1]

During an IVF procedure, the woman is treated with hormones to stimulate the production of more than one egg, or oocyte, during a menstrual cycle. These eggs are "harvested" and fertilized outside of the body. In most cases up to three fertilized oocytes are returned into the woman's uterus in order to raise the probability that one of them will ultimately settle in the womb. Commonly only 30 percent of such procedures result in pregnancy, which means that often the treatment has to be repeated. Since the whole process of hormone treatment and harvesting the oocytes usually takes a heavy toll on a woman's organism and psyche, it is generally preferred that the number of such processes be kept as low as possible. Therefore more embryos or fertilized eggs are created than are usually needed for a single treatment. Those extra embryos are frozen and can be kept over a period of several years for later use without significantly losing their potential to develop successfully into human beings through pregnancy.

The ethical problem of what to do with frozen embryos arises when they are no longer needed for the purpose for which they were created. This is often the case when the couple who donated the oocyte and the sperm have separated or divorced, or when one or both of the partners have died. This might also be the case after an IVF treatment has been successful and the couple do not want any additional children. It has often been suggested that the problem can be solved by freezing the sperm and the oocytes separately. For biological reasons, however, only the fertilized egg obtains a substantial rate of success (that is, nidation and pregnancy) after freezing.[2] Therefore it has been suggested from the beginning that the unwanted embryos could be used for research purposes, so that in this way their inevitable destruction would serve some benefit.

These issues were discussed in the late 1980s and early 1990s by Muslim religious scholars. In the fall of 1989 a committee of internationally renowned *fuqaha'* and medical doctors, at a meeting of the Islamic Organization of Medical Sciences (IOMS) held in Kuwait, issued a recommendation (*tawsiya*) stating explicitly that frozen embryos could be used for research purposes according to Islamic law. In the spring of 1990 an almost identical committee met at the annual meeting of the Islamic Fiqh Academy (IFA, arab. Majma' al-fiqh al-islami) of the Organization of Islamic Conferences (OIC) at Jedda to discuss the same issue again, relying on an almost identical body of expert studies. This time the scholars arrived at the opposite conclusion and issued a decree (*iqrar*) according to which the creation of frozen embryos should be avoided during IVF treatments. When such embryos occurred, they should not be used for research purposes. How was such a fundamental change of opinion possible within such a short period of time?

Terminological inconsistencies, legal developments outside countries with predominantly Muslim populations, selective information, and especially the manipulation of discussion processes at international meetings brought about these two contradicting results. The publications of the IOMS and the IFA contain, among other things, the expert studies presented at the respective meetings as well as the transcripts of the public discussions surrounding these studies. These sources offer the opportunity to analyze contemporary Islamic legal statements as a result of a particular process rather than of normative texts, which are often formulated in such a way as to present these texts as independent of time and space.[3]

None of the aspects that influenced the legal statement of 1990 is a particularly Islamic phenomenon. On the contrary, Muslim legal experts, being human beings, might sometimes act according to external influences. In the second half of the twentieth century and particularly since the 1970s, Islamic law has witnessed a growth in the number of international Sharia committees, such as the Majma' al-buhuth al-islamiya at al-Azhar, the Islamic Fiqh Academies of the OIC, of the Muslim World League or of India, and the IOMS. These institutions and organizations were created to promote "group *ijtihad.*" In other words, the legal statements of these committees are not the expression of one single scholarly mind but are the result of negotiations among many such minds. Therefore techniques for directing discussions, such as those used in parliamentary sessions, have entered the decision-making process used by these committees.[4]

In our concepts of how Islamic law is currently applied, the assumption is often made that there would be a gap between the "Islamic norm," the letter of the law, and "Islamic practice," whether by "lay" Muslims or by religious judges, the *qudat,* who seemingly often attempt to find ways of evading the worldly application of Islamic norms.[5] In this dichotomy of "norms" on the one hand and "practice" on the other, the statements of the IOMS and the IFA would clearly be on the "norms" side: since both work internationally, they do not have the ability to force individual nation-states to put their statements into law or even practice. In addition these statements are formulated as broad guidelines, not as detailed laws.

This dichotomy can be criticized in several ways. First, the statements of the international legal committees are integrated into the legal reasoning of Islamic judges (as I learned in extensive discussions with *qudat* from Palestine and Tuareg Niger at Bern, Switzerland, during the "Islamic Family Law Contested" workshop in February 2006). Whether or not these statements are actually applied in legal practice, it can be inferred that they are at least integrated into the *qudat*'s decision-making process. Second, the normative statements of the IOMS and the IFA are not simply taken from traditional legal textbooks; such statements are already a result of negotiations among "real Muslims."

Prelude: *The IOMS Meeting of 1987*

In 1987 the question of how to proceed with frozen embryos was discussed for the first time at an IOMS meeting. Two short studies about the Sharia point of view were presented by two medical doctors (no studies of *fuqaha*' were presented): Ma'mun al-Hajj 'Ali Ibrahim and 'Abdallah Basalama. The first argued that a fertilized egg before nidation differed significantly from an embryo after nidation and therefore did not have the same *hurma* rights, the rights of bodily integrity. Consequently an embryo that had not been implanted in the womb might be used for research purposes. Basalama maintained the contrary and demanded that all frozen embryos be implanted in the uterus of the woman from whom the egg cells were taken.[6] He did not address the question of what should happen with the fertilized eggs if the woman died, the couple got divorced, or the couple did not want to have more children.

During this discussion the religious scholars were also divided. Muhammad al-Ghazzali from Egypt and Badr al-Mutawalli from Kuwait, for example, contended that in classical *fiqh* the aborted embryo is treated differently than birthed human beings. For example, the fine for an abortion was lower than the fine for killing a human. In addition it was claimed that even the ensouled embryo would have to be buried and yet was not given a name. They concluded that embryos did not have the same *hurma* rights and could therefore be used for scientific research.[7]

Muhammad al-Mukhtar al-Salami from Tunisia maintained that human dignity could not be exclusively linked to human life, as could be easily inferred from the respectful treatment of human corpses. According to his view, human dignity would start with fertilization of the egg, although one could not speak of human life at this point. He added that the classical *fuqaha* issued their rulings at a time when human life could be diagnosed only at a comparatively late stage of pregnancy. According to Salami, modern science had shown that the potential to develop into a full human being would exist from the time when the egg was fertilized.[8] To attack an embryo at this stage would consequently be an attack on human life during its early stages.[9]

The final recommendation (*tawsiya*) of this meeting was somewhat vague. First, the text encouraged researchers to develop techniques to store sperm and eggs separately, thus indicating that the creation of frozen embryos should be avoided.[10] In a second step, it allowed three options for how to deal with frozen embryos: "letting die," "killing," and "use for science," adding that the first of the three would be the lesser of the three bad options.[11] However, this way the text implied that using frozen embryos for research purposes would be a possible option. In addition the *tawsiya* reiterated the IOMS recommendation of 1983 that any IVF treatments should be allowed only for legally married couples and that any kind of third-party donation or surrogacy should be strictly forbidden.

"Islamic Embryology"

During this discussion, the Saudi Arabian sheikh ʿAbd al-Sattar Abu Ghudda made an interesting remark during a longer argument against what he termed an "exaggerated protection of fertilized eggs" (*mubālagha fī iʿtāʾ al-ḥurma li-hadhihi l-buwaiḍa al-mulaqqaha*):

> Let us return to the definition of the word "embryo" (*janīn*). Linguistically, janīn comes from *ijtinān,* i.e., covering, hiding. In the *sharīʿa,* the legal experts broadened the term to metaphorical use. Therefore they attributed the term janīn to the fruit of the womb (*ḥaml*) since its earliest stages [of development]. But I found clear textual evidence that this attribution was a metaphor of the *Shāfiʿī* scholars. . . . It has been related that the Imam al-Shafiʿi said that the real/descriptive use (*al-istiʿmāl al-haqīqī*) of the term *janīn* is only for the period after the muḍgha-stage, and that for the stages before that period the term is only used metaphorically. Al-Shafiʿi says in [his book] *al-Umm:* "in order to be a *janīn* it has to have passed the stages of *muḍgha* and *ʿalaqa,* so that it shows some human shape."[12]

Abu Ghudda's distinction between a linguistic definition and a Sharia definition of the same term is typical of the discussions among Muslim religious scholars.[13] His first definition refers to the fact that in Arabic most words are derived from "roots," that is, a particular combination of three consonants, which defines one or several broader semantic fields. For example, the root *k-t-b* is related to writing, and words derived from this root are somehow related to this basic meaning: *kitab* means "book" or "writing," *maktub* means "written," and *katib* "writer." The root *j-n-n,* from which *janin* is derived, means "to cover, to become dark." In this context it has become a common interpretation that *janin* means "embryo," because the embryo is covered in the womb.[14] Sometimes this interpretation is linked to the Qur'anic passage "He makes you, in the wombs of your mothers, in stages, one after another, in three veils of darkness" (Q 39:6).[15] This way, the question of whether the term *janin* can be applied only to intrauterine embryos or also to extracorporeal ones transcends the realm of mere linguistic exercise in the discourse of Muslim religious scholars because of the Qur'an's central position.

Such talk of semantics and metaphors is far from marginal in bioethical discussions. For example, in the Anglophone debate about embryonic stem cell research, the term *embryo* became a highly contested issue. Supporters of such research argued that the term would be too unspecific. Rather, terms such as *blastocyst* or *zygote* should be used, since the term *embryo* would evoke pictures of a fetus with legs and a head, that is, resembling human shape. Therefore the term would emotionalize the whole debate, whereas other terms were more accurate and "more sober," as it were. Opponents of this view, who wanted to continue the use of the term *embryo,* deemed this argumentation a mere rhetorical maneuver aimed at smoothing the path toward research on early stem cells. Interestingly both sides claimed to represent the "real" objective scientific view.[16] The cloning debate among contemporary Muslim religious scholars also demonstrates the relevance of terminology. Apparently some of the *'ulama'* had a simplistic understanding of cloning (*istinsakh*), since its Arabic term is derived from the root *n-s-kh,* which refers to taking a mere copy, primarily of a book.[17]

The second part of Abu Ghudda's quoted statement refers to an embryological concept that has developed around Qur'an 23:12–14: "Man We did create from a quintessence (of clay); Then We placed him as a drop (*nutfa*) in a place of rest, firmly fixed; Then We made the sperm into a clot of congealed blood (*'alaqa*); then of that clot We made a lump (*muḍgha*); then we made out of that lump bones and clothed the bones with flesh; then we developed out of it another creature."[18]

From this passage, Muslim religious scholars developed the concept that during pregnancy the embryo goes through three major stages of development: the *nutfa, 'alaqa,* and *mudgha* stages. This concept was usually linked to a hadith from the *Sahih al-Bukhari* in which the Prophet Muhammad stated: "Each one of you collected in the womb of his mother for forty days, and then turns into a clot (*'alaqa*) just like that (*mithla dhālika*), and turns into a lump (*muḍgha*) just like that, and then Allah sends an angel and orders him to write four things, i.e., his provision, his age, and whether he will be of the wretched or the blessed (in the Hereafter). Then the soul is breathed into him."[19] This passage is commonly understood to indicate that the three stages of embryonic development would last 40 days each, and therefore the whole process until the soul is breathed into the embryo would take 120 days.[20] This act of ensoulment would be the meaning of the rather unspecific Qur'anic statement "then we developed out of it another creature," at the end of the quoted sura. In classical *fiqh,* these passages formed the textual basis for the *'ulama*'s rulings about abortion, because *nutfa, 'alaqa,* and *mudgha* were understood to represent three consecutive stages in which the embryo increasingly showed features of human shape. Historically, in order to assess abortions, it was first necessary to establish whether an abortion had occurred at all. Since abortion commonly took the form of inducing a miscarriage, it was difficult to tell without any doubt that the "thing" that had come out of a woman's uterus was an embryo. Consequently most religious scholars stated that this could be proven only by human features such as a hand or a head, which in their understanding developed only in the later stages of their *nutfa-'alaqa-mudgha* model.[21] Al-Shafi'i's statement quoted by Abu Ghudda that the term *janin* should be applied only to stages of antenatal human development beyond the *mudgha* stage has to be seen within the context of this traditional Qur'anic embryology. Thus Abu Ghudda's intervention aimed at the fundamental question of whether the rulings of classical Islamic jurisprudence about abortion, which basically accord the unborn with rights of bodily integrity and protection of life, could also be applied to extracorporeal fertilized eggs.

One of the problems of this embryological model is that it contradicts scientific observation, as was already known to *fuqaha'* at least by the nineteenth century.[22] The fundamental Qur'anic passage mentions seven stages: clay, *nutfa, 'alaqa, mudgha,* bones, flesh, "another creature." The clay stage is generally understood to refer to the creation of Adam, not of every embryo. The last stage, "we developed out of it another creature," was commonly equated with ensoulment at the 120th day after the *nutfa, 'alaqa,* and *mudgha* stages had passed. However, the formation of bones in the embryo's body, which is described in the Qur'an to follow the *mudgha* stage, starts around the thirty-fifth day after conception.

These discrepancies have led to considerable efforts starting in the 1980s, when the issue of an "Islamic Embryology" was discussed more systematically because of the rapid development of reproductive medicine at that time to reinterpret the Qur'anic passages in light of modern science. Basically such efforts fall into the framework of the so-called "Islamization of Sciences," which aims at proving that all discoveries of modern science have already been revealed in the Qur'an or at least do not contradict it, which would prove its divine origin. The embryological concept of Muhammad 'Ali al-Bar, a Saudi Arabian doctor and medical consultant at the IFA, presented in his book *The Creation of Man between Medicine and the Qur'an,*[23] has become particularly influential. Al-Bar argues that the movements of the embryo would become willing movement only after the 120th day of pregnancy, a result of particular neurological developments at that time. In this context, the existence of a will is seen as an indicator of ensoulment. Therefore it is argued that the traditional concept of ensoulment at the 120th day of pregnancy would be proven correct by modern science.

However, in spite of al-Bar's claim simply to prove the correctness of traditional embryology, his interpretation constitutes a fundamental transformation of the traditional concept.[24] First, in al-Bar's book, the Qur'anic stage "then we developed out of it another creature" is no longer equated with ensoulment. On the contrary, the two are described as two consecutive stages.[25] Second, al-Bar states that five consecutive stages from *nutfa* until "clothing the bones with flesh" would take eight weeks[26] and would consequently be in accordance with the findings of modern science. Ensoulment would occur at the 120th day.[27] However, the calculation of traditional Islamic embryology leading to the concept of ensoulment at this time rests on the premise that the first three stages, *nutfa*, *'alaqa*, and *mudgha*, would last 40 days each, that is, much longer than the period he accords in his model to the first five stages. Therefore al-Bar's concept changes the basis of this calculation without adapting its result.

Whatever the flaws of this new "traditional" concept, it represents the predominant mindset in the *'ulama*'s debates, especially with its claim to present scientific evidence for ensoulment at the 120th day of pregnancy. However, the fundamental and terminological issue raised by Abu Ghudda, which is whether the new genetic entity created by the merging of sperm and oocyte already has to be termed an embryo or whether that term must be reserved for later developments growing out of this entity, has still not been settled in the forums of contemporary Islamic legal debates such as the IOMS. For example, during discussions about human cloning at the 1997 IOMS meeting at Casablanca, 'Ali al-Bar considered it necessary to raise the issue again by arguing that the term *janin* should be replaced by *laqiha*, which would translate as "fertilized egg"; however, no final consensus was achieved.[28] Therefore the issue of the applicability of the term *janin* to fertilized eggs, and conversely the issue of the applicability of classical Islamic legal rulings about abortion to them, remained unsettled. In this situation, the issue of frozen embryos was raised again at the 1989 IOMS meeting and the 1990 IFA (Jedda) conference.

The IOMS Meeting of 1989: Embryo Research Is Allowed Explicitly

At the 1989 IOMS meeting, the issue was discussed on a much broader basis than at the 1987 meeting described above. Three studies of *fuqaha'* were presented, usually linking the issue of frozen embryos to the question of using aborted embryos for research purposes.[29] Only two of these studies are presented here in some detail, because the third one, authored by the Jordanian 'Umar al-Ashqar, simply summed up the IOMS recommendations of 1985 and 1987, stating that the creation of frozen embryos should basically be forbidden, although embryo research could be allowed under strict conditions once the embryos had been created for some reason. Ashqar added that there was no need of further discussion because the *tawsiyat* of 1985 and 1987 had already treated the topic sufficiently.[30] The other two studies were presented by the two Jordanians ʻAbd al-Salam al-Ibadi and Muhammad Naʻim Yasin. The first argued that the creation of frozen embryos should be avoided. If it occurred, the embryos should be implanted in the uterus of the woman from whom the eggs were taken. Yasin argued to the contrary that under certain conditions frozen embryos could be used for research purposes.[31]

Ibadi defined abortion as "ejecting" the embryo (*ikhrāj aw ilqā' al-ḥaml*) from the female body before or after nidation.[32] In this way, he could treat the issue of using aborted embryos and frozen embryos together. He considered the use of aborted embryos for research purposes as unproblematic, because the embryo would already be dead under the condition that the abortion had not been started for research purposes.[33] Concerning the question of frozen embryos, he argued that the majority of classical *fuqaha'* would have opposed abortion. Therefore the use of frozen embryos for research could not be allowed, and the embryos should be implanted in the mother's uterus.[34]

Muhammad Naʻim Yasin argued that life would exist since the fertilization of the egg, but only through ensoulment at the 120th day would it become human life. This would not imply that abortion before ensoulment could be easily allowed, because the classical *fuqaha'* did not link their rulings that forbade abortion to ensoulment but based it on the embryo's potential to develop into a human being. However, in classical *fiqh*, abortion was allowed in case of a grave necessity (*darura*)—for example, if pregnancy threatened the mother's health. Since killing the embryo before ensoulment would not equal the killing of a human being, the saving of the mother's life would have more weight. Therefore the basic question concerning the scientific use of frozen embryos would be whether the expected benefit would outweigh the expected damage.

There would be two parties, Yasin proceeded, who would experience damage by the destruction of extracorporeal embryos: the parents and the embryo. If the parents would consent to this procedure, they would not suffer any damage, because the realization of their wish to have children would not constitute an absolute necessity in the Sharia. Concerning the embryo, the basic argument would be its potential to grow into a human being once it would be implanted in a uterus. However, there would be cases in which such an implantation could not be recommended for medical reasons. In addition there were cases in which it could not be allowed according to the Sharia, because any form of in vitro fertilization implying procreation outside of the framework of an existing legally valid marriage would be forbidden. Therefore the embryo could not be implanted after divorce or if the donor of the oocyte or the sperm had died. In other words, those embryos would suffer no legal harm by their destruction because according to the Sharia, they could not have developed legally into a human being anyway.[35]

During the discussion at the IOMS meeting, religious scholars such as Yusuf al-Qaradawi and ʿUthman Shabir from Jordan supported Yasin's view.[36] At the end of the 1989 meeting, the following sentences were added to the recommendations of the 1987 meeting: "The opinion of the majority (with which some disagreed) is that the destruction of the fertilized eggs before their nidation in the uterus is allowed, no matter how this destruction is brought about. So according to this opinion there is no reason to forbid scientific experiments in accordance with the Sharia. During these experiments, the egg cells must not be multiplied. Some disagreed entirely with this view."[37]

The IFA Meeting of 1990: Embryo Research Is Strictly Forbidden

In March 1990 the IFA of the OIC at Jedda organized a similar meeting, at which the primary focus was again issues of organ transplantation, thus forming a comparable context for the discussion of frozen embryos. For this question, the relevant passages of the decree issued at the end of the meeting read as follows: "First: In view of what has become reality concerning the possibility to store non-fertilized oocytes for later use, it is necessary to restrict the number of fertilized eggs to the number necessary for a single treatment, in order to avoid a surplus of fertilized eggs. Second: If for any reason such a surplus of fertilized eggs is brought about, they ought to be left alone without medical intervention, so that the life of this surplus may end in a natural way."[38]

In this way, the decree was even more restrictive than the IOMS recommendation of 1987, which had considered the possibility of using frozen embryos for scientific research by stating that it would be among the worst of three possible ways to deal with frozen embryos. This obviously diametrically opposed opinion is even more surprising given the fact that in the proceedings of the 1990 IFA meeting, the studies concerning frozen embryos are almost identical to the studies of the IOMS meeting of 1989.[39] The discussion at the IFA meeting can be analyzed in two steps, first through the framing of the discussion and then through the interaction among the participants.

The Framing of the Discussion

In contrast to the 1989 IOMS meeting, at the 1990 IFA meeting some of the authors of the studies were not in attendance. Muhammad Naʿim Yasin, who had argued for a scientific use of frozen embryos, was notably absent, whereas ʿAbd al-Salam al-Ibadi, who had taken the opposite stand, was present. Ibadi was the deputy head of the IFA at that time.

In addition the studies were not discussed. The discussion transcripts make it clear that the respective papers were not at hand during the meeting. Rather, an oral summary of the three studies was presented by Ahmad Raga'i al-Gendi, the IOMS assistant general secretary. After several remarks about the pros and cons of the scientific use of embryos, he pointed out that Germany and Australia had recently passed restrictive laws concerning embryo research.[40] In his summary of the three *fiqh* studies presented at the IOMS meeting, he devoted the most time to Ibadi's study (sixteen lines in the transcripts), then the study of 'Umar al-Ashqar (ten lines), and then the study of Yasin (four lines), which had been by far the most extensive of the three studies. His summary of Yasin's study is worth quoting verbatim: "The study of Doctor Muhammad Na'im Yasin is quite extensive, about sixty-seven pages, but he tended to declare it forbidden (*haram*) to use the highest possible number of oocytes; concerning the issue of how to deal with the embryo after ensoulment, he tried to be as restrictive as possible, too. He also declared the use of embryos *haram*, but he was able to say that before the 120th day, it would be possible to have differing opinions."[41] In other words, the studies that had opposed the scientific use of embryos were given much more space than the study allowing it. The contents of this study, in turn, were presented in an abridged manner.

The Discussion

The ensuing public discussion was not an open debate about how to deal with frozen embryos; rather it consisted of a mere reading and then consideration of each paragraph of the IOMS recommendations from 1987 and 1989. Therefore the course of the whole discussion was heavily influenced by the IOMS texts. When it was time to talk about the paragraph allowing embryo research under certain conditions, which had been added in 1989, Bakr b. 'Abdallah Abu Zaid, head of the IFA and chair of the panel, intervened immediately by referring the discussion of this paragraph to the nonpublic committee of the IFA, which would eventually formulate the final decree to be published at the end of the meeting.[42]

During the discussion, Abu Zaid intervened several times, especially when criticism was formulated by medical doctors who were lobbying for a scientific use of frozen embryos. For example, medical doctors criticized the IOMS recommendations from 1987, which had differentiated between the "letting die" and the "killing" of embryos. In practice, they argued, there would be no difference between the two, since in the former case one would throw the embryos away, thereby killing them. In their view, there would be only two options: "killing without any benefits" and "killing with possible benefits."

Abu Zaid, who was chairing the discussion, responded that this would risk commercialization. The issue of proper conduct in relation to frozen embryos would touch on the basic questions of humanity. Therefore it would be impossible to argue that strict legal rulings should guarantee this proper conduct because such rulings are made by men and are usually bypassed in practice. Abu Zaid proceeded by stating that the majority of those present would opine that the creation of frozen embryos should be avoided.[43] A short time later the general secretary of the IFA, Muhammad al-Habib Ibn al-Khuja, agreed with the medical doctors that there would be no difference between "letting die" and "killing." The third option from the IOMS recommendations of 1987 and 1989, the use of embryos for scientific experiments, should be rejected by refusal to discuss the issue at all.[44]

The transcripts also make clear that the passing of the embryo protection law in Germany had a decisive impact on the discussion among the *fuqaha'*. According to this law, the creation of frozen embryos during IVF treatments must be avoided. This aspect had already been discussed at the IOMS meeting of 1989.[45] During the IFA meeting six months later, however, this issue received much more attention. Ahmad Raga'i al-Gendi pointed especially to new techniques that would allow the creation of the exact number of embryos needed for a successful IVF treatment. These techniques had already been mentioned in the IOMS recommendation of 1989. When asked at the IFA meeting six months later why the recommendation still allowed the use of frozen embryos, Gendi answered that these techniques were not yet available in the Middle East; therefore the German solution could not be easily transferred to Islamic countries.[46]

What Gendi most probably had in mind was the technique of freezing the oocyte after the sperm has entered but before the two nuclei have merged. Such techniques, not to mention the separate freezing of egg and sperm, have a much lower success rate than freezing the fertilized egg, a piece of information that had already been introduced into the debate among the religious scholars at the IOMS meeting of 1987.[47] This is an important point, since it has to be kept in mind that frozen embryos are created in the first place in order to lower the negative physical and psychological consequences for women receiving IVF treatments. The whole ethical and legal discussion about frozen embryos starts only once they are no longer needed for achieving pregnancy, the purpose for which they had originally been created.

As stated above, the discussion at the IFA meeting followed the pattern of simply reading out and discussing the IOMS recommendations of 1987 and 1989, transferring the discussion of the most controversial issue embryo research to a nonpublic committee. These recommendations encouraged scientists to develop techniques to create the exact number of embryos needed for IVF treatments. At the IFA meeting in 1990, it was stated that such techniques were now available and should be applied in order to avoid any discussion about how to properly deal with frozen embryos. This view was voiced in particular by prominent members of the IFA such as 'Abd al-Salam al-Ibadi and Muhammad al-Mukhtar al-Salami, the former mufti of Tunisia.[48]

The committee for drafting the final decree of the IFA meeting consisted primarily of outspoken opponents of a scientific use of frozen embryos, such as ʿAbd al-Salam al-Ibadi, Muhammad al-Mukhtar al-Salami, and Ahmad Raga'i al-Gendi. Against this background, the contents of the decree hardly came as a surprise.

Conclusion

On the one hand, contemporary "normative" texts of international *fiqh* institutions are the result of negotiations among the members of these institutions. Such negotiations can be influenced by particular historical circumstances, such as the absence of Muhammad Naʿim Yasin at the 1990 IFA (Jedda) meeting. On the other hand, there are structural factors that might occur repeatedly, several of which have been identified in the preceding essay and none of which is a particularly Islamic phenomenon: lack of terminological and semantic clarity, manipulation of discussions, and influence from legal developments and debates in other places of the world. Examples of the latter aspect are, for example, Muhammad al-Mukhtar al-Salami's reference to European legal developments in a statement during discussions at the 1987 IOMS meeting and the scientist Haitham Khayyat's quoting of a WHO conference report in discussions about cloning at the 1997 IOMS conference at Casablanca.[49] From the same meeting, another case of manipulation of public discussions by a chairman can be provided: during the discussions of the draft version of the final recommendations, Walid al-Tabataba'i, a representative of the Kuwaiti Health Ministry, criticized the text. On the one hand, he argued, cloning was declared *haram* on a basic level, but on the other hand, it forbade only foreign companies or interest groups from doing research on this technology. He suggested broadening the passage from "on the part of foreign entities (*jihāt ajnabiya*)" to "on the part of foreign and local entities (*jihāt ajnabiya wa-maḥalliya*)." Ahmad Raga'i al-Gendi answered: "Concerning the topic of locality, we do not intend to give local entities the opportunity to conduct such research. We close the door because the foreign entities closed the door to research there [in their respective countries] and consequently they will come to the developing countries (*al-duwwal al-nāmiyya*) in order to conduct this research under different names. For this reason we close the door in front of them from now on." ʿAbd al-Rahman al-Awadi, who chaired this discussion, obviously felt that this response did not explain why the "local entities" were not mentioned in the final recommendations, and he promptly stated: "Because of the lack of time: please [next speaker], Doctor Saʿid Salam."[50]

Such acts of manipulation of discussions have to be seen as the inevitable result of the formation of forums of contemporary *fiqh*, in which several individuals, religious scholars, and scientists alike have to agree on one final text. This restricts considerably the possibility of expressing dissent in these texts, which is a common feature in classical *fiqh*. This is nicely illustrated by a statement of the

Moroccan professor of Islamic studies Sa'id Rabi' shortly after Tabataba'i's intervention. He took issue with the wording "building on these propositions, about which all attendants [of the conference] agreed, some expressed the opinion that cloning should be forbidden." He said, "I cannot imagine that there was an agreement, and there was dissent at the same time."[51]

The creation of committees of *'ulama'* since the 1960s aimed at changing certain features of traditional *fiqh,* primarily the restricted geographic scope of a certain ruling.[52] Setting up institutions such as the Islamic Fiqh Academy, which comprises representatives of all legal schools (*madhahib*), Sunni as well as Shiite, was a deliberate attempt to create Sharia institutions of transnational authority and consequently to unify the *'ulama*'s statements on a given issue. To a certain degree this attempt was successful.[53] However, as the above quotation shows, this change has created new problems, such as the possibility of influencing the committee's final statements by a variety of means and strategies. Such strategies are part of a deliberative process. In this sense, they can be interpreted as ways to create authority within the structure of these committees.[54] Undoubtedly, references to the religious texts as well as legal and ethical principles of the Sharia remain primary markers of authority. However, the example of this debate on frozen embryos shows that the framing of these principles and textual references during a discussion might be even more important than the references themselves.[55] Students of Islamic bioethics are therefore well warned not to take pronouncements of these forums to be "what Islam says" in a simplistic manner, but rather as one position in an ongoing process of ethical inquiry.

NOTES

1. These developments have been treated extensively in the work of Marcia Inhorn. See, for example, her *Local Babies, Global Science.*

2. See Henning Rosenau, "Der Streit um das Klonen und das deutsche Stammzellgesetz," in *Recht und Ethik im Zeitalter der Gentechnik: Deutsche und japanische Beiträge zu Biorecht und Bioethik,* ed. Hans-Ludwig Schreiber and others (Göttingen: Vandenhoek and Ruprecht, 2004), 142.

3. The latter has been the approach of the groundbreaking studies of medical and bioethical issues in contemporary Islamic law of the 1980s and 1990s, such as Ebrahim, "Islamic Ethics"; Krawietz, *Die Hurma;* and Rispler-Chaim, *Islamic Medical Ethics.*

4. An analysis of the wording and way of presenting the decrees and recommendations of the mentioned committees in the 1980s and 1990s shows how these committees initially allowed the expression of dissent in these texts. See, for example, the recommendations of the IOMS meeting in 1983 about the beginnings of life in 'Abd al-Raḥmān al-'Awaḍī, ed., *Al-Injāb fi dau' al-Islām* (Kuwait: al-Munaẓẓama al-Islāmiyya li-l-'Ulūm al-Ṭibbiyya, [1984?]), 351; or of the meeting of the IFA of the Muslim World League on surrogate motherhood in *Majallat majma' al-fiqh al-islāmī* 2, no. 1 (1986/87): 323–27, esp. 327. Eventually

this practice vanished, and the evaluation of a certain issue from the *Sharia* point of view was presented as much more static than discursive.

5. See, for example, Nahda Younis Shehada, "Justice without Drama: Observations from Gaza City Sharī'a Court," in *Gender, Religion and Change in the Middle East: Two Hundred Years of History,* ed. Inger Marie Okkenhaug and Ingvild Flaskerud (Oxford: Berg, 2005), 13–28.

6. 'Abd al-Raḥmān al-'Awaḍī and others, eds., *Al-Ru'ya al-islāmiyya li-ba'ḍ al-mumārasāt al-ṭibbiyya,* 2nd ed. (Kuwait: al-Munaẓẓama al-Islāmiyya li-l-'Ulūm al-Ṭibbiyya, 1995), 443–49 (Bāsalāma) and 450–55 (Hājj 'Alī Ibrāhīm). It is interesting to note that the latter restricted himself to presenting scientific information and its medical interpretation, whereas the former referred primarily to questions of embryology in the Qur'an and classic treatises of Islamic law. This mixing of moral, religious, and medical assessments of scientific information is not uncommon in studies presented by medical doctors at meetings of the IOMS or the IFA (Jedda).

7. Al-'Awaḍī and others, *Al-Ru'ya al-islāmiyya li-ba'ḍ al-mumārasāt al-ṭibbiyya,* 670, 727.

8. The standard counterargument to this point is that the fertilized oocyte depends on the uterus to develop into a full human being.

9. Al-'Awaḍī and others, *Al-Ru'ya al-islāmiyya li-ba'ḍ al-mumārasāt al-ṭibbiyya,* 673f, 738.

10. As noted above, it is, of course, possible to store sperm and oocytes separately, but the success rate of fertilization of such cells is very low.

11. Al-'Awaḍī and others, *Al-Ru'ya al-islāmiyya li-ba'ḍ al-mumārasāt al-ṭibbiyya,* 757.

12. Ibid., 671–72.

13. For another example, see 'Abd al-Fattāḥ Maḥmūd Idrīs, *Al-Ijhāḍ min manẓūr islāmī* (Cairo: self-published, 1995), 16.

14. Ibid.; 'Umar Sulaymān al-Ashqar, "Al-Istifāda min al-ajinna al-mujhaḍa au al-zā'ida 'an al-ḥājja fī l-tajārib al-'ilmiyya wa zirā'at al-a'ḍā'," in *Ru'ya islāmiyya li-zirā'at ba'ḍ al-a'ḍā' al-bashariya,* ed. 'Abd al-Raḥmān al-'Awaḍī (Kuwait: al-Munaẓẓama al-Islāmiyya li-l-'Ulūm al-Ṭibbiyya,[1992?]), 396–97.

15. Al-'Awaḍī and others, *Al-Ru'ya al-islāmiyya li-ba'ḍ al-mumārasāt al-ṭibbiyya,* 725.

16. William H. Danforth and William B. Neaves, "Using Words Carefully," *Science* 309 (September 16, 2005): 1816–17; Françoise Shenfield, "Semantics and Ethics of Human Embryonic Stem-Cell Research," *Lancet* 365 (June 18, 2005): 2071–73; editorial, "Playing the Name Game," *Nature* 436 (July 7, 2005): 2.

17. Thomas Eich, "The Debate about Human Cloning among Muslim Religious Scholars since 1997," in *Cross-Cultural Issues in Bioethics: The Example of Human Cloning,* ed. Heiner Roetz (Amsterdam: Rodopi, 2006), 302. Another example comes from the field of organ transplantation, where it has been shown that differing metaphorical conceptualizations of the human body have an impact on an individual's willingness to donate or receive organs. For example, if a person has a more mechanistic picture of the human body, describing the heart as a pump, he is more willing to donate or receive such an organ than if he describes the heart as the seat of personal emotions or even the soul. See Russell W. Belk, "Me and Thee Versus Mine and Thine: How Perceptions of the Body Influence Organ Donation and Transplantation," in *Organ Donation and Transplantation: Psychological and*

Behavioural Factors, ed. James Shanteau and Richard Jackson Harris (Washington, D.C.: American Psychological Association, 1990), 139–58; Robin Saltonstall, "Healthy Bodies, Social Bodies: Men's and Women's Concepts and Practices of Health in Everyday Life," *Social Science and Medicine* 36, no. 1 (1993): 7–14.

18. This translation is based on Yusuf Ali, who uses the word *foetus* in the passage "then of that clot we made a lump." See also the passage about Muhammad ʿAli al-Bar's writings on embryology below.

19. Abū ʿAbdallāh Muḥammad b. Ismāʿīl al-Bukhārī, Saḥīḥ al-Bukhīrī (Cairo: Dār wa-maṭābiʿ al-shaʿb, 1960–69?), 8:152.

20. In another view held by a small but considerable minority of Muslim religious scholars, ensoulment occurs on the fortieth, forty-second, or forty-fifth day after conception. This view is based on another hadith of Muhammad (see, for example, Marion Holmes Katz, "The Problem of Abortion in Classical Sunni *fiqh,*" in *Islamic Ethics of Life: Abortion, War, and Euthanasia,* ed. Jonathan E. Brockopp [Columbia: University of South Carolina Press, 2003], 30–31). For the sake of clarity, this view is not treated in this article.

21. On these issues, in much greater detail, see Holmes Katz, "Problem of Abortion"; and Thomas Eich, *Islam und Bioethik: Eine kritische Analyse der modernen Diskussion im islamischen Recht* (Wiesbaden: Reichert, 2005), 26–50.

22. Muḥammad Amīn Ibn ʿĀbidīn, *Ḥāshiyat Radd al-muhtār ʿalā al-durr al-mukhtār,* 3rd ed. (Cairo: Maṭbaʿat Muṣṭafā al-Ḥalabī, 1984), 1:314–15.

23. Muḥammad ʿAlī al-Bār, *Khalq al-insān bayna al-ṭibb wa-l-Qurʾān,* 11th ed. (Jedda: al-Dār al-Saʿūdiyya li-l-Nashr wa-l-Tauzīʿ, 1999).

24. Strictly speaking, al-Bar presents two slightly differing embryologies at two parts of his book, which differ in some details of his terminology for the stages between *muḍgha* and ensoulment (al-Bār, *Khalq al-insān,* 360, 370).

25. Al-Bār, *Khalq al-insān,* 360.

26. Ibid., 370.

27. In his two models, al-Bar does not make any statement about when ensoulment occurs. However, he mentions the 120th day in another passage of his book (al-Bār, *Khalq al-insān,* 354).

28. ʿAbd al-Raḥmān al-ʿAwaḍī and others, eds., *Ruʾya islāmiyya li-baʿḍ al-mushkilāt al-ṭibbiyya al-muʿāṣira* (Kuwait: al-Munaẓẓama al-Islāmiyya li-l-ʿUlūm al-Ṭibbiyya, 1999), 360. Another example for considerable discussions about the term *janīn* without clear results can be found in the proceedings of a meeting of Jordanian medical doctors and *ʿulamaʾ* in 1992, where issues of reproductive medicine were discussed; see Jamʿiyyat al-ʿulū m at-ṭibbiyya al-Islāmiyya al-munbathiqa ʿan niqābat al-aṭṭibāʾ al-Urduniyya, *Qadāyā ṭibbiyya muʿāṣira fī ḍauʾ al-sharīʿa al-Islāmiyya* (Amman, 1995), 99–126.

29. In the program of the meeting (*barnāmaj al-nadwa*), the section was entitled "Aborted Embryos and Possibilities of Their Use" (*al-ajinna al-mujhaḍa wa-madā al-istifāda minhā*); see al-ʿAwaḍī, *Ruʾya islāmiyya li-zirāʿat baʿḍ al-aʿḍāʾ al-bashariya,* 17–18.

30. Al-ʿAwaḍī, *Ruʾya islāmiyya li-zirāʿat baʿḍ al-aʿḍāʾ al-bashariya,* 395–96.

31. Muḥammad Naīm Yāsīn, "Ḥaqīqat al-janīn wa-ḥukm al-intifāʾ bihi fī zirā ʿat al-aʿḍāʾ wa-l-tajārib al-ʿilmiyya [The reality of the embryo and the ruling about making use of it in organ transplantation and scientific experiments]," in Al-ʿAwaḍī, *Ruʾya islāmiyya li-zirāʿat baʿḍ al-aʿḍāʾ al-bashariya,* 277–374; and ʿAbd al-Salām al-ʿIbādī, "Ḥukm al-istifāda

min al-ajinna al-mujhaḍa au al-zā'iḍa 'an al-ḥājja [The ruling about making use of aborted and supernumerary embryos]" in Al-'Awaḍī, *Ru'ya islāmiyya li-zirā'at ba'ḍ al-a'ḍā' al-bashariya,* 375–92.

32. Al-'Awaḍī, *Ru'ya islāmiyya li-zirā'at ba'ḍ al-a'ḍā' al-bashariya,* 377.

33. Ibid., 378–79.

34. Ibid., 388–89. 'Ibādī also did not address the question of what should happen with the fertilized eggs if the woman died, the couple got divorced, or they did not want to have any additional children.

35. Al-'Awaḍī, *Ru'ya islāmiyya li-zirā'at ba'ḍ al-a'ḍā' al-bashariya,* 294–344.

36. Ibid., 418–19.

37. Ibid., 648.

38. *Majallat majma' al-fiqh al-islāmī* 6, no. 3 (1990): 2151–52.

39. Only one study by the medical doctor Georges Abouna was missing, and another study by Bakr b. 'Abdallah Abu Zaid from Saudi Arabia, the head of the IFA, was added. In this study Abu Zaid did not really deal with the issue of frozen embryos. Rather, he discussed whether it would be legal to transplant organs from a baby who was born with almost no brain. He used this discussion primarily to criticize the concept of brain death, which had been accepted by the IFA some years before. On this particular IFA decision, see the contribution of Budiani and Shibly in this volume and Grundmann, "Scharia, Hirntod und Organtransplantation," 27–46.

40. Gend meant the Gesetz zum Schutz von Embryonen, BGB1. I (1990), 2746 (Germany), and the Infertility Medical (Procedures) Act from 1984 and its following amendments (Australia). See John Leeton, "The Early History of IVF in Australia and Its Contribution to the World (1970–1990)," *Australian and New Zealand Journal of Obstetrics and Gynaecology* 44 (2004): 495–501.

41. *Majallat majma' al-fiqh al-islāmī*, 2084.

42. Ibid., 2131.

43. Ibid., 2125.

44. Ibid., 2126–27.

45. Al-'Awaḍī, *Ru'ya islāmiyya li-zirā'at ba'ḍ al-a'ḍā' al-bashariya,* 404, 421.

46. *Majallat majma' al-fiqh al-isl m,* 2118–22. It has to be noted that nobody asked the obvious question of whether those new techniques had been introduced into the Middle East during the six months between the IOMS and the IFA meetings of 1989 and 1990.

47. Al-'Awaḍī and others, *Al-Ru'ya al-islāmiyya li-ba'ḍ al-mumārasāt al-ṭibbiyya,* 677; see also Jam'iyyat al-'ulūm, *Qadāyā ṭibbiyya mu'āṣira,*103.

48. *Majallat majma' al-fiqh al-islāmī*, 2114–16, 2118, 2120, 2122.

49. Al-'Awaḍī and others, *Al-Ru'ya al-islāmiyya li-ba'ḍ al-mumārasāt al-ṭibbiyya,* 674; al-'Awaḍī and others, *Ru'ya islāmiyya li-ba'ḍ al-mushkilāt al-ṭibbiyya al-mu'āṣira,* 488.

50. Al-'Awaḍī and others, *Ru'ya islāmiyya li-ba'ḍ al-mushkilāt al-ṭibbiyya al-mu'āṣira,* 525.

51. Ibid., 526. The relevant passages of the conference's final recommendations are on pages 509–13.

52. Reinhard Schulze, *Islamischer Internationalismus im 20. Jahrhundert: Untersuchungen zur Geschichte der Islamischen Weltliga* (Leiden: Brill, 1990), 301f.

53. For example, this can be seen from a newspaper comment about a highly controversial statement by the *mufti* of Egypt in spring 2007, where it was said the issue should be referred to the IFA. It was argued that the issue at hand (so-called hymen repair) should not be left to the plurality of differing opinions usually expressed in fatwas (*al-Ḥayāt* [February 19, 2007], 9).

54. On Islamic ethics as a deliberative process, quite similar to that of Western bioethics, see Manfred Sing's paper presented at the Penn State conference and published as "Sacred Law Reconsidered: The Similarity of Bioethical Debates in Islamic Contexts and Western Societies," *Journal of Religious Ethics* 36, no. 1 (March 2008): 97–121.

55. For a historical example, see David S. Powers, "Kadijustiz oder Qāḍī -Justice? A Paternity Dispute from Fourteenth-Century Morocco," *Islamic Law and Society* 1 (1994): 332–66.

SHERINE HAMDY

Rethinking Islamic Legal Ethics in Egypt's Organ Transplant Debate

The public media debate over Islam and organ transplantation in Egypt[1] can serve as a case study in the production of Islamic legal-ethical[2] positions. Discussion of two opposing fatwas issued on organ transplantation demonstrates that in order to properly analyze Islamic positions, we must study the social context in which they are issued, as well as the position of the mufti and his understanding of the practice at hand. Disagreement over the permissibility of a given medical technology, it can be argued, may have more to do with opposing views on the nature of that technology and its benefits to society than with diverging approaches to Islamic scripture or legal tenets.

Organ transplantation, which has been described as "the most intensely social of all medical practices,"[3] is a major subject of disagreement in Egypt. Although kidney transplantation is carried out from living donors and cornea transplants are procured from systemically dead cadavers in some of Egypt's public and private hospitals, efforts to initiate a national organ transplant program have consistently failed in the Egyptian Parliament for nearly three decades. Opponents to organ transplantation have argued that the fact that there is a black market in human organs is the inevitable result of a practice that recasts God's creation into a mass of interchangeable parts: such denigration of divine wisdom could not lead to benefit, which is why this practice has caused so many social and political problems.[4] For those pushing for a national program, resistance to organ transplantation is a symptom of backwardness, which hinders Egypt's technological progress and contributes to its inability to crack down on the illicit organ trade. Such a view assumes that technological advances in medicine necessarily lead to benefit, and that the actual problems of organ trade and theft are caused by "backwardness" and "corruption" that should and can be regulated by the Egyptian state. The question about the permissibility of this medical practice is waged heatedly in the official and state-opposition newspapers; on state television; in the parliament;

among politicians, academics, physicians,[5] and Islamic legal scholars; and among ordinary people.[6]

What is the place of Islam or, more precisely, Islamic legal ethics in this debate? This question, namely whether religion explains the reluctance in Egypt to pass a law that would organize a national program, is debated in normative as well as descriptive terms. That is to say, there is genuine disagreement as to whether Islam should have any objection to what is essentially a medical issue, and whether Islam in fact does explain why there have been obstacles to establishing a national program. Of course, "Islam" is not a monolithic agent; it is Muslims who debate practices and interpretations of their religious texts in various ways, depending on social and historical contexts. Yet, "Islam" is represented as a monolithic agent in much of the Egyptian national media, including around the debate on organ transplantation. Many commentators, politicians, physicians, and journalists have maintained that Islam has nothing to do with resistance to organ transplantation, and they cite as their evidence the fact that Saudi Arabia[7] and Iran[8] both have national programs for transplantation from both living and brain-dead donors. These two countries, they point out, operate under Islamic law, while Egypt does not.[9] The argument made by those who are considered proponents of organ transplantation is that the resistance in Egypt must then be caused by something other than Islam, namely the uncontrolled black market in body parts and reports of organ theft that have tainted the public perception of organ transplantation. Shaykh Muhammad Sayyid Tantawi, as grand mufti of Egypt and later in his position as rector of al-Azhar University,[10] condoned the practice and declared that it was a "medical, and not religious," question.

In contrast Shaykh Muhammad Mutwali al-Sha'rawi, famous throughout Egypt for his widely popular television show, which has aired on Fridays years after his death, had maintained that one cannot ethically donate organs that belong to God. "How can you give a kidney that you yourself do not own?" he had asked. This sentiment has resonated profoundly with many Egyptians, and my fieldwork among patients diagnosed as "in need of" kidney transplants, their family members, and their physicians reveals a complex array of factors that help explain why this is the case.

Sha'rawi (d. 1998) was an immensely popular figure in Egyptian social life who had never held an official post as state mufti. His opinion against organ transplantation was offered spontaneously in a television interview in the 1980s, which sparked a heated controversy; he was subsequently vilified in the Egyptian media. In contrast, Tantawi held the positions as state mufti and later as rector at al-Azhar and was generally perceived as a figure who facilitated state interests. During his tenure in both positions he held firmly to his stance that organ transplantation was permissible under certain circumstances. Yet, among most of the dialysis patients I interviewed, all the Islamic scholars, and even many transplant physicians, it was Sha'rawi's opinion that was most often cited and held the deepest resonance among patients in need of kidney transplants. Contrasting the positions of the two scholars can help elucidate why this was the case.

Sha'rawi: Shaykh of the People

Shaykh Muhammad Mutwali Sha'rawi remains an immensely popular and well-loved figure throughout Egypt. The Danish scholar Jakob Skovgaard-Petersen has remarked that while researching in Egypt he would enter Egyptian friends' homes and find that the Qur'an and Sha'rawi's book of fatwas were the only two books there.[11] During the course of my fieldwork, no other Islamic scholar's name was invoked as often as his in discussions about organ transplantation.

While certain erudite Islamic scholars were known for their scholarly language, Sha'rawi was known for his ability to speak to "the common people" (*al-'awwam*) and to make classical learning accessible, a talent that made him a household name. While some of the Egyptian intelligentsia, particularly journalists writing for the mainstream press, considered Sha'rawi to be a "hard-headed extremist," the vast majority of middle-class Egyptians, including religious scholars, expressed a tremendous amount of respect for Sha'rawi and credited him with reawakening Muslims with a sense of spiritual awareness and piety.

Sha'rawi's opinions against particular types of medical interventions were made in the context of telling pious Muslims that they need not fear death and reminding them that the Qur'an bears the ultimate truth.[12] He was constantly speaking against the assumption that new technologies have made Islamic teachings outdated or irrelevant. In stating that "we belonged to God," Sha'rawi iterated a phrase that was an established premise of religious belief, but he used it to challenge many assumptions about medical technologies as well as the authority of other Islamic authorities, particularly those functioning in official state positions.[13]

By reformulating the idea that we belong to God as a response to a specific medical technology, Sha'rawi contested prevailing views of biomedicine. Among these views are the following: a) that the body is to be viewed as property owned by the self, a major premise of much of post-Enlightenment Western bioethics; b) the technological imperative to "transcend mortality," in which death is defined as the "biological demise," over which technology must triumph;[14] and c) self/body contradictions foregrounded by the practice of organ transplantation.[15] In reasserting humans' obligations toward their Creator, Sha'rawi insisted: a) that we do not own our bodies as we own property, b) that death is the exalted encounter with the divine, and c) that the self and body are integrated through practices of worship and devotion. For someone who is a religious scholar, or in the position of *da'iyya* (one who calls people to Islam), none of these statements is in itself new or controversial; each is a clear tenet of Muslim faith. It was the context in which these statements were uttered that caused so much controversy in the Egyptian public sphere.

One of the earlier explanations of Sha'rawi's position on organ transplantation is outlined in *al-Liwaā' al-Islāmi,* a weekly, self-described "Islamic" newspaper, dated February 26, 1987. Sha'rawi there premised his argument on the fact that suicide is explicitly forbidden in religion.[16] The prohibition against the premeditated taking of one's self forms the basis of Sha'rawi's argument: that one does not own one's own body in order to act freely with it, that there are limits, and that these limits (God's command) are inscribed in the divine Revelation.

In keeping with his general message and role in Egyptian society, Sha'rawi did not employ legal reasoning or tools of legal theory to make his case. He was instead interested in asserting a particular disposition that humans should have toward their Creator and toward their bodies as God's creation. He viewed organ transplantation, and the discursive field of "gift of life" that surrounded it,[17] as an arrogant imposition on the correct relationship that worshipers should cultivate toward their Creator. His reasoning was as follows:

> One cannot donate something that one does not own; in that case the donation would be invalid. The human being does not own his whole self and does not own some or parts of his self (*dhātihi*). The human being does not own his body. Rather, this body is the property of God, most exalted and High. He is the One who created it. No one can claim otherwise. It is God who gives the gift of life (*huwa alladhī wahhabahu al-ḥayāt*).
>
> So a person, no matter who he is or what he accomplished, can never claim to have given the gift of life. Or to have created life. God is the One who makes [a person] die whenever He wills and no one on this earth could supersede His will by preventing death, nor by making a person on the verge of death (*'alā qayd al-ḥayāt*) live a single second beyond his final time.[18]

Sha'rawi explained that devout humans should be conscientious at every moment, contending that it is God who owns every intricate mechanism and part of their bodies. He described the functions of the body, voluntary and involuntary, as signs of God's will (*ayat Allah*) and as indications that God enacts his will through humans in diverse ways. The involuntary cellular mechanisms of the body are signs for humans that God owns and controls their bodies through his ultimate will. Voluntary movements are signs that humans are responsible and can will certain actions, but God ultimately controls and judges them. According to Sha'rawi, God tries some of his servants by depriving them of certain bodily functions, and this in turn serves as a sign that the body is ultimately controlled by divine will.[19]

What was most troubling about this formulation to many of Sha'rawi's critics was that this reasoning could be read as a passive acceptance of any disease or affliction and as a challenge against the Prophet's teachings that believers should "seek treatment" for every illness. This was the basis of the media attack launched against Sha'rawi for his position. Sha'rawi was indeed challenging the presumption that afflictions are abhorrences to be rectified, and he stated that instead they are among the signs of God's perfect wisdom. Sha'rawi contested the notion that the body is something we should seek to control, for this was an arrogant imposition on God's creation and the fact of God's total and ultimate power.[20]

Sha'rawi thus articulated a position that strikes at the very heart of biomedical philosophy. As Bryan Turner has put it: "At least in the West (during the classical and Christian eras) the body has been seen to be a threatening and dangerous phenomenon, if not adequately controlled and regulated by cultural processes."[21] For Sha'rawi, who took a position that could be traced to a long tradition of Muslim philosophical thought, a state of heedlessness of divine omnipotence (*ghafla*) distances people from the ontological reality that it is God, not us, who is in control of every infinitesimal bodily process. Turner, following Erving Goffman, notes: "Any loss of control over our bodies is socially embarrassing, implying a loss of control over ourselves."[22] In contrast, Sha'rawi suggested that loss of immediate control (as in a paralyzed person's lack of control over limb movement or a blind person's loss of visual control) would bring the afflicted person closer to the ontological reality that the body belongs to God and is ultimately subject to divine omnipotence.[23]

Sha'rawi aimed to challenge the notion that humans should presume to control or own their bodies, that humans could prolong life or thwart death. The fact that we cannot tell our hearts when to beat or stop was, for Sha'rawi, a divine sign to remind humans to cultivate the proper disposition of utter submission and gratitude to God.[24] In the Islamic tradition, it is not the flesh of the human body that is the source of sin or evil; rather, the fallacy of the human being is the tendency to forget and neglect God's omnipotence. Thus the path to salvation in Islam is the constant remembrance (*dhikr*) of God, the appreciation of God's mercy, the understanding that all of creation is a reflection of God's signs to which humans should submit in gratitude (*shukr*). This is not generally disputed among Muslims. However, what is contentious is Sha'rawi's implication that the imperative to treat an affliction nullifies the opportunity to view this affliction as a sign from God. Many physicians and patients would counter that medicine, too, is a divine sign, a point that Sha'rawi readily admitted.[25] Indeed, Sha'rawi never opposed hemodialysis or blood transfusions for patients with kidney failure. The question then becomes, at which point does medical treatment pull us away from a disposition of God-awareness and piety? Why do particular medical treatments endanger such a disposition while others do not? What is particular about organ transplantation such that its status as "treatment" becomes obscured by its complicity in turning away from God's will?

Lesley Sharp and others have critically analyzed the persuasive discourse around the "gift of life" that drives the moral imperative of organ transplantation in the United States.[26] This phrase had little resonance in Egypt, where it was a given that only God owns this imperative. Sharp has noted that the rhetoric of the "gift of life" obscures the (monetary, violent, gory) origins of body parts through its association with "the very fabric of American (and in effect, assumed Judeo-Christian) ideals surrounding altruism when one quite literally gives of oneself to others in need."[27] This religio-ethical discourse has driven the medical practice of organ transplantation in the United States, and some in Egypt adopt similar language and also speak of organ donation in terms of self-sacrifice.[28] Yet, many others in Egypt, most notably Sha'rawi, questioned organ transplantation's claims to the religious ideals of self-sacrifice and altruism. Sha'rawi explained why organ donation did not represent altruism, by contrasting it with the imperative to risk one's life in order to save someone else:

> Those who have permitted organ donation do not have the justification to say that they are "saving the life" of another. Saving life is an imperative owned by God alone. My plea to those scholars and doctors for whom the humanitarian spirit and love has dominated their work, is for them to stay far away from arrogance and rebelliousness toward God's creation. They have issued a new opinion that says that this is "saving life." My response to such an opinion is: don't destroy the religions in order to "save life."
>
> Now this does not mean that we do not take precautions or cures, or that we do not take medicine for illness, for it is God who created illness and God who created its medicine. Just as there is a difference between donating the whole body and donating its parts, so is there a difference between donating the effects of the body and the effects of the parts. For me to donate the effects, this is permitted and commanded in the religion. For example, even if I were to lose a body part [in saving a person from a fire], the goal here was for me to donate my abilities of movement to save a person from the dangers of burning, and in any case this all could not happen without the will of God.[29]

By stating that in any case all events are willed by God, Sha'rawi sought to remind proponents of organ transplantation that even when a person donated a kidney so that the recipient might live, it was God who ultimately saved this life—not the donor, not the surgeon, not the technology.

While his position was clear and uncompromising, it was not until Sha'rawi uttered his position on national television, a year after this *al-Liwā'* article, that he indeed attracted a substantial amount of controversy and adversity in the Egyptian press.[30] He had been a guest on the television program *From A to Z* in December 1988.[31] Sha'rawi was vociferously condemned in the press by journalists and physicians for taking what was perceived and depicted as an extreme and nonsensical position. Newspapers reported that Sha'rawi was against medical treatment and thus breaking with the tradition of the Prophet that encouraged seeking healing in illness.

My research into this intricate debate complicates the views of these journalists on two levels. The first concerns the genre in which Sha'rawi had spoken. Sha'rawi was not making a legal argument about the permissibility of organ transplantation, and for many specialists in Islamic jurisprudence (*fuqaha'*), his position was not perceived as such. Rather, Sha'rawi was speaking from the perspective of a *da'iyya,* one who calls people to Islam and urges the cultivation of proper dispositions toward God as Creator and God as the sole dealer in life and death. Other Islamic scholars condemned the media for having mistaken Sha'rawi's statement about piety by wrongly rendering it a legal judgment. Second, my work among patients and physicians revealed that while many held a tremendous amount of respect for the late Sha'rawi and were familiar with his position, it was not blindly or prescriptively followed as such. Rather, the statement that the body belongs to God, a commonsense articulation of many religious teachings, was a signifier for a wide range of meanings, depending on the specificities of each case. This statement was constantly taken up, commented on, reframed, and reinterpreted, depending on the situation in which it was uttered.

Sha'rawi remained one of the few voices among public religious figures who opposed organ transplantation and other interventionist medical technologies. His argument that the body belongs to God is, in fact, a truism in Islam, and no Muslim scholar would argue against it. However, the question remained as to whether this precept necessarily led to a prohibition against organ transplantation. When legal scholars employed the legal tools of necessity (*darura*) and overall benefit (*maslaha*), the majority came to judge organ transplantation to be permissible under several conditions (consent of donor, benefit to recipient, no harm to donor, no financial transaction).

Organ Donation as Altruism: Tantawi's Fatwa

In the fatwa on transplantation that Tantawi issued during his tenure as Egypt's grand mufti, he too begins with the explicit statement that the body belongs to God. Tantawi, in fact, reiterates many of Sha'rawi's earlier arguments, even though his fatwa ultimately permits organ donation.[32] Tantawi begins with an elaborate explanation of the human body as being owned solely by God and therefore its elevated stature in Islamic belief. Like Sha'rawi, he refers to the prohibition of suicide as evidence that one cannot do what one wishes with one's body but rather must abide by the command of the Creator, who endowed humans with their bodies as a trust. After an elaborate discussion that reads much like Sha'rawi's arguments, Tantawi remarks that the fact that God owns our bodies is evidence of the prohibition of the sale or commodification of any body part. Tantawi then notes that unlike other scholars, he distinguishes between the selling of an organ and donating it out of love or concern for the welfare of the recipient, which he states is surely a noble act that God will generously reward. Tantawi ultimately permits organ donation under the conditions of the dire need of the recipient, the clear overall benefit, and the avoidance of undue harm to the donor, which must be assessed by a doctor of confidence.[33] Tantawi asserts that the Sharia honors the human being in life and in death and aims to lessen suffering, and that the medical field could help toward these goals. Throughout the fatwa Tantawi appears to make many implicit references to the words of Sha'rawi, using Sha'rawi's arguments to prohibit organ commodification rather than organ transplantation more generally.

By including stipulations of permissibility, these types of fatwas appeal to the logic and rationalism embedded within Islamic legal reasoning. If the aim of the Sharia is to uphold the ultimate spiritual and material benefits of the Muslim *umma*, then a practice aimed at treatment or the improvement of quality of life would, by this logic, be permissible as long as it does not contradict any current religious principles. This leads us back to the thorny question of how "benefit" is to be determined. This is why the production of fatwas and the use of tools such as *maslaha* (public benefit or social good) must be studied within their specific social contexts, taking into account the particular worldview, political persuasions, education, and outlook of the particular muftis.[34] With this in mind, we can ascertain that religious scholars' differing positions on a practice such as organ transplantation may have less to do with their different approaches to Islamic legal tenets than with their views of the practice at hand and its relationship to state institutions. While Tantawi seems less apt to question the medical benefit of the procedure, leaving this task to the medical experts, Sha'rawi was clearly influenced by the negative effects of organ transplantation that he witnessed or heard about in Egypt, and particularly the black market in human organs. However, Sha'rawi did not state that these reasons formed the basis of his position. Rather, he cited the detrimental effects of transplants as evidence that his position was correct. In his rebuttal argument to his critics, he had stated: "I spoke about organ transplantation and I said: it is *haram*. And I have [a right to] my opinion. Because the human being does not own his own body. And most cases of organ transplantation fail anyway and do not succeed in their goals. The one who receives a transplant remains seriously ill and suffering for the two or three months that he lives."[35]

Sha'rawi's "clarification" hints at contingencies of organ transplantation that may have also influenced his position: he argued that most organ transplants failed and that the recipients would remain ill. For those, like Sha'rawi, who based their position on the idea that transplants are not permissible because the body belongs to God, the failure of organ transplants to secure benefits for the recipients was further evidence of God's displeasure and further indication that this was not suitable "treatment" (morally or scientifically).

Other opponents of organ transplantation invoked the legal tool of *sadd al-dhara'i'* ("blocking the means"), which is used to forbid something that is not itself forbidden (*haram li-dhatihi*) but leads to things that are forbidden (*haram li-ghayrihi*).[36] In yet another article in *al-Liwā' al-Islami,* Dr. 'Abd al-Salam al-Sukari, a professor of Islamic law, noted that those who have used the tools of *maslaha* (social benefit) and *darura* (necessity) have premised their findings on civil law from non-Muslim countries, while Egyptians should base their reasoning firmly in the Sharia. As he further argued, the fact that organ transplantation has led to such clearly horrific practices as a black market in human organs and bodily exploitation should be the basis of its prohibition, according to the tenet of *sadd al-dhara'i'*.[37]

Still others have argued that it is the role of the mufti to research, rather than assume, to what extent organ transplantation is a safe and efficacious procedure, before issuing a fatwa. This latter group of muftis, such as Shaykh 'Ali Gum'a, solicit information about graft survival, patient well-being, or other indications that would help judge the "social welfare" (*maslaha 'amma*) of this medical procedure. The fact that Sha'rawi evidently did not believe that this medical procedure in fact benefited organ recipients contributed to the position he took. Yet, throughout his lifetime Sha'rawi insisted that his position was based on the simple fact that God as Creator owns our bodies.

Sha'rawi was reluctant to appeal to the legal tools of reasoning, such as *maslaha,* which are now the most familiar modes of reasoning for approaching a novel medical procedure such as organ transplantation.[38] This is why his position was unrecognizable to many other Islamic legal scholars as a fatwa, and this is also why he was open to such a virulent attack in the mainstream press. At the same time, as Birgit Krawietz has noted, many have expressed misgivings about the overuse of *maslaha* to legitimate all "modern" practices;[39] Sha'rawi's refusal to do so fit with his popular role as someone who was "firm in the tradition." Sha'rawi spoke in absolutist, black and white terms, which held great appeal to those who considered the secularization of Egyptian society a threat to their way of life. He criticized a medical practice that held dubious promise or benefit to the vast majority of Egyptian patients. Further, the fact that he drew on such basic tenets of Islam, suggesting that invasive medical technologies have threatened these beliefs, struck at a particular vulnerability in Egyptian society: the distrust and mismanagement of biomedical institutions, particularly within the context of their privatization and an eroded welfare state, the desacralization of the body, and the vulnerability of the poor to bodily exploitation.

Rethinking Our Assumptions of Islamic Legal Ethics

There was much ado in the Egyptian press about Sha'rawi's and Tantawi's differing opinions on organ transplantation. Many journalists and commentators stated, in exasperation, that the scholars' lack of agreement demonstrated that Islamic authorities had no place in assessing questions about medical practice. Indeed, with the difficulties surrounding efforts to implement a national organ transplant program, a pressing question in Egypt has been: Why has there been no agreement over "the" Islamic position on organ transplantation? If the rector of al-Azhar (Tantawi), who arguably holds one of the most authoritative positions in the Sunni Muslim world, has argued that the practice is permissible, then why is there continuing opposition to a national organ transplant program, presumably on "religious" grounds? Are there, in fact, other reasons why this debate has taken the shape it has?

While these are clearly important questions to ask, I would add a slightly different one could be added to frame this discussion: What drives the desire to codify a single Islamic response, and why has it failed? What are the underlying assumptions in this question about the constitution and boundaries by which something is considered to be "Islamic" in its reasoning such that it will be acceptable to all Muslims? What assumptions are being made about the locus of Islamic authority from which such a formulation would issue forth?

As demonstrated above, positions or fatwas by scholars should not be taken as "givens" conveying "the" Islamic opinion. Rather, we must inquire into the specific context to understand how that opinion was produced and how it remains contingent upon fluctuating social factors. It is clear that Sha'rawi was not convinced about the medical benefit of organ transplantation. In contrast, Tantawi assumed that the procedure could save lives and that Egyptian medical institutions could be entrusted with the task of dealing with body parts. Social factors necessarily influenced the scholars' positions. Their rulings about the practice at hand were based on specific understandings and assumptions about its benefit and risks.

Thus we need to question the formulation of consolidating the Islamic opinion, given both the complex and variable methodologies that may be employed in Islamic legal ethics toward engaging a new dilemma. Organ transplantation as a medical practice is complex, multi-sited, widely variable, and a moving target: rates of donor and recipient survival; graft survival; pharmacological considerations in immunosuppressants, including cost and toxicity, organ type, experience of the disease, potentials of intensive care treatments for brain-dead patients, preservation and transportation of organ grafts, and allocation, are all highly variable depending on the particular times and resources of the places in which this practice is carried out. Furthermore, all these factors are considered to be under the domain of the Islamic legal scholar who determines the permissibility of such a practice. Yet, to ask what the Islamic position on organ transplantation is presumes that both "Islamic legal ethics" and "organ transplantation" are separate, static entities that are easily recognizable and the same everywhere.

Shaykh 'Ali Gum'a, the current grand mufti of Egypt, explained in an interview (June 2004) that viewpoints such as Sha'rawi's represent a *madhhab,* a particular way of seeing things. This should not be confused with a fatwa, a legal opinion or answer to a question; nor should it be seen as a recommendation, let alone prescription, for someone's particular case. Sha'rawi's *madhhab* does not answer the question about whether or not a particular person can receive a transplant in a particular way. 'Ali Gum'a argued that for the media to have taken up Sha'rawi's position and read it as a prohibition against anyone ever having a transplant is a misapplication and misunderstanding of how Islamic jurisprudence works. According to Shaykh 'Ali Gum'a, the case of a healthy mother donating a kidney to her sick child who will benefit from such an operation poses an entirely different set of ethical questions than does the case of a poor man trying to sell his kidney to alleviate himself from debts or the case of a heart-beating, brain-dead donor who may be declared "dead" in order for his organs to be procured. Shaykh 'Ali Gum'a further insisted that two hundred years ago (that is, before the devastating effects that colonialism had on traditional institutions of learning), ordinary people (*al-'awwam*) knew the difference between a fatwa and a *hukm* (general rule). Yet, he argued, irresponsible media and "entertainment-style journalism" have contributed to distorting people's understandings of how Islamic jurisprudence should be applied. Others remarked that the media treats the muftis as if they are popes and then derides them for not, in actuality, having such authority.

For Shaykh 'Ali Gum'a, the fact that the same mufti might render one person's decision to receive a transplant permissible and another's impermissible is, moreover, a feature of how Islamic jurisprudence is supposed to work. In his terms, Islamic jurisprudence (*fiqh*) is "like a yo-yo: Something that is forbidden in one situation, like eating pork, is considered permitted and even obligatory in a situation of starvation." Yet, he conceded that because the general population has lost an understanding of the mechanisms of Islamic law, the media has explained contradictory fatwas as evidence that Islamic scholars have "differed in opinion" and that they therefore do not know how to respond to this question. This has resulted in a blow to the scholars' credibility, in the minds of many people. From Shaykh 'Ali Gum'a's perspective, a fatwa issued during the very early stages of organ transplantation, when there were many cases of both donor and recipient death during or after operations, should look different than a fatwa issued decades later, after the availability of powerful immunosuppressants such as cyclosporine, which dramatically increased donor and graft survival. Shaykh 'Ali Gum'a's solution to the question of organ donation from consenting donors is to form a committee comprised of experts from many fields, including Islamic law, that reviews different cases. Furthermore, he insisted that people need to be reeducated through the media, formal education, and the law about the mechanisms of Islamic legal ethics.

ʿAli Gumʿa also argued against Shaykh Tantawi's statement that "this is a medical, not a religious, question." The practice of organ transplantation is not confined to medical facts or surgical expertise. Shaykh ʿAli Gumʿa pointed out that the definition of "brain death" (which was consolidated by an ad hoc committee of the Harvard Medical School in 1968) was not merely a technical matter but was, since its inception, essentially linked to the question of organ transplantation. This practice necessarily involves political and economic incentives that cannot be divorced from the realm of social relationships that are clearly under the purview of Islamic law.

Conclusion

For those scholars making judgments about the permissibility of organ transplantation, practical considerations about efficacy, graft survival, surgery risks, toxicity of postoperative medical treatments, and financial costs—questions that might be located within the realms of political economy, public health, epidemiology, medical science, sociology, or pharmacology—are, in fact, formative of Islamic legal-ethical opinions about permissibility. This is true even for those (such as Shaʿrawi) who did not consciously acknowledge the contingency of these social factors in the making of his fatwa. Other muftis with whom I spoke articulated that such factors must be within their purview of analysis for assessing the ultimate "benefits" or "risks" posed by a particular practice. Furthermore, this feature of Islamic legal ethics, which Baber Johansen has described as a sacred law based on the contingencies of social realities,[40] is not merely one conceptualized by muftis or those who have attained formal legal scholarship; patients and physicians, too, consider practical questions to be formative of their decisions about religious permissibility. Whether or not their bodies could tolerate years on hemodialysis and whether or not they could financially afford to consider transplant are factors in their opinions about what is the correct thing to do from an "Islamic" perspective.[41]

Social analysts, including leftist journalists in Egypt, have claimed that practical considerations, such as the financial cost of organ transplantation or the availability of immunosuppressive drugs, prove that this question is not "Islamic." They are correct, if by "Islamic" they are speaking about timeless theological truths, such as those expressed in the statement "It is God who owns our bodies." This statement in and of itself is not adequate for explaining why organ transplantation has provoked so much ethical debate. The question to be asked is this: What social factors, such as ideas about efficacy, treatment access, cost, benefit, procurement, medical side effects, and trust in medical practice, make this statement meaningful? Further, we should ask how such statements become available and later resignified as they travel from the mouths of popular Islamic scholars—in the press, on television, through official fatwas—to the general populace, culminating in a national debate.

NOTES

1. This essay includes the results of research conducted in Egypt (2001–4) as a much larger project on organ transplantation, Islam, and biomedical ethics in Egyptian life. This research was generously supported by the National Institutes of Health, the National Science Foundation, the Social Science Research Council, and the Charlotte Newcombe Foundation.

2. I take Islamic legal-ethics to be partly included in *fiqh* (jurisprudence) but also present in other sources, such as *taṣawwuf* (Sufism), *'aqīda* (creedal theology), or *adab* (etiquette).

3. Nancy Scheper-Hughes, combined review of Thomas Koch, *Scarce Goods: Justice, Fairness, and Organ Transplantation* (Westport, Conn.: Praeger, 2002); and Margaret Lock, *Twice Dead: Organ Transplants and the Reinvention of Death* (Berkeley: University of California Press, 2002), *American Anthropologist* 105, no. 10 (March 2003): 172–74.

4. These arguments are simplified here for the sake of brevity. In fact, there are several different arguments made against organ transplantation. The first looks at the denigration of the human body (as a collection of spare parts), which should instead be conceived of as a trust (*amana*) from God. In this formulation, the fact that there is an organ trade or that recipients do not live long after the transplants or that each has merely traded in one lifelong illness for another one, posttransplant (of living with immunosuppressants), or that there is harm to the donor is proof of God's displeasure but is not the basis on which organ transplantation is rendered impermissible. Others begin with the fact that there is an organ trade that has unacceptable outcomes and side effects, arguing that because there is more harm than benefit, Islamic law must render the practice impermissible on this basis. While both arguments are similar and evoke the negative consequences of organ transplantation, they begin with different premises; one argument considers unacceptable problems as the premise of its impermissibility, the other as its outcome.

5. While many physicians are ambivalent about the practice, only a small and loud minority of physicians has worked actively to block the passing of the law. These physicians, headed by Dr. Safwat Lotfy, an anaesthesiology professor with the faculty of medicine at Cairo University, are convinced that organ transplantation is morally wrong, that it would lead to moral devastation in Egypt, and that procuring organs from brain-dead patients is akin to the murder of terminally ill patients. It is interesting that these physicians have had a much larger role in the obstacles posed toward legislation than any Islamic scholars have; the majority of Islamic legal scholars appointed by the state have declared the practice permissible under several conditions.

6. Sherine Hamdy, "Our Bodies Belong to God: Islam, Medical Science, and Ethical Reasoning in Egyptian Life" (Ph.D. diss., New York University, 2006).

7. See Abdullah A. al-Khader, "Cadaveric Renal Transplantation in the Kingdom of Saudi Arabia," *Nephrology Dialysis Transplantation* 14 (1999): 846–50.

8. See Ahad J. Ghods, "Renal Transplantation in Iran," *Nephrology Dialysis Transplantation* 17 (2002): 222–28. In 2000 the draft law was refuted by the Guardian Council after it had passed parliament. In 2002 it was de facto enacted by a directive of the Health Ministry.

See S. M. Akrami and others, "Brain Death: Recent Ethical and Religious Considerations in Iran," *Transplantation Proceedings* 36 (2004): 2883–87; Javaad Zargooshi, "Iranian Kidney Donors: Motivations and Relations with Recipients," *Journal of Urology* 165 (2001): 386–92. My thanks to Thomas Eich for clarification on this point.

9. Egypt's legal system is derived from French and English codes, a legacy of colonial rule. However, the constitution states that the Sharia is the major source of the law, and the personal status courts and family law technically function under the Sharia, resulting from the fact that secular governments have long considered religion to reside in the private domain. Many scholars have noted that the result of drawing on European code has been in some cases a much more rigid interpretation of Islamic law than had previously been customary (see, for example, Carl W. Ernst, *Following Muhammad: Rethinking Islam in the Contemporary World* [Chapel Hill: University of North Carolina Press, 2003], 128; see also Judith Tucker, *In the House of the Law: Gender and Islamic Law in Ottoman Syria and Palestine* [Cairo: American University of Cairo Press, 1998]).

10. The rector of al-Azhar has traditionally been viewed as holding one of the highest positions of authority in the Sunni Muslim world.

11. Jakob Skovgaard-Petersen, *Defining Islam for the Egyptian State: Muftis and Fatwas of the Dār al-Iftā* (Leiden: Brill, 1997).

12. These fatwas/responsa are to be found in the compilation by Muḥammad Mutwallī al-Sha'rāwī, *Al-Fatāwā al-kubrā*, 2nd ed. (Cairo: Maktabat al-Turāth al-Islāmī, 2002).

13. Ironically Sha'rawi had close ties to the state: his television program installed through the state-owned media and having served as minister of religious endowments (*awqaf*) under President Sadat. However, part of his popular appeal had to do with his ability to seem independent from state authority, and at times even critical of it.

14. Margaret Lock, "Transcending Mortality: Organ Transplants and the Practice of Contradictions," *Medical Anthropology Quarterly* 9 (1995): 391.

15. Donald Joralemon, "Organ Wars: The Battle for Body Parts," *Medical Anthropology Quarterly*, n.s., 9 (1995): 335–56; Lock, "Transcending Mortality"; Margaret Lock, *Twice Dead: Organ Transplants and the Reinvention of Death* (Berkeley: University of California Press, 2002); Lesley A. Sharp, "Organ Transplantation as a Transformative Experience: Anthropological Insights into the Restructuring of the Self," *Medical Anthropology Quarterly*, n.s., 9 (1995): 357–89; Sharp, "The Commodification of the Body and Its Parts," *Annual Review of Anthropology* 29 (2000): 287–328; Sharp, "Commodified Kin: Death, Mourning, and Competing Claims on the Bodies of Organ Donors in the United States," *American Anthropologist* 103 (2001): 112–33.

16. In much of his language, he speaks of what is permitted or forbidden in the religion (*al-dān*), rather than in Islam. The presumption is that Islam is the religion, the ultimate seal of prophecy in a long perennial philosophy of divinity and creation.

17. In fact, I rarely heard the language "gift of life" while I was doing fieldwork in 2001–3, and when I did, it came from a few physicians but never from patients. My guess is that with the initial practice of organ transplantation in Egypt came, too, an imported discourse that had originated in North America. However, by the time of my fieldwork this discourse had little salience with those involved in the debate (except among those who consciously argued against it).

18. *Al-Liwā' al-Islāmī*, February 26, 1987; my translation from the Arabic.

19. Ibid.

20. Ibid.

21. Bryan S. Turner, "The Body in Western Society: Social Theory and Its Perspectives," in *Religion and the Body,* ed. S. Coakley (Cambridge: Cambridge University Press, 1997), 20.

22. Ibid., 19.

23. *Al-Liwā' al-Islāmī,* February 26, 1987.

24. "[A person] cannot order his own heart to beat if it stopped, nor can he, if it stopped, tell it to beat again" (Sha'rawi quoted in ibid.).

25. Ibid.

26. Sharp, "Commodified Kin"; Renée C. Fox and Judith P. Swazey, *The Courage to Fail: A Social View of Organ Transplants and Dialysis* (Chicago: University of Chicago Press, 1974); Lock, *Twice Dead.*

27. Sharp, "Commodified Kin," 16.

28. This discourse is most likely to be found in parent-to-offspring donations.

29. *Al-Liwā' al-Islāmī,* February 26, 1987.

30. Television is an exceedingly popular and influential medium in Egyptian life. See Lila Abu-Lughod, *Dramas of Nationhood: The Politics of Television in Egypt* (Chicago: University of Chicago Press, 2005).

31. *Min al-alif il al-yā',* presented by Tariq Habib, December 23, 1988. Thanks to Dr. Reem Saad, who first alerted me to the importance of this television episode.

32. Dār al-Iftā' al-Miṣriyya, subject number 3510, Human Organ Transfer, December 1, 1993, issued by His Honor Doctor Muḥammad Sayyid Ṭanṭāwī.

33. For a discussion of the doctors of confidence in contemporary fatwas on medicine in Egypt and in Egyptian society more broadly, see Hamdy, "Our Bodies Belong to God."

34. Skovgaard-Petersen, *Defining Islam for the Egyptian State;* Opwis, "*Maṣlaḥa* in Contemporary Islamic Legal Theory," 182–223.

35. Cited in Muḥammad Mahjūb Muḥammad Ḥasan, *Muḥammad Mutwallī al-Sha'rāwī: min al-qarya ilā al-'ālamiyya* (Cairo: Maktabat al-Turāth al-Islāmī, 1990). More than a decade later Sha'rawi was quoted as saying that God had disgraced those who had permitted organ donation in a case when a patient was mistakenly declared to be dead (*Rūz al-Yūsuf* [May 18, 1998], 84).

36. This legal tool is accepted in only some of the schools of jurisprudence *(madhāhib).* An example is a ruling in which the Prophet forbade a creditor from accepting a gift from his debtor lest it become a means to usury. It is usury that is explicitly forbidden in Islam, not the accepting of gifts from creditors; yet, the latter is prevented from leading to the former. See Kamali, *Principles of Islamic Jurisprudence.* Felicitas Opwis, a theorist of Islamic law, describes *sadd al-dharā'i'* as the principle of eliminating pretexts and as a prime example of substantive rationality: whenever a formally legal transaction leads to something contrary to the purpose of the law, it is considered illegal and void, such as a deferred sale (*bay' al-ājāl*) that results in charging illegal interest (*ribā*) (Opwis, "*Maṣlaḥa* in Contemporary Islamic Legal Theory," 192).

37. *Al-Liwā' al-Islāmī,* July 14, 1988.

38. Birgit Krawietz has written extensively on the use of Islamic legal theory in twentieth-century Egypt in cases of new medical procedures: for example, "*Ḍarūra* in Modern

Islamic Law: The Case of Organ Transplantation," in *Islamic Law: Theory and Practice,* ed. Robert Gleave and Eugenia Kermeli (London: I. B. Tauris, 1997), 185–93.

39. In the case of organ transplantation, Krawietz writes: "I cannot imagine a comparable test case which offers such a scope of issues with regard to conceptions of maslaha" (ibid., 187).

40. Johansen, *Contingency in a Sacred Law.*

41. Hamdy, "Our Bodies Belong to God."

THREE

Norms and Their (Non-) Application

Overview

While the establishment of norms is central to the ethicist's task, the violation or evasion of those norms seems to be an endemic part of society. Whether the subject is American Catholics using contraception or Iranian women letting a bit of hair peek out of their head scarves, human beings seem ready to take normative statements only so far. Moreover, when it comes to matters of life and death, they abandon those norms quickly. This does not mean that rules have no purpose; indeed rules are essential to the orderly functioning of society. It does suggest that Muslims follow rules no more blindly than the rest of us.

Once we accept this fact, the full complexity of Muslim medical ethics is revealed. The essays in this section address specific topics in particular contexts, focusing on the ways that established norms are applied, or evaded. Moreover they address ethical issues that arise from new medical procedures: for example, sterilization operations, in vitro fertilization (IVF), and organ transplants. Through questionnaires, interviews, and participant observation, the authors provide thick descriptions of these ethical dilemmas.

The first essay, by Susi Krehbiel Keefe, is based on interviews with women in Ugweno, a region in Tanzania where sterilization has become a common form of contraception. The population of Ugweno is unique in several aspects, one of which is that it contains half Muslims and half Christians. Krehbiel Keefe finds that women from each religious tradition use similar arguments to justify their sterilization, which is particularly surprising for the Muslim population, since sterilization is commonly considered forbidden by the *'ulama*. Interestingly the women as well as the local imam view sterilization far less critically than they do other forms of contraception, such as the birth control pill, injections, or intrauterine devices, which they regard as having negative side effects. This also contradicts the general attitude of international Muslim religious scholarship, which allows nonpermanent forms of contraception. In her study Krehbiel Keefe draws a picture of significant changes over the last ten to twenty years because of the introduction of contraception programs. They are justified with the Malthusian axiom that reduced numbers of children lead to better living conditions for the families and development of the community, an idea that has become widely accepted in Ugweno.

Viola Hörbst's study looks at the opposite problem, male infertility preventing couples from having children in Bamako, Mali. As in Tanzania, religious precepts are only one factor among several at play in these situations of severe social and psychological crisis. A patriarchal society such as Mali views male infertility as a major stigma for the husbands, which highly impacts on gender relations. Therefore such couples keep the truth secret, while the wives endure social abuse in an environment that presumes that they are "the problem."

Hörbst's essay shows that modern technologies of reproductive medicine have changed social strategies for dealing with age-old problems. Solutions that would have been tried years ago are abandoned in favor of IVF treatments abroad. As a result, the very idea of family changes from a socially defined entity to a biologically defined one. For example, Hörbst discusses a traditional solution to male infertility whereby an infertile husband's brother sleeps with the wife and impregnates her. The resulting child is raised within the family and is recognized as the offspring of the husband. The introduction of modern reproductive technologies considerably narrows these spaces of maneuverability, both by allowing the genomic determination of the biological father and by opening up possibilities for the couple to have a child "of their own." Therefore changes wrought by IVF technologies are much more far-reaching than they might first appear.

The third essay in this section, by Debra Budiani and Othman Shibly, uses similar methodologies to examine issues surrounding kidney transplants in Egypt. Their in-depth interviews expose complex perceptions and motivations that complicate any desire for simple ethical precepts. In this case, however, the legality of the procedure is not entirely clear, adding a new layer of ethical concern. Whereas family-planning issues are mostly private affairs in Tanzania and Mali, the system of illegal organ trade in Egypt has become a full-blown public scandal. In response, the Egyptian government has placed severe restrictions on organ donation.

Budiani and Shibly interviewed Egyptians who have chosen to go around the rules, despite the fact that they consider their actions to be both illegal and ethically questionable in the mind of God. Interestingly vendors and buyers alike invoke the religion-based obligation to care for their families, primarily their children, in order to justify their acts. In other words, for religiously minded Egyptian kidney vendors and buyers, it is necessary to view their behavior not as a blunt turning away from religious norms but as a weighing of two competing religious norms. Therefore their acts cannot be viewed simply from the perspective of the statement "religious norms say one thing, but what people actually do is another." A simple dichotomy of norms versus practice is insufficient to describe a much more complex reality.

The final essay in this section also addresses state regulation, this time of clinics that provide artificial reproductive technologies (ARTs) in and around the Arabian peninsula. Using the foundation of his own experience as director of an ART center, Hamza Eskandarani surveys the legal framework for centers of in vitro fertilization and shows that even within the same country different IVF centers can have differing working procedures. In addition he finds that where government guidelines exist, they are not closely monitored, and so norms are not put into practice.

Two similarities in these final two essays are worth noting. First, in both cases government enforcement of legally defined norms is lax. In Egypt, this lax enforcement seems to be positive, since it allows for a kidney transplant that would otherwise not be possible. One must also wonder whether similar issues operate in the case of the IVF clinics surveyed by Eskandarani: Do couples take advantage of lax enforcement to undergo procedures that would otherwise be restricted by law? In both these cases, lax enforcement seems to allow a measure of patient autonomy that would otherwise not be available, but they also raise serious questions about justice. The second similarity, then, is the activist stance taken by these authors in advocating for greater justice. For Eskandarani, this means greater vigilance on the part of clinics and government inspectors alike to ensure that "Islamic directives" are followed. Budiani and Shibly are likewise concerned that "Islamic edicts" against organ trafficking are implemented, and they have helped found an organization, the Coalition for Organ-Failure Solutions, to find pragmatic solutions to these problems. This combination of scholarship and advocacy may be uncomfortable for some, particularly theoretical or historical ethicists who maintain a certain distance from the objects of their investigation. For others, however, the combination is quite natural; indeed, any other stance could be seen as ethically questionable, since both ART and organ transplantation hold out the promise of life for the individual patients involved.

As each of these essays demonstrates, highly local applications of norms have international repercussions that demand our attention. Men from Africa travel to Europe for fertility treatments, and Europeans travel to the Middle East to obtain organ transplants. In such cases treatment options are increased, but only for a certain, wealthier segment of society; moreover, they may be based on a system that exploits poorer, defenseless members of society. We may be witnessing here not the way that norms restrict practice, but the way that practice can challenge, and perhaps change, ethical norms in these societies.

SUSI KREHBIEL KEEFE

Competing Needs and Pragmatic Decision-Making

Islam and Permanent Contraception in Northern Tanzania

Both Sub-Saharan African and Muslim populations are known for their high fertility and resistance to family planning and contraception. However, a fertility transition in Sub-Saharan Africa is under way,[1] incorporating both the use of IUDs (intrauterine devices) and sterilization.[2] The findings of Hollos and Larsen from Ugweno, Tanzania, the site of my fieldwork, are striking; they indicate that 33 percent of women of reproductive age who have ever used contraception had sterilization.[3] These findings, when contrasted with sterilization rates for continent (2 percent), country (2 percent), and regional area (about 7 percent), indicate that women are choosing an unexpected method of contraception in this area.[4]

Beginning in 1988 Tanzania, with the assistance of the United States Agency for International Development (USAID), implemented a program called "Permanent and Long-Term Methods" (PLT).[5] The PLT program is the largest project funded by USAID/Tanzania. The cornerstone of PLT is promoting female sterilization.[6] UMATI, Tanzania's family-planning association, was responsible for the logistics of implementing the program. By 1991 UMATI trained twenty-one counselors and fourteen mini-laparotomy teams of doctors and nurses to begin working in all regions of the country.[7] One of these teams visited the Ugweno Health Unit once a month from 1992 to 1997.[8] On the country level, USAID's sterilization program has been deemed largely unsuccessful. However, the staggering numbers of women with sterilizations in the Kilimanjaro region (around 7 percent) and Ugweno village (33 percent) demanded further inquiry.

Today approximately one-third of Tanzanians identify themselves as Christian, and another third as Muslim. Those constituting the remaining third practice one of the country's numerous indigenous religions. The Muslim population is most heavily concentrated on the Zanzibar archipelago and in the coastal areas of the mainland. There are also large Muslim minorities in inland urban areas. Ugweno is approximately 50 percent Lutheran Christian and 50 percent Sunni Muslim, which is a somewhat unusual situation, since most communities are predominantly Muslim or Christian. Remarkably, sterilization in Ugweno is accepted by both Sunni Muslim and Lutheran Christian women. This unusual finding prompted investigation as to why women are choosing a permanent method of contraception, especially since the broader cultural context is conventionally considered to be unreceptive to both contraception and sterilization.[9]

My fieldwork among the Northern Pare in Ugweno sought answers to the following questions: What are women's motives and explanations for the decision to seek sterilization? How is sterilization negotiated in marital and family contexts and in light of wider community norms? What are individual perceptions of religious doctrine regarding family planning, and how do interpretations of these doctrines on both individual and communal levels influence reproductive decision-making? Specifically, how do women and men manipulate, adopt, and construct their understanding of Islam and Islamic mandates regarding family planning to achieve their own goals? A series of in-depth interviews that I conducted in 2000–2001 revealed that individuals in Ugweno pragmatically construct reproductive lives that challenge overly deterministic understandings of the relationship between religion and contraceptive practices.

Islam and Individual Reproductive Practice

Many researchers, and many Muslims, still associate Islam with resistance to contraception, or with its outright prohibition.[10] At the same time, fertility rates are decreasing and contraceptive use is increasing in many parts of the Muslim world. Some scholars have argued that the widespread assumption that Islam is hostile to family planning draws on, and feeds into, a much wider pattern of portraying Muslim societies as dominated by Islam.[11] Obermeyer's research, in contrast, provides a good example of how more nuanced understandings of Islam question such a "naturalized" relationship between Islam and family planning.[12] Her work in Tunisia and Iran demonstrates that different cultural, social, political, and economic situations color the interpretation of Islam, thereby affecting women's lives, status, and reproductive choice in multiple and diverse ways. Obermeyer shows that religious ideologies can be used to suppress women and support gender hierarchy; alternatively, women may use the rubric of religious law and belief to critique society and to expand their options.

With respect to family planning in particular, Islamic texts do not present a major obstacle in and of themselves. As Musallam argues, "since the Quran said nothing about contraception, and there was nothing like the Christian concept of the 'Church' in Islam, there existed no 'Islamic' attitude independent or above that of the jurists" who relied on hadiths to determine their opinions.[13] There are, in fact, a large number of hadiths on contraception.[14] Most frequently noted are the many hadiths that refer to the fact that the Prophet condones the use of coitus interruptus (withdrawing before ejaculation):[15] "With the absence of an explicitly religious provision, Muslim jurists were able to argue to their own satisfaction that contraception was proper. . . . Their method was grounded in the third source of Islamic law: *qiyas,* reasoning by analogy."[16] This permissive stance on coitus interruptus has been taken to apply to all nonterminal methods of contraception. Sterilization specifically poses greater difficulty because the finality of the method is seen as interfering with divine will, and therefore Muslim religious scholars have not condoned its use.[17] A study in Somalia concludes that "tubal ligation [sterilization] is never an option; it causes permanent infertility and is an assault to women's sexuality, their ability to produce more children and hence their status in society."[18] Recent research continues to demonstrate that some Muslims are reluctant to use contraception because of Islam.[19] Sargent and Cordell note that men cite with conviction Islamic doctrine as an explanation for their opposition to contraception, while women increasingly justify contraception in response to French government policies and biomedical encouragement.[20]

As political, social, and economic structures change, so do the considerations and attitudes governing marriage and reproduction. These attitudes are both culturally variable and dynamic. My research in Tanzania further demonstrates that women, men, and religious leaders interpret and understand Islam and family planning according to their own sets of needs, expectations, and experiences. This leads to sometimes differing interpretations that overlap between groups and individuals. Important here is that there is not one "right" or "correct" understanding of what Islam permits and what the community supports. The presence of these multiple ideologies allows women to make pragmatic choices based on their own life circumstances, without feeling that they are violating Islamic moral code. Evidence from Ugweno challenges any straightforward connection between Islamic ideology and practice. Observing and examining people's discussions and decisions about family planning reveal the multiple ways that people interpret, adopt, and work within prescribed religious doctrine. This interactive approach allows a more complex, nuanced lens with which one can examine this relationship beyond merely that of listing the laws, norms, and restrictions in place to constrain behaviors. People can, and do, deny and manipulate cultural norms proscribing reproductive behavior. An analysis of family planning and religion demonstrates how people actively adapt to and re-create their culture.[21]

The Pare of Ugweno, Tanzania

Ugweno is a rural area situated in the Northern Pare Mountains in northeastern Tanzania in the Kilimanjaro region. The region is sizable, with 13,200 square kilometers and a population of 1,108,699 (5.4 percent of Tanzania's total population). The population of Ugweno, a major subdivision of the Pare, consists of approximately 20,000 inhabitants. Ugweno is divided into four wards, each of which contains two villages. My research was conducted in two centrally located subvillages within Kifula village: Masumbeni (population 4,200) and Kisanjuni (population 2,500).[22]

Regarding religious affiliation, approximately half of the Ugweno Pare are Lutheran Christian, and the other half are Sunni Muslim. These distinct religious groups live together amicably. Intermarriage is common, and religious conversion is frequent. Observation alone indicates that Muslims are generally less well off, that they have more children and less education, and that their access to economic opportunities and resources is limited. Most people in Ugweno attributed these differences to the fact that Muslim children must go to the madrasa (Qur'anic school), which distracts them from government school and other development opportunities. Furthermore, people discussed the fact that Christianity explicitly encourages people to actively pursue "development" and a more "modern" lifestyle (including all methods of family planning), whereas Islam allegedly does not encourage these endeavors.[23]

In comparison, within Tanzania the Kilimanjaro region has high levels of education for both sexes—second only to Dar es Salaam in the level of female education.[24] The total fertility rate for women of reproductive age in the Kilimanjaro region is 5.71 live births per woman of childbearing age.[25] Eighty-six percent of women knew of a modern method of contraception, but only some 24 percent of women and 15 percent of men reported using a modern method.[26]

In 1998 Hollos and Larsen[27] conducted a survey of 393 women of reproductive age (twenty to forty-nine years) in Kifula, a subvillage of Ugweno. The survey covered a range of questions, including contraception, value of children, as well as birth and contraceptive histories. Forty-two percent of women reported having used contraception at some point, and 39 percent were using contraception at the time of the survey. Fifty-one percent of these women used modern, reversible contraceptives (pill, IUD, injection, or implant), 33 percent were sterilized, 12 percent used withdrawal and the calendar method, and 4 percent did not report a method.[28] The survey concluded that female sterilization was significantly higher for women with more than four children, regardless of age: "The sterilized women in the survey present a profile that is very different from the women using modern contraception. These women are less educated, have more children and are in a more traditional union. The choice of sterilization is determined primarily by the number of children the woman has already had and not by her other characteristics."[29]

Research Methods and Sample

The bulk of my research was based on in-depth, unstructured, open-ended interviews with women, men, local religious leaders, and hospital workers. Interviews were conducted exclusively in the local language, KiSwahili, over a four-month period in 2000–2001. In conjunction with the interviews, I participated in community activities (funerals, weddings, send-offs, and religious and school events) and local discussions throughout the course of the research project. Furthermore, I lived with a local family and participated in family activities, events, visits, and discussions. Participant observation provided context and background to the interview data.

In-depth interviews were conducted with forty women (half had been sterilized, and half had not) between the ages of thirty-three and fifty-one. The method of selection began at the local clinic. Nurses suggested contacting several women who were known to be open, and those women recommended others. Women from the two groups were chosen to match, as much as possible, in age, education, and religion. The interviewees had between one and ten children each; the women who were sterilized had an average of six children each, and those without sterilization had an average of four children each. The average number of years of school was the same for both groups (six and one-half years), with a range from four to twelve years of schooling for the entire group. Of the women who had been sterilized, 30 percent reported using a modern method of contraception before being sterilized, while 70 percent of the women who were not sterilized had used a modern method of contraception at some point. Muslims comprised one-fourth of the women who were sterilized and 45 percent of the women who were not.

A questionnaire with open-ended questions was developed and administered to each of the forty women. Subjects covered in the questionnaire included basic demographic information, fertility and contraceptive history, and religion (importance in life and knowledge of acceptability of family-planning use). In the final month of the project, five women were selected from each group to participate in follow-up interviews, which included in-depth interviews with their husbands.

In addition I interviewed several other individuals: the director of the Kilimanjaro regional office of UMATI for information on institutional goals, methods, history, and demographics; a USAID representative in Dar es Salaam regarding the Permanent and Long-Term Methods (PLT) program; and the local *daktari* (medical assistant) and family-planning nurses in Ugweno. I met with this last group each week throughout the duration of the fieldwork to discuss their understanding of how sterilization is negotiated, their perceptions of the women who chose to be sterilized, and the key concerns and changes they may have noted in the women choosing to be sterilized since the program's initiation. In addition I observed weekly maternal and child health sessions.

Findings: *Ethnographic Portraits of Three Women and a Local Imam in Ugweno, Tanzania*

The portraits of three women, two who were sterilized and one who was not, illuminate the experiences and thoughts of both sterilized and not-sterilized women.

An interview with a local imam (Muslim leader/teacher) highlights the ambiguity that exists regarding Islam and family planning in this community.

Aina Ibrahim

Age: Forty-five years old
Number of children: Seven
Contraceptive history: Never used contraception, not sterilized
Marital information: Married at age eighteen; husband not supportive of contraceptive use

Aina has never used modern family planning, but she definitely thinks it is a good thing. At the time of the interview, six of her children were still living at home. Aina's youngest child was four years old, and her oldest child had two young children of her own (all of whom were at that point living in Aina's household). Her children were spaced between two and three years apart with the aid of breast feeding (a natural method of birth control). Regarding family planning, Aina said: "Family planning is good for spacing your family and for making sure you have fewer children. For me, it is too late now. I wanted to use family planning, but my mother in-law, she didn't like it. She threatened to put a curse on us if we used family planning. She had no education and she thought that many children meant that we would have everything we needed. When I was younger it was not so important to me and I did not realize how much easier my life would be with fewer children. My mother in-law, she lived with us and she would know if we only had a few children because my mother had many children and she had many children too. My husband, he likes the idea of family planning, he wanted me to use it, but he was also afraid of his mother, so we did not use family planning."

In discussing family planning, Aina acknowledged that people in Ugweno were receptive to family planning and to *maendeleo* (economic development activities). Although she had never used family planning, Aina was aware of the different family-planning options and had opinions about which were good and which were bad. She said, "Pills, injection, condoms, withdrawal, these are some of the methods I know. I have never used any of these, but people talk about how bad pills are, many complain of pains, blood pressure, bleeding. But still, so many women use pills. Norplant, Norplant is good, I have never heard anyone complain." I asked Aina why she thought so many people used pills. She responded, "the pain and inconvenience of the pills are not so great when they can choose the number of children they will have and they can space their children as they want without having to rely just on God." In this discussion about various methods of family planning, Aina distinguished sterilization from the rest. Unlike hormonal methods, there are few, if any, rumors associated with sterilization. She also confirmed that most people—not just those women who have had them—have a positive view of sterilization. She said, "*Sterilization* is good for those women who are finished completely with having children, they just have to go to the hospital once, and then they are free. There are no problems and no side-effects. Then they can do whatever they want."

Aina and I conferred about family planning and life in Ugweno on several occasions. Several times she mentioned that Muslim women have more difficult lives than Christian women do. With respect to Islam and family planning, specifically, she noted differences between Christians and Muslims. The main difference she identified was that the Lutheran Church actively encourages family planning for men and women, while the Sunni Muslim leaders and the Qur'an do not encourage women to use contraception. In fact, she said, Muslim leaders never talk about family planning. Speaking about normative statements of her own Islamic religion about family planning, Aina said, "*hawaruhusu sana,*" which translates as "they really do not permit/allow it." Aina noted that family planning is not allowed or permitted "because they say it is God who gives you children . . . but you have to give them a good life." She said that Muslim women know that family planning is bad because they learn this at the madrasa school and read it in the Qur'an. Many Muslim women, however, use family planning despite this knowledge, although they do not talk about it at the mosque. Aina explained that "basically, women do what they want. They decide what is best for themselves."

Clearly there is a contradiction between perceived religious ideology and cultural practices of women in Ugweno: women have to make decisions about themselves and their families despite going against their religious leaders. Observing the difficulties of raising a large family and the benefits of family planning, Aina claimed: "Our lives, they are hard. Now many Muslim women and men see how family planning and other things, like development and education, have helped the Christians, so now they also want to have fewer children and they want to take care of their children better so that everybody can have a better life. Family planning helps us with that. So, many women use family planning anyway, even though Islam and the Qur'an say that we should not use family planning."

The fact that many women have sterilizations, despite a perception that Islam does not allow it, was not a problem for Aina (or other Muslim women in Ugweno). Rather, Aina saw that women are empowered by family planning to "do what they want" and need to do. For Muslim women, this often means using family planning and having sterilization despite contradictory cultural, social, and religious messages.

Aina undoubtedly thinks that her religion, Islam, is the most important thing in her life; she does not, however, always agree with how Islam works for women. She spoke candidly about Muslim women in Ugweno: "For Muslim women things are different. They are not as free as the Christian women. Their husbands keep them from doing more. They have less education, they are less free, and they get less development. Christian women have better lives than Muslim women." Aina was referring to the fact that many Muslim women are not allowed by their husbands to participate in development efforts that specifically target women—many of these efforts are run by missionary groups that come to help Christians specifically.

Aina's account illustrates knowledge of and devotion to Islam but also sympathetic sentiments regarding the use of family planning. Aina did not use family planning, despite wanting to, because she had several factors working against her: namely, her mother-in-law and her husband. Her lack of family planning use is not attributable to Islam per se, but Aina did articulate the conflict that contemporary women face when negotiating family-planning use and religion. She will, however, encourage her daughters and sons to use family planning.

Aina has a positive view of sterilizations and even at some point had a desire to use contraception. She draws a connection between a better life, smaller families, and contraception. Her account further demonstrates that Muslims in Ugweno are starting to desire family planning more and more, largely in an effort to achieve the same positive outcomes they perceive Lutherans to have developed.

Mama Maharage

Age: Forty-two years old
Number of children: Nine
Contraceptive history: Never used contraception, sterilized
Marital information: Married at age eighteen; husband not supportive of contraceptive use but condoned sterilization after birth of twins

Mama Maharage had her first child when she was eighteen and then had a child every two to three years thereafter until 1993, when she had twins. In 1993 she decided to "take action" and to get *funga kabisa* (sterilization). Mama Maharage explained, "Family planning . . . it is a good thing, but for me it is too late! People these days, young people, they like family planning. They want few children. They think, there are so many diseases . . . if you have fewer children you can take better care of each one. Only people who don't know about family planning or women who have jealous husbands do not use it. . . . I know of pills, Norplant, sterilization, and condoms. I learned about these methods at the clinic from the nurses when I took my children in for their immunizations." Mama Maharage never used family planning to space her children because she feared possible side effects from hormonal and barrier methods. She decided to have a sterilization because "otherwise I would have twenty children instead of just nine!" Sterilization also enabled her to end childbearing: "*funga kabisa* is the best method, you don't have to worry or think about it every day. You also don't have to worry about it not working. It is one time and then you are finished; it is permanent. Then you are free and have no problems."

We discussed why she never used family planning before being sterilized. She recalled:

> When I first got married I wanted to have babies. In addition family planning was really new here. We didn't really know anything about it. And from the things that we did hear, it seemed pretty risky. My husband and I were not sure about it. We also were not sure about our children. We did not want to be using family planning and ruin our chances to have the number of children we wanted. My husband never really liked to talk about planning how many children we wanted. After our first child we talked about it, but we knew many women who took action and had so many problems. We decided not to take any action. But after we had the last two, the twins, we talked about it more. He agreed with me that I could not keep having pregnancies and that we could not afford to pay for more children to go to school. So, we decided that I should have a sterilization. I needed his permission for the nurses, so it was good that he agreed.[30] I know a lot of women with a sterilization now and they all really like it. There are no side-effects, and it was so easy. Now the pill, that has too many side-effects, I would never want to use that. I've heard so many bad things about the pill, IUD, injections and even Norplant. Why would I want to take these things? You don't know what they are going to do inside of you. With a sterilization you know what can happen to you: nothing!

Mama Maharage said that the best number of children to have is four but that if she were getting married today she would have only two. She sees a direct connection between a poor quality of life and having too many children. She said that *maisha si rahisi* (life is hard) when one has so many children. She also wishes that she had had the courage to use family planning earlier and had not waited so long to have a sterilization. Some of her friends did use family planning at earlier stages and have smaller families: "[They] have better things; they have all those things that I do not have . . . they have nice furniture, their children are all able to go to school, and they have plenty of food. They are free to do the things that they want. They have the ability to develop, to continue in a good way. Those who have few children have a good chance of developing their families. For me, I still have to work to pay for primary school fees.[31] My daughters are still young. This is hard for me." Her interpretation of Islam now would "permit/allow us to use family planning" (*wanahurusu uzazi wa mpango*): "At this time, the leaders, they encourage family planning. They say that we should use family planning, that it is important, and that we should decide for ourselves. In the past, they would say you are interfering with God's work, now it is up to everyone to decide for yourself."

Mama Maharage's case illustrates the anxiety that women and men in Ugweno have about the side effects of hormonal contraceptives. Furthermore, sterilization is seen as being in a completely different realm than that of hormonal contraception.

Mama Maharage also discussed Islam and the Islamic leaders in Ugweno as being supportive of and encouraging family planning and contraception—quite different from the views of Aina, thus revealing the multiplicity of views that exist locally regarding family planning and contraceptive use.

Lilian Yasini

> *Age:* Thirty-six years old
> *Number of children:* Four
> *Contraceptive history:* Used IUD, the pill, injection, and is now sterilized
> *Marital information:* Married at age twenty-two; husband supportive of contraceptive use and sterilization

Lilian works five days a week as a nurse at the Kifula hospital. After completing primary school she received two years of nurse training from the government. Lilian was married at the age of twenty-two, after her training. She grew up in a Lutheran household and married her Muslim husband for love. She said that converting to Islam was a difficult decision, especially because it meant becoming a second wife.

Lilian acknowledged that her position as a second wife is improved because of her job and economic independence. Lilian has "only four children." One year after her last child was born, she had a sterilization with the support of her husband. Her husband was supportive "because he understands how difficult our life is, but he wanted to have four children first" and because he already had four children with his first wife. Throughout her childbearing years, Lilian used different methods to space her children. She used the loop (IUD) for three years, injections for three years, and the pill for only a few months because she suffered from its side effects. For her, family planning was not a difficult issue. As a nurse, she understands the benefits and, because of her training, realizes that side effects are sometimes part of the process. Having a sterilization made the most sense to Lilian. With respect to family planning, Lilian said that Muslims like family planning but that this is largely a result of the educational efforts made by the clinic. It is unrelated to understandings of Islam, which she thinks "protests family planning because it goes against the commandments of God."

Lilian's forty-two-year-old husband, Yasini Shabani, reported that he initially wanted to have six children because "this is the number I could feed well and take to school." He has fathered eight children between two wives. He now thinks that four children is the best number and that any more than six would make life difficult. To him, family planning can help achieve the number of children that one can care for. He explained, "Islam and the Qur'an teach people to have a number of children that you can feed and take care of, so we can use family planning to make sure that we have the number of children we can feed and take care of."

Imam Mohammed

Given the multiple—and seemingly contradictory—views that circulate in Ugweno about the religious acceptability of family planning, discussions with local imams were valuable. At the time of the interview, Mohammed had been an imam (leader and teacher of local Muslims) in Ugweno for forty-three years. He had spent at least twelve years in Dar es Salaam, Zanzibar, and Mombasa (Kenya) studying Islam. He teaches Muslims in Ugweno religious knowledge, conducts prayers at the main mosque, and teaches women and children about the Qur'an at the madrasa (the Qur'anic school). Mohammed appears to be influential in the community; discussions with women and men in Ugweno made it clear that his teachings and understandings of Islam influenced their own understandings of Islam significantly, especially with regard to family planning. While it is unclear if women and men would approach Mohammed specifically about their personal decision to have sterilization, it is clear that Mohammed presented and discussed his own interpretations and understanding of the Islamic position on issues such as family planning, and sterilization specifically.

My conversations with Mohammed highlighted the intense ambiguity that exists with respect to Islam and family planning in Ugweno. More than once he specifically stated: "Islam does not support the use of family planning, but the Qur'an says we should use family planning, but not the kind you find at the clinic: not the tablets. The Qur'an suggests breastfeeding your children for a long time. We encourage this because it is written in the Qur'an." His explanation for why women should not use "tablets" was either "it interferes with God's will" or "we know of the harmful side-effects of this family planning." He did, however, say that "family planning is important, but as Muslims we should not do it." When asked if he thinks that Muslims in Ugweno use family planning, he said, "Yes, they go [to the clinic]. We even encourage them to go . . . but we do not agree with the tablets because of the side-effects." Mohammed never discussed sterilization separately from family planning. Clearly, however, even the local religious experts offer Ugweno Muslims some latitude to act pragmatically within Islamic strictures. From comparisons with other research, it is not surprising that Muslim leaders in Ugweno do not necessarily agree.[32]

Why Are Women in Ugweno Getting Sterilized?

Four major themes—*funga kabisa, hamna athari, maisha si rahisi,* and *maendeleo*—emerged from the analysis of interviews, conversations, and observations in Ugweno. Together they describe why women choose to have sterilization in a religious and cultural context conventionally expected to be resistant to permanent methods of contraception. These themes consistently came up in general conversations about family planning and, more specifically, about female sterilization.

Funga kabisa is the KiSwahili term for "completely closed off," "finished completely," and "female sterilization." For those women who had been sterilized and also for those who had not consistently articulated a positive view of sterilization, permanency was not a negative aspect of *funga kabisa;* instead, it was one of the major benefits. Women talked about sterilization as only "a one-time thing." They view sterilization as a method that is guaranteed and has no side effects. Once you have a sterilization, you can "be free." The perception is that it is an appropriate method for women who are finished with childbearing and no longer need to hold onto their reproductive capabilities. Christian women have no religious restrictions on their ability to use any form of family planning. Muslim men and women, however, have contradictory messages and understandings of what is permitted for them by their religion.

Hamna athari is the KiSwahili term for "no negative, harmful, or inconvenient side effects." Sterilization is associated with *hamna athari* because, unlike hormonal methods of contraception, it is considered free from side effects. In general, women expressed an extreme dislike for hormonal methods and their subsequent side effects. Hormonal methods are judged to be unhealthy, a nuisance, unpredictable, and ineffective. Despite all of this, many women still use hormonal methods because if they are not finished with childbearing and want to limit their family size, they have no other choice. Sterilization, on the other hand, is distinguished as a healthy and safe method by all the women interviewed. The health center in Ugweno has three primary family-planning and maternal- and child-health nurses, all of whom stress this aspect of sterilization. They actively encourage women in Ugweno who are finished with having children to consider the procedure. This undoubtedly has a serious impact on women who trust the wisdom of the nurses at the clinic. The fact that no woman in Ugweno has had complications or problems associated with a sterilization is extremely significant in a place where stories, rumors, and misconceptions circulate about hormonal and barrier methods. Throughout my research there was no mention of a negative association with or consequences of sterilization. Concomitantly rumors about male sterilization frequently arose—usually with laughter and joking about how men are afraid. It should also be noted that sterilization and reversible methods of modern contraceptives are provided free of charge by the local clinic.

Maisha si rahisi is the KiSwahili phrase for "life is not easy." Women discussed their desire for smaller families, usually four children, in terms of the general difficulty and cost of living. They talked about general, and daily, obstacles in their lives. Women are well aware of the costs—financial and social—of having many children. For most of the women interviewed, it was too late to have a small family; however, they hoped that their daughters would have fewer children. A primary concern was the cost of education. In Ugweno, education is seen as the key to improving one's chances in life. An educated child has the necessary skills and tools to become successful in life and therefore is able to provide for his family. Education is undeniably expensive for people with little access to cash. Now, when women and men discuss their options, sending only some of their children to school is no longer the only choice; having fewer children, through the use of family planning, is increasingly a viable preference. The Tanzanian government recently eliminated school fees for primary school education, but there are still many costs associated with sending a child to school (uniform, books, supplies). To fully benefit from education, however, completing secondary school is necessary. Therefore the decision to educate a child has farther reaching ramifications in terms of a family's budget. Entrance exam fees for secondary school and secondary school tuition are both prohibitively expensive. In such a context—where educating children is expensive—family planning is viewed positively by men and women despite cultural traditions and norms that support having many children.

Maendeleo is the KiSwahili term for "development" (as in economic or sustainable development). Women in Ugweno are deeply concerned with being "modern" in various contexts, and attaining the benefits of "development" is an important aspect of that. As Ann Anagnost said about the one-child policy in China: "I began to ask myself whether the meaning of having fewer children had expanded from a remedy for under-development to become a sign of the modern itself. . . . In China the project of modernization suffuses everyday life with its language, with its reform of practices, and with both people's consciousness of commodities—their access to them or their lack thereof—and the practical uses. Commodities become the markers of a stage of development, the tangible indicators of a society's wealth and vigor."[33]

Anagnost's observation in China parallels what women and men were saying in Ugweno. With regard to family planning, a smaller family ideology is pervasive despite general pronatalist cultural traditions and tendencies. This changing ideology does not always translate into small completed family size, but today people in Ugweno subscribe to values linked to their own notions of "modernization" and "development"—words frequently used by women and men in the village. Some of the benefits of a small family that women articulated were: increased economic opportunities, a healthier family, more food, and increased education for each child. These benefits are conceptualized within a "modern" context. Family-planning decisions are made within that framework. A smaller family, despite certain cultural disadvantages, is a trade-off; nevertheless it is considered advantageous in the "modern" context. When asked, people in Ugweno responded unequivocally that they use family planning more than people in other areas of Tanzania do because "we have better education and *maendeleo.*"

Conclusion

The ethnographic portraits and interviews presented in this article point to the ambiguity that exists within Ugweno regarding Islam and family planning—themes that Obermeyer, Jeffery and Jeffery, and others point to in the larger discourse on Islam and family planning. Sterilization, however, is the exception. Islamic religious experts do not condone this form of family planning, and yet, in Ugweno, Tanzania, we find examples of Muslims undergoing the procedure. Aina put it best when she said, "Yes, many Muslim women use family planning; they just do not talk about it at the mosque. Basically women do what they want, they decide for themselves." It was never mentioned by women, men, or Muslim leaders that sterilization was worse than other family planning methods prohibited by Islam. This research thus demonstrates that local people's perceptions of Islamic rules about family planning—and sterilization specifically—are individual and cannot be considered at the community level. Women, however, are consistent in their belief that sterilization is the best method of contraception and that Islam does not permit use of family planning nor of sterilization. Nevertheless individuals, specifically women, are able to define their own approach by manipulating the rules or by resisting them.

Research on reproduction and family planning, and especially on sterilization, has tended to consider African women in a context of family relations, where expectations about women's fertility are rigidly constructed. Similarly Muslim women are portrayed as living in a context where Islamic religious proscriptions regulate behavior. This supposedly results in choices and ideals that are diametrically opposed to a "modern" paradigm of contraceptive use. Anthropological demographers have demonstrated, however, that women in Africa may have agendas other than those that the Western world imposes on them when it comes to reproduction and family planning.[34] Women in Ugweno contradict our expectations about rural Muslim African women and the acceptability of permanent contraception. Decisions of sterilization are embedded in women's narratives of their own health, happiness, well-being, and freedom; in terms of their families' health, happiness, and well-being; and in terms of achieving certain goals for their families. For many women, these goals justify the choice to use contraception—despite the stance they perceive Islam to have on their use of family planning.

In Ugweno the women, couples, families, and religious and social communities are not homogenous units with uniform beliefs about family planning. What makes them different? What unites them? Aina, Mama Maharage, and Lilian all demonstrate that women and couples are working within a cultural system, and a set of norms and traditions, to achieve their own life goals. All of these women have different life constraints and opportunities, and yet each arrives at her own reproductive decisions and conclusions based on what is best for her. Islam clearly plays a role in terms of how women, men, and couples navigate and negotiate their options. In Ugweno religion matters, but religious doctrine may be less important than one might expect. Islam, despite its great variation internationally, nationally, and even locally, is often a domain of analysis that is presumed to unite groups of people. Clearly, however, people interpret and manipulate their understandings of Islam in pragmatic ways, and individual life situations lead to different decisions within the same ideology.

NOTES

1. See J. C. Caldwell and P. Caldwell, "The Fertility Transition in Sub-Saharan Africa," in *Fertility and the Current South African Issues of Poverty, HIV/AIDS and Youth* (Cape Town: Human Sciences Research Council, 2002), 1.

2. Today sterilization is the world's most widespread form of birth control, accounting for over a third of contraceptive use worldwide and almost half in developing countries (Population Reference Bureau, *Family Planning World Wide: 2002 Data Sheet* [Washington, D.C.: Population Reference Bureau, 2002]).

3. M. Hollos and U. Larsen, "Marriage and Contraception among the Pare of Northern Tanzania," *Journal of Biosocial Science* 36 (2004): 267.

4. Bureau of Statistics and Planning Commission and Macro International Inc., *Tanzania: Demographic and Health Survey 1996* (Calverton, Md.: Macro International Inc. and Bureau of Statistics and Planning Commission, 1997).

5. L. A. Richey, "'Development,' Gender and Family Planning: Population Politics and the Tanzanian National Population Policy" (Ph.D. diss., University of North Carolina at Chapel Hill, 1999), 3.

6. Ibid., 267.

7. Ibid.

8. Personal communication with Ugweno Health Unit nurse, 2000.

9. Cf. D. Hogan and B. Biratu, "Social Identity and Community Effects on Contraceptive Use and Intentions in Southern Ethiopia," *Studies in Family Planning* 35, no. 2 (2004): 79–90; Hollos and Larsen, "Marriage and Contraception"; S. A. Kridli and S. E. Newton, "Jordanian Married Muslim Women's Intentions to Use Oral Contraceptives," *International Council of Nurses* 52 (2005): 109–14; S. Philliber and W. Philliber, "Social and Psychological Perspectives on Voluntary Sterilization: A Review," *Studies in Family Planning* 16 (1985): 1–29.

10. H. Comerasamy and others, "The Acceptability and Use of Contraception: A Prospective Study of Somalian Women's Attitudes," *Journal of Obstetrics and Gynaecology* 23, no. 4 (2003): 412–15; K. L. Dehne, "Knowledge of, Attitudes towards, and Practices Relating to Child-Spacing Methods in Northern Burkina Faso," *Journal of Health, Population, and Nutrition* 21, no. 1 (2003): 55–66; C. Sargent and D. Cordell, "Polygamy, Disrupted Reproduction, and the State: Malian Migrants in Paris, France," *Social Science and Medicine* 56, no. 9 (2003): 1961–72; Hogan and Biratu, "Social Identity"; Kridli and Newton, "Jordanian Married Muslim Women's Intentions."

11. L. Abu-Lughod, "Zones of Theory in the Anthropology of the Arab World," *Annual Review of Anthropology* 18 (1989): 267–306; R. Jeffery and P. Jeffery, *Population, Gender, and*

Politics: Demographic Change in Rural North India (Cambridge: Cambridge University Press, 1997).

12. C. Obermeyer, "Reproductive Choice in Islam: Gender and State in Iran and Tunisia," *Studies in Family Planning* 25, no. 1 (1994): 41–51.

13. B. F. Musallam, *Sex and Society in Islam: Birth Control before the Nineteenth Century* (Cambridge: Cambridge University Press, 1983), 13.

14. Ibid.

15. Jeffery and Jeffery, *Population, Gender, and Politics;* Musallam, *Sex and Society;* Obermeyer, "Reproductive Choice in Islam"; A. Omran, *Population in the Arab World: Problems and Prospects* (London: Croom Helm, 1980); N. Youssef, "The Status and Fertility Patterns of Muslim Women," in *Women in the Muslim World,* ed. Lois Beck (Cambridge, Mass.: Harvard University Press, 1978).

16. Musallam, *Sex and Society,* 17.

17. Obermeyer, "Reproductive Choice in Islam"; Omran. *Population in the Arab World;* Youssef, "Status and Fertility Patterns."

18. Comerasamy and others, "Acceptability and Use of Contraception," 414.

19. Hogan and Biratu, "Social Identity"; S. A. Kridli and K. Libbus, "Establishing Reliability and Validity of an Instrument Measuring Jordanian Muslim Women's Contraceptive Beliefs," *Health Care for Women International* 23 (2002): 870–81; Sargent and Cordell, "Polygamy, Disrupted Reproduction, and the State."

20. Sargent and Cordell, "Polygamy, Disrupted Reproduction, and the State."

21. A. Carter, "Agency and Fertility: For an Ethnography of Practice," in *Anthropology Theorizes Reproduction: Integrating Practice, Political Economic, and Feminist Perspectives,* ed. S. Greenhalgh (Cambridge: Cambridge University Press, 1995), 55–85.

22. Hollos and Larsen, "Marriage and Contraception"; M. Hollos and U. Larsen, "Which African Men Promote Smaller Families and Why? Marital Relations and Fertility in a Pare Community in Northern Tanzania," *Social Science and Medicine* 58 (2004): 1733–49.

23. Hollos and Larsen, "Marriage and Contraception"; Hollos and Larsen, "Which African Men?"

24. Bureau of Statistics and Planning Commission and Macro International Inc., *HIV/AIDS Indicator Survey 2003–4* (Calverton, Md.: Macro International Inc., 2005). Statistics indicate a gendered bias among the uneducated: 21.5 percent of women and 13.8 percent of men have no education; 31.9 percent of women and 33.9 percent of men complete primary school; and 5.7 percent of women and 8.1 percent of men have a secondary level of education or more.

25. Bureau of Statistics and Planning Commission and Macro International Inc., *Tanzania,* the most recent DHS with regional-level data.

26. Slightly higher numbers of men (26.7 percent) and women (37 percent) in the Kilimanjaro region reported using a method of contraception.

27. Hollos and Larsen, "Marriage and Contraception."

28. Ibid., 267.

29. Ibid., 269.

30. In the first years of the program a husband's permission was required; that changed after 1994.

31. These are no longer "fees" per se but the costs associated with attending school, such as uniforms and books.

32. Dehne, "Knowledge," notes that imams in the same village in Burkina Faso have conflicting notions of what is permitted by Islam with respect to family planning.

33. A. Anagnost, "A Surfeit of Bodies: Population and the Rationality of the State in Post-Mao China," in *Conceiving the New World Order: The Global Politics of Reproduction,* ed. F. Ginsburg and R. Rapp (Berkeley: University of California Press, 1995), 29.

34. C. Bledsoe and others, "Constructing Natural Fertility: The Use of Western Contraceptive Technologies in Rural Gambia," *Population and Development Review* 20 (1994): 81–113.

VIOLA HÖRBST

Male Infertility in Mali

Kinship and Impacts on Biomedical Practice in Bamako

To offer a situated understanding of Islam[1] in postcolonial Mali, Benjamin F. Soares describes Mali "as a place of many contradictions and often jarring juxtapositions and synthesis."[2] This phenomenon also holds true for many other African societies and nations. Nominally 90 percent of Mali's 10.6 million inhabitants consider themselves to be Sunni Muslims,[3] but the "non-Islamic" figures prominently. Following Soares, "juxtapositions include Islam, on the one hand, and what we might call 'fetishism,' 'animism,' 'paganism' or African 'traditional' religion on the other; Muslim and non-Muslim; African and Western."[4] To illustrate his claim, Soares draws our attention to the backyard of the main Friday mosque situated in the heart of Bamako. There, Islamic commodities are presented next to ingredients for traditional rituals of African religion or medicine. These "dried and cured animal parts . . . are bought and sold alongside copper vessels used in writing magical and therapeutic texts and a wide array of plant medicines."[5] Just a few steps away, biomedical or Western pharmaceuticals are sold at the neighboring market found in the dense roads of Bamako's center.

This juxtaposition leads to entanglement and blurring of boundaries with regard to medical conceptualizations and practices, especially those concerning such delicate spheres as fertility and infertility. In general, Malians suffering from marital infertility consult biomedical practitioners in governmental and private clinics. However, they also seek out a variety of so-called traditional experts, such as marabouts (*karamogow*),[6] who base their treatment on botanical knowledge, the Qur'an, amulets (*gris-gris*), and the influence of spirits. Malians may also visit hunters (*donzonw*), who treat via botanical, mineral, and animal products and refer to ancestral forces, fetishes or charged objects (*boli*), and spirits for their diagnoses and therapeutic interventions.[7] Further, they approach herbalists (*furabolaw*), who emphasize their knowledge and practice of phytotherapy and sometimes their cooperation with biomedical institutions, while embedding their treatments in different interpretations of Muslim or animistic concepts of human being.[8]

Islamic-oriented "traditional practitioners" seem to be inclined to either monogenetic or duogenetic perceptions of procreation as offered by Islam—that is, perceptions of conception that emphasize the active part of either one (mono) or both (duo) partners.[9] Hunters and ritual specialists relying on animism tend toward a duogenetic model of conception.[10] To varying degrees, all of these specialists are informed of the biomedical duogenetic model of conception. While their explanations concerning the cause and treatment of infertility can greatly differ, the male factors causing marital childlessness are well known to all of them. Nevertheless, in everyday social life in Mali there is a strong tendency to consider women solely responsible for childless marriages. In communications and family dealings, the possibility of male infertility is considered the "unspeakable" or even the "unthinkable."

Anthropologists have argued that reproductive questions are not simply an individual matter, pointing out that "reproduction lies at the intersection of group interests, including families, households, kinship, ethnic, and religious groups, states, and international organizations."[11] Nevertheless most studies—and especially those concerning Sub-Saharan Africa—have focused on women. As Dyer and colleagues point out, this fact may be caused by "the understanding that in African countries women carry the main burden of infertility as they appear to be 'blamed,' often solely, for a couple's childlessness."[12] An investigation of people's experiences, practices, and processes of decision-making when marital childlessness is a result of male-factor infertility can address the question of how the diagnosis of male-factor infertility affects marital relations in Mali and how biomedical treatment strategies are responding to these specific conditions. An outline of the basic background of family life and the general features of handling marital childlessness resulting from male or female factors, including some of the major therapeutic options, could help anthropologists and others "understand why men and women behave the way they do."[13]

Methods and Research

The data presented in this article are based on preliminary fieldwork that was carried out in Bamako between November 2004 and February 2005.[14] The project focused on women experiencing marital infertility. In addition it was intended to gain an overview of therapeutic landscapes. Therefore explorative research centered predominantly on three major sites. First I carried out participant observation during consultations in different governmental hospitals and in one private clinic, in which treatment by in vitro fertilization has been offered since the end of 2003. In addition to informal talks with the biomedical and paramedical professionals during the consultations and beyond, I conducted semistructured and open-ended interviews with various gynecologists. Qualitative research methods were used, including participant observation. Here the term *qualitative research* does not refer to the use of open-ended, narrative, or semistructured interviews with each informant one or two times, but rather formal interviews and informal talks that were repeated on a regular basis. This method made it possible to enter into a communication process to receive nuances and details including individuals' ambivalences within decision-making processes, their experiences, and their evaluations and opinions concerning the researched issues. Participant and nonparticipant observations were carried out by attending informants at events taking place and by cross-checking information gained through communication via participating in everyday lives—for example, at clinics.

The second realm of explorative research was made up of nonbiomedical specialists such as hunters, ritual specialists, marabouts, and traditherapists, with whom semistructured interviews were conducted. The third domain consisted of five women belonging to the ethnic groups of Soninke, Bambara, and Malinke, which are all of Mande origin.[15] I worked with these women in order to gain insights into everyday life experiences and attitudes toward means for solution of infertility and childlessness. Concerning the women's social and educational backgrounds, they can be roughly grouped as members from the middle class to the lower upper class. Visits at their homes, chatting about different topics, and talking informally about infertility shed light on their family contexts. Besides these informal conversations and participant observation, I recorded open narrative as well as semistructured thematic interviews with each woman. In addition I accompanied two of them during biomedical consultations. Whenever possible, information about infertility was cross-checked with Malian women and men who were not affected.[16]

Toward the end of my stay in Bamako, the husbands of two of the women I worked with contacted me to talk about their position and experiences as well. One of them was assumed to be the cause for marital childlessness; the other one, Boubaker, knew that he was diagnosed as infertile. Analysis of the stories of these husbands and their wives was based on questions about how male infertility affects marriage and biomedical treatment strategies. These reflections are to be taken as "informed hypotheses,"[17] which are followed up in a research project on perception, utilization, and transformative potential of new reproductive technologies in Bamako.[18] As background some insights into Malian "local moral worlds"[19] can provide a better understanding of specific Malian contexts and configurations.

Marriage, Family Life, and Childlessness in Bamako

Predominantly, the goal of marriage in pronatalist Mali is producing children. Above all, procreation is considered a kind of duty toward the extended family as well as toward the parents. With marriage, women "retain *de jure* membership in their kin group and do not give up their lineage names"[20] but become members of their husbands' family households. Concerning normative rules between marital partners, wives have to be obedient to their husbands and respect their husbands' overall authority and decisions. In addition husbands are taken as their wives' social superiors. Consequently they are implicated by the social conduct and activities of their wives.[21]

In general married women live within their husbands' extended family compounds. Here they have quite a weak position: in their husbands' patrilineage, wives are attributed with an outsider status.[22] They can improve their situation by showing high respect and working hard for all elder family members, in particular their mothers-in-law. Above all, having children will strengthen the wife's standing with regard to her daily working load, respect shown to her by in-laws, and her influence in decision-making concerning family matters. Moreover children might shield her—at least for some years—from polygyny.

According to Malian legislation, couples can choose whether to marry under the rules of monogamy or those of polygyny. Nevertheless, when a couple originally had chosen marriage within the rules of monogamy and then the husband wants to marry another wife, the fact that he had originally chosen monogamy is no obstacle. Following Muslim rules as written down in the Qur'an, a man may marry as many as four wives.[23] Thus the husband has simply to ask his wife whether she agrees with his decision in favor of polygyny. As women explained to me, the wife will be better off to agree, so as not to run the risk of divorce or harassment.

Polygynic marriage arrangements are widespread in Mali and are partially feared among Malian women, especially if marriage does not result in procreation. In general, in these cases women are initially held responsible—at least by the husbands' families. Simultaneously, for many women, pressure exerted by in-laws starts within a few months up to one year if their marriages do not result in pregnancy. A woman is then increasingly harassed by her mother- and sister-in-law or co-wife with snide remarks and open insinuations about her "unworthiness" for not giving birth to children and "not being a full female person."[24] Male infertility as the cause of childlessness is not assumed; within families it is rather taken as the "unspeakable" or even as the "unthinkable." In narratives, male infertility is often equated with impotency, thus deeply disrupting a man's personal, masculine, and sexual identity. As regularly pointed out to me, male infertility is the absolute shame and disgrace to a man and his family. Without children, as one man put it, "you are not a man; nothing will remain from you, no one will remember you—you are born for nothing." Subsequently, men often refuse to subject themselves to sperm analyses; in cases of bad results, men often keep them secret from their families. Grosz-Ngaté states that for men, shameful situations, acts, or conduct "can be tantamount to social death."[25] Additionally she cites a proverb that her informants used to underline this topic: "If you find a woman in trouble, help her. But if you find her in a shameful situation, leave her because she will get over it. If you find a man in trouble, leave him because he can get out of it on his own. But if you find him in a shameful situation, get him out of it because otherwise he might die."[26]

Social Options for Handling Childlessness

Most Malians suffering fertility problems are ready to move heaven and earth for "finding a child," as they call it. Social means to ameliorate the consequences of childlessness for Malian women and men include extramarital sex, polygyny, and fostering children. To foster children is a common social practice in Bamako. Nearly all the women and men I worked with had foster children, but all women expressed fears that the identity of the children's biological mother would not be kept secret and that, sooner or later, the children would go back to their real parents despite whatever the foster parents are doing.[27] In some literature, child fostering is presented as an alternative for biological motherhood or fatherhood "that [has] hitherto adequately handled and cushioned the problem of infertility."[28] From the affected women's perspective, however, fostering children alleviates neither their weak position nor their stigmatization within their husbands' families, since they did not bear the children themselves. Subsequently, to foster children is not seen as providing a conclusive solution for their "infertility." Rather, data from this study suggest that, from both affected women's and men's points of view, social parenthood does not equate with biological parenthood in Bamako.[29]

Polygyny—at least from the husbands' and patrilineal families' points of view—seems the ideal solution for marital childlessness. From the affected women's point of view, co-wives are feared and are seen as an augmentation of pressure, especially if co-wives bear children. The childless woman's position within marriage and within the extended family is then weakened further while the insinuations and offensive comments mount.

In some cases, if important family members assume that male infertility is the reason for childlessness, one further social option is to discreetly send a male family member to the wife for the purpose of impregnating her. Moreover the wife is advised to sleep with her husband on the same day. A child conceived in this way would officially be seen as the infertile man's procreation, as he is married to the mother. Additionally Bamako healers who suspect that the husband is the cause for marital childlessness recommend that the affected woman have clandestine extramarital sex while also sleeping with the husband on the same day. Thus, in both cases, no one can tell who indeed fathered the child without genetic testing. Only within the field of diffuse assumptions, secrecy, and uncertainty might "induced adultery" or extramarital sex seem to be acceptable as a solution by all actors involved—wife, husband, and extended family.

Therapeutic Avenues to Overcoming Infertility and Childlessness

In addition to the social means described above, there are also a variety of therapeutic avenues. Generally, if women do not conceive within six to twelve months after marriage, they start looking for therapeutic means or are requested to do so by their in-laws, husbands, and friends. Such therapies may include ingesting phytotherapeutic and mineral products, inserting such products into the vagina, or washing the body with these substances. Additionally pilgrimages to saints' tombs or to powerful places are conducted, and sacrifices for ancestors are made. Moreover spirits and charged objects are used via consultations of hunters and diviners.

However, to stimulate pregnancy with these latter means generally comes at a cost: if a child is born, that child must be named by the charged object's (*boli*) name or a name chosen by the hunter in charge of the *boli* and the treatment. The belief is that if this requirement is not correctly fulfilled, the child will die sooner or later. As a result, people quite often object to such means. On the one hand, giving the child its first name (*togo*) is not only an important social ritual but also a meaningful act for his personal features by the patrilineal family members.[30] On the other hand, interventions involving animistic spirits, objects, and powers are commonly considered prohibited by Islam. Women and men affected by infertility eventually resort to methods and means that might be deemed un-Islamic and thus forbidden in the eyes of religious leaders.[31] For example, Salifa, one of the affected women I worked with, is clearly devoted to Islam in her daily practices. Nevertheless, Salifa admitted that she regularly consults diviners and animists, despite the fact that the powers, objects, and spirits they work with are said to be prohibited by Islam: "A Muslim doesn't have to do that but often—Allah may forgive me—I am doing it. At least, by going there, I never do anything malicious to someone else, but I am visiting them to know about my problems. I have never done anything malicious to someone else."[32]

Salifa never tells her mother-in-law about consulting diviners and animists. She talks with her only about visits to Islamic-oriented practitioners or about visits to biomedical institutions, which are unanimously accepted by Muslim rules.[33] In addition to these so-called traditional modes of treatment, childless women and to some extent men in Bamako commonly resort to biomedical diagnosis (for example, hormonal analyses, echography, hysterosalpingography) and biomedical treatments by hormonal pharmaceuticals and surgical interventions (for example, laparoscopy, tubal insufflation).

All of these different therapies may be used simultaneously, though some are not used to completion. When women suffering from infertility have financial means, they visit different traditherapists, marabouts, or hunters in Bamako or in remote areas, in addition to consulting different biomedical governmental institutions and private clinics. In general, Bamakonian couples in pursuit of conception are pragmatically oriented toward a positive outcome.[34]

In Vitro Fertilization and New Reproductive Technologies in Bamako

Women and men participating in these case studies knew about IVF from French television, as well as from rumors spread about well-known Malian female bards (*griottes* or *jelimusow*) and artists, ministers, or even friends who had undergone IVF treatment in Europe or overseas. Additionally knowledge was passed by Malian migrants in Europe or overseas, by Malian gynecologists, and via the Internet. Two of my informants had already experienced one or more IVFs—unsuccessfully—in the Ivory Coast, England, and France. Two more were planning future treatments in Germany and Canada.

Detailed information about the means and interventions through which conception would be achieved seem to be of secondary interest—especially with regard to the underlying conceptions and ideologies concerning fertility and infertility. While the "importance of adhering to Islamic prohibitions and expectations"[35] concerning the means of so-called traditional and religious interventions was in some cases an issue of discussions, pragmatic handling and secretly bypassing prohibitions concerning those modes of consultation that are deemed non- or un-Islamic modes of treatment preponderated in affected women's and men's activities. With respect to IVF, the general Sunni Islamic position that "in vitro fertilization is allowed, as long as it entails the union of ova from the wife with the sperm of her husband and the transfer of the resulting embryo(s) back to the uterus of the same wife"[36] was equally represented and underlined by statements from medical and religious experts and from affected and nonaffected women and men. As long as IVF was restricted to the egg and sperm of the marital partners, women and men did not make critical statements about the technical modes of reproduction, referring neither to the act of fusing cells outside of the body nor to the fact that third parties' agents were used in the act of procreation. Sperm or egg donation was sometimes considered prohibited by Islam, but another crucial point made (especially by men) was that children conceived in this way would not be the biological children of the married couple. Clearly, however, affected women criticized the unclear and diffuse way that biomedical practitioners give information. Additionally women expressed mistrust concerning gynecologists' competence and integrity, and they assumed that many of them were pursuing, above all, financial fortunes.

Against this background is the question of how male-factor infertility affects marital relations and biomedical treatment strategies. Boubakar and Bintou's story illuminates the possible answers to this question.

Boubakar and Bintou: A Couple's Life Story, in Short

In 1982 Boubakar, then thirty years old, and Bintou, twenty-two years old, were married. It was an arranged marriage, but Bintou stated that it was love at first sight for both of them. One year passed without pregnancy. By then, her in-laws had already started making allusions and insinuations. Bintou visited a gynecologist in Mali, who told her to be patient as nothing was wrong with her. When Boubakar received a grant to go to France in 1984, he took Bintou along with him. There, Boubakar subjected himself to diagnostic procedures, after which he openly told Bintou as well as the couple who hosted them that he was suffering from severe oligospermia.[37] The gynecologist told them that treatment with medications would be possible, but without guaranty. The gynecologist dissuaded them from insemination and in vitro fertilization (IVF), as neither intervention would likely be successful. Instead, he proposed to use donor sperm for an insemination or IVF. Boubakar clearly rejected this opportunity, arguing that a child conceived in this way would not be his "real," that is, biological, child. A short time later Boubakar offered Bintou a divorce, but she refused. Bintou told me that marriage is meant to last through the good days as well as the bad days. She emphasized that she not only loves her husband but also wanted to save him from his depressive mood and shame.

The following year they returned to Bamako, where they continued to live within the compound of Boubakar's extended family. Urged by her mother-in-law, Bintou started to undergo a variety of traditional treatments. Together with Boubakar, she went to several nonbiomedical healers, including non-Islamic ones. With all of them, Boubakar openly divulged his diagnosis. Within his family, however, he kept his diagnosis secret—except from his father. Neither his siblings nor his mother knew that Boubakar was the reason for the couple's childlessness. Bintou was increasingly harassed by the family's insinuations and offensive commentaries. Only her father-in-law defended Bintou against these snide remarks.

The situation was getting better for Bintou in 1987, when Boubakar received an appointment in a nongovernmental organization, and they left the extended family's compound in Bamako. They lived first in another Malian town and then in another African country. When her father-in-law died in 1989, her in-laws started to pressure Boubakar even more to take another wife. However, Boubakar told Bintou that this would never be the case as he knew that his condition, not hers, was the reason the couple could not conceive.

In 1991, when Boubakar and Bintou lived for a short period in England, they underwent IVF using their own gametes. As forewarned by the French gynecologist, this intervention was without success. In 1996 they traveled to the Ivory Coast in order to make a second attempt, again based on their own gametes; this too failed. Bintou stated that Boubakar let himself be easily convinced by the two biomedical practitioners to undergo IVF even though he knew that IVF was not recommended in cases of male-factor infertility such as severe oligospermia. Bintou angrily added that Boubakar robbed her of the possibility of getting pregnant through donor sperm by rejecting this possibility, saying that a child conceived in this way would not have been his own biological offspring. She openly told me that she evaluated things differently than he did.

After their return to Bamako in 1994, they lived apart from the extended family in their own house. For Bintou, this new—to some extent—independency of her in-laws ameliorated the heavy burden of stigmatization, insinuations, and sneering remarks. Although her in-laws continued this behavior, Bintou did not have to see them each day. In their own house she and Boubakar lived with two foster children from Boubakar's brothers, whom they received in 1989. Bintou told me that Boubakar agreed to serve as foster parent only to children from his patrilineage. Boubakar refused to receive children from Bintou's siblings, with whom Bintou would have had more direct influence. Nevertheless, having foster children did not stop Bintou's in-laws from making offensive comments concerning her failure to give birth. One day, when the foster daughter was five years old, Bintou's mother-in-law bluntly told the little girl the truth, that Bintou is not her real mother, although the little girl did not know anything about this before. Additionally her in-laws continued to exert pressure on Boubakar to marry a second wife.

Influences on Marital Relations

Since his diagnosis twenty-three years ago, Boubakar has suffered inner turmoil and hardships. He told me openly that he can work at only 10 percent capacity since reflecting on his problem gnaws at him each day. He also stated that the decision of whether one bears his own children is decided by Allah and that therefore his infertility is not his own fault. He knows that he should accept this, but it is difficult. As a scientist, he further pointed out that he should officially confess his infertility and speak openly about it. He should build a self-help group to stop male infertility from being such a stigma and taboo, from which many Malians are suffering. However, as Boubakar summarized, it is just too difficult for him to do this.

Clearly Boubakar is suffering through his infertility and feels himself strongly stigmatized. He is suffering even more because of his inability to meet his own values of sincerity and officially confess to his infertility. Because of his childless marriage, he told me, he did not receive some professional appointments and was also refused a stronger position in his own family despite being the one to gain the biggest portion of money and means for the extended family. Clearly Boubakar and Bintou have suffered deeply, but how did his handling of infertility shape power dynamics within his marriage and his family?

Implications for Marriage and Family

From a strategic perspective, at first glance it seems that guarding his secret within his family saved Boubakar from negative consequences. Even so, Boubakar continuously suffers from not meeting expectations of honesty by guarding his diagnosis from his family. He escaped shame, stigmatization, and marginalization, while Bintou had to shoulder these for him. Boubakar escaped the probable chance of "induced adultery" within the family. In addition, since Boubakar knew his diagnosis, Bintou could not discreetly find a solution through extramarital sex.

Boubakar also lost some of his marital domination. Male infertility carries with it the possible disruption of divorce. In cases of male infertility, it is a legal and religiously accepted possibility to grant a Malian woman divorce upon her request. Subsequently there is the permanent threat for Boubakar that his wife will disclose his secret.

Guarding a secret is a strong topic in Malian narratives, especially when depicting gender relations and family affairs. For noblemen, it is a highly idealized, valued, and expected virtue, whether concerning the secrets of ritual groups, secret societies, or family matters.[38] In popular discourse women are assumed to readily disclose secrets. Therefore they are shielded from family secrets. As some Malian men explained to me, male abilities to guard secrets and keep silence are a kind of defense against female powers.[39] Nevertheless male infertility, which is one of a man's most intimate and delicate secrets, will be revealed sooner or later to his wife. Thus the husband is somewhat at his wife's mercy, as his wife has the power to uncover his secret or not; she can protect her husband or expose him to the greatest disgrace.

As in Boubakar's case, the husband is permanently pressured by his kin to take a second wife. When the husband knows he is infertile, a second wife is a new danger. If the second wife does not get pregnant within the locally expected time (three months to one year), rumors start circulating concerning his fertility. Thus, holding on to his first wife is a kind of defense against revealing his infertility.

From the first wife's perspective, through guarding her husband's secret against all odds, she can augment her personal value and prestige, fulfilling a high level of obedience and respect toward her husband. While the wife has to endure the hardships of stigmatization and marginalization, she also holds a pledge of power against her husband. Thus she can escape polygyny by strengthening the emotional bond with her husband and by influencing him with regard to important decisions. As Boubakar told me, he is eternally grateful to Bintou for accepting him with his infertility.

Second Marriage with Fanta

For Bintou, the situation changed dramatically when, in 2003, Boubakar, who was then fifty-one years old, married Fanta, forty-one years old. Officially Boubakar named Bintou's infertility as his reason for taking a second wife, but to everyone's surprise, Boubakar chose not a young woman in her twenties but a woman already in her forties and only two years younger than Bintou. From Boubakar's perspective, the age of his second wife might allow him some space to argue and hide his own problem when questions arose concerning offspring of this second marriage.

Until this time, Bintou had guarded her husband's secret—within and beyond his family. Confronted with the second marriage and, in particular, with the reason Boubakar offered to the family, she told her brother- and mother-in-law about her husband's infertility and thus the reason for her childlessness. Moreover she told her mother-in-law during an argument that she, Bintou, was the one who saved her son from death and thus made the highest gift to her mother-in-law.[40]

Bintou ascribed Boubakar's decision to marry a second wife not only to specific in-laws' pressure but also to his increased interest in and adherence to Islam. Within the previous five years, Bintou told me, he had intensified his studies of the Qur'an as well as his visits to the mosque, becoming more and more devoted to Islamic esoteric aspects and to some religious personalities.[41] Bintou believed that this is how Boubakar became fascinated with the wonder that happened to Abraham according to the Old Testament: while Abraham and Sarah lived childless for many years, Abraham eventually had sons with a maidservant; then, at last, Sarah—although being of relatively high age—conceived and bore a son.[42] In one talk with me, Boubakar, as well, raised this issue and talked about his belief in such wonders evoked by devotion.

All in all, for Boubakar, the second marriage created serious problems. Since Bintou openly told his secret to his family, he is permanently at danger that she will disclose it publicly too. Moreover, since his second wife did not conceive after one year of marriage, he is under heavy pressure to prove his fertility.

Social Dynamics Affecting Biomedical Avenues of Male Infertility's Treatment

When I met Bintou and Boubakar in 2004, Boubakar had recently decided to undergo another treatment. The result of his sperm testing by then was azoospermia. Thus discussion was under way to undergo a testicular biopsy in Europe to get at least some (premature) sperm for an "Intracytoplasmatic Sperm Injection" (ICSI). With ICSI, as long as a single viable spermatozoon can be retrieved from an infertile man's body—including through painful testicular biopsies or aspirations—it can be injected directly into an ovum under a high-powered microscope, thereby producing live offspring for men who would never have otherwise procreated.[43] However, the gynecologist favored a hormonal treatment with gonadotropins, which have to be applied for twelve to eighteen months.

From an economic viewpoint, the recommended hormonal treatment is considerably expensive. Costing approximately fifteen hundred euros for one month and eighteen thousand euros for one year, the expense roughly matches three attempts with ICSI. If an ICSI has to follow the hormonal treatment, it would become even more expensive. Adding to these challenges, another year with hormonal treatment would be needed. This is an important disadvantage, as Boubakar is already in his fifties and both his wives are in their forties.

However, two further social aspects favor such a decision. First, a successful hormonal treatment not only would heal Boubakar's bodily functions but also would be the only way for him to fully restore his offended male identity, according to standards of the Malian perceptions about male infertility.[44] Second, Boubakar told me directly that because of his polygynic life now, he faces a dilemma when undergoing ICSI. On one hand, Islam and fairness would demand that he give both women the same chances. On the other hand, he would give priority to Bintou, because for twenty-two years she had accepted him with his problem, had defended his life, and had carried the burden of all social consequences. With hormonal treatment, which would be geared exclusively for him, this dilemma could be bypassed.

Given the prevalence of polygyny in Mali, it is certain that other males are affected by this predicament too. Thus, treating male infertility while simultaneously bypassing female bodies could be of substantial significance for the gynecologist, for whom gaining experience with such a treatment would be crucial. Additionally a treatment reducing interventions on women's bodies would enable a husband, in this case Boubakar, to prevent his wives from gaining another pledge against him, whereas with ICSI, the women would undergo the greater part of the procedures and risks. The choice of hormonal treatment could also erase the permanent danger that his wives would disclose his secret.

Appropriations Concerning Consultation

In addition to these influences on consultation, therapy, and social handling or decision-making processes within the spheres of infertility, specific Malian communicational and behavioral etiquette determined by membership in social categories of distinction is also an important factor. Mande categories of social distinction and their impact on communication constitute a complex feature of Malian everyday life. Basically Mande society can be divided into three main social categories: the *horonw*, often translated as noblemen; the *nyamakalaw*, composed of different branches of professional groups such as smiths (*numuw*), bards (*jeliw*), and leather-working artists (*garankew*); and the *jonw*, formerly slaves.[45] Often misunderstood, these social categories do not imply fixed hierarchical structures. Rather, they are interwoven constellations of influence and power, which according to perspective and situation can encompass aspects of domination and subordination for all involved parties. In daily practice these relational structures allow a creative ability to interact beyond deterministic or static imperatives.[46] All three categories are connected to various tasks, abilities, duties, and rights of professional, political, and social levels with specific norms and leading values of behavior and communication, especially concerning interactions with members of the same category or different ones. For all interacting persons, membership in one of these social categories is often recognizable through their patronyms (*jamu*). In each communication between foreigners, asking for the patronym after formal greetings is the first question, which then may lead immediately to distinct patterns and forms of conduct. In Bamakonian narratives behavior, communication, and general conduct of *horonw* should be ideally guided by values of politeness, respect, and modesty as the basis for honor and dignity, leading to a distinct reserve concerning speech, intimacy, and emotions. As pointed out to me, this conduct is meant to avoid any feeling of shame and to show neither weak points nor secrets of the family.[47]

Many aspects of participant observation in consultations reminded me of my interlocutors' complaints that their doctors rarely gave clear and unambiguous information regarding diagnosis or prognosis. They often left the doctors' offices with uncertainty and ambiguity about the statements made. As Zobel mentions, the speech-dominating principles of *horonw*—respect, self-control, shame, and restraint—result in applying an indirect style of communication with use of metaphors, ambiguous statements through allusions and proverbs, which contribute to inefficient communication in some spheres.[48]

When the gynecologist in the private clinic was asked about his opinion concerning social etiquette's role in consultation, he told me: "With artisans and former slaves, there are no problems at all because they won't show shame. They directly tell the truth and openly name the reason for which they are coming. But nowadays, this has changed. Many become wealthy and don't like to be remembered that they belong to the social category of artisans or slaves, as these categories are a bit lower than nobles. Thus this has no impact on my communication any more."[49] However, he explained that joking relationships do have an impact: "Here in Mali, noble women do not openly tell why they are coming for a consultation. I use joking relationships to gain their trust, because this is needed first. And I not only use my father's family's bonds of joking relationships but the ones of my mother's family as well."[50]

Joking partners (*senankunw,* singular: *senankun*), traced back to alliances between ancestors, can be established between families bearing different patronyms, but they can also be effective between ethnic groups or social categories as a whole.[51] As Brand describes, they are in opposition to relations governed by respect: "Between *senankunw* almost everything can be said without fear or shame: whereas on the one hand most serious insults are taken as jokes, on the other hand, a *senankun* is the obvious person to tell the truth. Conflict is excluded between *senankunw:* it is inconceivable to become angry at one's *senankun,* no matter how provocative his or her behaviour."[52]

At the heart of this conduct and behavior lies the knowledge that one's *senankun* knows your weak point, as one of Zobel's informants described the matter.[53] A joking partner "gives the appearance of saying the 'plain truth,'" thus he is allowed to be shameless,[54] while members of different *horonw* families, not being allied by joking relationships, have to avoid, at any cost, acting shameless as well as revealing family secrecy. Honor and respect are outweighed through the bonds of a joking relationship that exists between specific families and can be recognized by patronyms. In joking relationships everything can be said without shame.[55] Thus, in using joking relationships, the gynecologist enables an open and direct exchange of information, which is one of biomedicine's inherent bases for treatment. Relying also on his maternal family's bonds, the doctor enlarges the group with which he can communicate in this way.

This short, ethnologically informed impression of consultations highlights the fact that the above-mentioned values of conduct are an important context for women and men suffering from infertility because they shape the pragmatics of communication within therapeutic interactions. This becomes even more important since childlessness and infertility are delicate and intimate issues concerning the honor and shame not only of the wife and husband, respectively, but of both their families as well.

Concerning his communication of information in general, the gynecologist told me: "I committed myself to honesty. Thus I am openly and honestly telling the people what is the point. But how I tell it and to whom I am communicating, that is different." The gynecologist further outlined that if the problem of infertility lies within the man, then he will schedule a prostate massage for that man. At this event the gynecologist will tell the patient that he, and not his wife, is the cause for marital childlessness. Moreover the gynecologist will recommend that the patient not disclose this information to his wife, so as to avoid divorce or even worse problems.

With respect to the wife, in such a case, the gynecologist tells her that both she and her husband have some problems but that all of this can be managed by treating both of them. If the woman already suspects that her husband might be the problem for their childlessness—for example, when the husband was already married and then divorced because of childlessness, but then his ex-wife became pregnant with another man—in such cases, then, the gynecologist tells the woman that her husband has minor problems but that without him she cannot get pregnant.

Conclusion

The notion of male-factor infertility in Mali threatens men's identities, their masculinity, and their honor. Thus, keeping male infertility secret is a crucial aspect of its social management in Bamako. There is a strong tendency to allow a level of uncertainty from which further options and hopes can be drawn. Biomedical diagnostics, which are aimed at removing doubt and producing final decisions, contradict the social handling of male infertility in a secret and nebulous manner. On the one hand, it can shift the power relations within marriages to a slight advantage for the women. On the other hand, gynecologists adopt their style of consultation as well as their treatment strategies to these social values. They also take local customs of communication, gender relations, social organization, and religious concerns into account. In this way, the clearness and finality of biomedical diagnostics are balanced in favor of secrecy and uncertainty in regard to information and consultation politics. Since most Malian gynecologists are men and favor a hierarchy of the sexes, they are subtly shaping the consultations to the advantage of their male patients. In so doing, they not only affect women's reproductive health but also perpetuate definitions "of what is important and what is not" from a male perspective "without taking heed of women's perceptions and felt needs."[56] This trajectory of influence is to some extent reflected in women's criticism concerning information practices in biomedical consultations and their general mistrust with respect to biomedical practitioners' competencies and professional integrity.

Within these fields of tension, devotion and adherence to Islamic rules are clearly moral factors in Mali that impact not only the decision-making processes in the realm of fertility and infertility but also what is communicated and how that is done. Nevertheless Islam forms but one system of references amid others.[57] Concerning communication and interaction, distinct social categories—and resulting demeanor—form other important dimensions of reference. Muslim references concerning values and norms of conduct are subjected to varying interpretations in Mali; moreover, they merge and compete with other systems of references regarding behavioral values (for example, social categories of distinctions; economical, educational, and political positions; and adherence to secular values). The importance assigned to Islamic rules and expectations vis-à-vis other systems of references seems to depend on a variety of factors, including the historical role Islam plays within the tradition of single families or lineages and from which region a family originates. Determining which diverse systems of references are balanced, which are dominate, or which are overthrown when it comes to decision-making also depends on the dimension and content of the problem at hand. Moreover it is important to determine to what extent the consequences of decisions touch or implicate family concerns, as in the issue of naming children. As choosing children's names is a highly valued task for the father and his kin, this forms a particularly difficult problem to ignore, especially since names cannot be hidden away and do serve as social markers.

In cases where it is possible to hide the transgression of what are perceived to be Islamic rules—such as discreetly looking for extramarital sex—it seems to be easier for people to go beyond Islamic rules, because of the desperation caused by infertility, for example. The pragmatic handling of avenues for solution to infertility suspends these systems of reference, causing them to be interpreted in various ways or even overlooked. The issue of how pragmatics are culturally, socially, and religiously shaped in different societies should be followed up in studies of how Islam impacts health-related decision-making.

NOTES

1. I am grateful to Dorothea Schulz and particularly to the editors Thomas Eich and Jonathan Brockopp for their comments on an earlier draft.

2. Benjamin F. Soares, "Islam in Mali in the Neoliberal Era," *African Affairs* 105, no. 41 (2005): 79; compare Sargent, "Reproductive Strategies," 46.

3. John L. Esposito, "Mali, Islamin," in *Oxford Dictionary of Islam,* ed. John L. Esposito (Oxford: Oxford University Press Inc., 2003); compare Sargent, "Reproductive Strategies," 35. Besides, in Mali, "9 percent practice African traditional religions, and 1 percent are Catholic" (Esposito, "Mali, Islamin," 189). The Maliki school of jurisprudence is historically and traditionally practiced. Moreover the Tijani brotherhood is an important Muslim institution in Mali (Sargent, "Reproductive Strategies," 46), although the majority of Malian Muslims are not members of any brotherhood (personal communication with Dorothea Schulz, November 2006).

4. Soares, "Islam in Mali," 79.

5. Ibid., 80.

6. "Marabout" is a "westernized form of Arabic *murabit,* referring to a saint or to a person living in a Sufi hospice" (John L. Esposito, "Marabouts," in *Oxford Dictionary of Islam*). According to Soares, during colonial times in Mali, all Muslim religious personalities and members of Muslim lineages, "who specialized in religious activities and conformed to such norms, were those the French glossed as marabouts" (Benjamin F. Soares, *Islam and the Prayer Economy: History and Authority in a Malian Town* [Ann Arbor: University of Michigan Press, 2005], 26). Moreover, "These marabouts ranged from the renowned to the relatively unknown and included village imams, Quranic school teachers and scholars, as well as amulet makers" (Soares, *Islam and the Prayer Economy,* 54). Up to the present time, religious personalities, independent of their actual positions, are named "marabouts" in French everyday speech. The word *karamogow* or *moro* is used in Bamanan carrying the meaning of teacher or wise men.

7. Instead of *fetish,* I prefer to use the term *charged object* or *objects that are charged with some kind of power referring to the non-human domain* (Peter Geschiere, *Village Communities and the State: Changing Relations among the Maka of South-Eastern Cameroon since the Colonial Conquest* [London: Kegan Paul International, 1983]).

8. For further discussion on hierarchies assigned to different religious-therapeutic domains of expertise and experts and the impossibility of drawing clear analytical distinctions between them, see Dorothea E. Schulz, "'God Is Our Resort': Islamic Revival, Mass-Mediated Religiosity and the Moral Negotiation of Gender Relations in Urban Mali," unpub. habilitation, Free University of Berlin.

9. See Marcia C. Inhorn, *Quest for Conception: Gender, Infertility, and Egyptian Medical Traditions* (Philadelphia: University of Pennsylvania Press, 1994), 52. See also Corinne Fortier, "Le lait, le sperme, le dos. Et le sang? Représentations physiologiques de la filiation et de la parenté de lait en islam malékite et dans la société maure de Mauritanie," *Cahiers d`Études Africaines* 40 (2001): 103.

10. See Germaine Dieterlen, *Essai sur la religion Bambara,* 2nd ed. (Brussels: Editions de l'Université de Bruxelles, 1988), 82.

11. Matthew R. Dudgeon and Marcia C. Inhorn, "Men's Influences on Women's Reproductive Health: Medical Anthropological Perspectives," *Social Science and Medicine* 59 (2004): 1381. See also Carole H. Browner and Carolyn F. Sargent, "Anthropology and Studies of Human Reproduction," in *Medical Anthropology: A Handbook of Theory and Method,* ed. Thomas M. Johnson and Carolyn F. Sargent (New York: Greenwood Press, 1990), 215–29.

12. S. J. Dyer and others, "'You Are a Man because You Have Children': Experiences, Reproductive Health Knowledge and Treatment-Seeking Behaviour among Men Suffering from Couple Infertility in South Africa," *Human Reproduction* 19, no. 4 (2004): 960; compare Sylvie Schuster and Viola Hörbst's "Introduction" to the special issue devoted to *Reproductive Disruptions: Perspectives on African Contexts, Curare* 29, no. 1 (2006).

13. Dudgeon and Inhorn, "Men's Influences on Women's Reproductive Health," 1381.

14. I am grateful to the HWP program of the University of Munich for a postdoctoral grant, which made this fieldwork in Bamako possible. Moreover I am grateful to the Münich Universitätsgesellschaft, which helped fund expenses during fieldwork.

15. Mande refers to some ethnic groups (in Mali, Guinea, Ivory Coast, Senegal, and the Gambia) sharing related languages and having similar sociopolitical, economic, and religious institutions. Moreover they all trace their history back to the Mali Empire. The majority of Mali's numerous ethnic groups are of Mande origin. See Clemens Zobel, *Das Gewicht der Rede: Kulturelle Reinterpretation, Geschichte und Vermittlung bei den Mande Westafrikas* (Frankfurt am Main: Peter Lang, 1997), 11; Saskia Brand, *Mediating Means and Fate: A Socio-political Analysis of Fertility and Demographic Change in Bamako, Mali* (Leiden: Brill, 2001), 13.

16. Concerning their helping hands, I am especially grateful to Alou Dembele, Sako Fanta Damba, Diahara Bagayogo, Astrid Blaschke, Fatim Traoré, Seydou Bouaré, Djedi Diakité, Gabriel Magatma Konaté, Salif Togola, Rokia Sanogo, Keneya Yiriwaton (ATTHDB), Minta Fousseyni, Radio Bamakan, and all the women and men plagued by childlessness, who cannot be named because of anonymity. For this latter reason, in this essay all names of informants are changed.

17. John L. Comaroff and Jean Comaroff, "Of Fallacies and Fetishes: A Rejoinder to Donham," *American Anthropologist* 103, no. 1 (2001): 150–60.

18. I am grateful to the Deutsche Forschungsgemeinschaft for funding this research project starting in November 2006.

19. Arthur Kleinman, "Local Worlds of Suffering: An Interpersonal Focus for Ethnographies of Illness Experience," *Qualitative Health Research* 2 (1992): 127–34.

20. Maria Grosz-Ngaté, "Hidden Meanings: Explorations into a Bamanan Construction of Gender," *Ethnology* 28, no. 2 (1989): 177.

21. Grosz-Ngaté, "Hidden Meanings," 171. For Muslim rules, compare Sargent, "Reproductive Strategies," 37, where an imam states: "It is the husband's obligation to 'show his wife the correct road' (moral direction)." Sargent explains: "To validate this contention he cited verses from the Qur'an (1974) stating that men have a status superior to that of women (Qur'an 2:228, 4:30), men's right to repudiate wives (Qur'an sura 2:229), and women's obligation to be obedient (Qur'an sura 4:34)."

22. Grosz-Ngaté, "Hidden Meanings," 177.

23. See Sargent, "Reproductive Strategies," 37; Qur'an 4:3.

24. Concerning the context of full female personhood, Brand writes: "One has to be circumcised, get married, have children and grandchildren in order to achieve full personhood" (*Mediating Means and Fate,* 17). See also Dieterlen, *Essai sur la religion Bambara,* 94. Moreover, Grosz-Ngaté explains, "A woman who has no sons, whose sons die or do not return from labor migration, but who otherwise has shown her commitment to the kin group in her actions is respected and assured of a place in old age. Nonetheless her personhood, like that of her male counterpart who finds himself with sons, remains incomplete" ("Hidden Meanings," 179).

25. Grosz-Ngaté, "Hidden Meanings," 170.

26. Ibid., 171.

27. Viola Hörbst, "Infertility and In-Vitro-Fertilization in Bamako, Mali: Women`s Experience, Avenues for Solution and Social Contexts Impacting on Gynecological Consultations," *Curare* 29, no. 1 (2006).

28. See Godfrey B. Tangwa, "ART and African Sociocultural Practices: Worldview, Belief and Value Systems with Particular Reference to Francophone Africa," in *Current Practices and Controversies in Assisted Reproduction,* ed. E. Vayena, P. J. Rowe, and D. P. Griffin (Geneva: World Health Organization, 2002), 57.

29. See Brand, *Mediating Means and Fate,* 241–42.

30. For more information on this topic, see Hörbst, "Infertility and In-Vitro-Fertilization."

31. See Schuster and Hörbst, "Introduction."

32. Salifa, interview, December 2004. Salifa's expression of making something "malicious" refers to sorcery.

33. Soares discusses the general topic of Islamic, non-Islamic, and un-Islamic secret objects and secret knowledge within healing practices concerning the western region of Nioro in Mali (Soares, *Islam and the Prayer Economy,* 153–80).

34. It is interesting that Bernhard Hadolt and Monika Lengauer, in "Kinder-Machen: Eine ethnographische Untersuchung zur Handhabe von ungewollter Kinderlosigkeit und den Neuen Reproduktionstechnologien durch betroffene Frauen" (Ph.D. diss., University of Vienna, 2003), found the same result in their study of IVF patients in Vienna, Austria.

35. Sargent, "Reproductive Strategies," 36.

36. Marcia C. Inhorn, "Religion and Reproductive Technologies: IVF and Gamete Donation in the Muslim World," *Anthropology News* 46, no. 2 (2005): 14–18. Compare with Dudgeon and Inhorn, "Men¥s Influences on Women¥s Reproductive Health," 1389.

37. "Oligospermia" means less than twenty million sperm per milliliter of ejaculate. According to WHO guidelines, the normal finding in an ejaculate is more than twenty million sperms from which 50 percent or more show forward mobility and 30 percent show normal morphology; "Azoospermia" means no spermatozoa in the ejaculate (http://www.med-direct.com/mens-fertility/semenf.html; accessed October 4, 2006).

38. See Grosz-Ngaté, "Hidden Meanings," 174–75. In the achievement of personhood for men, "the importance of silence, of knowing when to speak and when not to speak" (Grosz-Ngaté, "Hidden Meanings," 174) is matching the importance of speech.

39. See Sory Camara, *Gens de la Parole: Essai sur la condition et le rôle des griots dans la société Malinké* (Paris: Mouton, 1976), 76; Grosz-Ngate, "Hidden Meanings," 180–81; Clemens Zobel, "Les genies du Kòma: Identités locales, logiques réligieuses et enjeux socio-politiques dans les monts Manding du Mali," *Cahiers d`Études Africaines* 36, no. 4 (1996): 639–40; Brand, *Mediating Means and Fate,* 20–21.

40. This seems to refer to Grosz-Ngaté's statement on the crucial importance of shame for men in Mali, for whom shameful situations, acts, or conduct "can be tantamount to social death" ("Hidden Meanings," 170–71).

41. Soares argues that he prefers the term *esoteric sciences* to *maraboutage* because this realm of knowledge and practice is intimately tied to secrets. In addition the term highlights "acquisition through human and/or divine channels," because it has fewer European and Christian referents as "the occult"; moreover, esoteric sciences point to the political economy of knowledge, such as "the divide between those select persons who know and use these sciences . . . and those men and women who make appeals to the knowledgeable ones" (Soares, *Islam and the Prayer Economy,* 129).

42. *Luther Bibel* (Stuttgart: Deutsche Bibelgesellschaft Stuttgart, 1985): Genesis 16:1–16; 18:10–14; 21:1–7.

43. Dudgeon and Inhorn, "Men's Influences on Women's Reproductive Health," 1389.

44. According to Gannon and colleagues, "in most societies motherhood is the ultimate expression of being a woman" (Kenneth Gannon, Lesley Glover, and Paul Abel, "Masculinity, Infertility, Stigma and Media Reports," *Social Science and Medicine* 59 [2004]: 1170). For masculine identities, the role as worker and provider is emphasized, with fatherhood forming but a marginal aspect. In particular, to impregnate a woman is underlined in masculine identity. Thus male-factor infertility forms a disruption to manliness in the sense of "emasculation," as Dyer and colleagues summarize ("You Are a Man because You Have Children," 966). This emasculation is reflected in "the common conflation of the terms of impotency and infertility" (Gannon and others, "Masculinity, Infertility, Stigma," 1170), which also might play a major role in Mali.

45. Zobel mentions that the majority in Mande society are noblemen, whereas only about 10 percent of the population belong to professional groups of craftsmen (*Das Gewicht der Rede,* 47).

46. See Zobel, *Das Gewicht der Rede,* 21; Jan Jansen, "Griot's Impression Management and Diplomatic Strategies," in *Mande–Manding: Background Reading for Ethnographic Research in the Region South of Bamako (Mali),* ed. Jan Jansen (Leiden: Leiden University Press, 2004), 131–61.

47. See Zobel, *Das Gewicht der Rede;* Brand, *Mediating Means and Fate;* Jansen, "Griot's Impression Management."

48. Zobel, *Das Gewicht der Rede,* 146–47.

49. Interview with ynecologist, December 2004, Mali.

50. Ibid.

51. See Zobel, *Das Gewicht der Rede,* 134, 139.

52. Brand, *Mediating Means and Fate,* 20.

53. Zobel, *Das Gewicht der Rede,* 136.

54. Jansen, "Griot's Impression Management," 21.

55. Besides, there are some forms of joking relationships between certain categories of in-laws too, such as between grandparents and grandchildren, between children and mothers' brothers, with the younger siblings' spouses, and sometimes between age-mates (Brand, *Mediating Means and Fate,* 19).

56. Dudgeon and Inhorn, "Men's Influences on Women's Reproductive Health," 1380.

57. Sargent comes to similar conclusions concerning the management of contraceptive decision-making processes by Malian migrants in Paris. She also hints to other dimensions of influences, writing that "Qur'anic references to modesty, chastity and obedience are subject to debate" (Sargent, "Reproductive Strategies," 38).

DEBRA BUDIANI *and* OTHMAN SHIBLY

Islam, Organ Transplants, and Organ Trafficking in the Muslim World

Paving a Path for Solutions

Organ trafficking[1] is gaining worldwide attention as indicators suggest that the market in organs is a global phenomenon that continues to expand. Research findings, particularly since the 1990s, have revealed grave consequences from the marketing of human organs.[2] These include the following: an increasing reliance on commercial donors via sophisticated international brokers; identified health, economic, social, and psychological consequences for donors, including a compromised ability to continue manual-labor jobs, incomplete payment of the agreed price for an organ sale, and a lack of donor follow-up and general welfare concern; and a subsequent undermining of deceased and altruistic donorship.

In much of the Muslim world, some fatwas (guidelines based on Islamic law) that have been issued deem paid donation to be *haram* (forbidden) and thus condemn the trade. These edicts largely exist alongside state laws within the Muslim world that also prohibit the sale of human organs. The majority of Muslim scholars have agreed that organ donation is permitted based on the conditions that a) it will help the recipient with certainty; b) it does not cause harm to the donor; and c) the donor donates the organ or tissue voluntarily and without financial compensation. Many countries in the Middle East began transplantation programs, particularly renal transplants, in the late 1970s and early 1980s, and living donors continue to be the main source of organs. Despite these various mandates, organ trade also operates in and via the Middle East and elsewhere in the Muslim world. Results of a survey among transplant specialists in twenty-one countries in the Middle East indicate that donations from living, unrelated donors is a prominent issue facing regional organ transplant programs.[3] Furthermore, many countries in the region do not have entities to administer fair and just practices of organ distribution; rather, they rely on the market as the distribution mechanism. A discussion of some of the dynamics of organ trafficking in the Middle East, in other predominantly Muslim countries, and in the particular case of Egypt forms the backdrop to one cultural question: to what extent have Islamic rulings provided guidelines on transplants and how are these engaged with other bioethical discourses on transplants? Finally we discuss an initiative to bring together advocates, including the *'ulama'* (religious scholars), bioethicists, state officials, and key stakeholders—for example, patients, donors, medical professionals, laboratories, and health-insurance companies—with an aim to collectively bridge guidelines with practical solutions to the problem of organ trafficking in the Muslim world.

Regional Dimensions of the Global Trade:
Organ Trafficking in the Middle East and Muslim World

The international trade in human organs, particularly kidneys, has especially flourished in developing countries where organs from nonliving donors are not adequate or available and where there are marked disparities in wealth. For example, Persian Gulf countries with transplant programs have no or low numbers of nonliving donors, and patients from these countries have relied heavily on poor, recruited, living donors as suppliers of human organs from countries such as India, Pakistan, the Philippines, Eastern Europe, and increasingly China. Elsewhere in the region the lower classes within countries are solicited and compensated for living, unrelated donations. For example, Egyptian law requires that a donor and a recipient must share the same nationality in order to obtain a license for a transplant in Egypt, and the vast majority of donors are poor Egyptians who have been solicited for donation. Many countries in the region have thus been involved in both the demand and supply sides of the global organ trade and in hosting trafficking routes: Istanbul has been a significant transplant host for North American and Israeli patients who receive Moldovan kidneys; Pakistani, Indian, and Indonesian donors supply organs to transplant tourists from the Subcontinent and the Middle and Far East; and recent trends in Kuwait and Saudi Arabia facilitate the trade within their borders almost exclusively via donors from East and Southeast Asia.

Because nonliving donation is scarce or nonexistent in the region, few countries in the Middle East transplant organs such as the heart, heart valve, or pancreas. Liver transplants have begun to increase in recent years and mainly consist of partial liver procurements from living donors. A recent study on issues of renal transplantation in Middle Eastern countries identified eleven prominent problems.[4] One of these problems is that paying living, unrelated donors is considered an "easy way out" of the scarcity problem.[5] Further, some physicians encourage commercial transplantation and thus profit financially while debates on solutions continue. The study also reports that few countries in the Middle East have centers to coordinate nonliving organ donation and that there is thus also an absence of planning of organ procurement with transplant centers. Another prominent issue related to transplants in the Middle East is the lack of effective health insurance and minority groups' lack of trust in the health system, because of the inaccessibility of the health system and lack of social justice for many minorities.[6] Similarities in some of the featured problems of transplants exist amid diverse policies among Islamic countries, but there are key differences as well. For example, Saudi Arabia and Qatar permit procuring organs from the nonliving, while Egypt and Pakistan rely entirely on living donors. A country as resourceful as the United Arab Emirates has no transplant procedures whatsoever.

Among countries that permit living donations, a further distinction is in the policies of dealing with living, unrelated donors. Despite a consensus among Islamic jurists as reflected in fatwas that have been issued on paid donations (discussed further below), the Islamic Republic of Iran was, until recently, the only country worldwide that legalized commercial kidney donations; the state also recompenses donors for kidney donations. This policy is a state attempt to fill the demand for kidneys and standardize the low prices. Javaad Zargooshi, an Iranian urologist who has conducted follow-up studies on Iranian organ donors, reports significant negative consequences for donors' quality of life[7] and argues that the system has also failed to satisfy supply, has damaged the ability to advance altruistic and cadaveric donation, has decreased the price of kidneys, and has been unable to eliminate a coexisting black market via a regulated market in organs.[8] Despite these concerns and a consensus in fatwas against organ vending, Kuwait and Saudi Arabia have also recently passed legislation to legalize commercial trade in organs from deceased donors, and there are efforts to legalize the trade from living donors in Saudi Arabia. The United Arab Emirates and Yemen do not share this policy on living donations, but both states sponsor their nationals to seek care abroad for transplants since these are not available in their home countries. That is, they assist Emirati and Yemeni patients to fund the costs of transplant surgery abroad and the cost of purchased organs. The reliance on living donors, within or outside patients' home countries, presents significant moral dilemmas to both donors and recipients. A case taken from Egypt illustrates such complexities.

The Case of Egypt

In Egypt legal restrictions prohibit the procurement of organs from nonliving donors.[9] This renders living donors as the only source for organs, mainly kidneys and partial livers, for transplant. In addition to a strong sense of the sanctity of the dead, legislators and religious authorities share concerns about the procurement of organs from nonliving donors without prior consent or advanced directives; they also worry about misdiagnosis of brain stem death and the difficulties of regulating transplants.[10] Furthermore, several publicized scandals have colored Egyptians' views, including evidence of doctors procuring organs or tissues from nonliving donors without proper consent procedures and the use of living bodies of poor Egyptians as a source of kidneys by wealthy patients from the Persian

Gulf.[11] As mentioned, legislation prohibits organ procurement from the nonliving, prohibits payment for an organ donation from the living, and requires recipients and donors to be of the same nationality. Many draft laws to regulate organ transplants and the distribution of organs beyond these policies, however, have failed to be enacted in the People's Assembly. In the absence of federal policies that address living donors, the national Doctors' Syndicate provides the only framework from which doctors, patients, and donors maneuver to regulate transplants by issuing a license for each transplant surgery. Accordingly national policies and fatwas work to inhibit living, unrelated organ donorship or prohibit commercial living donorship. Patients in need of transplants and their doctors are thus left with narrower alternatives for managing "scarcities."

Within this context, transplant doctors estimate that at least 90 percent of kidney donors are in fact unrelated, recruited, and compensated.[13] The number of licensed kidney transplants is estimated between five hundred and one thousand per year. Dozens of partial liver transplants are performed annually in Egypt, and the number has been increasing rapidly over the last few years. Although presently there are more efforts to secure related donors for partial liver transplants, this may well soon change, following the trend of kidney donors. Among requirements for obtaining a transplant license from the national Doctors' Syndicate, a patient must state that there are no suitable related donors available when unrelated donors are presented, and both the donor and the patient must state that the donation is voluntary and not compensated or "gifted." The syndicate does little beyond this to verify donor-recipient relations and transactions. Furthermore, a significant percentage of transplants are performed without licenses, particularly for non-Egyptian donors and recipients.[14] Mahmoud and Soheila's story illustrates the conditions of transplants in Egypt.

Mahmoud, a thirty-five-year-old father of two young sons, is a laborer from the city of Asyut in Upper Egypt. He had been undergoing dialysis for seven years as a treatment for his end-stage renal failure when Debra Budiani (co-author) met him in a large public hospital in central Cairo. Mahmoud described the onset of his condition when he experienced symptoms of "nefisi te'eel" (heavy breathing) and fatigue while working as a laborer in Saudi Arabia. After consultations with seven doctors, one doctor noticed that Mahmoud's creatinine levels were markedly above range and immediately prescribed dialysis. Soon after his diagnosis Mahmoud returned to Egypt, where he paid between 85 and 160 Egyptian pounds per dialysis session, an average of approximately 20 dollars, depending which of two surgically created dialysis sites, in his forearm or his abdomen, were used. Mahmoud explained: "Ghaseel iddam [dialysis, literally 'washing the blood'] is painful and tiring and makes me too sick to go to work many days. On the days that I do not go for dialysis I also feel very weak when my blood pressure is too low and I have burning pain in my arm and stomach where they attach the machines. All of the patients are there getting dialysis together in one room and the staff are harsh on patients, shouting around us. They are not suited to work there and it makes us all very tense. My family has been waiting for me to get better from these treatments. I need to work to take care of my wife and sons. I am Sa'eedi [from Upper Egypt] and we provide for our families so that our wives do not have to work."

The cost of dialysis averaged about 85 percent of Mahmoud's normal monthly income, which he was increasingly unable to generate because of his condition. Via the combined funds from his savings from working in Saudi Arabia, the assistance of his extended family, and token government assistance, Mahmoud financed the remaining costs of his dialysis treatments for the following six years. Mahmoud also sought and tried various alternative therapies ranging from locally produced homeopathic regimes to an imported drug from Germany. Yet, the outcomes of these pursuits were insignificant, and his doctors suggested that Mahmoud consider a transplant. It was an option that Mahmoud had been avoiding, since he knew that it would be difficult to afford at approximately thirty thousand Egyptian pounds (five thousand dollars), but he also thought that it would end his reliance on costly dialysis treatments.

Mahmoud's wife, brother, and sister volunteered to be potential donors. None of them matched adequately in tissue typing and blood tests. Two months before Budiani's meeting with Mahmoud, he identified a suitable unrelated donor via the assistance of a laboratory. Soheila, a woman from a village town outside of Cairo, presented the minimum 65 percent matching criteria and soon met with Mahmoud and the lab's agent to establish an agreement of donorship. Mahmoud explained: "Soheila is a strong woman, muhaggaba [wears a headscarf], and I feel that she is a good person. Like me, she wanted to do what was required to help raise her children and give them a future. I knew from the doctors that it does not hurt a healthy person to give a kidney and this is why I let my wife and brother and sister think of donating a kidney to me. If I were able, I would have donated to them also. The sheikhs say that it is *haram* [Islamically prohibited acts] to buy an organ. But Soheila and her kids also can survive on the money that I give to her for saving my life. We know that saving a life pleases Allah and doing something like this deserves rewards in this life and after."

Soheila, a thirty-two-year-old woman and mother of three children, and her husband were in dire financial debt when they discussed the option of a kidney sale to generate funds. Budiani met Soheila days before that transplant surgery, in which she would donate her left kidney to Mahmoud. She explained:

> Because of my kids and my house we had a very large debt. We took a loan for a small house and couldn't pay yet so I could have gone to jail. If I didn't pay they would take my house or send me to jail. My husband and I decided that it is better for me to be the one of us to give a kidney because my husband can work and

earn money in other ways and take care of me and our children better than I could if one of us falls sick from this operation. Giving my kidney is also better than working in "furnished apartments" [an expression that refers to apartments owned by single men with a reputation for hosting female visitors for sex]. This is against my dignity and I wouldn't want to go and do such things. If I get any other job it will not pay me enough to even afford the transportation and I would be leaving my children alone. I didn't want to do *haram* and steal for money. I don't like working and I prefer not to work and have my husband support me. There is still no other way to get such money so I decided still to give my kidney.

I read the Qur'an to make me feel more relaxed. No one of my friends or family know where I went or what I am doing except for my husband and eldest son who are taking care of my two smaller children until I recover.

After their agreement with the laboratory's broker, Mahmoud submitted an application for the transplant license, which is issued by the Egyptian Doctors' Syndicate and required for all transplants. In a meeting with the syndicate, Mahmoud was required to state that he had no relatives who could qualify as a matching donor. He and Soheila also stated under oath that there was no payment or gifting to the donor for the organ and that the donorship was completely voluntary. Both denied accordingly, and soon after that Mahmoud was granted an official license for the surgery and scheduled it with the surgeons, the hospital, and Soheila.

In the days that followed, Mahmoud and Soheila were given preoperative treatment and preparations, and although they were in separate wards for men and women, doctors and hospital staff referred to them as husband and wife. An hour before the onset of the surgery, Mahmoud's brother handed a cash payment of seventy-five hundred Egyptian pounds to Soheila's husband with a commitment to pay the remaining half after the surgery. This sum constituted a little over a third of the total price that Mahmoud paid for the entire cost of the surgery.

Following the renal transplant, Mahmoud's response to the new kidney satisfied his doctors as his immune system produced minimal resistance. He remained in isolation for several weeks and then returned home to Asyut for continued care. Soheila was assisted by nurses and patients' visitors in the hospital room that she shared with three other female patients. When she was able to walk down the hall to meet with her husband, he assured her that he had received the remainder of the payment and that he and the children were eager for her return home, where she could continue to rest for another day.

Eight months after the surgery Mahmoud was recovering well and began to carry out normal activities. While he said that the transplant gave him a new sense of freedom from the exhausting dialysis treatments, he also felt financially exhausted from the high costs of the immunosuppressant drugs that he would need for the rest of his life. Soheila traded in her personal wealth in gold and used the funds that her kidney earned to pay off her and her husband's debts. She complained of occasional dizziness and wished she could afford further medical attention. She explained that she had been afraid to undergo the operation but prior to the surgery would not show her fear or any hesitancy that may have inhibited her ability to donate. She also said that she was afraid of how her health would be in the months and years ahead. In a statement about her afterlife, Soheila said that she knew "that many sheikhs and muftis say that it is *haram* to sell an organ. But I pray that Allah will forgive me and be happy that I did what I could to support my children."

Soheila and Mahmoud's story illustrates the complex situation of transplants in Egypt and the deep moral reasoning they each undertook in a decision-making process amid narrow choices. For each, the desperation to survive and obligation to support their children took priority over other ethical considerations, particularly religious rulings on the buying and selling of organs. Further, Mahmoud reasoned that restoring his health via a transplant not only would enable him to further support his wife and children but also would work to support Soheila and her children. For Soheila, there was more honor and dignity in selling a kidney than in working outside of her home. She emphasized her moral limits and explained that she sold her kidney not out of greed but because of her high moral standards and that given these intentions, she prays for Allah's understanding.

Soheila and Mahmoud's case is similar to many of the donor-recipient relationships in Egypt, in which brokers and laboratory recruits match donors to recipients. A broker handles the agreement of the donor's compensation, usually in the amount of approximately seventeen hundred to thirty-five hundred dollars, and a license for the transplantation is obtained under false pretenses from the Doctors' Syndicate. It has been less common that low-income organ-failure patients have been recipients, such as Mahmoud, who was able to afford his kidney and surgery through the relatively high income he gained working in the oil-rich gulf economy. Yet, as more government subsidies are being provided for transplants and more public hospitals are performing these surgeries in Egypt, poorer patients are better enabled to receive transplants, particularly from related donors when the organ is donated free of charge. The price awarded to donors, however, is not secured and has consistently declined in recent years. From existing information about donors in Egypt, Soheila tends to represent many organ donors in being a) solicited from an underserved and/or vulnerable community and b) being threatened by poverty and debt. Data on the gender ratio of organ donors in Egypt is consistent with global trends and suggests that the number of unrelated male donors significantly exceeds the number of female donors in Egypt.[15] However, the number of unrelated female donors, particularly between the ages of twenty and thirty, does appear to be growing, and thus Soheila represents a growing trend.

Soheila's and Mahmoud's narratives provoke thought also about capitalism (and the far-reaching benefits derived from the oil-rich gulf economy), globalization, and modernization. For example, government programs to support transplant tourists, or permit organ sales within a country, exist because it is often cheaper and more convenient than supporting patients on dialysis long-term; other countries are simply wealthy enough to buy the convenience of organ supplies for their nationals. Most important, the narratives also demonstrate how the current operations of transplants and absence of donor registries facilitate exploitative practices in the procurement of organs and the social inequalities in their distribution. Despite attempts to outlaw solicited donations in Egypt, the present system does little to end it, and so the trade persists, presenting few other options to an exploited underclass of donors such as Soheila and recipients such as Mahmoud.

Islamic Declarations, Other Bioethical Guidelines, and Implementation

In response to the emergence of a market for organs, most ethicists worldwide, Islamic jurists among them, began issuing guidelines to denounce these practices. Islamic jurists of the Board of the Islamic Fiqh Academy (a part of the Organization of the Islamic Conference) issued a *qarar* (resolution) on death and transplants at the Third International Conference of Islamic Jurists meeting in Amman, Jordan, in 1986.[16] This *qarar* declared the following: "A person (is) considered legally dead, and all the Sharia's principles can be applied, when one of the following signs is established: 1. Complete stoppage of the heart and breathing, and the doctors decide that it is irreversible. 2. Complete stoppage of all vital functions of the brain, the doctors decide that it is irreversible, and the brain has started to degenerate."[17]

These guidelines thus paved a way for permitting donation from brain-stem-dead and nonbeating-heart donors, and a variety of consent requirements have been incorporated across the Muslim world. Working within these guidelines, the twelfth session of the Council of Arab Ministers of Health (Khartoum, March 1987) devised the Unified Arab Draft Law on Human Organ Transplants, which states: "Specialist physicians may perform surgical operations to transplant organs from a living or dead person to another person for the purpose of maintaining life, according to the conditions and procedures laid down in this law."[18] That law also addresses the subject of organ sales and indicates that the sale, purchase, or remunerated donation of organs is prohibited, and no specialist may perform a transplant operation if he knows the organ to have been acquired by such means.

Although it is difficult to assess how this draft law has been utilized since 1987, numerous other consistent fatwas and statements have been issued against compensated organ donation since these initial declarations. These range from sources such as the Islamic Charter of Medical Ethics (a document issued to the

World Health Organization), to regional societies such as the Islamic Medical Association of North America (IMANA), to book-length statements such as that from Kuala Lumpur.[19] Corroborating fatwas have also been issued by Egypt's Dar al-Ifta (fatwa office). As for Egypt, these fatwas have influenced the heated discourse on transplants as well as national policies that aim to protect Egyptians from nonnational transplant tourists but have not protected Egyptians from conationals in need of organs.

Although these fatwas and regional draft laws incorporate distinctive discourse and reasoning, they share a condemnation of paid donation with other international declarations, including the WHO's Human Organ and Tissue Transplantation Report (2003), the World Medical Association's Statement on Live Organ Trade (1985) and Resolution on Physicians' Conduct Concerning Human Organ Transplantation (1994), and the long-standing statement of the international Transplantation Society. Thus, despite the few countries that have legalized organ sales, there is largely a consensus among Islamic and other biomedical statements against the exploitation of individuals for organ donation via financial incentives.

Maqasid al-Sharia

These declarations have made clear an intolerance of the exploitation of the poor as a source for organs via financial gain. Like national policies in the region, fatwas have thus far largely not addressed the subject of organ donation from the perspective of the *maqasid al-sharia* (goals of Islamic laws, developed by al-Shatibi and others) that require universal social justice and respect of human rights. More specifically, *maqasid al-sharia* focus on preserving the goals and spirit of laws in practice. In the case of transplants, the aforementioned requirements are essential but must also work in tandem with efforts to assure that certain groups of society (the privileged) are not benefiting more, or at the price of, other groups (the underprivileged) in donating as well as receiving organs. Laws implemented in the spirit of *maqasid al-sharia* aim toward nonexploitative practices for obtaining organs as well as providing equal access to these scarce supplies, regardless of race/ethnicity, religious identity, class, or financial situation.[20] Most striking in existing Islamic and other bioethical statements is the neglecting to recommend, and insist on, the establishment of specific tools of assuring implementation of just transplantation practices. Working toward operationalizing *maqasid al-sharia* jointly with other Islamic and bioethical statements can help pave the way for solutions to the problems of exploitation and privilege as in the current practices of organ trafficking, particularly in the Muslim world.

Paving a Path for Solutions

As demonstrated, despite Islamic and other bioethical guidelines and laws against it, the organ trade still thrives globally as well as in the Middle East and Muslim world. This sober reality of the expansion of the global trafficking of human organs, and particularly the grave consequences it has for organ donors, has fueled an initiative to implement the ethical guidelines that speak against this practice. The Coalition for Organ-Failure Solutions (COFS) is a nonprofit international health and human rights organization committed to combating organ trafficking and ending the exploitation of the poor and vulnerable as a source of organ supplies.[21] COFS consists of experts from a variety of disciplines, including Islamic and other medical ethicists, medical professionals, social scientists, policy analysts, and human rights activists and lawyers, predominantly from the Middle East and other Muslim countries.

A project of implementing Islamic and other bioethical solutions raises the question that fatwas on transplants have thus far failed to address: namely, how do we advocate for this cause according to Islamic edicts? COFS started its work in the Middle East in 2006 with special attention to Egypt and the unique circumstances of the organ trafficking situation there. It has formulated a strategy to bring together advocates, including the *'ulama'*, decision-makers, and key stakeholders, for example, patients, donors, medical professionals, laboratories, and health insurance companies. The aim is to collectively seek practical solutions to the problem of organ trafficking globally, while focusing on regionally and locally appropriate solutions for the Middle East and the Muslim world. COFS recognizes that patients resort to an organ trade because of lack of available alternatives. Accordingly COFS is committed to calling for state accountability toward establishing alternative solutions for organ supplies and distribution. This includes a procurement and distribution entity and a protocol of nonexploitation and fair distribution. Such a system may rely on a campaign to increase deceased donations, promote concepts of altruism from related and close-kin donors, and advance emerging proposals and models of altruistic organ sharing. Additionally COFS works to prevent further exploitation of potential commercial living donors and provides outreach services to individuals who have already been commercial living donors. Outreach services include clinical follow-up and health services that are direct results of the commercial living organ donation, health education about best practices after an organ donation, the facilitation of donor support groups, employment/income generation assistance when these abilities have been compromised as a result of a donation, and referral to legal services. These services not only provide support to an otherwise abandoned group of exploited individuals but also work to provide the otherwise overlooked data on donor outcomes and quality of life. While Muslim societies, like societies elsewhere, continue to grapple with protocols for dealing with the global search for organ supplies, they should be informed of the heavy consequences of a market trade in organs and, in turn, advance solutions based on existing Islamic edicts and based on the concepts of *maqasid al-sharia*.

Conclusion

In sum, the phenomenon of the trafficking of humans for organs operates globally, including in the Middle East and the Muslim world. Research and analysis emerging since the late 1990s have begun to reveal some of the grave consequences of this trade. Emerging literature has also shed light on the complex concepts and discourses that surround this problem. Within the region Islamic rulings have provided guidelines on transplants that condemn solicited and compensated organ donation and thus the exploitation of the poor for organs. *Maqasid al-sharia* concepts have been employed less frequently, but they are important in emphasizing the role of social justice in the equitable distribution of organ supplies.

These measures have not yet made a significant impact on the organ trade. In response, COFS has emerged as an initiative to advance these guidelines toward more practical solutions to combat the organ trafficking problem. Among its aims, COFS seeks to further engage the *'ulama'* for building an appropriate road map to carry out this mission. This is one step toward applying Islamic and other biomedical ethical discourse to action.

NOTES

1. Scholars grapple with various terms to describe this phenomenon, including "organ trafficking," "transplant tourism," "organ trade," and "organ fraud." According to the United Nations Trafficking Protocol, organ trafficking occurs where a third party recruits, transports, transfers, harbors, or receives a person, using threats (or use) of force, coercion, abduction, fraud, deception, or abuse of authority or a position of vulnerability for the purpose of removing that person's organ(s). Where children are concerned, the removal of an organ(s) facilitated by a third party constitutes trafficking with or without considerations of deception or coercion. Third parties may include brokers or others such as medical professionals or laboratories acting as brokers. Global decreases in prices for organs, such as kidneys, indicate that the market is expanding. Additionally countries such as China and Pakistan have significantly increased hosting transplant tourists.

2. George M. Abouna, "Ethical Issues in Organ and Tissue Transplantation," *Experimental and Clinical Transplantation* 1, no. 2 (2003): 125–40; George M. Abouna, "Negative Impact of Trading in Human Organs on the Development of Transplantation in the Middle East," *Transplantation Proceedings* 25, no. 3 (1993): 2310–13; George M. Abouna and others, "Experience with 130 Consecutive Renal Transplants in the Middle East with Special Reference to Histocompatibility Matching, Antirejection Therapy with Antilymphocyte Globulin (ALG), and Prolonged Preservation of Imported Cadaveric Grafts," *Transplantation Proceedings* 16, no. 4 (1984): 1114–17; Debra Budiani, "Consequences of Living Kidney Donors in Egypt," presentation and proceedings of WHO and MESOT meetings, Kuwait, 2006; Lawrence Cohen, "The Other Kidney: Biopolitics Beyond Recognition," in *Commodifying Bodies,* ed. Nancy Scheper-Hughes and Loïc Wacquant (London: Sage, 2002), 9–30; Abdullah Daar, "Money and Organ Procurement: Narratives from the Real World," in *Legal and Social Issues in Organ Transplantation,* ed. Theo Gutmann and

others (Munich: Pabs Publishers, 2004); Daar, "South Mediterranean, Middle East, and Subcontinent Organ Transplant Activity," *Transplantation Proceedings* 33, nos. 1–2 (2001): 1993–94; Daar, "Organ Donation—World Experience: The Middle East," *Transplantation Proceedings* 23, no. 5 (1991): 2505–7; Daar, "Ethical Issues: A Middle East Perspective," *Transplantation Proceedings* 21, no. 1 (1989): 1402–4; Madhav Goyal and others, "Economic and Health Consequences of Selling a Kidney in India," *Journal of the American Medical Association* 288, no. 13 (2002): 1589–93; M. A. Masri and others, "A Comparative Study of HLA Allele Frequency in Lebanese, Arabs, United Arab Emirates and East Indian Populations," *Transplantation Proceedings* 29 (1997): 2922–23; A. Riad, "Current Issues and Future Problems of Transplantation in the Middle East: Syria," *Transplantation Proceedings* 33 (2001): 2632–33; Nancy Scheper-Hughes, "Commodity Fetishism in Organ Trafficking," in *Commodifying Bodies,* ed. Scheper-Hughes and Wacquant, 31–62; Nancy Scheper-Hughes, "The Ends of the Body: Commodity Fetishism and the Traffic in Human Organs," *SAIS Review: A Journal of International Affairs* 22, no. 1 (2000): 61–80; Nancy Scheper-Hughes, "The Global Traffic of Human Organs," *Current Anthropology* 41, no. 2 (2000): 91–224; F. A. M. Shaheen and others, "Current Issues and Problems of Transplantation in the Middle East: The Arabian Gulf," *Transplantation Proceedings* 33 (2001): 2621–22; Zargooshi, "Iranian Kidney Donors," 386–92; Javaad Zargooshi, "Quality of Life of Iranian Kidney Donors," *Journal of Urology* 166 (2001): 1790–99.

3. Shaheen and others, "Current Issues and Problems of Transplantation," 621–22.

4. Ibid.

5. Ibid., 2622.

6. Ibid.

7. Zargooshi, "Quality of Life."

8. Personal communication and statements from a draft manuscript of Zargooshi's forthcoming work.

9. The first author, Debra Budiani, has conducted research on organ transplants in Egypt from 1999 through the present. Her research has included structured and unstructured interviews with donors, recipients, religious leaders, state officials, laboratories, and doctors. For further details, see Budiani, "Facilitating Organ Transplants in Egypt: An Analysis of Doctors' Discourse," *Body and Society* 13, no. 3 (2007): 125–49.

10. For a more extensive discussion on the resistance to procuring organs from the non-living in Egypt, see Budiani, "Facilitating Organ Transplants in Egypt."

11. Joelle Bassoul, "Egypt's Illegal Organs Trade Thrives on Poverty," Middle East Online (April 4, 2006), http://www.middle-east-online.com/English/egypt/?id=16154; Gihan Shahine, "When Does the Soul Depart?," *Al-Ahram Weekly* 420 (March 11–17, 1999), http://weekly.ahram.org.eg/1999/420/fe2.htm; Shaden Shehab, "Between Life and Death," *Al-Ahram Weekly* 528 (April 5–11, 2001): 528.

12. Budiani, "Facilitating Organ Transplants in Egypt."

13. Hamdy al-Sayyed, the head of the Doctors' Syndicate of Egypt, estimated that approximately one-third of transplants conducted in Egypt are unlicensed and that it is difficult to control this practice (personal interview, August 7, 2006).

14. Budiani, "Consequences of Living Kidney Donors."

15. As discussed earlier in the introduction to this volume, the Islamic Fiqh Academy was established as an independent organization formed by renowned Muslim scholars

worldwide. Their objective is to respond to new challenges that Muslims confront by concluding resolutions based on Islamic laws and *fiqh* and its sources from the Qur'an and Sunna.

16. Cited in Daar, "Organ Donation," 2505.

17. Cited in ibid.

18. Abul Fadl Mohsin Ebrahim, *Organ Transplantation: Contemporary Islamic Legal and Ethical Perspectives* (Kuala Lumpur: A. S. Noordeen, 1998).

19. Jamāl al-Dīn 'Aṭiya, *Nahwa taf'īl maqāṣid al-sharī'a* (Damascus: Dār al-Fikr, 2001).

20. For more information on COFS, see www.cofs.org.

HAMZA ESKANDARANI

Ethical and Legal Implications in Assisted Reproductive Technology

Perspective Analysis of the Gulf Cooperative Council States

Assisted reproductive technology (ART) has raised more interest and more ethical concerns than any other medical practice. Many countries have imposed legislative measures and guidelines in order to regulate ART practice and to circumvent any resulting ethical and legal dilemmas. The results of a survey on the presence and implementation of rules and regulations for ART practice in the Gulf Cooperative Council (GCC) states, which include Saudi Arabia, the United Arab Emirates, Kuwait, Oman, Qatar, Bahrain, and Yemen, suggest that the lack of legislative regulations and proper guidelines for ART practice in GCC states is cause for ethical and legal concern.

Introduction

Infertility has been defined as the inability to conceive after one year of regular, unprotected sexual intercourse.[1] Although infertility affects 8 to 15 percent of couples worldwide, depending on the region,[2] a large portion of this percentage can now be successfully treated with assisted reproductive technology (ART). For nearly three decades ART has been considered a feasible alternative for the treatment of infertility. It has helped many couples to become parents, achieving a conception rate of around 30 percent per cycle in many good centers.[3] However, the use of human egg cells (oocytes), sperm, and embryos for the treatment of infertility and their use in research has provoked intense religious, ethical, and moral debate in both the Arab and Islamic world and elsewhere.[4] Further, ethical and moral dilemmas may arise for some couples when confronted with supernumerary embryos that cannot be transferred because of the risk of multiple pregnancy; in turn, this poses the dilemma of either reducing the number of fertilized embryos, aborting these embryos, or increasing the health risk for the mother.

In addition other ethical issues are raised by new technologies to preserve and manipulate these embryos. For example, one solution to the problem of leftover embryos is cryopreservation, but this then raises further concerns: How long should gametes and embryos be stored? What happens if one of the partners dies or becomes mentally incapable, or the couple divorce or separate while embryos are in storage? Embryos created outside the womb can also be tested for serious genetic disease and chromosomal anomalies in a process known as "Preimplantation Genetic Diagnosis" (PGD). This offers important advantages to couples at risk for these anomalies; yet, it also raises troublesome ethical and legal issues because of its extensive manipulation of embryos. Some have also raised concern about its potential for eugenic selection of offspring as well as its use in sex selection.[5]

Although ART has many positive aspects, it has nevertheless opened the door for negative uses. This problem is compounded when clinics lack basic regulations, such as a proper set of guidelines to follow, acquisition of mandatory licenses, supervision by an independent statutory body, and the implementation of disciplinary action. Among such negative aspects is the possible misuse of spare or supernumerary embryos: they could be used for research, taken from the treated couple without their consent, or mistakenly given to another couple for transfer. These pitfalls warrant the need for tighter supervision by an independent statutory body to prohibit misuse; in particular, ministries of health should look carefully into the ethical and legal issues of ART.

Data Collection

Two sets of data from the IVF centers in the GCC states were collected and analyzed: 1) data on legislative measures and guidelines imposed by the governing bodies of each GCC country; and 2) information on the implementation of any such regulations by the IVF centers and also the distribution of training literature on dealing with possible ethical dilemmas. A questionnaire consisting of two tables (see below) was sent to the managers of all IVF centers in the GCC countries.

Results

All GCC states have legalized ART exclusively for married heterosexual couples seeking infertility treatment. Currently there are fifty licensed IVF centers serving a total population of approximately fifty-five million people. Their distribution is as follows: twenty-seven centers are located in Saudi Arabia, ten in Kuwait, seven in the United Arab Emirates, three in Bahrain, and one each in Qatar, Oman, and Yemen. Last year the average number of IVF/ICSI cycles per center was approximately 250 (ICSI stands for Intracytoplasmic Sperm Injection, a treatment for male-factor infertility). Moreover the highest number of centers per inhabitants is in Bahrain, where three units serve six hundred thousand inhabitants (that is, five centers per million) and perform 883 IVF/ICSI cycles per million, which is considered an excellent service number when compared to some European countries that have an average of one and a half centers per million inhabitants and perform 856 IVF/ICSI cycles per million.[6] By contrast, Yemen has the lowest number of centers per inhabitants of the GCC countries: one center per nineteen million inhabitants and 26 IVF/ICSI cycles per million.

All GCC centers employ IVF/ICSI programs, but few use assisted hatching, a technique to drill holes, usually by laser beam, in the walls of the fertilized oocytes, facilitating their implantation in the uterine wall following embryo transfer. However, PGD techniques, which are focused mainly on "Fluorescent In Situ Hybridization" (FISH) analyses, are practiced in three centers in Saudi Arabia. Such techniques use fluorescent dyes that display the chromosomes of the resulting embryos, thus revealing the qualitative and quantitative status of such embryos.

While statute laws, such as the prohibition of any kind of surrogacy donation,[7] are always enforced, few guidelines have been introduced by all concerned ministries of health. Compliance with such guidelines is left to the discretion of the regional licensing office or the treating center.

A questionnaire was sent to each of the concerned assisted conception centers, and sixteen of them (32 percent) agreed to answer the questions listed in tables 1 and 2 below. Nine of these centers are in Saudi Arabia, two in Bahrain, and one each in Kuwait, the United Arab Emirates, Oman, Qatar, and Yemen. Because of suspicion that there would be discrepancies between official government guidelines and actual practice, copies of the questionnaire were passed on to the concerned IVF centers directly rather than to the government licensing offices of the countries. The result is a more realistic picture of how centers interpret and adhere to government guidelines. In the tables the category "government" refers to the perception of that government's regulations, not the actual existence of government regulation.

With regard to the process of regulating centers to practice IVF, the Saudi Arabian government scored much higher, meaning that centers in Saudi Arabia perceived their government as exercising greater control over IVF centers than did their counterparts in other GCC countries. In addition centers in Saudi Arabia apparently scored higher in self-regulation compared to other corresponding centers (table 1; note that the column "X" refers to the average response on a scale where a score of 3 indicates that the item is imperative, 2 for possible, 1 for not sure, and 0 for not available). These results could come from the strong legislative measures for licensing recently imposed by the Saudi government. Therefore it seemed reasonable to analyze the data in two different groups: countries with no government legislative measures versus Saudi Arabia. The standard deviation, however, is very high for data obtained from all IVF centers, whether in Saudi Arabia or not. This inconsistency reflects the extra precautionary measures taken by some centers, but it means that the only significant differences in the data are found in two areas: the awareness of government ART guidelines and the requirement for obtaining a license. See tables 1 and 2.[8]

TABLE 1. Comparison of average scores on the legalization of IVF centers to practice

Category	Saudi Arabia (9 centers)				Other GCC states (7 centers)			
	Government		*Center*		*Government*		*Center*	
	$\bar{X}$	SD	$\bar{X}$	SD	$\bar{X}$	SD	$\bar{X}$	SD
Are there any ART regulations to be followed?	2.33	1.32	2.33	1.32	0.75	1.50	1.41	2.50
Are there any ART guidelines to be followed?	1.78	1.39	3.00[a]	0.00	1.25	1.50	1.73[a]	1.50
Is there any official body that accredits gynecologists to work in ART?	2.33	1.32	1.00	1.50	2.00	1.41	1.50	0.00
Is there any official body that accredits embryologists to work in ART?	2.00	1.50	1.00	1.50	2.00	1.41	1.50	1.00
Are there requirements of IVF center to obtain license?	3.00[b]	0.00	1.00	1.50	2.25[b]	0.96	1.50	1.00
Has the IVF center been inspected by official body for license?	2.67	1.00	1.00	1.50	2.00	1.41	0.00	0.00
Is there any surveillance by licensing body of the IVF center?	0.67	1.32	0.56	1.13	1.50	1.73	0.00	0.00
Is there any mandatory submission of data for IVF center to the licensing office or official body?	0.89	1.36	1.00	1.32	1.00	1.15	0.00	0.00
Is there any written disciplinary action that can be taken against any violation?	1.67	1.58	1.22	1.48	1.00	1.41	1.50	0.00
Could violation lead to suspension of license or imprisonment?	1.78	1.30	0.89	1.17	2.25	0.96	1.00	0.00
Could violation lead to other forms of punishment?	1.33	1.32	1.11	1.27	1.25	1.26	1.50	0.00
Does the official body approve or inspect the release of information to the press for the purpose of advertisement?	1.44	1.42	1.33	1.58	1.00	1.15	1.73	1.50

Does the official body approve adverts for the IVF center in advance?	1.44	1.42	1.33	1.58	1.00	1.41	1.50	0.00
Does the official body inspect biostatistical data of the center prior to their publication?	0.33	1.00	1.00	1.50	0.00	0.00	0.00	0.00
Total score	23.67	6.44	17.78	12.35	19.25	8.85	11.00	11.14

[a, b] Significantly different ($P<0.05$)

TABLE 2. Comparison of average scores on guidelines related to treatment cycles of IVF centers

Category	Saudi Arabia (9 centers)				Other GCC states (7 centers)			
	Government		*Center*		*Government*		*Center*	
Are there any regulations and/or guidelines for the following:	$\bar{X}$	SD	$\bar{X}$	SD	$\bar{X}$	SD	$\bar{X}$	SD
Number of pre-embryos to transfer								
Transfer limits of pre-embryos	0.67	1.32	2.78	0.44	1.25	1.50	2.0	1.41
Requirement for patient's counseling prior to or during the IVF treatment cycle	0.56	1.13	2.56	1.01	1.25	1.50	1.75	1.26
Genetic counseling for severe male-factor infertility	0.33	1.00	2.89[a]	0.33	1.50	1.73	1.50[a]	1.29
Requirements for patient's good mental and physical health	0.22	0.67	2.56	0.53	1.25	1.50	1.25	1.26
Mandatory presence of husband at time of embryo transfer	0.22	0.67	2.33	1.00	1.50	1.73	1.50	1.29
Age limits to female patients undergoing treatment cycles	0.22	0.67	1.22	1.30	0.75	0.96	0.75	1.50
Prerequisite for patient's consent forms	0.33	1.00	2.00	1.32	1.00	1.15	0.50	1.00
Mandatory submission of data for IVF center to the licensing office	0.33	1.00	3.00	0.00	1.50	1.73	2.25	1.50
Freezing sperm	0.56	1.13	1.33	1.32	1.25	1.50	0.75	1.50

TABLE 2. (*continued*)

Freezing embryos	0.22	0.67	1.78	1.39	1.25	1.50	1.50	1.29
Freezing ovarian tissues	0.56	1.13	2.78[b]	0.44	1.25	1.50	1.50[b]	1.29
Limiting period of gamete/embryo freezing	0.22	0.67	1.00	1.32	1.25	1.50	0.75	1.50
Micromanipulation	0.44	0.88	2.67	0.50	1.25	1.50	1.50	1.29
Preimplantation Genetic Diagnosis	0.56	1.13	2.11	1.27	1.25	1.50	1.50	1.29
Clinical/laboratory written protocols	0.44	0.88	1.33	1.41	1.25	1.50	0.75	1.50
Moral status of the conceptus (embryo research)	0.22	0.67	2.22	1.30	1.50	1.73	1.75	1.26
Prior approval for research from the ethical committee/licensing office	0.22	0.67	1.78	1.39	1.50	1.73	0.75	1.50
Sex preselection	0.67	1.32	2.22	1.30	1.25	1.50	1.25	1.50
All handling, processing & utilization procedures of gametes are witnessed appropriately	0.22	0.67	2.11	1.27	1.00	1.15	1.00	1.50
Embryo reduction	0.67	1.32	2.33	1.32	1.75	1.50	1.75	1.26
Maximum limits for daily dose of FISH stimulation	0.22	0.67	2.11	1.27	0.75	1.50	1.25	1.50
Ovarian stimulation (pointless attempt) with concomitant helpless testicular sperm extraction	0.22	0.67	0.89	1.05	1.00	1.15	0.75	0.96
Minimum resting period between successive IVF/ICSI treatment cycles	0.44	0.88	1.33	1.32	0.50	1.00	1.00	1.15
Maximum limits of receiving IVF/ICSI treatment cycles per patient	0.22	0.67	0.67	1.00	1.00	1.15	0.50	1.00
Imposed limits toward cost of treatment	0.22	0.67	0.44	0.88	0.50	1.00	0.50	1.00
	0.22	0.67	1.00	1.32	1.00	1.15	1.00	1.15
Total score	9.44[c]	20.68	49.44[c]	9.59	30.50	35.33	31.25	28.91

a, b, c Significantly different ($P<0.05$)

With regard to the treatment cycles of IVF centers (table 2), the picture from Saudi Arabia is quite different. Governmentally set guidelines scored low, with very high standard deviation, compared to guidelines by corresponding centers and other GCC countries. This could be caused by individual centers' misinterpretations of government guidelines and/or the lack of governmental guidelines; in either case, differing guidelines from the respective centers could be evidence of compensatory measures taken by the centers. However, IVF centers in Saudi Arabia had higher scores than those in other GCC countries did regarding the presence of guidelines for specific procedures; these scores were significantly higher in two cases: patient counseling and embryo freezing (see table 2). The average scores from tables 1 and 2 are compared in table 3.

TABLE 3. Comparison of average scores of guidelines set by countries

Country	Legislations of IVF center		Guidelines related to treatment cycles	
	Mean	*SD*	*Mean*	*SD*
Saudi Arabia	41.44	18.08	58.89	25.99
Other GCC	30.25	11.32	61.75	52.73
P Value	>0.05	<0.05		

Appraisal of the results above indicates that certain guidelines introduced in Saudi Arabia a few years ago, such as those that legalize the practice of IVF centers, remain the governing yardstick for ART practice, as evident from the high average score of 23.67 in table 1. Mandatory regulations, in the form of royal decrees, have just recently been proposed, but the adoption of these regulations is not complete. In other GCC countries, the existing guidelines for licensing IVF centers focus mainly on the suitability of the place and the credentials of the working team. One interesting finding is that most centers do not require the presence of the husband during the embryo transfer (table 2). From an Islamic point of view, the husband's presence at the time of embryo transfer is mandatory to make sure that he is still living and that death or divorce has not terminated the marriage. It is also worth noting that there is no clear stance on the ethics of embryo reduction among these centers. The prevalence of anecdotal guidelines over government regulation appears to result in either the ignorance of many important ethical aspects of IVF treatment or the lack of understanding of Islamic directives.

Conclusions

The GCC states follow the Sharia (Islamic law) in all their ordinances. Although tight control has been imposed over many facets of medical practice, such as the prohibition of abortion except in extreme cases where there is a threat to the mother's life and of human cloning, some technological and scientific applications have been left unaddressed. When it comes to ART centers, part of the reason that a similar level of control has not been imposed could have to do with the fact that Muslim scientists have not sufficiently explained the sorts of vital control measures that could be introduced. But it must also be admitted that ambiguity on certain issues continues to linger. For example, jurists are divided on whether to condone the techniques used for selecting the sex of the embryo for reasons such as balancing the ratio of boys to girls in a family; there is also disagreement on whether to destroy some embryos during multiple pregnancies, thus increasing the chance that the remaining embryo(s) will survive the pregnancy.

Lack of legislative regulations and proper guidelines for ART practice in GCC countries is a cause for legal and ethical concern—as in, for example, the case of a husband dying before embryo transfer or the question of determining which embryo(s) to select for reduction. The effects of this lack of regulation can be seen on three levels. First, the statutory bodies in each participating GCC country have failed to ensure that standards of quality are adhered to and that violations of these standards are punished. They have also dismissed the imposition of a national or regional ART registry. Second, to avoid accusations of malpractice, many treating centers increase the number of pre-embryos per transfer, offer cryopreservation of surplus embryos, or send patients to countries overseas that allow embryo reduction. Third, counseling, if offered to patients, is rarely performed by professionals such as social workers. This runs the risk that some patients form misconceptions or have difficulty understanding ART procedures. Other patients, if properly informed, might not countenance IVF and the extracorporeal creation of a human embryo at all. In light of these concerns, several recommendations are proposed in order to refine the control of ART practice and safeguard its application from possible ignorance or misconduct.

Recommendations

Two important domains have been suggested in order to regulate ART practice in most GCC countries:[9] first, the legislative act, in its broader terms, for the regulation of ART practice, which should be approved by a supreme council or authority; second, the statutory body detailing all aspects of an ART code of practice. Accordingly all IVF centers would have to be licensed for their facilities, procedures, and all professionals involved. Moreover penalties for violations should be imposed. In this way, compliance to such measures would be beneficial for any legal and ethical concerns as exemplified above.

The statutory body will have four central objectives:

To set certain guidelines and regulations. It will be treated as the code of practice.

To safeguard ART practice by monitoring the centers' compliance to the set guidelines and regulations. This will include revoking licenses, penalizing offenders, and imposing controls on scientific research.

To provide logistic support, advice, and necessary assistance in explaining the legislative measures to all practicing centers or to any new setup.
To supervise the annual national ART registry and to provide guidelines through which data collection from various IVF centers/units can be achieved annually.

The suggested statutory body could be established for each country separately or could be formulated regionally for the GCC states. Although the full implementation of these central objectives is a daunting task, it could be attainable provided that the concerned countries appreciate such need and commit themselves by providing necessary support.

NOTES

1. P. I. Rowe and others, *WHO Manual for the Standardized Investigation and Diagnosis of the Infertile Couple* (Cambridge: Press Syndicate of the University of Cambridge, 1993), 1–83.

2. Ibid.; E. Greenhall and M. Vessey, "The Prevalence of Subfertility: A Review of the Current Confusion and a Report of Two New Studies," *Fertility and Sterility* 54, no. 6 (1999): 978–83.

3. A. Taylor and P. Braude, "Ethical Issues Related to the Use of Human Gametes and Embryos in Research and Subfertility Treatment," *Biochemist (Bulletin of the Biochemical Society)* 16, no. 2 (1994): 3–8; J. Gunby and S. Daya, on behalf of the IVF Directors Group of the Canadian Fertility and Andrology Society, "Assisted Reproductive Technologies (ART) in Canada: 2001 Results from the Canadian ART Register," *Fertility and Sterility* 84, no. 3 (September 2005): 590–99.

4. S. A. A. Hijawi, "Human Infertility: Ethical Implications of Modern Researches in Genetics," in *Proceedings of the Islamic Educational, Scientific and Cultural Organization (ISESCO) Seminar, Doha, Qatar, February 13–15, 1993* (Doha, Qatar: ISESCO Publication, 1993), 213–25; V. H. Eisenberg and J. G. Schenker, "The Ethical, Legal and Religious Aspects of Preembryo Research," *European Journal of Obstetrics and Gynecology and Reproductive Biology* 75, no. 1 (1997): 11–24; Inhorn, "Religion and Reproductive Technologies," 14–18; J. Carter, *The Issue at Hand: IVF and the Obligations to Embryos,* posted on the Evangelical Outpost blog, http://www.evangelicaloutpost.com/archives/001363.html, accessed June 14, 2005.

5. K. Cloonan, C. Crumley, and S. Kiymaz, "The Historical, Scientific, Cultural, and Economic Aspects of Gender Preselection," *Developmental Biology,* edited by S. F. Gilbert, 7th ed. (Sunderlland, Mass.: S. Nauer, 2003). Online, http://www.devbio.com/article.php?ch=21&id=185, accessed April 16, 2003. A paper on fetal sex selection was presented by Vardit Rispler-Chaim at the Penn State conference, published as "Contemporary Muftis between Bioethics and Social Reality: Pre-selection of the Sex of a Fetus as a Paradigm," *Journal of Religious Ethics* 38 (March 2008): 53–76.

6. A. Nyboe Andersen, L. Gianaroli, and K. G. Ngren, "Assisted Reproductive Technology in Europe, 2000: Results Generated from European Registers by ESHRE," *Human Reproduction* 19, no. 3 (March 2004): 490–503.

7. Hijawi, "Human Infertility."

8. Data were analyzed using the SPSS software program (version 12.0). All tests were two-sided, and the level of significance was set at $P<0.05$ (P for probability, meaning the chance of something being true or occurring accidentally is less than 1 in 20). First, a scoring system was used for each respondent's reply, with a score of 3 indicating that the item is imperative, a score of 2 for possible, 1 for not sure, and 0 for not available; then a total score was obtained for each ART center. Therefore, for table 1, the highest total score is 3 x 14 = 42 and the lowest is 0 x 14 = 0. For table 2, however, the highest score is 3 x 27 = 81 and the lowest is 0 x 27 = 0. As the standard deviations of scores were high and the number of observations was small, nonparametric tests were preferred. The Mann-Whitney test was used for comparison between Saudi Arabia and other gulf countries in the average scores. Wilcoxon Signed Ranks test was used for comparison of scores on guidelines set by government and those set by center for each country.

9. H. A. Eskandarani, *Assisted Reproduction Technology, "State-of-the-Art"* (Rabat: Islamic Educational, Scientific and Cultural Organization [ISESCO], 1996).

FOUR

Muslims in Clinical Settings in North America and Europe

Overview

For medical ethics, the clinical setting is where ethical theory meets its most serious test. Speculation on the importance of key principles, such as *maslaha* (societal welfare) or nonmaleficence, dissipates in the face of the urgent demands of the intensive care unit and the changing technological environment of the modern hospital. The three essays of this section include numerous case studies, all of which focus on attitudes toward end-of-life issues among members of Muslim communities in Toronto, Canada, and Antwerp, Belgium.

Unlike the essays in the previous section, where the focus was on the application of Islamic norms in Muslim countries, this section focuses on Muslim minority populations. The Muslim communities of Toronto and Antwerp both have long histories, but whereas Canada (and Toronto in particular) has a tradition of assimilating large numbers of immigrants into a multicultural society, Moroccans in Belgium are often separated by class and language in addition to culture and religion. Moreover the Muslim population of Antwerp is fairly homogenous, having arisen from particular historical circumstances; in contrast, the Muslim population of Toronto is extremely diverse.

These three contributions therefore are essays in comparative ethics largely out of necessity; contrasts in religion, culture, and language form the context of every ethical interaction in these cities. In such a situation many problems can arise between Muslim patients and non-Muslim medical practitioners; these form the context for the first essay, by Iqbal Jaffer and Shabbir Alibhai, but the authors further complicate matters by looking at a minority within a minority. Their essay considers several end-of-life issues (organ transplantation, autopsy, and euthanasia, for example) as viewed by the Shiite community of Toronto. Shiites have been largely neglected in literature about Muslim medical ethics, and as Jaffer and Alibhai demonstrate, Shiites' end-of-life ethics differ both in substantive judgments and in the sources used for obtaining those judgments. The essay is based primarily on a detailed interview with Sayyid Muhammad Rizvi, a leading cleric in the North American Shiite community. This interview demonstrates that Shiite Islam knows much stricter hierarchies of religious learning than does Sunni Islam. The assessments of certain religious scholars (grand ayatollahs) are determinative for large communities of followers in a much stricter sense than is the case in the Sunni world. Moreover the legal reasoning of Shiite scholars depends far more on the principle of *'urf*, customary knowledge or common sense. This means that some important Shiite scholars refuse to accept the brain-death criterion, since it has not yet become customary knowledge; among Sunni scholars brain death has become widely accepted since the 1980s.

The following essay, by Shabbir Alibhai and Michael Gordon, undertakes comparative work in a more traditional sense by placing normative judgments from Shiite Islam side by side with judgments from Orthodox Judaism. They find significant similarities, such as in the presumptions that human life is infinitely valuable and that illness must be treated. In both religious traditions, the idea of weighing the value of life per se, and assessing the quality of that life, is largely abhorred. For both Orthodox Judaism as well as Shiite Islam, however, there is a key difference between withholding medical help from a person who has entered a stage of dying and withdrawing life support that has already been put in place.

In both these essays the authors describe case studies based on their broad clinical experience. These case studies reflect the complex and changing nature of the clinical environment, where a patient's health can suddenly deteriorate or improve. They provide a valuable method for testing ethical intuitions and demonstrate the importance of imagining ethical dilemmas in advance of a pressure-filled clinical scenario. They also reveal, however, the many ways that well-intended actions may go awry in the clinical environment. This method of considering hypothetical cases also forms a bridge between this section and the next, since case studies are a widespread method for teaching ethics in medical schools.

The final essay in this section, by Stef Van den Branden and Bert Broeckaert, uses very different methods to approach similar issues. Their study is based on a series of qualitative interviews with working-class Moroccan immigrants in Belgium to assess their attitudes toward end-of-life issues. They found a broad consensus that illness and healing are gifts from God, a view that is shared by medical doctors and religious experts of Moroccan origin but is opposed to the views of most Belgians. Further, assessments of ethical issues by these immigrants were strongly influenced by stories they had heard from relatives in Morocco. However, the interviews also made clear that Moroccans in Belgium, despite differences in language and religion, are highly influenced by their local environment.

The challenges faced by medical professionals in Antwerp and Toronto are symptoms of increased global migration. As Van den Branden and Broeckaert argue, "Europe can no longer cling to a Christian or secular conceptual frame of reference to explain general attitudes towards ethical decisions." This sentiment holds for North America as well, both urban and rural communities. The case studies and interviews presented here provide much food for thought; they suggest the need for a strong support staff, including chaplains and social workers, to face these challenges. They also recommend that nurses and physicians be provided basic information on the needs and concerns of their Muslim patients. In the end, however, these studies make it clear that there is no "Muslim patient," and no single set of ethical presumptions holds for all Muslims everywhere. In the stress-filled clinical environment, nothing can replace honest questions put by a sensitive, caring health-care worker.

IQBAL H. JAFFER *and* SHABBIR M. H. ALIBHAI

The Permissibility of Organ Donation, End-of-Life Care, and Autopsy in Shiite Islam
A Case Study

"I will apply dietetic measures for the benefit of the sick according to my ability and judgment; I will keep them from harm and injustice."[1] For hundreds of years these words of the Oath of Hippocrates have formed the basis of Western medical ethics. However, in many parts of the world, and within various religio-cultural traditions, medical ethics are influenced by other guiding principles.Shiite Muslims in North America, specifically Toronto, Canada, understand the practices of medicine from their own doctrinal sources and through the rulings of specific jurists, and this understanding affects critical decisions made surrounding the end of life, particularly the practices of organ donation, end-of-life care, and autopsy.

Medical practice is a constantly changing art, and what may have been true ten years ago may not be so now. Although modern medicine has witnessed some spectacular successes in improving life expectancy and treating many illnesses, increasing medical complexity has led to unique challenges for adherents of age-old faiths such as Islam. Moreover, trying to understand the issues and implications of current medical practice through the eyes of a religion that is centuries older than current medical practice is difficult without the aid of an expert in that religion or in the specific medical field. To this end we conducted interviews with experts in each of the respective fields, and we consulted the primary sources of Islam, the Qur'an and hadith. In addition several secondary sources were used to gain an understanding of ethics and for a commentary on the specific issues involving modern medicine and ethical practice.

Our clinical experience and encounters with members of a large Shiite community in Toronto, Canada, have shown that this population's interactions with the health-care sector were often strongly shaped by their interpretations of Shiite Islam. Some of these interpretations were different from the extensive published literature on Sunni persceptions of important medical issues. In addition some of these interpretations appeared to vary depending on which Shiite jurist was being followed.

This situation is not unique to Toronto. In many large North American cities, such as Toronto and Dearborn, Michigan, large Shiite communities are situated within larger local Muslim populations. Given that there appear to be notable sectarian differences in medical ethical positions, it is important to highlight the Shiite perspective for the benefit of health professionals and patients.

Additionally, during these encounters with the Toronto Shiite community, several issues came up recurrently on both specific medical decisions and the context within which those decisions were made. Thus the methodology of decision making was reviewed, and a summary of common decisions made is shown in table 1 at the end of this essay. This approach helps to clarify the issue for nonexperts in the field and provides a succinct representation of the main issues of this discussion.

It is important to note, however, that ethical decisions within Shiism are dependent on the specific issue, the grand ayatollah being followed by the patient in question, and the specifics of each case. There may also be important ethnocultural nuances that impact on the implementation of any religious decisions. As such, two case studies highlight some of the important issues presented and typify some important bioethical issues.

Context

The backdrop of Toronto, Canada, was chosen as the focus of this work for several major reasons. Primarily it is the location from which both authors hail and where the respective work was undertaken. Moreover, within the greater Toronto area (GTA) a large Shiite Muslim community is spread over several mosques and community centers and comprises a significant minority within the greater Muslim population of the GTA. The spread of the Shiites in the GTA is a result of ethnicity and geography. The Shiite community in Toronto numbers between five thousand and ten thousand people and consists of members of several ethnic communities, including but not limited to East Africans of Indian descent (Khojas), Arabs (Iraqi, Lebanese, and others), Iranians, Afghanis, Pakistanis, Indians, and smaller ethnic groups and converts. Though the various mosques or religious centers create unique subcommunities, members of the community as a whole often get together during the religious festivals—for example, to celebrate the end of Ramadan—in order to hold joint prayers. Although upward of five thousand people have attended such gatherings, this number is somewhat smaller than the population of the larger Shiite community in Dearborn, Michigan; even so, it represents one of the largest concentrations of Shiites within North America. Additionally the Toronto community is home to one of the most well respected clerics within the North American Shiite community, Sayyid Muhammad Rizvi, who is the local spiritual leader of the Khoja community.

Twelver Shiism, so called because of followers' belief in the line of twelve divinely appointed Imams who succeeded the Prophet Muhammad upon the latter's death, is the most widespread form of Shiism in North America. According to Shiite doctrine, the twelve Imams (direct descendants of the Prophet through his son-in-law 'Ali) are the only people capable or worthy of authoritatively interpreting the Qur'an and hadith and of guiding the community on religious and spiritual matters.[2] This lineage of Imams ended with the Mahdi, who was born in 868 and will return at a time appointed by God in order to fulfill his mission to restore the world to peace and justice. Until his return the Shiite community is guided in matters of law (*fiqh*) by the *'ulama'*, religious scholars who are considered to be the representatives of the last Imam.[3]

The most learned scholars are given the title *marja' al-taqlid* (example of emulation), also known as grand ayatollahs or *mujtahids,* who guide the community at large with their fatwas (edicts). At any given point in time there may be several grand ayatollahs; however, one is generally favored by a particular community. Currently the majority of the Toronto community follows Grand Ayatollah Sayyid 'Ali al-Husseini al-Sistani, who is based in Iraq. A much smaller portion of the Toronto community follows Grand Ayatollah Sayyid Abu l-Qasim al-Khu'i, who died in 1992. The choice of a grand ayatollah to emulate is a personal one and can vary among communities and even within families. Ayatollah al-Khu'i was the grand ayatollah for most of the non-Iranian Shiite community prior to his death in 1992, and he also served as Ayatollah Sistani's teacher and mentor. Their ideas are similar; however, in general, Ayatollah al-Khu'i's rulings tend to be more permissive than Ayatollah Sistani's rulings.[4]

Sources for This Study

A structured interview with Sayyid Muhammad Rizvi, the primary source for this study, was held at his office at the Islamic Shia Ithna-Asheri Jamaat of Toronto (ISIJT) in 2004. Sayyid Rizvi is employed as a resident *'alim* by the ISIJT, a nonprofit organization comprised primarily of East African Khoja Shiite Muslims in the greater Toronto area. The ISIJT operates five religious centers with funds generated from membership fees and donations from members of the Shiite community. Sayyid Rizvi functions as a spiritual leader to the membership, leads congregational prayers (including the Friday prayer), recites sermons at one or more of the religious centers on a weekly basis, and guides the community in its religious affairs. In his capacity as resident *'alim,* Sayyid Rizvi regularly fields a variety of questions related to *fiqh,* predominantly by followers of Grand Ayatollah Sistani, including questions concerning medical ethics.[5]

Independent interactions by the authors with a variety of Toronto Shiite Muslims in the clinical environment have confirmed that Sayyid Rizvi is frequently looked to for advice on medical ethics by members of the ISIJT and by other Shiite Muslims residing in the GTA. This broader Shiite Muslim community includes people from a variety of ethnocultural backgrounds, including Arabs, Indo-Pakistanis, and Iranians. These Muslims often emulate other grand ayatollahs and have sought advice from Sayyid Rizvi to clarify rulings of those other jurists. Sayyid Rizvi appears to have scholarly knowledge of the rulings of several current and recently deceased grand ayatollahs.

Sayyid Rizvi has published articles on the subject of bioethics within the Shiite framework and continues to do his own research within the field.[6] He has translated a variety of religious texts from Persian and Arabic into English, including a book of fatwas for followers of Grand Ayatollah Sistani. In addition he comes from a distinguished family of religious scholars; his father was a prominent *'alim* within the Indo-Pakistani community internationally.

The interview was conducted at Sayyid Rizvi's office on December 3, 2004, and was structured according to the following questions:

How often do Shiite doctrines change vis-à-vis bioethical topics, and what is the driving force that causes these changes: new advances in medicine, a better understanding of current medical practice by jurists?

Is organ donation permitted?
- From human to human?
- From non-Muslim to Muslim?
- From Muslim to non-Muslim?
- From animal to human?

Is live organ donation permissible, or is it restricted to posthumous transplantation? If it is not permissible, what is the rationale behind that decision?

Has this decision ever been different under the understanding of a different *mujtahid*?

In cases of people who are considered to be "terminally ill," what sorts of options do they have under Islamic law for the remainder of their lives?
- Are they allowed to refuse medication that might prolong their lives?
- Are they allowed to refuse medical intervention that might prolong their lives?
- Are they allowed to ask to be "helped" to die?—whether those they are asking can or cannot do so is irrelevant.
- Are they allowed to provide advance directives that, in case they are not conscious to do so, give medical teams the right to "remove them from respirators"?
- Are they allowed to sign organ donation cards, which give organ transplant teams the opportunity to harvest their organs upon their death?

At what point, if any, with a comatose patient is the family allowed to remove the respirator?
What if treatment is causing the family undue financial hardship?
What if treatment is causing the family undue emotional hardship?
Is there a distinction, in Islamic understanding, between sanctity of life and quality of life?
Is an autopsy permissible? Under what circumstances or restrictions?
Why do Muslims bury their dead so quickly, compared to Western burials?
What rights, if any, does the corpse have? What sorts of actions would violate these rights?
Is a person allowed to donate his body to medical science? Why or why not?

Because of the complexity of the issues and the various elements involved in the answers, at times, the interview tended to retain a broad focus. The interviewer (Iqbal Jaffer) took notes during the interview and then created a transcript, which was submitted to Sayyid Rizvi for his approval of the content and for clarification of the issues, if required. Additionally Sayyid Rizvi was e-mailed during the write-up of this study to clarify any changes in position that may have arisen since the time of the interview, as he had indicated that some positions, specifically concerning organ donation, were being reevaluated by Ayatollah Sistani.

Concepts within Shiite Medical Ethics

Within the context of Shiite scholarship over several centuries, Islam considers death to be a natural part of life. Though Islam would not suggest that life is meaningless and not worth living, Sayyid Rizvi explained that death is considered liberation of the soul from the body. It is a necessary step in moving forward toward the ultimate goal of achieving paradise. These ideas have been presented within the Qur'an and the Sunna of the Prophet and the Imams. The Qur'an promises, "Every soul shall have a taste of death: And only on the Day of Judgment shall you be paid your full recompense. Only he who is saved far from the Fire and admitted to the Garden will have attained the object [of life]: For the life of this world is but goods and chattels of deception" (Q 3:185).[7]

According to Sayyid Rizvi, this verse spells out exactly what is to happen to a person and what his obligations are during this life. There is the promise of death and of heaven and hell, and there is the mention of the fact that this life is fleeting, and the ultimate goal is to avoid the fire (hell) and to attain the garden (heaven). Essential, from Rizvi's perspective, is the statement that the life of this world is "chattels of deception" and that it is not to be desired. These principles keep the believing men and women focused on their ultimate destiny.

The Qur'an also states, "Nor take life—which Allah has made sacred—except for just cause. And if anyone is slain wrongfully, we have given his heir authority [to demand qisas (retribution) or to forgive]: but let him nor exceed bounds in the matter of taking life; for he is helped [by the Law]" (Q 17:33). Rizvi reinforced that it is evident from this verse that life is sacred and that it should not be taken lightly. This command forms the basis of ethics in approaching matters of death. In virtually every situation considered throughout this study, the premature cessation of life was strictly abhorred by Grand Ayatollahs Sistani and al-Khu'i, as it is in violation of the basic tenets of the Qur'an and the will of God as expressed therein.

The statement above automatically begs the question that if the Qur'an condemns the taking of a life, what is its position on the saving of one? To this, the Qur'an replies: "On that account: We ordained for the Children of Israel that if any one slew a person—unless it be for murder or for spreading mischief in the land—it would be as if he slew the whole people: and if any one saved a life, it would be as if he saved the life of the whole people. Then although there came to them Our apostles with clear signs, yet, even after that, many of them continued to commit excesses in the land" (Q 5:32). In referring to this verse, Sayyid Rizvi suggested that the saving of a life in Islam according to the Qur'an is equated with saving the whole community. Thus there is a strong impetus for saving a life, and an even stronger one against taking a life unnecessarily.

From Qur'an 5:32, Sayyid Rizvi explained that we obtain a clear prohibition against taking a life, and the blessings associated with saving one. It is with the aid of this guiding principle that issues of end-of-life care are understood and specific issues have been interpreted by all Shiite grand ayatollahs in recent times. This principle ensures that the idea of euthanasia should be refuted categorically. It serves to actively preserve life and thus acts as the "anti-euthanasia" principle. Furthermore, Sayyid Rizvi explained that the verse also encompasses the idea that the preservation of life is meritorious, which fulfills the promise of the Qur'an in 2:155: "Be sure we shall test you with something of fear and hunger, some loss in goods or lives or the fruits (of your toil), but give glad tidings to those who patiently persevere."

This verse is further strengthened by the strict condemnation of suicide from the hadith of the Prophet and the Imams. For example, the sixth Imam, Ja'far al-Sadiq, said, "One who commits suicide is not from among us."[8] This verse also shows that God in the Qur'an commends those who persevere patiently. In fact, those who persevere are to be given good tidings—which in Qur'anic terms are meant as the good tidings of paradise.

We move from the theoretical perspective of saving life to situations where this principle is invoked. It is of particular importance in the life of the average person when he or she is critically ill and the prognosis is questionable. Another situation wherein families face confusion is the concept of brain death. Brain death has become a relatively established concept in the medical world in the past decade.

However, it has posed difficulties for families and has raised numerous questions for Shiite jurists.

Sayyid Rizvi explained that in Twelver Shiite jurisprudence, there are three main classifications of definitions: *shar'i*, *'ilmi*, and *'urfi*. A *shar'i* definition means something that is covered clearly by the Sharia, such as prayer. Here there are virtually no differences of opinion among generations of grand ayatollahs. An *'ilmi* definition is something that is arrived at by science or technology, such as the true horizon or phases of the moon. The last of these is the *'urfi* definition, which is the conventional definition—essentially the one that is understood by most laypeople. It is this logic that is most relevant in issues surrounding brain death. According to Sayyid Rizvi, Grand Ayatollah Sistani has considered the definition of death as *'urfi*. Grand Ayatollah Sistani does not consider brain death as equivalent to actual death, as it is not appreciable through normal senses; it requires machines such as an electroencephalogram. Therefore, unlike the majority of Sunni scholars, Grand Ayatollah Sistani does not consider brain death to be an acceptable definition of death at present. This fatwa is similar to one issued by Grand Ayatollah Khu'i. Sayyid Rizvi added during the interview that the only situation in which brain death is considered differently from life (but also from the traditional definition of death) is from a fatwa by the Iranian grand ayatollah Makarim Shirazi, who states that if a patient is considered brain dead, his power of attorney ceases to be valid, but the patient is not dead until he achieves "heart death."

We have alluded to the rapid changes in medicine affecting religious decision-making processes and how they impact families and jurists alike. Another scenario where this dilemma presents itself is in the context of the appropriateness of pursuing aggressive medical care near the end of life. This may manifest in two separate situations. First, a patient with a progressive illness (for example, cancer) may reach the point where standard treatments have failed, and he/she is left with the option of pursuing a palliative approach (one that focuses primarily on comfort care) or opting for further aggressive (often experimental or highly toxic/risky) measures, if available. The second scenario involves a patient with one or more chronic serious illnesses who experiences an acute deterioration because of either disease progression or a superimposed acute illness (for example, pneumonia). In discussions with Sayyid Rizvi about these situations, we learned that from a Shiite perspective, decision-making in this context hinges on a main factor: the issue of continuity of life. If, said Sayyid Rizvi, there is a reasonable chance that the ailment afflicting a person is curable or treatable and that person has several months or years of life left, then it becomes the person's religious imperative to pursue that treatment. However, if the prognosis for that disease has a poor outlook, then the person is allowed, religiously speaking, to seek a more conservative (and palliative, if applicable) course of treatment.

A palliative course of treatment implies that death will be forthcoming quickly. However, an oft-repeated statement within Shiite ceremonies of mourning is "Every soul shall have a taste of death in the end to Us shall ye be brought back" (Q 29:57). Believers are reminded that every soul will succumb to death and that it is a natural part of life. Rizvi also added (and advises Shiite Muslims) that there are limits to all things.

Though death is never easy to handle, in some scenarios it is particularly difficult for both families and medical practitioners, especially if the death was unexpected or sudden. In many such cases, autopsies may be requested by the physicians involved in order to ascertain the true cause(s) of death. According to Rizvi, the position of all Shiite jurists, including Sistani and al-Khu'i, is that an autopsy is considered to be a desecration of the body; it is a practice that is abhorred and to be refused by the family if requested. There are, however, important caveats to this position. In Sayyid Rizvi's experience, two such situations exist. Perhaps the more common, in his and our clinical experience, is when an autopsy is required by law. This usually happens through the office of the jurisdiction's coroner or equivalent health officer, which orders an autopsy to determine the cause of death when the death seems suspicious, accidental, or a result of criminal activity. In such situations, because it is a primary duty to follow the laws of the land where one resides, Sayyid Rizvi has advised families to oblige and allow the autopsies to be performed without hindrance to the authorities. These are considered extenuating circumstances in the eyes of Shiite jurists, and therefore the families bear no responsibility in the desecration of those bodies. The second situation, in Rizvi's experience, involves performing the autopsy to better understand the cause of death when the person was suffering from an illness that was not well defined or understood from a scientific point of view. In this situation, the autopsy is often requested to better characterize the illness with the hope of finding new treatments for others suffering from similar symptoms. Sayyid Rizvi explained that in this situation, both Sistani and al-Khu'i would permit an autopsy to take place if the life of another person was likely to be saved through the knowledge gained by the autopsy.

A natural question that arises from this concept of desecration of the body concerns the concept of donating one's body to medical science. All students of anatomy, including doctors, have benefited over the ages from the goodwill of people who have donated their bodies for the furthering of knowledge by allowing them to be dissected and studied. However, this practice, says Rizvi, is frowned on by Shiite jurists. It is still considered to be a desecration of the body and therefore is to be discouraged among Shiites. This begs the question: How do Shiite societies further the study of anatomy among their students if they have no bodies from which to learn? To this Rizvi answers that Shiite jurists would prefer that the body of a non-Muslim be used first to further the study; if no non-Muslim donor can be found, it then becomes permissible to use the body of a Muslim, but only if it is likely that the knowledge gained will assist in the saving of life and, furthermore, that this knowledge cannot easily be gained through less morally reprehensible means.

In discussing desecration of a body, mention should also be made of the practice of organ donation. With greater advances in immunosuppressive therapy and the science of transplantation, medical science has been able to remove organs from a dead person and transfer them to a living person with increasing success. In the world of organ donation, the practice is considered to be one of the noblest things that one person can do for another and is a truly altruistic act.[9] The question that is then posed to jurists is: Do the nobility of the act and the altruism of the donor supersede the desecration of the dead? Sayyid Rizvi noted that there are a variety of opinions as far as organ donation is concerned. These opinions correspond to specific scenarios that are predicated by the status of the donor (alive or deceased, human or nonhuman), the type of organ (dispensable/minor versus indispensable/major), and the type of recipient (Muslim or non-Muslim).

Medically speaking, organ donation is possible in limited circumstances between a living human and another living human, from a dead person to a living person, and from an animal to a human (although this is limited in scope). Sayyid Rizvi noted that though medical distinctions exist, religious distinctions also exist. In the eyes of jurists, two major distinctions are significant, those of minor and major organs. A minor organ is considered to be any tissue that can regenerate (for example, blood, marrow, skin, and a portion of liver) or a portion of nonregenerative tissue that the donor can survive without (for example, a second healthy kidney and a portion of lung). Major organs are those that cannot regenerate and the loss of which would be detrimental to the health of the donor.

Having considered the above medical and religious distinctions, Sayyid Rizvi noted that Grand Ayatollahs Sistani and al-Khu'i both allow the donation of minor organs during life. Additionally they also approve the receipt of any minor or major organ that comes from someone else (whether a human or nonhuman donor) in order to save one's own life. As mentioned above, all Shiite jurists consider the saving of one's own life to be of great importance and a religious duty. Rizvi clarified that where the distinction arises is in the issue of posthumous (after-death) donations. Grand Ayatollah Sistani disapproves of the donation of any organ after death. Additionally he considers a will or organ donation card that indicates the desire to donate organs to be invalid for that purpose. In recent times, however, Sistani has allowed for the organ donation after death only if the life of another Muslim depends on it. This holds true even if a will or testament stating this does not exist.[10] Rizvi pointed out that this differs for Grand Ayatollah al-Khu'i, who allows posthumous donation of all organs, as long as that donation does not desecrate the body beyond recognition. Rizvi clarified this position by saying that al-Khu'i ruled it acceptable to donate the organs of the internal cavity of the body but that any donation that will alter the outward appearance of the body (for example, eyes or skin) for the funeral is not allowed. Both Sistani and al-Khu'i approve of the donation of any tissue from an animal to a human being that will save the human's life—even if that animal is considered *najis* (ritually impure), as is the case with dogs and pigs.

Case 1

Salma was a sixty-two-year-old woman who underwent an elective gall bladder removal surgery (cholecystectomy).[11] She was otherwise in fairly good health. On the third postoperative day she was found without pulse and not breathing in her bed by a nurse doing on-call rounds. Cardiopulmonary resuscitation (CPR) was begun immediately; she was stabilized with a pulse and blood pressure and brought to the intensive care unit (ICU). Despite aggressive medical care, forty-eight hours later she remained completely unresponsive and required mechanical ventilation but had a stable pulse without medications. Various tests were done, including an electroencephalogram, and the family members were informed that Salma was brain dead. The ICU doctors proposed to withdraw all active care. Family members were not comfortable with this proposed plan and refused to withdraw care. Eventually the hospital ethics board became involved, and a Muslim chaplain on the hospital ethics board informed the family that there is a consensus among Muslim scholars that brain death is an acceptable criterion for death. The family, who were observant Twelver Shiite Muslims, were confused and sought clarification about the rulings of Grand Ayatollah Sistani in this matter.

Case 2

Abdul was a seventy-four-year-old man with chronic kidney disease requiring regular hemodialysis three times weekly. He developed fever, cough, and shortness of breath. He went to the emergency room and was admitted for pneumonia. After three days of antibiotics his condition worsened, and he suffered a small heart attack and became confused. The attending internist requested a do-not-resuscitate (DNR) order and suggested that Abdul not be admitted to the ICU if he deteriorated further, given his advanced age and poor prognosis. His wife was unable to make an immediate decision and requested more time to discuss issues with her family. In the middle of the night Abdul's condition worsened, and he required intubation, mechanical ventilation, and transfer to the ICU. Over the next few days he did not improve. The ICU physicians became more and more insistent on a DNR order and wanted to stop both his dialysis and mechanical ventilation. Abdul's wife tried to seek advice from leaders at her local mosque, but they felt uncomfortable commenting on this complex matter and referred her to a more learned scholar in Toronto. In the interim, Abdul developed a fatal complication from his infection and died. Abdul's family was suspicious about the circumstances of his death and wondered if something was missed. A sympathetic nurse encouraged Abdul's family to get an autopsy to determine the cause of death and satisfy themselves about whether he had received optimal medical care.

Commentary/Analysis

Although these scenarios represent composites of actual cases encountered by us and/or Sayyid Rizvi in clinical practice, they are fairly representative of the challenging issues faced by patients, families, and religious advisers. Salma's case was typical of a patient who is declared brain dead. This issue is becoming increasingly common in the technologically advanced intensive care units of hospitals in highly industrialized countries. Nonmedical readers may not appreciate the tremendous innovations in medical practice in the past few decades. Prior to the 1960s, and specifically prior to the introduction of CPR and mechanical ventilation, the concept of brain death simply did not exist; the definition of death had remained relatively unchanged since the time of Hippocrates. The past few decades have seen an explosion in medical technology such that artificial devices and medications can keep critically ill patients alive far more successfully than ever before. This came at a price, including the recognition that, in the absence of any measurable brain electrical activity, physicians could keep the heart and lungs, and thereby the rest of the body, of a brain-dead person alive for weeks or months. However, if the brain were dead, the body would never be able to come off the machine, and the person would never regain consciousness.

Similar to every other major faith-based ethical paradigm, Shiite medical ethics has had to confront the issue of brain death and whether it represents an alternate, acceptable definition of death. Sayyid Rizvi is quite familiar with this issue, having consulted patients facing this issue in the greater Toronto area and elsewhere. He has researched and provided opinions from Grand Ayatollahs al-Khu'i and Sistani on this matter. As mentioned earlier, according to Sayyid Rizvi, both jurists have ruled that brain death does not meet the *'urfi* definition of death presently. As such, Salma's family and others in a similar situation would be advised by scholars such as Rizvi to refuse to withdraw active care such as a mechanical ventilator. An important bioethical point that has come up in our clinical practice and is worthy of mention here is that Shiite jurists such as Sistani and al-Khu'i consider the withholding of medical interventions to be morally distinct from the withdrawal of them. In other words, if Salma were found to be brain dead prior to having been intubated and attached to a mechanical ventilator, then further medical treatment would not be necessary (because there would be no hope of recovery). However, if she were found to be brain dead after being intubated, which is more commonly the case, then mechanical ventilation could not be stopped (that is, the machine could not be "unplugged") until she died of other causes.

More problematic at a practical level than the treatment of a patient who meets medical criteria for brain death is that of a person who is acutely critically ill and has an underlying serious chronic medical illness, exemplified by Abdul's case. This can create difficulties for families of such patients. On the one hand, if there is any hope of curing a person within a reasonable amount of time,[12] or if life can be prolonged, then aggressive treatment should be provided and any do-not-resuscitate (DNR) order is considered invalid. Following the reasoning outlined above, although this life is fleeting and transient, it is still imperative for every person to try to live as long as possible and do what is necessary to prolong life. Furthermore, Rizvi pointed out that any person involved with the care of a person who can be fixed or cured is required by Islamic law to do everything within his or her power to continue therapy—to do otherwise would make them accountable in the eyes of God.

On the other hand, if there is no hope of a cure, then a person is not required to undergo "heroic measures" to prolong life. If indeed a person is terminally ill, that person is not required to accept a respirator, a heart-lung machine, or any extra medicine (such as chemotherapy) but is required to continue oral feeding and hydration,[13] and any DNR order that states the above is valid in this case. Rizvi explained that the most important thing to consider vis-à-vis the issue of life-sustaining treatment such as ventilators is that the decision should be based on whether there is a reasonable hope of cure or reversal of the condition. However, once life-sustaining treatment has been initiated, it cannot be removed or withdrawn until a natural organ death overcomes the person. Rizvi emphasized that neither brain death nor lack of response to treatment is a sufficient criterion to permit withdrawal of life-sustaining treatment, according to Sistani. This can pose a dilemma for a doctor and a family. If the patient is given an intervention in the hope of reversing the current medical illness but the situation turns out to be irreversible (and the patient is terminal), the patient ends up on life-sustaining therapy that cannot be withdrawn (for that would hasten death) but cannot benefit medically because the illness is irreversible (for example, progression of severe lung disease).

In situations such as these, Rizvi explained that the correct option is to err on the side of attempting to prolong life and put trust in God to manifest his will (that is, cause the patient to die when God wishes). It is also important to remember that if all measures have been taken to prolong life and the person dies anyway, then the family can be comfortable that they have fulfilled their responsibility to the sick person and can accept the decision that God has chosen for their loved one. Rizvi mentioned an oft-cited verse from the Qur'an in which God instructs humankind to "say, when afflicted with calamity: 'To Allah We belong, and to Him is our return'" (Q 2:156). This principle is to be taught to all believing Muslims at all times, and it is especially important in the grieving and consolation process following the death of a loved one.

In the case of Abdul, then, his pneumonia should originally have been treated because pneumonia is usually quite responsive to treatment. Once he deteriorated further, the appropriateness of ICU care for him, given his advanced age, chronic kidney failure, and recent heart attack, would have to be carefully considered. In such cases Rizvi has previously inquired of the medical team whether they felt the deterioration was caused by a potentially reversible illness or was a progression of an underlying, terminal, or incurable disease. In thes cases he has advised that aggressive care be encouraged, whereas in the latter, he has suggested it be discouraged, based on the opinions of Grand Ayatollah Sistani.

Abdul's case also touched on the issue of autopsy. In such cases Rizvi has advised families that the desire to clarify cause of death is not a sufficient criterion to allow, on religious grounds, an autopsy to take place. However, if Abdul were suffering from a mysterious or emerging illness that was poorly understood, and if an autopsy had a significant chance of obtaining knowledge that could be used to treat other victims of the same condition, then it would be justifiable. Alternatively, if a criminal investigation or coroner's inquiry were proceeding and an autopsy were deemed to be a necessary component of that process, then it would be permissible.

Limitations

There are several important limitations to this study. First and foremost, it covered only specific issues related to end-of-life care. We focused on the rulings of Grand Ayatollah Sistani and at times contrasted them with those of Grand Ayatollah al-Khu'i. Given the differences of opinion among current Shiite jurists, caution must be applied when extrapolating these views to those of other Shiiite *'ulama'*. Moreover our focus was on a particular Twelver Shiite community in Toronto, Canada, and much of our understanding was gleaned from one scholar (Sayyid Rizvi). Whether our findings would differ significantly if we sought out another *'alim* in another part of the world, whether Western or other, is unclear.

Because of space restrictions and our methodological approach, we did not explore in detail issues about comparative rulings among Shiite and Sunni sources. Nor did we discuss interactions between Shiite Muslim health-care professionals and non-Muslim patients or between Shiite Muslim patients and secular hospital ethics boards, particularly where differences of opinion exist or different frameworks are applied to decision making (for example, principlism versus Shiite medical ethics). Each of these issues is important, however, and deserves further exploration.

Conclusion

An attempt has been made to better understand the principles and practices of Shiite medical ethics as interpreted by modern scholars and jurists. This study focused on end-of-life care issues and highlighted some of the principles and moral reasoning that are involved in these cases, as well as touching on the complexities of medical practice. This area requires further academic scrutiny as some issues are evolving both medically and bioethically. The study of Shiite biomedical ethics is an important and yet relatively undescribed field of study.

TABLE 1. Summary of findings

	Ruling	Clarification
Organ Donation		
From Non-Muslim	Permissible	
From Nonhuman	Permissible	
From Muslim	Permissible	
To Non-Muslim	Permissible	
To Muslim	Permissible	
Posthumous donation	Permissible (al-Khu'i) Not permissible (Sistani)	Ayatollah Sistani does not allow for posthumous donation unless the life of a Muslim can be directly saved by the donation.
End of Life Care		
Withdrawal of care	Not permissible	Withholding and withdrawing care are not considered morally equivalent by Sistani or al-Khu'i
Withholding of care	Permissible	If person has a terminal condition and no reasonable hope of survival or prolonging life
Food, water	Mandatory	Considered to be part of basic care by Sistani and al-Khu'i
Extraordinary measures	Unclear*	This terminology has not been used by most current Shiite jurists
Experimental therapy	Unclear	This issue is primarily discussed within the context of withholding care
Autopsy	Not generally permissible, considered abhorrent	Permissible to save another's life or if mandated by state, but not for medical or scientific research

*Currently this question has not been brought to the *mujtahid* for his ruling. As it is considered a controversial issue, it may be several years before there is a clear opinion/ruling given on this subject. For our current purposes, it may be best to suggest that one seek an opinion at the local level that can then be referred to Grand Ayatollah Sistani for further review.

NOTES

1. Ludwig Edelstein, *The Hippocratic Oath: Text, Translation, and Interpretation* (Baltimore: Johns Hopkins University Press, 1943), http://www.pbs.org/wgbh/nova/doctors/oath_classical.html, accessed February 13, 2005.

2. Moojan Momen, *An Introduction to Shi'i Islam* (New Haven, Conn.: Yale University Press, 1985), 150. We are speaking here, as in the rest of this essay, in the sole context of Twelver Shiism. This is not to be confused with any other form of Shiism.

3. Ibid., 165.

4. This is according to a personal interview with Sayyid Muhammad Rizvi, conducted by Iqbal Jaffer in Toronto, 2004.

5. Shabbir Alibhai has had clinical discussions with Sayyid Rizvi in which Sayyid Rizvi sought medical input from him on complex clinical cases.

6. Personal interview with Sayyid Muhammad Rizvi, Toronto, 2004.

7. The translation of the Qur'an is by Yusuf 'Ali.

8. Ayatullāh Sayyid Abu l-Qāsim al-Khū'ī, *Rationality of Islam*, http://al-islam.org/rationality/2.htm, accessed May 31, 2007.

9. The perception of this act as altruistic may be unique to Western civilizations; see Hamdy's discussion of this issue in the essay titled "Rethinking Islamic Legal Ethics in Egypt's Organ Transplant Debate" in this volume.

10. "Contemporary Legal Rulings in Shī'ī Law in Accordance with the Rulings (Fatāwā) of Ayatullah al-'Uzma al-Sayyid'Ali al-Husayni al-Seestani," as found on http://al-shia.com/html/eng/books/contemporary/index.htm, accessed May 31, 2007. In this scenario, Sistani also specifies that if the excision of the organs is done without a will indicating that it is the preference of the deceased to do so, the person who removes the organs is liable to pay the *diya* (blood money). If, however, the excision occurs with the indication through a will that it was the deceased's wish to be a donor, then there is no *diya* to be paid. On a practical level, in Western societies in most cases it is not the decision of the donor who will receive the organs after the donor's death. Therefore it would be exceedingly difficult to ascertain that the recipient would be a Muslim. In such a situation, it is not presently clear whether Sistani would deem it permissible to allow posthumous donation.

11. Names and specific details have been modified to protect patient confidentiality.

12. There is no standard definition of what is considered reasonable. Common sense must therefore be applied within each specific context.

13. Sayyid Rizvi pointed out that Shiite jurists distinguish the issue of oral feeding and hydration from that of aggressive care. This is because the former is considered part of basic care (which should never be withdrawn from a human being), whereas the latter can be withheld in specific circumstances as discussed above.

SHABBIR M. H. ALIBHAI *and* MICHAEL GORDON

A Comparative Analysis of Islamic and Jewish End-of-Life Ethics

A Case-Based Approach

"The life span of any civilization can be measured by the respect and care that is given to its elderly citizens and those societies which treat the elderly with contempt have the seeds of their own destruction within them."[1] Ethical dilemmas pervade modern medicine, especially in the care of older adults at the end of life. Issues such as the assessment of mental capacity, the use of advance directives (AD), do-not-resuscitate (DNR) orders, the approach to feeding disorders, and many others vex clinicians, patients, and their families daily. Although these issues are by no means restricted to older adults, they commonly occur in this patient population, and some issues, such as assessing mental capacity or the appropriateness of feeding tubes in advanced dementia, occur almost exclusively among elders. The question as to what is considered right or wrong in each of these situations is often greatly influenced by the religion of the patient, the family, and/or the clinician. Among other considerations, religious views often influence, either implicitly or explicitly, the medical decisions taken (or not taken).

Clinicians in Western countries will commonly come across adherents to Islam and Judaism among their older patients. Both faiths have carefully worked out positions on medical ethics. Many clinicians will not be of the same religious persuasion as their patients, and a lack of understanding of where the patient is "coming from" may cause confusion, misunderstandings, unnecessary conflict, or even untoward clinical events. By comparing and contrasting the positions taken by these two religions via a case-based approach, we intend to clarify the formal religious perspective for some of the relevant ethical issues in elder care.

For reasons of space, this essay is concerned with the Orthodox majority opinion among Sunni and Shiite sects. Where there are differences, the focus is on the Shiite perspective of the *Ja'fari madhhab* (school of thought) and reference to juridical rulings by recent *'ulama'* (religious scholars). Judaism has only one set of laws, with the Orthodox, Conservative, and Reform branches all agreeing on the form and principles of Jewish Law (Halacha—literally, "the way") but differing in the strictness of their adherence and approaches to interpretation of it.

In the following discussion offers an introduction to the formal, normative approach of both religions. Given the wide diversity of religious practice within each faith and different levels of adherence, we do not discuss how adherents would or should behave within their own religions but instead describe the formal approach taken by Orthodox Judaism and the orthodox Sunni/Shiite sects of Islam. Space does not allow us to be all-inclusive, nor to cover all aspects of this complex field for which a voluminous literature exists with respect to each religion. It must also be acknowledged that within these religious frameworks there is a process of evolution and ethical interpretation so that over time there may be some signficant adjustments to how individuals are expected to act, especially in the face of major changes in the world of medical technology and its profound impact on the care of patients, especially in what in the past were fatal or clearly end-of-life situations.

A much used and accepted (in the Western world especially) classification for discussing medical ethics involves Beauchamp and Childress's "four principles," which include autonomy, beneficence, nonmaleficence, and distributive justice.[2] While not all-inclusive, they do provide a useful starting point and framework for ethical considerations in general and for each religion in particular.[3]

Judaism

Judaism originated around 1500 B.C.E. At present there are approximately 13.25 million Jews (who acknowledge their affiliation or heritage) in the world—an increase of approximately 2.25 million from the end of World War II. The substantial loss of Jewish lives during the Holocaust has made contemporary demographics somewhat challenging. Of this number, the main population centers are the diaspora (8.3 million) and Israel (about 5.0 million), with North America having the largest diaspora population followed by Europe (the European Union and former Soviet Union have the greatest numbers). The rest are scattered all over the world, with a substantial number residing in Latin America. Of those who consider themselves Jewish, about 1.7 to 1.8 million, or approximately 13.5 percent of the population, identify themselves as observant or Orthodox in their belief and practices. The distribution of Orthodox and non-Orthodox (secular, conservative, reformed, for example) varies from country to country and community to community.

Jewish medical ethics is based on the concept of Jewish law (Halacha).[4] Halacha is derived from three main sources: the Torah (the first five books of the Old Testament of the Bible), the Talmud, and the Responsa (a collection of rabbinical opinions about the first two sources). The normative Orthodox approach toward Jewish medical ethics is presented here. Unlike the case of Islam, there are no significant theological differences within Judaism, that is, between the Reform, Conservative and Orthodox branches. All share essentially the same system of law and belief. However, the degrees of observance and practice differ between them, and not the rules of the system per se.

Within Judaism, the physician has clear obligations with respect to the duty to heal. The patient has a comparable obligation comprising the duty to be healed, which in practice enjoins him/her to both seek and follow medical advice. Sanctity of life is a paramount principle, and human life is deemed to be of infinite value. Although illness and death are considered natural parts of life, one is duty-bound to strive to save a life (short of doing so by committing murder, incest, or public idolatry).

Jews are considered responsible stewards of their bodies. Therefore autonomy for the individual, as espoused in secular principlism, is not a paramount feature of Halacha. Here, collective, in addition to individual values, are relevant, and often even more so. Relief of suffering is also important, as is the duty to care for one's parents in old age. The process of dying must be respected when it is clearly occurring, imminent, and irreversible (*goses*).

Beneficence is a major goal, as is nonmaleficence. The latter has taken on a new and even greater imperative since the Holocaust and the resultant harm done by medical practitioners to nonconsenting individuals.[5] In discussing Israeli legislation on medical ethical issues, Gross explains that for Jews, "sanctity of life is not only a religious norm but reflects the need of many Jews to persevere in the face of historical catastrophe."[6] There have, however, been some significant shifts within Israel to accommodate changes in the impact of modern medicine and the balance between sanctity-of-life issues and the avoidance of unnecessary suffering.[7] Distributive justice is an important concept, but the primary goal of medical practice is to secure maximum resources for the individual patient.

Islam

The laws and ethics of Islam come from four sources, only one of which differs between Sunni and Shiite sects. Both sects hold the Qur'an and the Sunna of Prophet Muhammad to be the first two sources and *ijma‘* (consensus) as a major source. Shiites place *‘aql* (reasoning) before *ijma‘*, whereas Sunnis hold *qiyas* (analogy) as the fourth source after *ijma‘*.

The Muslim has duties toward his Creator and fellow human beings, duties that cannot be separated from the attached rights.[8] The reciprocity of rights and duties exists between a Muslim and everything around him; no right exists in a vacuum.[9] For example, while Muslims believe that all healing comes ultimately from God, they have a duty to seek out medical attention when ill and a right to receive appropriate medical care.[10] In turn, the physician has clear obligations to heal.

Sanctity of life is a paramount principle. Every moment of life is precious and must be preserved. Only in rare circumstances (for example, for committing murder, idolatry, or adultery) is the taking of a person's life justified. However, Islam recognizes that death is an inevitable part of human existence. Thus treatment does not have to be provided if it merely prolongs the final stages of a terminal illness; in contrast, treating a superimposed, life-threatening condition is mandatory.

Human beings are considered to be responsible stewards of their bodies, which are viewed as gifts from God. Thus autonomy, while recognized within both Islam and Judaism, is of secondary importance.[11] Suffering is seen to have both positive and negative qualities. In particular, suffering is often seen as either a test from God for the believer or a punishment for (and expiation of) sins. At the same time, suffering is seen to come from either God or fellow human beings; while the former has redemptive properties, the latter is seen as unnecessary (from a divine perspective) and important to alleviate. Other important concepts include the obligation to feed and hydrate the dying person as well as the duties of children to care for their parents.[12]

When comparing Islamic medical ethics to secular principlism, beneficence and nonmaleficence are major, complementary goals. Distributive justice has played a relatively minor role in Islamic ethics to date, as the emphasis has been on the individual patient.

Three cases based on our clinical experiences illustrate the challenges and complexities of applying the ethical principles and concepts discussed above in clinical situations. These cases are composites; they are meant to be illustrative and do not represent actual patients. Key questions are provided after each case, followed by responses from Jewish and Islamic perspectives.

Case 1

An eighty-six-year-old, cognitively intact woman with coronary artery disease presents with a massive stroke. Over two months she remains unconscious with complete paralysis of one side of her body. Based on the opinion of her consultant neurologist, her chance of significant neurologic recovery (that is, regaining conscious awareness and use of limbs on the affected side) is virtually nil. She has no advance directive. Her family has strong religious convictions and requests a permanent feeding tube. While this discussion occurs, she develops a fever and cough and is diagnosed with pneumonia. The doctors ask the family if the pneumonia should be treated, given her poor overall prognosis.

The children insist that the doctors must under no circumstances tell the patient's elderly husband about her bleak long-term prognosis, as "the information would surely kill him." He is cognitively intact and keeps asking about his wife's condition.

Various questions and considerations should be taken into account at this point. Is it appropriate to insert or refuse to insert a feeding tube in this patient? Should her pneumonia be treated? How would you respond to the husband's queries?

Case 1 Response from a Jewish Perspective

In Judaism, the family's request for a feeding tube is understandable as it relates to the concept of the sanctity of life and the obligation to provide nourishment unless such feeding causes significant suffering. Pneumonia requires active treatment as long as the person is not clearly in the process of dying (*goses*). With respect to the children's request that their father not be told, when it is clear that informing him might truly offer a risk to his health, Halacha does enjoin the physician to withhold or at least to postpone bad news.[13] However, if possible, a truthful, supportive explanation would be preferable.

Case 1 Response from a Muslim Perspective

Islamic ethics would support the use of a feeding tube if there were a possibility of extending life (sanctity-of-life principle). Furthermore, there is a religious obligation to provide nourishment unless such an act shortens life. Nutritional support, at least enterally (using the person's own gut to absorb the nutrition), is considered by most Islamic scholars to be part of basic care rather than a medical treatment. The pneumonia would warrant treatment since it is potentially reversible and would not be viewed as a terminal illness.

It would be difficult to justify withholding information from the husband for two reasons. First, Islam holds that truth should be upheld at almost any cost, and deception is rarely justifiable, except in case of risk to one's life. Second, there is a formal hierarchy of decision-makers within Islamic law, and the patient's husband would be her surrogate decision-maker. Thus he would require information to make informed decisions on his wife's behalf.

Case 2

An eighty-four-year-old woman with mild dementia and stable congestive heart failure is admitted to a nursing home. Her husband, the surrogate decision-maker, presents the attending physician with a signed and witnessed advanced directive (AD), which states that under no circumstances does she want resuscitation (DNR), antibiotic therapy for life-threatening infection, or to be transferred to an acute-care hospital in case of acute illness.

How should the staff respond to these requests, especially if the requests go against their own religious convictions even in the face of an AD that would be deemed legal in the jurisdiction in which it was executed?

The patient falls ill and develops a decreased level of consciousness secondary to an infection. She is unable to communicate. How should the staff respond?

Case 2 Response from a Jewish Perspective

In Jewish law, the opinion of the staff is far less important than that of the surrogate. It is primarily to the husband that the AD speaks, and he is duty-bound to interpret the situation in its light. If he believes that his wife's requests do not contradict her deep-seated values, there would be no reason not to follow them. If he were a deeply religious person questioning a DNR order, he might want to get rabbinical advice to determine whether such a request contravenes Halacha. If the patient were an Orthodox Jew, she might have requested rabbinical input into her AD, which would now be of great value to the surrogate decision-maker.

When the patient developed a new infection with a decreased level of consciousness, there was a new immediacy because of the need to make an urgent decision about whether to treat her infection. Additionally, with her infection, she temporarily lost any ability to communicate her wishes. Her surrogate would still be expected to make decisions, with the staff having no formal role other than to provide the relevant clinical information. While Halacha might formally favor treatment if there were a chance of survival, the patient/surrogate may refuse such an approach, especially if the prognosis is grave, the suffering substantial, and the treatment effectiveness questionable (although some rabbis might differ on the imperative to treat the infection).

Case 2 Response from a Muslim Perspective

Although there is little published literature on the subject, Islam would probably acknowledge the role of ADs in communicating patients' wishes.[14] Although staff members cannot be forced to perform actions contrary to their own beliefs, the patient's expressed wishes must be respected. An observant Muslim might seek input from a local religious authority when formulating an AD. When the woman's level of consciousness deteriorates, these directives must still be respected. Although an observant Muslim would be obligated to accept treatment under Islamic law, one cannot compel someone to accept life-sustaining therapy if that person refuses it.

Case 3

An eighty-seven-year-old man with advanced lung cancer that has spread to his bones and other organs is admitted to an acute-care hospital for pain control. He is fed via a permanent feeding tube that was previously inserted into his stomach, but it aspirates food content into his lungs in the middle of the night, leading to an inability to breathe on his own. He is intubated, put on mechanical ventilation, and transferred to the intensive care unit. In the morning when the senior physician makes rounds, she is informed by the children that their father had told all of them that he would never want to "end his days on a machine," as did his late wife, who died of intractable congestive heart failure only several months previously. There is no written advance directive, but his clear wishes had been expressed verbally on multiple occasions in the recent past.

Several questions need consideration in this case. Should he have been intubated and put on mechanical ventilation? Can life support (that is, the ventilator) be discontinued in accordance with the patient's request, either as expressed directly or as transmitted to the team by the children?

Case 3 Response from a Jewish Perspective

With Halacha, intubation would be considered reasonable at the time of intervention, as the saving of a life would appear to be paramount. However, once the children inform the physicians that their father had clearly indicated his wish never to be intubated under such circumstances and since he has a terminal disease, according to Halacha, treatment could be discontinued.

The withdrawal of life-maintaining treatment would be acceptable on two counts: first, out of respect for the patient's autonomy; and second, since the patient suffers from terminal cancer, where discontinuation of treatment would be justified within the framework of a *goses* (someone whose death is imminent). In this situation, medical intervention that might disturb the imminent dying process would not be allowed.

Case 3 Response from a Muslim Perspective

Islam's position would favor intubation and mechanical ventilation unless aspiration were viewed as the final stage of a terminal illness rather than a potentially reversible life-threatening illness. Once it becomes clear that the patient would never have wanted to be intubated under such circumstances, the issue revolves around the permissibility of withdrawing life-sustaining treatment. The majority of Muslim scholars would allow withdrawal of the respirator, recognizing that this would lead to a rapid demise. However, a minority of scholars, including the majority of the Shiite sect, hold that withholding and withdrawing care are not morally equivalent. This is similar to the Jewish approach. In other words, while it would be permissible not to intubate in the first instance, once the patient is intubated, this treatment cannot be discontinued if this hastens death.[15]

Discussion

Clearly, with respect to end-of-life medical ethics, Islam and Judaism have much in common, in both principles and practice. Modern Judaism is particularly sensitive to the issue of nonmaleficence because of Jewry's experience of the Holocaust in general and Nazi medical "experimentation" on Jewish concentration camp captives in particular.[16]

In their formal expressions, however, the religions do differ in several domains (as outlined in table 1). Of cardinal interest, especially for health-care professionals practicing in North America, is how both faiths treat the principle of autonomy. As opposed to Western secular ethics, in which autonomy is the primary ethical principle, in both Islam and Judaism, autonomy (while respected) is less paramount in the decision-making process to the patient's health and welfare as judged by a duopoly of "experts"—clinician and cleric.

TABLE 1. Comparison of Judaism and Islam with respect to several principles and relevant issues in end-of-life bioethics

Principle/Issue	Judaism	Islam
Autonomy	+	+
Beneficence	+++	+++
Nonmaleficence	++++	+++
Justice	+	+
Role of family/community	+++	+++
Second religious opinion	+	+/-
Withholding truth	**	*
Moral equivalence of withholding or withdrawing treatment	*	**
Withholding nutrition	*	*
Use of AD	*	+/-

Key:
+ to ++++ : least to most important
* to *** : least to most acceptable
+/- : not well formulated

Evidence of the powerful effect of Halacha on all Jews, beyond its acceptance by the more observant, may be seen through an examination of a recently passed piece of "secular" legislation in Israel, the Patient Rights Act. (It is of interest to note that 80 percent of Israeli Jews are not particularly observant.) Despite its general support for patient autonomy, the law does provide a clause enabling the setting up of a hospital "ethics committee" (including physicians, lawyers, psychologists, and ethicists). This body may act in the court's stead to determine action when a competent patient rejects "life-saving" treatment. Compared to the previous act of 1966, this act allows a greater degree of decision-making to withdraw treatment in terminally ill patients either at their request or at the request of their surrogates. Prior to this new iteration of the act, scholars such as Gross criticized the previous act as an assault on autonomy and pointed out that the

Patients' Rights Act of 1966 "is probably the only example of legislation designed to override a patient's right to *informed* consent and to treat one against one's will."[17] The recent change with the new act allows for patients and surrogates to refuse treatment if they believe the treatment will not offer them significant well-being (primarily geared toward the dying patient). This law has just been introduced and is expected to have a profound effect on end-of-life decision-making and the processes in palliative care.[18] If similar laws have been enacted in any predominantly Muslim countries, we are not aware of them.

Within Judaism the patient is free to pick his or her physician and rabbi. However, when a rabbinical judgment is requested, no rabbinic "second opinion" is tolerated, although both cleric and physician are expected to consult as widely as necessary. From the point of view of the physician, there is no restriction on requesting a second opinion. As the new law in Israel takes effect, some of its influence is expected to influence practice in the diaspora as well, especially in the process of an ethics committee in which a rabbi (different from one's own chosen rabbi) is a member. Unlike the ethics committees as determined by law in Israel, in which a recommendation for treatment is expected, most North American ethics committees provide deliberation and advice to staff and families but have no authority for decision-making. In Islam, the local religious leader is looked upon to facilitate interpretation of religious rulings at the level of the individual patient. The existence, composition, and roles of ethics committees vary tremendously across Muslim countries. Of note, few ethics committees in North America, in our experience, include experts in Islamic law or bioethics.

Several important issues arise when considering commonly accepted secular bioethics principles. For example, both Judaism and Islam acknowledge and respect patient autonomy in general, yet they limit it in particular circumstances, such as suicide.[19] Because they consider life to be sacred, its preservation overrides almost all other religious commandments, as well as any right to autonomy. From the secular point of view of some clinicians, deferring to the judgment of a religious leader may appear to be an apparent dereliction of personal duty by religious Jews and Muslims, yet one could consider the patient's autonomy to be exercised via a conscious transfer of (most of) that autonomy to the chosen religious adviser.

Other principles function in a similarly nuanced fashion. For example, neither faith is particularly concerned about the issue of distributive justice, as they consider the patient to be the ultimate focus of attention without allowing (at least in theory) considerations of resource allocation to have influence. Regarding truth telling, the formal Islamic position is more concerned about disclosure, whereas Judaism is willing to allow the truth to be partially withheld if it is judged that the unadulterated truth would cause serious harm to a patient.[20]

There is a debate concerning whether the physician should be involved in the spiritual life of the patient,[21] and some literature suggests the beneficial impact of religious belief and prayer through faith on healing. However, this subject is in its infancy in terms of development and investigative scrutiny and is expected to be difficult to study scientifically. While this difficult question is not addressed here, a physician's faith can have implications for the care of patients. For example, some Orthodox patients may prefer a Jewish Orthodox physician, if available, because they assume he or she will be more sensitive to their religious needs and expectations.

In general Orthodox Jewish physicians are expected to follow the rules of Halacha, but these may be suspended if required for the care of their patients. For example, attending ill people on major holy days is expected, but the physician may walk to the hospital or sleep over rather than desecrate the holy day by driving, although if it were required by an emergency, that too would be allowed. When there is a significant conflict of values in a decision-making process, a physician may get advice from his/her rabbi or request that another physician undertake the care as long as this does not entail any compromising of the patient's well-being.

From an Islamic perspective, there is no formal recommendation for a Muslim patient to seek out a Muslim physician as opposed to a non-Muslim physician. Every Muslim patient is encouraged to find the most competent physician to provide medical care, irrespective of the physician's faith. One potential advantage of having a physician of the same faith as the patient is that the physician would likely be sensitive to the demands of religion on the medical care of the patient. A not uncommon scenario might involve a request from a non-Muslim patient to a Muslim physician that goes against the physician's beliefs. It is clear that a Muslim physician cannot be compelled to participate in medical acts that would be considered morally wrong (for example, active euthanasia). At the same time, a Muslim physician would not be expected to force her views on a patient (or act against the patient's expressed wishes) who may be behaving in a manner that is against Islamic teaching (for example, refusal of life-saving antibiotics as in case 2).[22] Some Western countries have enshrined within their codes of ethics a mechanism for transferring a patient to another physician in circumstances where the patient requests medical care that the physician is not prepared to provide on ethical grounds. Such a mechanism does not appear to have been formally discussed to date within Islamic bioethical circles.

Conclusion

Judaism and Islam have much in common with respect to medical ethics, but they do differ in some important aspects. Because of space limitations, only a sample of relevant issues is included here. The interested reader is referred to a recent comprehensive series on bioethics (www.cmaj.ca/cgi/collection/bioethics_for_clinicians_series) for detailed treatments of both religions as well as many others. As well, others have offered comparative and thoughtful analyses of religion and medical care.[23] We believe that comparing and contrasting formal religious approaches to geriatric ethical dilemmas is more than an interesting intellectual exercise; it can also provide the clinician with a range of possibilities for dealing with our increasingly multicultural societies and clientele. Moreover modern medicine and science continue to innovate in the area of health care, prolonging life, reducing disability, and improving quality of life. As such developments continue, all of us will have to find ways to make these innovations congruent with our underlying religious values. Adherents of Judaism and Islam deserve the support they need from their religion and religious advisers during the most difficult of life's situations.

NOTES

1. Attributed to Arnold Toynbee. We thank Mark Clarfield for helping to initiate this interfaith dialogue/discussion. Our thanks also go to Abdallah S. Daar, S. Muhammad Rizvi, and Shimon Glick for their insightful comments on an earlier version of this essay.

2. Beauchamp and Childress, *Principles of Biomedical Ethics.*

3. A. Steinberg, "A Jewish Perspective on the Four Principles," in *Principles of Health Care Ethics,* ed. R. Gillon (New York: John Wiley and Sons, 1994), 3–12; Serour, "Islam and the Four Principles," 75–92; K. Z. Hasan, "Islam and the Four Principles: A Pakistani View," in *Principles of Health Care Ethics,* ed. Gillon, 93–103. While principlism is a commonly used ethical framework in many Western countries, it is not commonly adopted in other parts of the world. A variety of other frameworks, both religious and secular, may operate in those settings.

4. G. Goldsand, Z. R. Rosenberg, and M. Gordon, "Bioethics for Clinicians: 22. Jewish Bioethics," *Canadian Medical Association Journal* 164, no. 2 (2001): 219–22.

5. R. J. Lifton, *The Nazi Doctors: Medical Killing and the Psychology of Genocide* (New York: Perseus Books, 1988).

6. M. L. Gross, "Medical Ethics Committees in Israel: Implementing the Israel Patient Rights Act and Terminating Life-Sustaining Treatment," *Israeli Medical Association Journal* 3, no. 6 (2001): 461–64.

7. J. Kunin, "Should Patients Be Told the Truth about Their Illnesses? Jewish Perspectives," *Israeli Medical Association Journal* 4, no. 9 (2002): 737–41; I. Marciano, "Knesset Approves Passive Euthanasia Law," YNet News (September 29, 2006), http://www.ynetnews.com/articles/0,7340,L-3180403,00.html.

8. A. Khan, "Islamic Philosophy and Medical Ethics," in *Islamic Perspectives in Medicine,* ed. S. Athar (Indianapolis: American Trust Publications, 1993), 103–5; Daar and al-Khitamy, "Bioethics for Clinicians," 60–63.

9. S. S. A. Rizvi, trans., *The Charter of Rights (Risalatu 'l-Huquq)* (Vancouver: Vancouver Islamic Educational Foundation, 1989).

10. H. Mavani, trans., *A Guide to Islamic Medical Ethics* (Montreal: Organization for the Advancement of Islamic Knowledge and Humanitarian Services, 1998).

11. K. M. Hedayat and R. Pirzadeh, "Issues in Islamic Biomedical Ethics: A Primer for the Pediatrician," *Pediatrics* 108, no. 4 (2001): 965–71.

12. Hasan, "Islam and the Four Principles."

13. Kunin, "Should Patients Be Told the Truth?"

14. A. F. Ebrahim, "The Living Will (*Wasiyat Al-Hayy*): A Study of Its Legality in the Light of Islamic Jurisprudence," *Medical Law* 19, no. 1 (2000): 147–60.

15. Mavani, *Guide to Islamic Medical Ethics* 8.

16. Lifton, *Nazi Doctors;* Gross, "Medical Ethics Committees in Israel."

17. Gross, "Medical Ethics Committees in Israel," 461.

18. M. Y. Barilan, "Dying with Dignity: New Euthanasia Law Provides Breakthrough for Synagogue-State Relations," YNet News (February 3, 2006), http://www.ynetnews.com/articles/0,7340,L-3180888,00.html.

19. Jonathan Brockopp discusses suicide within an Islamic context, along with its relationship with both euthanasia and martyrdom, in his essay "The Good Death in Islamic Theology and Law," in *Islamic Ethics of Life: Abortion, War, and Euthanasia,* ed. Jonathan E. Brockopp (Columbia: University of South Carolina Press, 2003), 177–93.

20. Kunin, "Should Patients Be Told the Truth?"

21. R. P. Sloan and others, "Should Physicians Prescribe Religious Activities?," *New England Journal of Medicine* 342, no. 25 (2000): 1913–16. Faiz Khan addressed this issue at the Penn State conference; his paper is being prepared for publication in the *Journal of Religious Ethics* as "An Islamic Appraisal of Minding the Gap: Psycho-Spiritual Dynamics in the Doctor-Patient Relationship."

22. *Islamic Code of Medical Ethics* (Kuwait: First International Conference on Islamic Medicine, Islamic Organization for Medical Sciences, 1981).

23. E. R. DuBose, ed., *Religious Beliefs and Health Care Decisions: A Quick Reference to 15 Religious Traditions and Their Application in Health Care* (Chicago: Park Ridge Center for the Study of Health, Faith, and Ethics, 1995); T. P. Hill, *The Challenges of Aging: Retrieving Spiritual Traditions, Special Topics in Health and Faith* (Chicago: Park Ridge Center for the Study of Health, Faith, and Ethics, 1999).

STEF VAN DEN BRANDEN *and* BERT BROECKAERT

Medication and God at Interplay

End-of-Life Decision-Making in Practicing Male Moroccan Migrants Living in Antwerp, Flanders, Belgium

As a result of the arrival of millions of migrants, European societies have undergone wide-scale demographic and cultural changes. Previous to 1956, for example, the Belgian government employed Italian laborers in its coal mines, a poorly paid and dangerous job. After 1956, the year of the great disaster in the coal mines at Marcinelles, the Italian state no longer wanted its employees to work in these situations, and Belgium started recruiting workers from other countries. The Moroccan government was eager to send workers from the impoverished Berber-speaking northern Rif areas of the country, resulting in the migration of a specific social cohort of the population: the generally uneducated and illiterate rural inhabitants. The Belgian experience with labor migration is similar to the situation in France and Germany, to name only two neighboring European countries where this is the case.[1]

Because of this type of demographic and cultural change, palliative care in Europe can no longer cling to a Christian or secular conceptual frame of reference to explain general attitudes toward ethical decisions. In Belgium, as in the majority of Western European countries, Islam has expanded to become the second-largest religion. However, this turn of events fails to be duly reflected in the public debate on euthanasia in Belgium or in any other Europe-wide biomedical debate.

This essay focuses on the way in which elderly Moroccan men in Antwerp (Flanders, Belgium) link their faith in God with the use and the effects of medication surrounding the end of life.[2] It should not be surprising that religious and ideological affiliation have a considerable impact on attitudes toward ethical decisions surrounding the end of life; yet, little in-depth research has been conducted in this area. In the limited amount of research that has effectively been performed on the topic, religion as a factor was invariably operationalized only on a rudimentary level, with little attention given to the attitudes of minorities in society in relation to ethical end-of-life decision-making.[3]

End-of-Life Decisions

"A doctor should never take someone's life or shorten it. No matter how he suffers, God is the one who decides about life and death. A doctor should try to soften the suffering as much as possible by using medicine. But he shouldn't kill." This statement by a Moroccan physician, who was trained in Belgium and practices there, reveals the importance of religious language when discussing end-of-life issues. It also highlights the salient issues at stake in any discussion of euthanasia among Moroccans living in Belgium. In international literature, the term *euthanasia* is understood and interpreted in a variety of ways. Often the term is found to be qualified by additional adjectives, such as active versus passive, direct versus indirect, and voluntary versus nonvoluntary, or involuntary. In response to the prevailing language confusion, and setting out from a strict definition of the term *euthanasia,* Bert Broeckaert compiled a typology with regard to ethical decision-making surrounding the end of life, for which he uses *end-of-life decisions* as an umbrella term. Not all of the seven elements in this typology are touched on in this essay, which deals only with issues of pain control ("the intentional administration of analgesics and/or other drugs in dosages and combinations required to adequately relieve pain"), voluntary euthanasia ("the administration of lethal drugs in order to painlessly terminate the life of a patient suffering from an incurable condition deemed unbearable by the patient, at this patient's request"), assisted suicide ("intentionally assisting a person, at this person's request, to terminate his or her life"), and nonvoluntary euthanasia ("the administration of lethal drugs in order to painlessly terminate the life of a patient suffering from an incurable condition deemed unbearable, not at this patient's request").[4]

Methodology

Broeckaert's typology of end-of-life decisions was broken down into seven cases that formed the basis for semistructured, in-depth interviews with ten Moroccan men, aged sixty and over, who were living in Antwerp.[5] In an attempt to map out the religious network of the respondents in as meaningful a manner as possible, and in order to guarantee the external validity of the study, we also interviewed two leading Antwerp Imams (Arabic: *fuqaha'* or *'ulama'*) and two Moroccan Muslim general practitioners.[6]

The age of the initial group of ten men varied between sixty and eighty, and all were practicing Muslims. The two Imams, ages thirty-two and thirty-four years, grew up as children in Antwerp, and one of them was born in Antwerp. The Muslim general practitioners were both born in Morocco. One was forty-five years of age and had a Riffian rural background (Berber). His colleague was thirty-eight and from Casablanca, a Moroccan urban environment. Both finished their medical studies at the Université Libre de Bruxelles (ULB Belgium) and were asked by the Moroccan embassy to locate in Antwerp.

The majority of the ten respondents had little or no command of Dutch, speaking Tamazight (a Berber language) or Moroccan Arabic as their mother language and Standard Arabic to a limited degree,[7] which necessitated the help of an interpreter. The interviews with the Muslim general practitioners were conducted in Dutch and French without the interpreter. The Grounded Theory Methodology acknowledges that resorting to the services of an interpreter is not a neutral element: his interventions did influence the research. This served to instigate a triple subjectivity situation, with due interaction between the three subjects of meaning creation: the respondent, the researcher, and the interpreter.[8] For the course of this article, quotes recorded as part of this study are used.[9]

Life as a Gift from God

The ten respondents described life as a gift that God offers humanity and which they as God's vice regents on earth are to administer in good stewardship. This good stewardship manifests itself through the Islamic way of life, which, in a concrete sense, is based on the rhythm of ritual events, including the strict observance of the five daily times of prayer. Nearly all respondents stated that they complemented these compulsory elements with voluntary prayers and days of fasting. These practices are closely associated with the vision of life as a test for which humanity is to be judged in the afterlife. Their descriptions of the importance attached to the compulsory and voluntary aspects of prayer showed the strong extent to which they think in terms of reward for good deeds in the hereafter. In this respect, several of the ten respondents distinguished between the value of a prayer said at home, the value of a prayer said at the mosque, and the value of a prayer said at the Haram, the mosque in Mecca:

> Brahim: When you go and pray at the mosque that gives you twenty-seven *ḥasanāt,* which is rewards, right, given by God, whereas if you only pray at home, that gives you just one reward, right, so that's a difference of twenty-six rewards. That is really one of the benefits that is important to motivate people really to go to the mosque, people of the same age group.

> Suleiman: *Ṣalāt,* praying at the mosque and together too, so on time at half past one and again at four today [a day during the month of Ramadan] when you do that at the mosque you get seventy points, right, *ḥasanāt,* seventy in Ramadan.

The vision of life as a gift from God who compels humanity to observe a good Islamic way of life is closely associated with the representation of God as being almighty. The omnipotence of God is represented in several ways: in God's capacity to judge humanity on Judgment Day; in the respondents' opinion that God is the Creator; and in the presumption that everything that happens in the world is a part of God's inscrutable plan. One respondent, Mohammed, indicated that even the success of the appointment made for the interview had been determined by God: "For example, we had an appointment at half past two; you came and I came, but in fact we have both come here by God. If you think about the way the appointment took place you came here and I came here all that has been taken care of by God." The same respondent also said that humanity suffers if God's plan with his creation is not respected: "We have to know first why these diseases actually exist in our time: it is because we do not follow the path set by God."

Illness and Healing

God's omnipotence also extends to the field of healing. If a person is ill, it is incumbent on him or her to seek to be healed. This view is reflected in the following quotations from Mohammed and Farid:

> Mohammed: That is . . . yes that is certain . . . because that is clearly in the Qur'an you always have to go and find the causes of healing. . . . It says so in the Qur'an, but if you want verses or texts or something like that, you need to go to people who study Islam.

> Farid: The Prophet Mohammed says you have to, in fact, you have to go and ask for medications.

When asked how they experienced growing older in the context of being an immigrant, four of the respondents referred primarily to physical ailments, usually rheumatism and diabetes, and expressed their feelings of homesickness for Morocco, immediately adding that a permanent return to Morocco is out of the question because of the life they have built for themselves in Belgium. This is a clear reference to the familiar return dilemma: ideally, respondents would prefer to return to Morocco but find it impossible to leave behind their life in Belgium, where they have responsibilities toward their immediate and extended families.

Four of the respondents testified to having problems in their relationships with their children. These are the same respondents who also mentioned suffering from typical age-related illnesses such as rheumatism and diabetes and who spoke of the communication problems they face when visiting a doctor, whether a general practitioner (GP) or a specialist. They also indicated that the language barrier is the underlying reason for frequenting a Moroccan GP. In this respect, the faith of the doctor was not of any relevance to any of the respondents in the context of treating physical ailments. Farid put this as follows: "First, Muslim or not Muslim does not enter into the discussion now; the discussion is about health, really, and I believe the gentleman as a doctor not as a Muslim. . . . What counts is really that he is a doctor who is capable to give an explanation and who can find a solution for a disease."

According to our respondents, God is the sole healer. Driss said, "The doctor is God." In addition God is also the only one to determine whether a person lives or dies. To substantiate this vision, they often referred to Qur'anic verses and Prophetic traditions. In this view, healing can be made to occur only when God wants the person to be healed. The emphasis placed by the respondents on the omnipotence of God also influences their views of the efforts put forward by doctors and of the effects of medication. In their view, human efforts to promote good health, including the use of medication, are only the means through which God is able to heal a person. Therefore, with regard to the role of doctors, there is a recognition of the physician's expertise, and yet this is consistently offset by a perspective that sees God as ultimately in control.

Brahim stated, "I take that medication, and I do this on basis of what I'm going to hear from the doctor, for example. The doctor has an understanding [of science] and knows better than I, but just because I'm going to take those medications, for example, doesn't mean that I'm going to be cured, right. Only God knows this." On the role of medication, Mohammed agrees with Brahim, stating, "You have to take the medications, but the healing comes from God. . . . You can only be healed by God. . . . God is the one who can heal someone. So taking those medications is simply an aid."

This perspective of the role of medication and of the efforts of physicians as means by which God can heal humanity does not mean that a person can just decide not to resort to physicians and medication. Quite the reverse is true. Time and again the respondents referred (often in vague terms such as "it says so in the Qur'an" or "the Prophet has said this") to elements in the Qur'an and the hadith, both of which encourage individuals to seek out healing.

Medication and the efforts brought to bear by medical specialists, however, are not the only way for God to bring healing. Here also the omnipotence of God is central. In this perspective, if a Muslim recovers from an illness, it is not clear whether this recovery occurred through the medication, through the attendance of the doctor, or through other means unknown to humankind.

To our respondents, the salubrious effects of medication are subordinate to the will of God. No amount of medication or therapy will bring actual recovery unless God wills it, for only God can take away the underlying cause of the illness. Doctors and medication are necessary means, although essentially they are considered to have a strictly symptom-countering effect and ultimately have no power to heal the human condition. Abdel maintained, "So we always count on God that this will bring a change for the better. But in fact, all you get is something for the pain, a painkiller or such. That's ok, but that is not really the way to get rid of the illness, is it? We give ourselves medications, in fact, for a temporary improvement or change for the better. That to me is a kind of road side assistance."

Pain Control and Euthanasia

This general conception of the effectiveness of medication also applies to palliative medication. To our respondents, the life-shortening effect that is often assigned (however falsely) to powerful analgesics does not pose a major ethical problem. Here too we come across the same view that holds that it is ultimately God and God alone who will determine the outcome of the treatment. He will determine whether or not the life of a patient is to end when the patient takes this type of medication. Controlling the pain takes precedence. A typical statement was:

> Ahmed: What is in fact important is that the patient must be free of pain and calm, and it must be perceived that [the medication] will not hurt his body, that his health is ok. Whether or not this shortens his life, that doesn't matter. What is important is that this person has to feel comfortable at that moment. . . . We can't say much about the shortening of days, etc., because as we said in the beginning, everything is determined by God. But if the doctor says, or has noticed, that this type of medication helps the patient, in fact, to stay healthy, that is ok.

One respondent, Brahim, reported that in the event of pain medication with potential side effects, he will always balance to what degree he is able to bear the pain. "Here in this case, I'm going to choose. But for me when this hurts, like real pain, then I'm going to choose medication. If I think I can handle the pain for example, then there is no need to take these medications."

The above quotations show that the use of pain medication is permitted, even necessary, as it helps the patient to stay focused on his religion and his trust in God. One respondent put forward an opposite view. Suleiman unambiguously asserted that pain medication with a double effect is not acceptable to Muslims. He linked his views to the conception that patiently bearing and enduring pain in life in this world serves as redemption for the punishment awaiting the person concerned in the hereafter for sins committed: "A Muslim will never accept this. A Muslim, the more he suffers, the more he goes to paradise. Okay? The more he suffers, the more God forgives his bad deeds from before. Maybe he has done bad deeds and by having this pain now, after dying. . . . In the Qur'an or in the hadith a Muslim believes that after much suffering, there he will be forgiven everything by God because he has suffered a lot."

Suleiman clearly expressed a point of view differing from that of the other respondents. To them, the (alleged) double effect of certain pain medication is not important from a religious point of view: after all, a person's life span is determined by God and by no one else. In other words, the majority of the respondents do not consider pain control to be an ethical dilemma.

While there is no absolute consensus among the respondents concerning the issue of pain control, there is a clear consensus when it comes to euthanasia. When the respondents were presented with the case of a patient who asked the doctor to end his suffering in an active and direct way by purposefully administering lethal medication, we invariably met a fierce aversion to this request. Some perceived it to be absolutely forbidden (*haram*), because of the duty of having to rely on God. In such a case they felt that the patient and the doctor were playing God, which is totally unacceptable. Ahmed's statement was typical: "That can not be discussed. That can not be discussed. It's absolutely *haram*. It's a sin, a sin, a real sin. It's suicide, and that's a real sin, so that can not be discussed."

One respondent, Driss, told us at the start of the interview that his wife had been taken to the hospital and was seriously ill. He said that he was not able to answer this question about the acceptability of euthanasia. He did not give his own opinion; neither did he refer to what he believed would be the normative Islamic vision: "This is a difficult question. I cannot answer." The respondent's personal experience seems to have prevented him from answering this question. Therefore we can hypothetically deduce that Muslims who are confronted with actual palliative situations might not have a clear answer.

External Validity of the Study Results

We presented the results to two Moroccan physicians and two Imams (*fuqaha'/'ulama'*) in Antwerp and distilled four elements. First, the physicians and the Imams all confirmed that our research results corresponded with their experiences. All referred to a lack of knowledge about science among the elderly, and in their opinion, this had to do with the respondents' illiteracy; eight of ten were indeed illiterate. Along these lines, it is interesting to note that when it came to the issue of the effect that a medication would have, our respondents believed that the physician might know which medicine would work and which one would not, but that it is not up to the physician to make a medical prognosis of the patient's life span. This clearly shows that our respondents do not rely primarily on a scientific paradigm to explain medical issues; they leave the science entirely up to the doctor and rely on their own theologically founded frame of interpretation. When we asked the physicians how they cope with this, they answered that the lack of medical understanding with the elderly sometimes creates difficulties when treating them:

> Hamid: If I have to talk to someone who does not read [sighs] I do not even try [laughs]. It is too frustrating. It is simple: they can not digest this, not understand this. Ignorance, pure ignorance, that's it. Not reading.

> Hussayn: Yes, eh, these people know nothing, right. There is nothing to explain, even if you do explain things, you don't get a result because they don't understand the logic.

The second conclusion is perhaps more surprising. We found that the physicians and Imams stress the same theological elements found in the respondents' stories.

God determines each person's life span (*ajal*). In other words, if the end of the life span comes, no one in any way whatsoever can postpone this end. The physicians even share the respondents' opinion that a doctor can act only within the life span predetermined by God. God intends that everyone take care of the life with which she or he has been entrusted by actively looking for a way to cure the disease, while realizing that God is the one who predetermines a person's life span:

> Hamid: God determined how long one should live. But who knows this? Only God does. He knows that X will become eighty years old. I, as a doctor, I don't know that. I do my best to prolong his life as long as possible, until you get to the day that God picked for you. That's it.

> Hussayn: Well, if the day is there, even if you administer all kinds of medicine, it will end; you will die. But if that day is still a long way ahead, if it is the right cure, He will let you live until that day. That's it. That's important to understand. We can never postpone this day to a later date. So, the final day of our life is determined. It's in the genes, right, genetics. There is nothing you can do about it. On that point, I agree with them. But it's a bit difficult to understand, you know, it's I, I understand them this way, how the day is yet to come and that one can always be cured and maybe without medicine, it's always possible, so eh, you can also get cured, but only until the day that has been predetermined. At that day, even if we administer medicine, very good medicine [smiles], it can't last very long anymore.

As is the case with the respondents, the interviewed Muslim physicians think of euthanasia as unmentionable, and all regard euthanasia from a religious point of view as forbidden.

> Hamid: No. A doctor should never take someone's life or shorten it. No matter how he suffers, God is the one who decides about life and death. A doctor should try to soften the suffering as much as possible by using medicine. But he shouldn't kill. Shouldn't kill. So, by lethal injection.

> Hussayn: My opinion or philosophy—eh, no—wants or eh—I'm against it, right. I'm against euthanasia. You said we have to control the pain, right? That is important until the end, but if you only mean euthanasia, no.

Our third conclusion is that physicians and Imams share the same fundamental complex vision on the role of God and the role of medical treatment (and medication). They do stress the presence of human reason within Creation. According to them, God created the universe and all its properties, including, for example, the fact that gravity on the earth and moon differs, the fact that human beings cannot breathe underwater, and that a person is burned by touching fire. In the same way, God created a cure for each disease. It is humanity's task to use intellect as the tool to discover curative means. In other words, humanity has to look for the means that will activate God's cure. One Imam compared it to hunger and the need to eat. When you are feeling hungry, it does not make sense to wait for God to take away your hunger. It is a person's task to look for food and to feed her body. This food will then activate the digestive system that God created, and the hunger will disappear. If someone struggles with her digestive system, she has to look for the medicine to cure it. According to these physicians and Imams, the healing effect of certain substances is God's wish and creation.

Also with regard to pain control, their vision runs parallel to the respondents' vision, on the one hand, but is more refined, on the other hand. The physicians consider it their task to keep the patient as comfortable as possible. However, the period of time over which the physician disposes to help the patient has been determined by God. The main difference between the physicians' and the respondents' perspectives is that the physicians recognize the intrinsic life-shortening action of pain medication. They think that a high dose of morphine shortens a terminal patient's life span in certain cases. The aspect of uncertainty, however, which also matters here, seems to leave sufficient scope, according to these physicians, to let God act as the one who makes the final decision: he eventually determines the moment of death:

> Hamid: It is my duty as a doctor to make life as comfortable as possible, not to prolong life as long as possible. You can't do anything about the life-shortening effect of some pain medication, you don't have an option. If I have to choose between a long or a comfortable life, I choose a comfortable life. Living while you really suffer is not living either. Having a shorter life, but of a good quality is better than having a long life without really living it.

As a fourth conclusion, we can say that the Imams, more than the physicians, stress God's absolute omnipotence: if God wishes so, he can reverse the universe's patterns. One Imam referred to the story about Abraham in the Qur'an that tells us that God protected Abraham from getting burned (Q 29:24). This reference shows us that God controls the universe and its patterns at all times in his capacity as the Almighty.

Statements by our respondents about the effects of medication have parallels with those by the physicians and the Imams, but the latter created a broader frame of reference by combining a more scientific view with the theological frame. Because the respondents' narratives lack both an understanding of and a belief in the scientifically determined effects of medication, their worldview seems to be at odds with the modern Western worldview. The physicians and the Imams put this theological vision in a broader frame in which modern science, to a varying degree, does have its place. As with scientists, the interviewed physicians and Imams search for patterns in the universe; the difference is that they see these patterns, as well as those substances that can cure illness, as having been created by God, together with the universe, in the first place.

Discussion

The vision of God as the sole determiner of the life span and the physician as the person who must try to cure the patient, or at least alleviate the pain, can be found frequently in literature on Islamic ethics.[10] Our respondents' visions on pain control show that there are different attitudes toward pain. The majority of our respondents considered pain to be a physical complaint that can be controlled. However, one of the respondents interpreted pain in a theological way, which means that pain is considered to be a physical discomfort that has to be endured without medication, because according to this theological interpretation, pain is seen as redemption of the punishment given for the sins in the afterlife. The literature mentions both interpretations.[11] Gatrad, Mynors, Hunt, and Sheikh argue that the respect for religious principles and the patients' clinical needs should be given due consideration when care providers are confronted with a theological vision that can limit options for the treatment of pain.[12] Research from McCarthy, Chammas, Wilimas, Alaoui, and Harif relating to pain management with children suffering from cancer in Morocco also shows the impact of experience-related elements, such as the socioeconomic situation of the patient and the resulting financial argument about whether or not to choose pain medication; their research shows that pain management is employed far less in Morocco because of a lack of structural and financial means.[13] Additionally, we should bear in mind that these are views expressed by Muslim men, not by Muslim women. In recent years the role of gender in pain perception and pain tolerance has become an important research topic.[14] It is particularly interesting to note the influence of gender on the role of religious knowledge in dealing with pain.[15] However, the influence of gender could not be studied in the present research. Our research did touch on the financial argument, however, regarding another ethical dilemma at the end of life. In reference to the question of the acceptability of withdrawing life-sustaining therapy, one respondent told us about a relative in Morocco whose life-sustaining therapy was stopped because of the high cost. Our study showed that respondents interpret euthanasia as an autonomous decision made by an individual that is unacceptable precisely because it denies God's role in matters of life and death.[16]

In the present study we did not talk to Muslims who were in actual palliative situations. We did not deem it appropriate to confront a religious minority, which in the field of palliative care is not often involved in research, during such a major emotional moment with these ethical and rather charged subjects. On the one hand, it is common knowledge that an asituational attitude measurement has only a limited predictive value with regard to the effective choices, which the same interviewees will make when they are confronted with the presented situations. On the other hand, it remains important to know that these people's consistent and strong rejection of any form of active termination of life is significantly different from the more open attitude generally found in Belgian society.[17] Many studies show that religiosity is an important factor in determining attitudes on end-of-life issues.[18] Nonreligious subjects often have attitudes opposite of those of our respondents.

It is worth reiterating that this study and its results have inevitably been controlled by the interpreter with whom we worked. The interpreter is a practicing Muslim man who is professionally involved in the Antwerp mosques, and we explored only the attitudes of observant first-generation Moroccan men aged sixty and over living in Antwerp. Therefore our findings may not apply to other groups, such as nonreligious Moroccan men.[19]

Conclusion

For the respondents in the sample examined, there is a strong focus on God and the afterlife. God's central importance can be seen in the respondents' perceptions of illness, recovery, medication, and the physician's role in the recovery process. On the one hand, the effects of medication and the physician's role are both placed second to the will of God, who seems to be the only one who can actually cure. On the other hand, radical pain control does not pose an ethical dilemma for the respondents since God alone controls the process of dying. Euthanasia, however, is totally unacceptable. Those who undertake it are seen as claiming a power to determine the life span to which they are not entitled and as shamelessly denying their dependence on God. Moreover they are seen as explicitly refusing to submit themselves to God's will.

NOTES

1. J. Leman, ed., *The Dynamics of Emerging Ethnicities: Immigrant and Indigenous Ethnogenesis in Confrontation* (Frankfurt: Peter Lang, 1998). For the situation in the Netherlands, see L. Lucassen, *The Immigrant Threat: The Integration of Old and New Migrants in Western Europe since 1850* (Urbana and Chicago: University of Illinois Press, 2005). On the situation in France, see O. Samaoli, *Yesterday's Immigrants, Today's Elderly: From the Maghreb, Aging in France,* http://www.gerontologie-migrations.fr/article.php3?id_article=7, accessed April 18, 2006. A European perspective on migration is offered by Leo Lucassen in "Old and New Migrants in the Twentieth Century: A European Perspective," *Journal of American Ethnic History* 21, no. 4 (2002): 85–101.

2. The work presented here is part of a broader-based research study (2002–6) on the attitude of Islam in general and of this population in particular toward ethical decision-making surrounding the end of life.

3. The majority of researches focus on Christian denominations (Catholic/Protestant). Believers of different faiths often receive the opportunity only to define themselves as other.

If, however, other religions were mentioned, we found, in order of appearance, Judaism, Islam, and Hinduism. Regarding the religion factor, one does not find any deeper questioning than religious affiliation. See A. M. Burdette, T. D. Hill, and B. E. Moulton, "Religion and Attitudes toward Physician-Assisted Suicide and Terminal Palliative Care," *Journal for the Scientific Study of Religion* 44 (2005): 79–93. As there are no duly tested research tools available to measure religious attitudes of Muslims in a migration context, we have endeavored to compile a workable operationalization of religion, adjusted to suit the target group. We chose to work with the five traditional dimensions of religion held out under the paradigm of C. Y. Glock and R. Stark in *Religion and Society in Tension* (Chicago: Rand McNally, 1965). Following F. H. C. Kemper, who examined the relationship between religion and well-being in first-generation Moroccan Muslim men in the Netherlands in "Religiositeit, etniciteit en welbevinden bij mannen van de eerste generatie Marokkaanse moslimmigranten" (Ph.D. diss., Katholieke Universiteit Nijmegen, 1996), we added a sixth dimension to Glock and Stark's model: the social dimension. This sixth dimension assesses social bonds and interwovenness with the religious community.

4. For a full description of the typology, see B. Broeckaert, "Ethical Issues at the End of Life," in *Palliative Care Nursing: Principles and Evidence for Practice,* ed. S. Payne, J. Seymour, and C. Ingleton (Birkshire: Open University Press, forthcoming); B. Broeckaert and the Flemish Palliative Care Federation, *End of Life Decisions—A Conceptual Framework* (Brussels: Federatie Palliatieve Zorg Vlaanderen, 2006), http://www.palliatief.be/, accessed March 30, 2007.

5. The cases that are relevant to the topics discussed in this essay are:

Case 4: Active life-shortening/life-terminating action, pain control: Do you feel that a person suffering unbearable pain should be given pain-reducing medication even if this has a life-shortening side effect?

Case 5: Active life-shortening/life-terminating action without the consent from the patient: A patient is in a deep coma and has been living like this for the past twenty or thirty years without the assistance of machines. Is it acceptable for a doctor to administer a lethal injection to this patient? Who is to decide this?

Case 6: Active life-shortening/life-terminating action, euthanasia: A patient is terminally ill, has only a few more weeks to live, and is suffering unbearable physical pain that cannot be relieved medically. Is it acceptable for the doctor to terminate this patient's life to put an end to his pain?

Case 7: Active life-shortening/life-terminating action, euthanasia in case of unbearable mental suffering: A patient is terminally ill, has only a few more weeks to live, and is suffering unbearable mental or psychological pain that cannot be relieved. Is it acceptable for the doctor to terminate this patient's life to put an end to his pain?

Regarding the final selection of the respondents, the reader is referred to the paragraph on the interpreter. The background of symbolic interactionism provided a suitable methodological and philosophical framework to set out in search of the experiential aspect of reality and the meaning attributed by respondents to reality. See M. Crotty, *The Foundations of Social Research: Meaning and Perspective in the Research Process* (London: Sage, 1998); L. I. Reynolds and N. J. Herman-Kinney, eds., *Handbook of Symbolic Interactionism* (Walnut Creek, Calif.: Alta Mira, 2003); K. Plummer, *Symbolic Interactionism,* 2 vols. (Aldershot:

Elgar, 1991); B. G. Glaser and A. L. Strauss, *The Discovery of Grounded Theory: Strategies for Qualitative Research* (New York: Aldine, 1967); A. Strauss and J. Corbin, *Basics of Qualitative Research: Techniques and Procedures for Developing Grounded Theory* (Thousand Oaks, Calif.: Sage, 1998).

6. During the first part of the interview, they were asked the same questions as those presented to the respondents. In the second part of the interview, we presented the findings of our interviews with the ten elderly Moroccan men to these supplementary interviewees.

7. We decided to study Moroccan Arabic because of the lack of possibilities to study Tamazight. For Moroccan Arabic, several courses were immediately available. We established international contact with the linguist Jan Hoogland (University of Nijmegen, the Netherlands) and started an intensive course in Moroccan Arabic with a local professional teacher and native speaker of Moroccan Arabic. The interviews made clear that the respondents' use of Tamazight contained a lot of Moroccan Arabic words.

8. B. Temple and R. Edwards, "Interpreters/Translators and Cross-Language Research: Reflexivity and Border Crossings," *International Journal of Qualitative Methods* 1, no. 2 (2002): 1–22. Nonetheless international studies resorting to the services of an interpreter have cleared up the role of the interpreter in the research only to a minimal extent. It is important to properly explain and clarify the role of the interpreter as part of our study. Only one interpreter was used during the research process, with the purpose of keeping variability in translations down to the bare minimum. The interpreter was a Moroccan male of thirty-nine, born in northern Morocco, and working for the Antwerp department of integration. He was a practicing Muslim with a professional interest in the aging Muslim population in Antwerp. The gender of the interpreter and the researcher meant that the scope of the study was limited to Moroccan men, which was important since the recruitment of respondents required not only a solid command of the language of the respondents but also a due knowledge of their cultural wonts and sensitivities. These proficiencies were important in persuading the candidates to take part in the study, in making and helping them keep concrete appointments, and in functioning as cultural experts. See A. O. Freed, "Interviewing through an Interpreter," *Social Work* (1988): 315–19; I. Kapborg and C. Berterö, "Using an Interpreter in Qualitative Interviews: Does It Threaten Validity?," *Nursing Inquiry* 9, no. 1 (2002): 55; S. Twinn, "An Exploratory Study Examining the Influence of Translation on the Validity and Reliability of Qualitative Data in Nursing Research," *Journal of Advanced Nursing* 26 (1997): 418–23; E. H. Bragason, *Interviewing through Interpreters,* http://www.psy.au.dk/ckm/newsletter/nb23/23–egil.htm, accessed October 10, 2004.

9. As the majority of respondents spoke little to no Dutch, in most of the cases these are translations put forward by the interpreter from Moroccan Arabic or from Tamazight. The study of Moroccan Arabic made it possible for the researcher to arrive at a better understanding of the results. On the one hand, this enabled the researcher to follow the course of the conversation during the interviews, and on the other hand, it proved beneficial to pay a good deal of attention to the words used by the respondents while transcribing the interviews. The interviews were digitally recorded (with the aid of a MiniDisc), transcribed using WavePad and Express Scribe software, and analyzed using MAXqda software for high-quality data analysis. The respondents' names have been changed to preserve their anonymity. Regarding this matter, it is important to stress that the quotations used in this

article are English translations, made by a professional translator, and are a written version of Dutch spoken words. Therefore a double filter is at work in quoting the respondents: on the one hand, the transcription of broken Dutch, and on the other hand, the translation of these materials into English. In the case of Suleiman, the quotations are the words used by the respondent himself. The occurrence of Moroccan Arabic words in the Tamazight of the respondents and the often-recurring formulations in the respondents' (Tamazight) answers made it possible for the researcher to gain an understanding of what was being said in Tamazight, although to a more limited extent than was the case with interviews in Moroccan Arabic.

10. J. E. Brockopp, "Islamic Ethics of Saving Life: A Comparative Perspective," *Medicine and Law* 21 (2002): 234; Rispler-Chaim, *Islamic Medical Ethics,* 95; A. Sachedina, "End-of-Life: The Islamic View," *Lancet* 366, no. 9487 (2005): 774–79.

11. We found Suleiman's view on pain attested in the following researches: Sachedina, "End-of-Life," 777; Daar and al-Khitamy, "Bioethics for Clinicians," 60–63; M. al-Jeilani, "Pain: Points of View of Islamic Theology," *Acta Neurochirugica,* supplement 38 (1987): 132–35; H. M. Ross, "Islamic Tradition at the End of Life," *Medical-Surgical Nursing* 10, no. 2 (2001): 83–87.

12. A. R. Gatrad and others, "Patient Choice in Medicine Taking: Religious Sensitivities Must Be Respected," *Archives of Disease in Childhood* 90 (2005): 984.

13. P. McCarthy and others, "Managing Children's Cancer Pain in Morocco," *Journal of Nursing Scholarship* 36, no. 1 (2004): 11–15.

14. S. K. Ahlawat, M. T. Cuddihy, and G. R. Locke, "Gender Related Differences in Dyspepsia: A Qualitative Systematic Review," *Journal of Neuroscience Nursing* 3, no. 1 (2006): 31–42.

15. C. Hayward and A. Madill, "The Meanings of Organ Donation: Muslims of Pakistani Origin and White English Nationals Living in North England," *Social Science and Medicine* 57 (2003): 389–401.

16. We regularly encountered this view in international literature: Brockopp, "Islamic Ethics of Saving Life," 233; Rispler-Chaim, *Islamic Medical Ethics,* 97; Sachedina, "End-of-Life," 778.

17. Studies conducted by the group European Values Study show that within Belgian society there is a lot of openness toward euthanasia: the study dates from 1999 and shows that only 22.4 percent of Belgians think euthanasia is rarely if ever unjustified. See K. Dobbelaere and others, *Verloren zekerheid: De Belgen en hun waarden, overtuigingen en houdingen* (Tielt: Lannoo, 2001), 156.

18. The acceptance of euthanasia decreased as the level of religious belief increased. See J. Cohen, I. Marcoux, J. Bilsen, P. Deboosere, G. van der Wal, and L. Deliens, "European Public Acceptance of Euthanasia: Socio-demographic and Cultural Factors Associated with the Acceptance of Euthanasia in 33 European Countries," *Social Science and Medicine* 63, no. 3 (2006): 743–56.

19. Time and again we tried, by using the snowball sampling technique, to contact non-religious first-generation men, but although some respondents did know nonreligious men, they did not want to pass us their names and addresses or contact them. Furthermore, the opinions of religious or nonreligious first-generation Moroccan women are still to be

studied. We can also ask whether there is a difference in the attitudes of first-generation Turkish men and women, nonreligious and religious, living in Antwerp. At present we have no idea about the kind of visions that men and women from later, second and third, generations living in Antwerp have, and so far we have not been able to compare them with the results of similar studies conducted in other Belgian cities besides Antwerp. Further studies, of course, can be conducted.

FIVE

Teaching Muslim Medical Ethics

Overview

Of all the disciplines touched on in this volume, pedagogy is perhaps the area that has had the least attention; yet, it seems fair to say that only through teaching will Muslim medical ethics become a discipline in its own right. The very nature of the teaching enterprise demands both a rational survey of the field and the identification of key sources. A careful choice of textbooks and paradigmatic cases help define the canon of what must be included in this discipline.

This section opens with two essays that describe some of the significant hurdles for the teaching of any course on Muslim medical ethics and concludes with one magisterial attempt at describing such a course. To begin, Hasan Shanawani and Mohammad Khalil surveyed the many articles that have appeared in this field. Using the popular search engine MEDLINE (developed and maintained by the United States National Library of Medicine), they identified, classified, and read through dozens of articles related to Islam and bioethics. They assessed these articles for their accuracy, depth, and breadth of focus. While they rated some of these sources quite favorably, the overall quantity and quality of publication is very much inadequate to the task of teaching Muslim medical ethics in a comprehensive fashion in medical schools and universities.

For the subsequent essay, Hassan Bella engaged physicians and clerics in Saudi Arabia in a broad-ranging content discussion of what he calls "Islamic medical ethics" (IME) and in the methods for teaching that content. To do this, he used the Delphi method, a controlled conversation that creatively engages a targeted group of experts in discussing complex topics. The method involves several rounds in which information is gathered, analyzed, and resubmitted to the entire group for their comments. These are then further analyzed and resubmitted, resulting in a useful trail of comments and revisions. The method is not meant to be conclusive as much as provocative, causing the group to consider the topic in great depth and producing important results. First, it underlines the difficulty of circumscribing a neat set of topics to be included in such a course. Second, it correctly points us to the task of method; that is, once the content of a course is agreed on, how does one teach it? Several creative answers are forwarded, all of which underline the very different interests, and needs, of medical school students in comparison with those in a liberal arts setting.

The pragmatic needs of the medical student define both the content (patients' rights, health insurance, dealing with the drug industry) and the methods (workshops, bedside teaching, case studies) of Islamic medical ethics for Bella's discussants.

In contrast, Abdulaziz Sachedina's model course emphasizes historical foundations, philosophical considerations, and reasoning processes. He begins his essay by emphasizing the philosophical foundations of ethical reasoning in the Islamic juridical tradition, pointing to what he sees as "sweeping, immature judgments about Islamic positions" in the medical literature. To correct this situation, Sachedina suggests the very combination of history, theory, and ethnography promoted in this volume. It is not that Bella is opposed to this sort of reflection; indeed, the majority of his respondents believe that history and theology should be an integral part of Islamic medical ethics. Nonetheless, in the final analysis, the contents and methods of Bella's and Sachedina's courses will, out of necessity, be substantially different.

As a final note, we point to the various terms of art at use in this section. While it may seem that "Muslim medical ethics," "Islamic medical ethics," and "Islamic bioethics" are much the same, they point to philosophical differences that can have a lasting effect. As noted in the introduction, the adjective *Muslim* was chosen to emphasize the contextualized nature of ethical reflection and to openly question the construction of authority in Muslim societies. The use of *Muslim* in this way is still fairly new, however, and still far less common than "Islamic," preferred by Bella and Sachedina. There is more at work here than fashion. Given the almost infinite variability of Muslim societies, the term *Muslim medical ethics* has built into it a presumption that it cannot be encompassed. It is inherently contingent, and therefore inherently unsatisfying. While we believe this position is theoretically defensible, others may find that it demands too much from liberal arts students in a course on comparative ethics; likewise, the severe time constraints of medical education may drive the instructor toward clarity, not complexity. This is an issue that can be resolved only by each teacher within her unique context, but at the very least every course addressing Muslim medical ethics ought to recognize and discuss the debates over authority, canon, and method that are essential to every academic field. Similarly the significantly differing orientations in these three essays should not be minimized, since they serve as a useful reminder of the many stakeholders in this nascent field.

HASAN SHANAWANI *and* MOHAMMAD HASSAN KHALIL

Reporting on "Islamic Bioethics" in the Medical Literature

Where Are the Experts?

With the advancements of science and medical technology in recent decades, new ethical dilemmas have functioned as the catalyst for a renewed religious bioethical discourse. Moreover, with a growing Muslim population in the West, interest among health practitioners in Islamic and Muslim bioethics has grown. This interest is made apparent by the increasing number of medical articles highlighting "Islamic positions" on various bioethical issues.

There is an active discussion in the medical community on bioethics questions in general and religious and Islamic bioethics in particular. However, the reports on Islamic bioethics in the medical literature appear to demonstrate less concern with questions that are often raised by Islamic studies scholars. Such scholars often take more interest in the complexities of Islamic studies in general and the Islamic ethics and legal discourse in particular.

This difference in focus is the basis of the first question we ask: Are Islamic bioethics papers in the medical literature conversant with any discourse of religious doctrine, or are these the works of medical experts with limited (if any) specialized training in such discourse? If religious doctrines are referenced, a second question becomes: What are the materials and approaches utilized? For example, are there references to medieval debates, for example, *al-tahsin wa-l-taqbih,* regarding whether good and evil (or right and wrong) can be known independent of Revelation?[1] What, if any, Islamic legal framework is assumed?

If an Islamic legal framework is assumed, our third, and perhaps most important, question is: Which methodologies are employed when utilizing and referring to Islamic thought? In other words, does the author refer to the positions and methodologies of the well-known schools of law (*madhhabs*)?[2] Does the author refer to Muslim jurists (*fuqaha'*) as authorities? Or does the author attempt to deduce his or her own conclusions by direct recourse to Islamic scripture? If so, which texts are utilized, and on what basis?[3]

These questions, while important to scholars of Islamic intellectual history, law, and ethics, seem to be ignored among medical practitioners with a professed interest and expertise in "Islamic bioethics." While articles in the religious studies literature thoroughly consider each of these questions, the questions seem to get short shrift, if any attention, in the medical literature.

There are many possible reasons for this. Medical practitioners are more often than not seeking to fill a void in order to satisfy practical, day-to-day concerns. This applied interest concerns itself primarily with the delivery of care to Muslim patients and by Muslim practitioners. It is less concerned with the philosophical and legal foundations that are the core interest of Islamic studies scholars. Their interest is less in developing ethical constructs and more in complying with them. In addition, because of their career research and intellectual focus, those writing for medical journals may not be aware, or are uncomfortable with, the methods and vernacular of Islamic studies scholars.

For Islamic studies scholars, these questions must be asked to maintain the integrity of their scholarly process. Issues of authority and the use of a consistent methodology form the yardsticks by which these scholars measure all legal and ethical decisions. Authors who come up short on these yardsticks lose legitimacy. The price paid for this emphasis is overlooking immediate questions of practical importance to physicians. Islamic studies scholars may not share the urgency of these bioethical issues and may not necessarily have to deal with the practical implications of this discourse. To that end, their peers and sources of criticism are rarely medical practitioners and researchers, and so there is little incentive to face their scrutiny in publication.

This difference in emphasis has led to a disciplinary and discursive schism. Potentially effective discourse that draws from both fields appears rarely, if at all. The result is twofold. First, Islamic constructs of philosophy and ethics are marginalized in the general discourse of medical bioethics, while meanwhile, recent developments in medicine and biology, with their ethical, legal, and social implications, receive relatively little or no attention by scholars devoted to the progress of Islamic studies.[4] Second, discussions of Islamic bioethics are often in the abstract and have little to do with Western Muslims who face these challenges daily.

While others may argue that discussions (such as those that occur at the Islamic Organization of Medical Sciences [IOMS], the Islamic Fiqh Academy in Jedda, al-Azhar, the Supreme Council of Iran, and others) are central to the discourse of Muslim religious scholars, we argue that such discussions and publications are virtually unknown to medical practitioners in North America and Europe, where most of the developments in biomedical research occur and where most standards of "best medical practice" are established. The practice of Islamic bioethics—be it at the bedside, in the research lab, or at a table establishing health policy—would greatly benefit from a closer relationship in the West of religious and biomedical scholarship.

For the research that forms the basis of this essay, we hypothesized that the majority of scholarship on MEDLINE makes little or no use of the discourse of Islamic studies; that available works are generally the products of medical experts with minimal specialized training in Islamic studies; and that majority of articles reviewed claim immutable authority and universal validity. Another objective was to quantify the number of articles that either report findings from anthropological or sociological studies of Muslim patients, or attempt to present a normative, "Islamic" view.

The results of our survey demonstrate that the majority of these articles make little or no use of the discourse of Islamic studies more commonly found in religious studies and Islamic studies journals. Furthermore, most of the articles fail to suggest the existence of such an exchange of ideas. As a result, they imply a monolithic, static nature to the canon of Islamic bioethical discourse. Some of the articles are less normative discussions of bioethics and more empiric reports of findings from anthropological or sociological studies of Muslim patients, despite being found under the heading of "bioethics."

Methods

To obtain a list of reports in the medical literature, we completed a literature search on MEDLINE, the journal search database for the U.S. National Library of Medicine (NLM) in Washington, D.C. It references approximately sixteen million citations dating back to 1950 (NLM Web site). We completed a basic Boolean search strategy on their PUBMED search engine (search completed September 26, 2005). Our search was "(Islam OR Muslim OR Arab) AND bioethics [sb]." The "bioethics [sb]" term refers to a strategy developed by the NLM to facilitate searching for citations to articles in the area of bioethics. We originally included the term *Arab* in hopes of obtaining citations from Arab countries, also deliberately excluding other regions for comparative analysis.

After this initial search strategy produced 497 citations, we individually reviewed each title and abstract to determine whether the paper was relevant to our study. We included any articles that broadly or specifically referred to issues of pregnancy, cloning, abortion, birth control, or assisted reproductive technology. We additionally included articles referring to solid organ transplantation, life support, end of life, hospice, palliative care, euthanasia, or death and dying. Any articles about general bioethics without a particular clinical subject were also included. To capture as many articles as possible, articles felt to be relevant by only one investigator were not excluded from analysis. We excluded articles that were not in English or did not expressly relate to the topics noted above.

This initial abstract/title review left 146 articles for further inquiry, and we subsequently read each article independently. We used a predetermined set of questions to assess each article. Each article was marked by the type of journal (specialty medical, ethics, nursing, social science, other). The geographic origin of the journal, first author, and patient population (where appropriate) was recorded. If a particular denomination or sect of Islam could clearly be identified in the report, it was recorded in our database.

Up to ten criteria were recorded as possible sources of Islamic jurisprudence: Qur'an, hadith or Sunna, *madhhabs*, group consensus statements, statements of individual scholars, citation of general legal principles, and fatwas from governments, religious institutions, and local entities. If the author made a statement without citing any source, this was also recorded.[5]

Results and General Findings

Of the articles that met our search criteria, 34 were excluded from further analysis (see table 1). This left 112 articles, which we used for our study.

TABLE 1. Articles excluded from further analysis

9	No reference in article to Islam
1	Not in English
24	Not obtainable from our university library consortium
34	TOTAL

Most of the articles we found were general pieces on bioethics (see table 2). Of the general articles, most were about multiple religions, and Islam was among the included faiths. We examined the "multiple faiths" articles to determine the relative weight given to each religious group. We found that while Islam received relatively less attention in a large number of the articles, the difference was minimal. However, in virtually none of the articles did Islam receive a substantially larger portion of the text of the article. It is to be wondered if the readership of most medical journals can assume at least a cursory understanding of basic precepts of Islam (or any religion, for that matter).

TABLE 2. Topics of the journal articles

General bioethics		47
Islam only	19	
Multiple religions	28	
Abortion / embryonic stem cells / birth control		40
"End-of-Life" (withdrawal of life support / hospice / brain death)		19
Organ transplantation		17
Empiric studies of Muslims		23

Geography of the Articles and Authors

We were interested in the question of where the discourse was occurring and where it came from. We hypothesized that a geographic discordance would exist between those who practice and write about medicine and bioethics and those with an interest in the study of Islamic law. The authors and journals (see tables 3 and 4) came from a variety of locations. Journals from the United States and Europe dominated the citations, but the greatest number of authors came from countries in the Middle East.

TABLE 3. Author geographic origin

Middle East		39
Israel	10	
Turkey	7	
Iran	5	
Kuwait	4	
Saudi Arabia	4	
United States		29
Europe		18
Africa		10
South Africa	8	
South Asia		5
Southeast Asia		4
Canada		4
Other		1
No location identified		3

TABLE 4. Journal geographic origin

Europe	47
United States	39
South Africa	12
Middle East	8
Canada	3
South Asia	2
Southeast Asia	1

These results reflect MEDLINE's focus on North American and Western European journals. Approximately two-thirds of journals indexed in MEDLINE are based in one of those two regions. Relatively fewer journals in MEDLINE come from Africa, Asia, and Eastern Europe. We speculate that we might find more citations from other more internationally oriented databases such as EMBASE, which is maintained in Great Britain and focuses less on North American journals. However, EMBASE has fewer citations and is used less by health practitioners in North America. It should also be noted that the removal of the term *Arab* in our search resulted in no loss of articles from this distribution. Of countries outside the United States and Europe, the most citations came from Israel (10), South Africa (8), and Turkey (7), with no other nations producing 5 or more citations in our search.

Despite the North American and European focus of the journals, it was notable that more often than not the authors of the reports originated from regions with large Muslim communities (table 3). Over half of the articles had authors from the Middle East, Africa, and South and Southeast Asia. However, not all countries contributed equally. Of countries outside of North America and Europe, Israel produced the most authors writing about Islam and Muslims, followed by South Africa and Turkey. We speculate that this is the result of closer ties between these countries and the North American / European academic enterprise.

Types of Journals, Types of Articles, and Their Subject Matter

We were particularly interested in the forums through which Islam was being presented to the medical community. These, we felt, would be reflected in part by the types of journals publishing these reports and would also be manifested through the types of articles found in our search. The journal origins of the articles found were as follows: sixty-three of the citations were found in specialty medical journals; twenty-five were in journals specializing in social studies of medicine and biology; thirteen were found in what we identified as ethics journals; seven had nursing care as their focus; and the remaining four articles were either primary news citations (for example, *New York Times*) or other non-peer-reviewed sources.

The fact that a majority of articles were found in medical specialty journals again reflects the disciplinary focus of MEDLINE. However, since most of these journals lack a disciplinary focus on ethics in general and religious bioethics in particular, we can only speculate about the quality of peer review of such articles. The lack of focus, coupled with the short length (typically fewer than three thousand words), of the reports was associated with a general superficiality of articles attempting to explain Islamic or Muslim positions on bioethics.

Empiric Studies of Muslims

We hypothesized that because of the disciplinary focus of MEDLINE on testable hypotheses and empiricism, more often than not articles citing Islam or Muslims would be attitudinal surveys, which are commonly published in the medical literature. Twenty-three of the articles were classified as "empiric studies." This figure changed with the inclusion of "South Asian" or exclusion of "Arab" into our search strategy, suggesting that some of the empiric studies included may not have been considered "Islamic." However, those articles that did fall out of our search strategy were all excluded in the second round of article exclusion (from 146 to 112). Of the twenty-three included articles, two were single cases of a bioethics issue involving a Muslim patient. Four were attitude surveys or focus groups of physicians, and two were of Islamic religious scholars. The remaining fifteen reports were attitude surveys of Muslims, mostly relating to issues of pregnancy and pregnancy termination.

While fewer than expected empiric studies were found, this reflects the focus of our original literature search and serial exclusion strategies. For comparison, MEDLINE was queried using the search term "(Islam OR Muslim) AND attitude" (search completed January 31, 2006). We found 315 citations, most of which would not have been excluded had they been found in our original search. Because our focus was not on empiric studies of Muslim attitudes on bioethics, this was not pursued further. However, the question of the relationship of bioethics scholarship to lay Muslim attitudes on bioethics questions is important and deserves further study.

Comprehensiveness and Depth of Islamic Citations

It is one thing to quote primary and secondary sources of Islamic law and another to deliberate on and interpret those sources so as to give them adaptability for coping with present needs. To the latter end, we evaluated the sources, as well as the depth, of quotations of primary literature made by the ethics authors. We also investigated the extent to which the intervening centuries of jurisprudence were evaluated. Also of interest was the diversity of viewpoints and schools cited in the name of "Islam."

The denomination of Islam mentioned most in the bioethics articles reviewed was overwhelmingly Sunni. Although denominations were not explicitly mentioned in the majority of the articles, we inferred a Sunni denomination based on the cited scholars, *madhhabs,* and use of hadith collections in the reports. Only five reports were exclusively about Shiites, and seven more explicitly mentioned both Shiites and Sunnis.

Sources of Jurisprudence

Although the Qur'an was the most frequently cited source of Islamic jurisprudence and principles of Muslim bioethics (see table 5), only slightly fewer than half (55 of 112) cited what most agree to be the bedrock of Islamic thought. Likewise, references to the Sunna, hadith in general, or to specific hadith were found in 34 articles. However, virtually none of the articles provided any interpretative analysis, much less a pluralistic analysis, of mentioned Qur'anic verses or hadiths.

TABLE 5. Number of articles citing a particular source as the basis of the author's stated opinion

Primary Sources	
Qur'an	55
Hadith/Sunna	34
Principles of Islamic Law	
Madhhabs	35
"Legal principles" (*maslaha*, etc.)	18
Historical or current citations	
Person	34
National fatwa	22
Regional/local fatwa	26
Group/organization ruling or consensus statement	24

Some reports made reference to principles or schools of Islamic jurisprudence. Thirty-five articles mentioned the *madhhabs,* with seven specifically mentioning a ruling by a *madhhab.* Eighteen articles mentioned at least one legal principle, such as *maslaha, qiyas, ijma', 'urf, ijtihad,* or others. Thirty-four articles mentioned a devotional scholar of Islam or Islamic law by name. Many of the persons referenced were historical figures (al-Ghazali [d. 1111], Rumi [d. 1273], Ibn Taymiyyah [d. 1328], and others), but several articles either cited or were full interviews with contemporary scholars, such as a recent grand mufti of al-Azhar, Ayatollah Sistani, Abdulaziz Sachedina, and Hassan Hathout, an obstetrician in the United States who has written extensively on Islamic bioethics relating to pregnancy.

There was a wide distribution for the number of sources mentioned. For this part of the analysis, only reports not categorized as "empiric studies" were used. Only five of the reviewed articles included more than five source categories as we categorized them. Thirteen reports mentioned five source categories, sixteen mentioned four, and thirteen mentioned three. Nearly half (forty-one of eighty-nine) articles mentioned fewer than three categorized sources. Fourteen reports mentioned only two categorized sources, and thirteen mentioned only one. The remaining thirteen articles that mentioned no source are described below.

Twenty-eight articles made no reference to any Islamic text or any sources of jurisprudence in their explanation of Islamic or Muslim bioethics. Fifteen of these twenty-eight articles were empiric studies of Muslims. These empiric investigations were generally attitudinal studies, either in a survey or focus-group format. The remaining thirteen articles (including the "author reply) had no citation of primary texts, made no reference to principles or schools of Islamic jurisprudence, and made no mention of contemporary or historical persons or organizations.[6] Of these thirteen articles, five were letters to the editor and were relatively shorter than the articles in general. Most of these articles were comparative studies of multiple religions.

Some of the reports cited actual individuals, such as the grand mufti of Jordan[7] or of al-Azhar.[8] A small number additionally referred to religious organizations, such as the Azhar fatwa committee and the Supreme Scholar Forum of Saudia Arabia.[9] In all of the articles there were fewer than thirty references to statements made by a Muslim professional society, Sharia council, or other organization with a professed interest and focus on either medicine or Islamic law. Conference meetings and symposia were cited in a small number of the references. Although the majority of reports were in North American and European journals, only four[10] mentioned any Islamic meetings or councils based in Europe. In the articles that mentioned these deliberative proceedings or centers of discourse, there was no mention of the deliberative process per se, any dissent, or points of contention. We concluded from this finding that few professionals with an interest in Islamic bioethics are turning to organized forums of discourse as the source from which they determine guidelines of best practice. The few that do cite such forums do so without depth of scrutiny.

Claims and Assertions of Universality

We found fewer than expected reports that explicitly framed the Muslim legal discourse as monolithic and referring to all Muslims around the world, although some did. One article, for example, claimed the existence of a central authority for Islam, referring to the Muslim Law Council of Great Britain as "a body that is to Muslims what the Vatican is to Catholics."[11] Others made broad statements about Muslims. One article commented that "Muslims prefer to die in their own homes."[12] Another article suggested, "Strict Muslims will not agree to organ transplants, and the subject should not be raised unless the family initiated the discussion."[13]

Several reports referred to Sunnis and Shiites monolithically. For example, one article noted that the fatwa it reports on "has the backing of . . . both the major Muslim groups, the Sunni and the Shia."[14] Only seven reports[15] specifically mentioned both Shiite and Sunni denominations in their attempt to characterize Muslim positions on bioethics issues. One article went so far as to claim that "Muslims have no sects. There are two major schools of thought in Islam, the Shia and the Sunni."[16] Although it is a common perception that Shiite Muslims follow a central authority, this perception was not specifically suggested in any of the reports we reviewed.

Answers to the question of which reports implied or explicitly stated a "universalist" or immutable theme to their understanding of Islam turned out to be more elusive than originally anticipated. We attempted to approach the question again, looking for articles that suggested that the process of establishing Islamic law was ongoing. Only five were agreed upon; these were the same five that gave reference to a deliberative process. An example of a relatively more comprehensive report is as follows:

> The general Islamic view is that, although there is some form of life after conception, full human life, with its attendant rights, begins only after the ensoulment of the fetus. On the basis of interpretations of passages in the Qur'an and of sayings of the Prophet, most Muslim scholars agree that ensoulment occurs at about 120 days (4 lunar months plus 10 days) after conception; other scholars, perhaps in the minority, hold that it occurs at about 40 days after conception.
>
> Scholars of jurisprudence do have some differing opinions about abortion. Abortion has been allowed after implantation and before ensoulment in cases in which there were adequate juridical or medical reasons. Accepted reasons have included rape. However, many Shi'ites and some Sunnis have generally not permitted abortion at any stage after implantation, even before ensoulment, unless the mother's life is in danger. Abortion after ensoulment is strictly forbidden by all authorities, but the vast majority do make an exception to preserve the mother's life. If a choice has to be made to save either the fetus or the mother, but not both, then the mother's life would take precedence. She is seen as the root, the fetus as an offshoot.[17]

We found the papers generally to be against both abortion and termination of life support before "complete" cardiac arrest. These findings were not without exception. For example, one reference suggested, "Prolongation of life by artificial means (such as a life support machine) is strongly disapproved of unless there was evidence that a reasonable quality of life would result."[18] As well as being a sweeping generalization, this contradicted the majority of reports we found.[19] However, this particular dissenting reference comes from the *British Medical Journal,* which enjoys one of the widest readerships of medical journals around the world.

Depth of Reference

Regardless of the number of sources referenced, we found in our review of the eighty-nine "nonempiric" studies that when reports noted sources of Islamic law and jurisprudence, they made only passing reference. In only a few articles (we would agree on only eleven)[20] did we feel that any reference to a deliberative process was made, or that there was anything other than full consensus on these issues. Of these eleven articles, four were arguably social science studies of Islamic law.[21] As an example, the ethics discourse that developed between Mu'tazilis and Ash'aris (which we would argue plays at least some role in every Islamic bioethics argument about a new medical technology) was referenced only once: "Within the different schools of thought different opinions exist, about the concepts of good and evil. For example between the Ash'arite- [*sic*] and the Mu'tazila schools."[22]

Discussion

This study analyzed articles discussing the position(s) of Islam on various biological and medical ethics issues, with emphasis on beginning-of-life and end-of-life issues. We observed that there is often a problematic geographical disconnect between the authors of these articles and the journals in which the articles are published. Observation was also made that many of these articles were published in specialty medical journals, which, given the subject matter, probably lack rigor of peer review. This seems to have been confirmed by our finding that most of these articles tended to be superficial in some way. Only a handful of articles adequately highlighted the rich, complex nature of "the Muslim body politic." Indeed, some of the articles presented Islam as a monolith, disregarding any diversity of opinions that might have developed since Islam's inception. Other articles resorted to a few isolated viewpoints, with some basing their normative positions on the views of just one scholar or institution.

From discussions with several of the authors of articles in this study, our findings reflect, in part, editorial bias rather than author bias. According to these authors, medical journal editors accepted relatively few of their articles. For those that they did accept, they demanded substantial shortening and simplification of complex issues relevant to their subjects. Determining how much of our findings reflect journal editorial demands over author demands goes beyond the scope of this article but is nonetheless deserving of further study.

It would be especially difficult for readers of many of these journal articles to learn that a rich variety of Muslim viewpoints exists, much less what those dissenting opinions might be. Equally surprising was the discovery that of all the articles studied, only seven mentioned a specific *madhhab* opinion. Even where there was a comprehensive inclusion of various viewpoints, not once was there an explicit elaboration of the methodology employed in reaching normative conclusions. Moreover most of the discussions in the articles appeared to speak of Islamic law as if it were divorced from specific regional contexts.

Our study has afforded important insights into the nature of these articles. Problems abound in the medical literature when the following questions are considered: 1) To what extent are the authors of these articles familiar with religious discourse and doctrines in general? 2) What are the general materials and approaches utilized, that is, if there is an apparent tension between "Reason" and "Revelation," how are such tensions resolved? Which approaches are utilized? 3) If a legal framework is used, what is the legal methodology employed, and are there sufficient references to the spectrum of scholarly viewpoints? Moreover, are specific regional contexts taken into consideration? It is important to note that the few somewhat comprehensive articles each focused on a specific regional context. If journal articles on the position(s) of Islam on various biological and medical issues are to be taken into consideration among Islamic studies scholars as satisfactory works of Islamic law and ethics, then these are some of the problems that will have to be addressed.

This study leads to another, more complex and challenging question. In discussing issues of Islamic bioethics, what is the relationship between medical professionals, biomedical scientists, and religious scholars? Is any one more deserving of authority than another? Some religious scholars believe that medical professionals without Islamic training deserve only a limited role in the discourse. One goes so far as to say:

> The Islamic world has become plagued with armchair pontificators who are self-declared experts and who decree what Islam is because they *will* it to be so . . . self-declared experts who claim to take the job of reforming Islamic thought without being minimally qualified to do so. Typically these magic-wand reformers are by profession engineers, medical doctors, or even social scientists who might be competent as sociologists or political scientists, but their knowledge and command of the Islamic intellectual tradition or its texts is minimal at best. Despite their poor knowledge of Islam, or perhaps because of their unfamiliarity with the Islamic intellectual tradition, these magic-wand reformers write . . . sweeping and unsubstantiated generalizations about what Islam is and what it ought to be.[23]

While this view is perhaps particularly uncomplimentary, authors should be careful not to stray far from their field of training, study, and expertise.

Our ultimate ambition is better collaboration among scholars of Islamic law, clinicians, and medical researchers. This study reveals that before this ambition might be realized, there is much to be done. There is a wide geographic distribution of journals and authors, with notable discordance between the two. In addition, while most government- and industry-funded medical research occurs in North America, Europe, China, and India,[24] and despite their large Muslim populations, there was a relative dearth of articles from those countries. Furthermore, few authors who asserted an Islamic or Muslim stance expressed nuanced positions that reflected a complex nature to the ethics questions put before them.

Several criticisms of this study can be made. Perhaps the most important is that it was based on a premise that medical journals are a proper forum in which to find elaborate discourse on Islamic law. In general, the degree to which religion is studied in the medical literature is a point of controversy. While some suggest that the number of articles addressing religion as a clinical issue may be increasing,[25] others suggest that the general presence of religion in (clinical) ethical discourse between peers is not.[26] The conclusion that might be drawn from this is that religion in general is not finding a place in bioethical discourse. If that premise is true, then the lack of Islamic bioethics articles may well be par for the course. That said, it is notable that similar searches for Jewish and Christian bioethics respectively produced nearly three times (1,384) and ten times (4,771) as many references as those resulting from the search for Islamic bioethics. The fact that Muslim bioethics articles are underrepresented in the medical literature has been reported elsewhere[27] and is arguably the biggest measure of the Islamic bioethics canon's inadequacy in the medical literature.

Another concern might be that MEDLINE misses an important set of references with its focus on Western Europe and the United States. This argument is real[28] and reflects a cultural dominance of Western Europe, North America, and Anglo-speaking nations and institutions in general. While we agree with this concern, we also believe that MEDLINE is the largest and most commonly used database for references, including most Muslim-majority countries (MEDLINE Web site). Furthermore, it is precisely this cultural context that is not being adequately analyzed through a prism of Islamic ethical construct.

Any one exploration of the depth of Islamic bioethical discourse is arbitrary and far from an adequate measure of its quality. For this reason, more collaborative efforts between physicians, researchers, patient advocates, general bioethicists, and scholars of Islamic law are needed, specifically in the United States, which has its own unique and diverse Muslim population; its own social and ethical issues relating to biology, health, and medicine; and its own forum for ethical discourse. While this survey of the state of Islamic bioethics in the medical literature is admittedly superficial, we hope that it sparks greater interest in collaborative efforts and focuses attention on a subject of profound importance and deserving of our collective attention.

NOTES

1. Generally it has been assumed that the Mu'tazilis and Twelver Shiites tended to place greater trust in the intellect (*'aql*) in making moral decisions, while the Ash'aris tended to downplay the role of the intellect. As for the Traditionalists, their most prominent representative, Ibn Taymiyya (d. 1328), assumed an ostensibly intermediate position. For a more detailed discussion of this medieval discourse, see A. Kevin Reinhart, *Before Revelation: The Boundaries of Muslim Moral Thought* (Albany: State University of New York Press, 1995); Sherman A. Jackson, "The Alchemy of Domination? Some Ash'arite Responses to Mu'tazilite Ethics," *International Journal of Middle East Studies* 31 (1999): 185–201.

2. These include the Hanafi, Maliki, Shafi'i, Hanbali, and Ja'fari schools of law.

3. In other words, which Qur'anic verses and hadiths (and hadith collections), if any, are referenced? And in interpreting the texts, how is priority assigned? For example, a pressing question that has led to much controversy in general bioethics circles is that of defining death and the end-of-life. While withdrawal of other "life-supporting" interventions (such as prayer and leeches) and the question of who "killed" a victim (say, if multiple

assailants stabbed the same person) were debated, the definition of death was a question largely ignored by Islamic scholars. The question was generally moot until the advent of mechanical ventilation in the 1960s and its widespread use in the decades after that. Now multiple controversies exist around "brain death," cardio-pulmonary resuscitation, artificial hearts, and organ transplants. These questions are being asked by Muslims around the world, with few answers available to medical practitioners.

4. Even within the devoted (non-MEDLINE referenced) bioethics literature, examples of more thorough, albeit still superficial, articles exist; see, for examples, Gamal Serour, "Islamic Developments in Bioethics," *Bioethics Yearbook* 5 (1997): 171–88; and Hassan Hathout, "Bioethics Developments in Islam," *Bioethics Yearbook* 3 (1993): 133–47. There are, of course, notable exceptions. For examples, we suggest the following books (which are, admittedly, not solitary articles): Rispler-Chaim, *Islamic Medical Ethics;* and Brockopp, *Islamic Ethics of Life.*

5. We felt that religion, geography, and culture might be conflated in the MESH-based categorization scheme that is the basis of MEDLINE searching. To assess the validity of our search, the authors implemented a PUBMED search using "South Asia AND bioethics [sb]" (search completed January 31, 2006), as well as with removing "Arab" from the original search term. The "South Asia" search produced 172 abstracts that were then reviewed for possible citations missed by our initial strategy. Removing the term *Arab* gave 398 citations, 99 fewer than our original strategy. In reviewing these articles, we noted that we would have included an additional 20 references, all of which were empiric studies. The 99 citations removed with the removal of the term *Arab* were also largely empiric studies.

6. K. M. Ajlouni, "Values, Qualifications, Ethics and Legal Standards in Arabic (Islamic) Medicine," *Saudi Medical Journal* 24, no. 8 (2003): 820–26; S. M. Alibhai and M. Gordon, "Muslim and Jewish Perspectives on Inappropriate Treatment at the End of Life," *Archives of Internal Medicine* 164, no. 8 (2004): 916–17; author reply 917; F. Berker, "Not Contradicting the Religion: Islam Has Been Putting an Emphasis on Family Planning for 14 Centuries," *Integration* 47 (1996): 4; A. M. Clarfield and others, "Ethical Issues in End-of-Life Geriatric Care: The Approach of Three Monotheistic Religions—Judaism, Catholicism, and Islam," *Journal of the American Geriatrics Society* 51, no. 8 (2003): 1149–54; Eisenberg and Schenker, "Ethical, Legal and Religious Aspects of Preembryo Research," 11–24; A. R. Gatrad and A. Sheikh, "Palliative Care for Muslims and Issues before Death," *International Journal of Palliative Nursing* 8, no. 11 (2002): 526–31; Michael Gordon and Shabbir M. H. Alibhai, "Ethics of PEG Tubes—Jewish and Islamic Perspectives," *American Journal of Gastroenterology* 99, no. 6 (2004): 1194; F. Moazam and A. M. Jafarey, "Pakistan and Biomedical Ethics: Report from a Muslim Country," *Cambridge Quarterly of Healthcare Ethics* 14, no. 3 (2005): 249–55; S. Naamane-guessous, "Traditional Methods Still Widely Used," *Planned Parenthood Challenges* 1 (1993): 14–16; S. Patterson, L. Balducci, and R. Meyer, "The Book of Job: A 2,500-Year-Old Current Guide to the Practice of Oncology; The Nexus of Medicine and Spirituality," *Journal of Cancer Education* 17, no. 4 (2002): 237–40; K. S. Prabhakar, "Cadaveric & Living Organ Donation: Natural Limitations; Possible Solutions; Singapore Experience," *Annals of Transplantation* 9, no. 1 (2004): 31–33; A. Sheikh, "Death and Dying—A Muslim Perspective," *Journal of the Royal Society of Medicine* 91, no. 3 (1998): 138–40.

7. S. S. Banwell and J. M. Paxman, "The Search for Meaning: RU 486 and the Law of Abortion," *American Journal of Public Health* 82, no. 10 (1992): 1399–1406.

8. Z. Badawi, "The Role of the Church in Developing the Law: An Islamic Response," *Journal of Medical Ethics* 28, no. 4 (2002): 223, discussion 229–31.

9. O. Asman, "Abortion in Islamic Countries—Legal and Religious Aspects," *Medicine and Law* 23, no. 1 (2004): 73–89.

10. "The Muslim Law (Shariah) Council and Organ Transplants," *Accident and Emergency Nursing* 4, no. 2 (1996): 73–75; D. Carlisle, "Life-Giving Fatwa," *Nursing Times* 91, no. 29 (1995): 14–15; S. D. Lane, J. M. Jok, and M. T. El-Mouelhy, "Buying Safety: The Economics of Reproductive Risk and Abortion in Egypt," *Social Science and Medicine* 47, no. 8 (1998): 1089–99; A. Siddiqui, "Ethics in Islam: Key Concepts and Contemporary Challenges," *Journal of Moral Education* 26, no. 4 (1997): 423–31.

11. Carlisle, "Life-Giving Fatwa."

12. A. R. Gatrad, "Muslim Customs Surrounding Death, Bereavement, Postmortem Examinations, and Organ Transplants," *British Medical Journal* 309, no. 6953 (1994): 521–23.

13. J. Green, "Death with Dignity: Islam," *Nursing Times* 85, no. 5 (1989): 56–57.

14. Ibid.

15. A. S. Bhashti, "Islamic Attitude towards Abortion and Sterilization," *Birthright* 7, no. 1 (1972): 49–51; Carlisle, "Life-Giving Fatwa "; M. M. Golmakani, M. H. Niknam, and K. M. Hedayat, "Transplantation Ethics from the Islamic Point of View," *Medical Science Monitor* 11, no. 4 (2005): RA105–9; B. Larijani and F. Zahedi, "Islamic Perspective on Human Cloning and Stem Cell Research," *Transplantation Proceedings* 36, no. 10 (2004): 3188–89; A. R. Omran, "Children Rights in Islam from the Qur'an and Sunnah," *Population Sciences* 9 (1990): 77–88; N. Sarhill and others, "The Terminally Ill Muslim: Death and Dying from the Muslim Perspective," *American Journal of Hospice and Palliative Care* 18, no. 4 (2001): 251–55; J. G. Schenker, "Assisted Reproductive Practice: Religious Perspectives," *Reproductive Biomedicine Online* 10, no. 3 (2005): 310–19.

16. Sarhill and others, "Terminally Ill Muslim."

17. Daar and al-Khitamy, "Bioethics for Clinicians," 60–63.

18. Gatrad, "Muslim Customs Surrounding Death."

19. We do not wish to imply that one position is more sound than the other(s). We highlight it only to illustrate the point that such discrepancies or disagreements exist in the literature. The existence of such disagreement is problematic insomuch as the supporters of such positions do not acknowledge dissenting views in their articles.

20. S. Aksoy, "A Critical Approach to the Current Understanding of Islamic Scholars on Using Cadaver Organs without Prior Permission," *Bioethics* 15, nos. 5–6 (2001): 461–72; M. al-Mousawi, T. Hamed, and H. al-Matouk, "Views of Muslim Scholars on Organ Donation and Brain Death," *Transplantation Proceedings* 29, no. 8 (1997): 3217; Daar, "Ethical Issues," 1402–4; A. F. Ebrahim, "Islamic Jurisprudence and the End of Human Life," *Medicine and Law* 17, no. 2 (1998): 189–96; Najma Moosa, "A Descriptive Analysis of South African and Islamic Abortion Legislation and Local Muslim Community Responses," *Medicine and Law* 21, no. 2 (2002): 257–79; Obermeyer, "Reproductive Choice in Islam"; F. Rahman, "Islam and Medicine: A General Overview," *Perspectives in Biology and Medicine* 27, no. 4 (1984): 585–97; V. Rispler-Chaim, "Islamic Medical Ethics in the Twentieth Century," *Journal of*

Medical Ethics 15, no. 4 (1989): 203–8; G. I. Serour, M. A. Aboulghar, and R. T. Mansour, "Bioethics in Medically Assisted Conception in the Muslim World," *Journal of Assisted Reproduction and Genetics* 12, no. 9 (1995): 559–65; Siddiqui, "Ethics in Islam"; J. Syed, "Islamic Views on Organ Donation," *Journal of Transplant Coordination* 8, no. 3 (1998): 157–60, 162–63.

21. Al-Mousawi and others, "Views of Muslim Scholars"; Moosa, "Descriptive Analysis"; Obermeyer, "Reproductive Choice in Islam"; Rispler-Chaim, "Islamic Medical Ethics."

22. A. van Bommel, "Medical Ethics from the Muslim Perspective," *Acta Neurochirurgica: Supplement* 74 (1999): 17–27.

23. Khaled Abou El Fadl, *The Great Theft: Wrestling Islam from the Extremists* (San Francisco: Harper, 2005), 108.

24. American Association for the Advancement of Sciences, *Guide to R&D Funding Data: International Comparisons* (Washington, D.C.: American Association for the Advancement of Sciences, 2006).

25. L. T. Flannelly, K. J. Flannelly, and A. J. Weaver, "Religious and Spiritual Variables in Three Major Oncology Nursing Journals: 1990–1999," *Oncology Nursing Forum* 29, no. 4 (2002): 679–85.

26. D. Lukoff and others, "Religious and Spiritual Case Reports on MEDLINE: A Systematic Analysis of Records from 1980 to 1996," *Alternative Therapies in Health and Medicine* 5, no. 1 (1999): 64–70.

27. P. Rodriguez del Pozo and J. J. Fins, "Death, Dying and Informatics: Misrepresenting Religion on MedLine," *BMC Medical Ethics* 6 (2005): E6.

28. A. Loria and P. Arroyo, "Language and Country Preponderance Trends in MEDLINE and Its Causes," *Journal of the Medical Library Association* 93, no. 3 (2005): 381–85.

HASSAN BELLA

Islamic Medical Ethics

What and How to Teach

The teaching of bioethics in a Muslim culture is as old as the Islamic faith. The Prophet Muhammad said: "I have been sent so that I may perfect good manners and ethical conduct,"[1] thereby emphasizing the sort of character formation that is central to moral life. The first known detailed textbook written on medical ethics in Arabic, *Adab al-Tabib* (The Physician's Etiquette), also emphasized character formation.[2] Razes, the famous Muslim physician, was one of the first to express his disapproval of physicians who "used their profession to blackmail patients or used illegal and dishonorable means"; he called them "pseudo-doctors."[3] Another Muslim scholar, Ibn Kabir, in his book *What the Doctor Should Not Fail to Know,* criticized some of his contemporary "ignorant" doctors who were not committed to ethics.[4]

Any Muslim doctor who is a committed believer must know the sources of moral obligation. Islamic law, the Sharia, is "based on a complete system of morality and therefore, can deal with problems that arise in medicine from a legal perspective."[5] This system leaves room for human rational judgment when dealing with the realities of life; it is also flexible enough to address new ethical dilemmas generated by advances in science and technology.[6]

In fact the three monotheist religions (Judaism, Christianity, and Islam) call for similar ethical principles and hence can contribute to "global bioethics." Even secular ethical principles find parallels in religious writings. For example, Beauchamp and Childress's four principles of medical ethics (beneficence, autonomy, justice, and nonmaleficence) are encapsulated in one verse in the Qur'an; "Behold, God enjoins justice, and the doing of good, and generosity towards [one's] fellow-men; and He forbids all that is shameful and all that runs counter to reason, as well as malfeasance" (Q 16:90).[7]

Despite this long and illustrious history, Islamic medical ethics is not well understood, and there is need to develop a bioethics educational program that is relevant to the culture of Muslim countries. Further, many medical schools in the Muslim world do not place enough emphasis on the teaching of medical ethics. The questions of how and what to teach in Islamic medical ethics (IME) have not been adequately addressed. For this reason, I engaged a group of Muslim medical professionals in Saudi Arabia in a process called the "Delphi method," which aimed at reaching a minimum consensus on what and how to teach in IME. I also drew on my personal experience as coordinator of undergraduate and postgraduate courses in medical ethics at the College of Medicine at King Faisal University and as chief editor of the *Journal of Family and Community Medicine.*

Rationale

Although Muslim scholars' writings on medical ethics were probably some of the earliest in the world, there is little literature today on Islamic bioethics in the Muslim world. A PubMed MEDLINE search with IME as key words produced only five publications in English and relatively few in Arabic.[8] This is all the more disconcerting given the increasing interest in medical ethics as a whole. In Western literature, the number of new articles in MEDLINE with "ethics" as a key word increased in the 1990s, and in 1993 this number reached a plateau of over three thousand a year.[9] In the United States, the National Institutes of Health established the Center for Clinical Bioethics.[10] The European Community and Canada are funding research projects and peer review panels for health ethics. There are more than ten ethics specialty journals. Even the major medical and science journals read by front-line health workers allocate more space for medical ethics. In the past decade books on Islamic medical ethics have been published. However, these books are not comprehensive. Besides, many do not address the ethical concerns generated by new developments in areas such as assisted reproductive technology (ART) and cloning.[11]

Obviously the need for both specialized comprehensive publications on IME and research on IME still remains. My research demonstrates, however, that there is currently no consensus on how and what to teach in IME. Even in Western schools, the debate continues on the best methods of teaching medical ethics. In their original articles on clinical medical ethics, Siegler and his colleagues anticipated that "the focus will shift from ethics courses, committees and consultants to an understanding on the part of most physicians and medical students that ethics is an inherent and inseparable part of good clinical medicine."[12]

Methods

To facilitate discussion with health-care professionals, a modified Delphi method—a combination of qualitative and quantitative methods—was used. In the Delphi method, experts in a subject are identified and invited to participate in the study. The researcher prepares questions on the research subject and sends them to participants for their opinion. The responses are then analyzed, and a summary of the results is presented to members of the group for their opinion. In a third or fourth round, arguments are presented, along with the evolving consensus and reassessment requested by members of the group.

The Delphi method is a controlled debate[13] and is effective in allowing a group of individuals, as a whole, to deal with a complex problem.[14] The process is based on the assumption that "composite opinion is better than any single expert opinion." In addition, "Delphi studies can provide consensus from experts about difficult questions where there was no previous agreement. They have been used extensively in many scientific disciplines to identify problems and essential elements in the area of inquiry."[15]

As the number of respondents is usually small, "Delphi do not (and are not intended to) produce statistically significant results, i.e.[,] the results provided by any panel do not predict the response of a larger population or even a different Delphi panel. They represent the synthesis of opinion of the particular group, no more, no less."[16]

Selection of Participants

Participants in the current study were carefully selected so that their knowledge, experience, and cooperation might yield valuable ideas on the main questions of the study: what and how to teach Islamic medical ethics.[17] The list of participants was composed of university teachers, religious scholars, and authors of papers and books on medical ethics. Most of them were in Saudi Arabia and served as faculty in the four main medical schools there.

These four institutions vary considerably in content and number of credit hours allocated to the teaching of medical ethics. Some of these schools offer medical ethics courses as early as the second year, and most of them offer it in the fourth year, including the College of Medicine, King Faisal University.

Data Collection and Analysis

The questionnaire included multiple-choice questions with a list of possible responses, all graded on a Likert type of psychometric scale: strongly disagree, disagree, neither agree nor disagree, agree, and strongly agree: teaching IME is essential for medical and health science students, graduates, and postgraduate students. Topics included subjects/titles that should be taught in IME; suitable methods for teaching IME; and when IME should be taught. The questionnaire also included open-ended questions, such as the following: What do you think are the obstacles to including IME in current curricula in medical schools that do not offer it? Would you like to suggest methods of teaching IME other than those provided in the multiple-choice questions? Of all the method(s) mentioned, which do you think is/are the most appropriate?

After the questionnaires were completed and returned, the author summarized the results and sent a second set to the respondents, giving them an opportunity to take a look at their original responses in relation to the group responses. The questionnaire data were analyzed manually using qualitative and quantitative methods of data presentation. Each participant in the study was assured of confidentiality of responses, and anonymity was preserved as inputs were private and not seen by others. The lack of diversity among participants, all of whom were male physicians of Saudi nationality, should be noted; their responses should not be regarded as typical of the Islamic world or even of Saudi Arabia.

Findings

The emphasis of this study was on two main questions of what and how to teach IME. However, results on questions about the importance of IME, who will offer it, and when it should be taught are also presented for the sake of completeness.

The first question was on why the participants thought it important to teach IME to undergraduate medical and health-sciences students. Seventeen of the eighteen participants who responded to this question strongly agreed or agreed that the teaching of IME would change knowledge and attitudes of the students. Twelve of the participants strongly agreed or agreed that it would positively influence the students' practice. However, six of the participants were not sure if teaching IME would change practices, and one participant strongly disagreed. Fifteen of the respondents agreed or strongly agreed that current curricula, despite being crowded, can accommodate IME.

The responses of the participants to the open question on the obstacles to teaching IME included the following:

"Most of our curricula are imported from outside our countries."
"Lack of awareness of those who design curricula of the importance of IME."
"Attitudes and backgrounds of academics and the way they were trained is the main obstacle."
"Some faculty are not convinced of the feasibility of teaching IME."
"Some faculty believe that the curriculum is already too crowded to allow the addition of this subject."
"Scarcity of experts in this area" is an obstacle.
"Lack of references, especially Arabic references."
"Lack of obligation to IME in practice."

On the question of what subjects should be taught in IME, a list of thirty-five subjects was composed. The results are shown in table 1. Some of the respondents did not answer some of the questions.

TABLE 1. Subjects to be taught in IME

Subject to be taught	Strongly agree	Agree	Not sure	Disagree	Strongly disagree
Introduction to the history of medicine & etiquettes of the medical profession	7	10		1	
Sources of morality & definition of ethics	10	7	1		
Prophetic medicine	10	6		1	1
Principles of current medical ethics compared to IME	12	6			
Qualities & attributes of a Muslim doctor	17	1			
Rights & duties of the physician	17	1			
Rights & duties of patient and relatives	17	1			
Ethical aspects of the medical record	8	9	1		
Dealing with the terminal patient, the brain dead, and the dead	12	5	1		
Code of Medical Ethics	11	6	1		
Patient confidentiality	17	1			
Religious duties of patients & doctors	12	4	2		
Patients' informed consent	15	3			
Covering "Awra" (patients' private parts)	11	3	1		
Ethical aspects of medical research	14	2		1	
Equality with patients	14	3			
Jurisdiction of seeking cure	9	5	2	1	1
"Ruqia" healing prayer	10	3	4	1	
Quarantine & community protection	6	8	3	1	
Medical rights of enemies in Islam	4	12	1	1	
Prioritizing for management during disasters and wars	5	12	1		
Women's work in medicine & health care	5	8	5		
Reproductive technology	5	11	1	1	
Assisted reproduction	8	6	1	3	
Abortion	12	6			
Artificial insemination & IVF	7	4			
Genetic engineering	7	4			
Choice of sex of the newborn	7	2	1	1	
Surrogate uterus	7	1	1	2	
Cloning	7	2	1	1	
Islamic view on health promotion	4	6	1		
Organ transplantation	5	6			
Treatment with stem cells	4	6	1		
Ethical aspects in health economics and allocation of resources; equity in health care	8	2	1		
The rights of children & adolescents	8	3			

The experts were asked to suggest additional topics to be taught in IME. They provided the following suggestions:

Quality of life
Telling the patient the truth
Relief of pain
Ethics consultations
Health insurance
Relation with medical and drug industry
Ethics of dealing with patients with special needs
Mercy killing
Plastic surgeries
Interrelationships between members of the health team
Ethical issues in international health
Ethical issues related to genomic project
Medical errors, malpractice, and accountability
Etiquette of communication in Islam and skills of dealing with patients and their families

Participants were asked for their opinions on how IME should be taught. Thirteen methods were presented, and participants were requested to agree or disagree with them. Their responses are shown in Table 2.

TABLE 2. Appropriate methods for teaching IME

Methods of teaching Islamic medical ethics	Strongly agree	Agree	Not sure	Disagree	Strongly disagree
Lectures	8	6	1		
Specialized Conferences	9	4			
Workshops	13				
Bedside teaching	4	1	1	5	1
Small research projects	3	6	1		
Simulated cases	5	5	1		
Internet based learning	2	5	1	2	
Supervised reading	2	2	4	2	
Research reports	5	3	3		
Self-learning	4	3		3	
Short essay examinations	2	8		1	
Multiple choice questions exams	3	4	1	2	
Debates	2	5		1	

Participants were asked to suggest methods other than the ones on the Likert scale. Responses are as follows:

Role models
Case analysis
Group discussions
Problems-solving exercises
Reviewing and summarizing books
Case studies
Use of manuals
Criticizing videotaped behavior of doctors
Smart dialogue

The participants thought the best or ideal methods were workshops, debates, lectures, role models, and "smart dialogue," in which the opportunity is provided for learners to listen carefully, think, and be prepared to consider other views.

Other suggestions from participants were also forthcoming. One of the experts suggested that the course should be named "Medical Ethics" rather than IME, which can be taught under the title of "Islamic View on Ethical Problems." The same expert called for a distinction to be made between "clinical ethics" and "medical ethics." Another expert remarked that there is a need for the adoption of agreed-on global practical medical ethics.

Discussion

The response rate achieved in the first round of this study was 65 percent. This was expected. According to the literature, a response rate of 40 to 75 percent in Delphi studies can be anticipated.[18] The current study panel was composed of twenty-two participants. This is also consistent with the norm in the Delphi method, with most studies using panels of fifteen to thirty-five people.

It was possible through structured communication in this study to reach a collective expert opinion on what and how to teach IME. The Delphi method is known to provide consensus from experts about issues on which there was no previous agreement.[19] The final round concentrated heavily on the full outcome of the Delphi process.

Will Teaching of IME Make a Difference?

The majority of participants believed that the teaching of IME would positively influence students' future practice. A sizable minority thought it would not. There was no change on this during the last round. The author tends to agree with the reservation of the five respondents who doubted that teaching of IME would make a difference, since the outcome would depend on the methods of instruction as well as the medical teachers being used as role models.

Western authors have questioned whether teaching clinical ethics made any difference.[20] These authors are primarily interested in the operational outcome for patients. In contrast, the teaching of ethics in Muslim cultures may serve additional purposes, including instilling knowledge of right and wrong. Deep knowledge in ethical issues would help a Muslim physician make the right decisions when confronted with real problems in daily practice. According to Islamic teaching, a doctor is held accountable for his conduct and decisions, not only in this world but also on the Day of Judgment.

A prospective evaluation of a medical ethics course in Saudi Arabia produced evidence of the importance of teaching IME. Ninety percent of the undergraduate students in the study regarded medical ethics as important. Graduate students recommended reenforcement of the course during postgraduate training.[21]

Most participants in the Delphi discussion felt that despite the overcrowding of the current curricula of medical schools, IME can be accommodated. This is a long-neglected subject that is no less important than many of the subjects taught in medical schools, especially those that are not directly relevant to medical practice.

Obstacles to Teaching IME

Although some obstacles to teaching IME were listed by the participants, more than one attributed these obstacles to a problem of attitude. Scarcity of experts in the area and the lack of availability of appropriate references should not be considered barriers but challenges to face. An important possible obstacle mentioned by one participant is that many in the medical profession assume that IME is taught automatically during practice or in clinical and nonclinical courses. However, contrary to this assumption, most consultations are brief. Many doctors claim that they do not have the time to discuss ethical issues with the patient or reassure him or her, and therefore teaching IME was unlikely. Even if IME is taught in different courses, how do we ensure that all important topics are covered?

What Is to Be Taught?

The majority of respondents agreed on the importance of the thirty-five IME subjects suggested. Most of these are basic and relevant to a doctor's practice. Many are specific to the Muslim culture, such as the religious duties of patients and doctors; *ruqia,* or healing prayer; and medical rights of enemies. Some of these topics are discussed in books on ethics written in Arabic or in proceedings of Muslim scholars and regular meetings of doctors on such issues. However, many other topics are extensively and rationally addressed in Western literature, such as patient informed consent, care of the dying, organ transplantation, and assisted reproduction. Even in the last round of the study some experts continued to suggest more topics.

One of the respondents objected to the teaching of what is known as "Prophetic Medicine" on the grounds that this would be part of alternative medicine rather than IME. This dealt with spiritual rather than organic health problems. The same respondent called for a distinction between "medical ethics" and "clinical ethics." Clinical ethics is "the identification, analysis and resolution of moral problems in patient care."[22] However, although IME is not all about patient care, the emphasis, as this participant rightly indicated, should be grouped with aspects of ethics related to patient care.

The objection of some respondents to teaching controversial issues, such as "surrogate uterus," cloning, and choice of sex of the newborn, is probably based on the assumption that such issues do not commonly occur in the Muslim world. This argument is not valid, as these are, in fact, live issues. Even if these issues do not arise now in some Muslim communities, that does not mean that they will not in the future.

It was not possible to reach a consensus on subjects such as "medical insurance," relation with drug companies, and the relief of pain. Some of the suggested topics, such as ethical aspects of "quality of life" and international health, are novel. Interestingly one of the religious scholars in the group of participants suggested the inclusion of Islamic etiquette of communication with patients and the skills of dealing with patients and their families. As for the experiences of non-Muslims, it is important and permitted to benefit from their opinions if these do not conflict with Islamic principles.

How Should IME Be Taught?

Surprisingly, more than half of the respondents disagreed or strongly disagreed with the suggestion of using teaching IME as part of bedside teaching. To some extent, the same was true for Internet-based learning, supervised reading, self-learning, and multiple-choice questions as means of teaching IME. As for bedside teaching, some participants tend to think that ethical aspects of patient management should not be discussed in front of patients. In fact, not all bedside teaching is done in front of patients. Furthermore there are occasions when ethical issues must be discussed directly with the patient concerned. Patients need to know their rights and obligations. Nonetheless this "requires staff with both clinical and ethical skills, and in most universities there are not enough faculty with such skills."[23] As for Internet-based cases, self-learning, and supervised reading, these are probably newer methods that some participants are not acquainted with, or they may have difficulty employing them in their teaching.

The participants gave valuable suggestions on more methods of teaching IME. These included use of manuals, case studies, and critiques of videotaped behavior of doctors. The use of these methods could be evaluated by qualitative research. Many of the participants insisted on "role models" as an excellent means of teaching IME. However, there is a problem here. Singer and colleagues referred to clinicians in influential positions who had no respect for their patients and in so doing damaged the education of medical students and residents in a way that no ethics education program can overcome.[24]

The participants were in almost full agreement about workshops, debates, and "smart dialogue" as methods of teaching IME. One participant rightly stated that what matters is not how much is taught but the ability of students to become self-learners, researchers, and capable of dialogue. Eighty-six percent of the students sampled in a Saudi study were in favor of joint discussion panels between religious scholars and medical staff, and 70 percent of the students preferred the problem-solving approach as a teaching method for IME.[25] In the last round an expert suggested seminars as a method of teaching IME. There was insistence on Web-based learning.

A World Health Organization (WHO) consultation in Geneva (October 1994) recommended that the teaching of medical ethics be a mandatory part of post-graduate and continuous medical education.[26] This, according to WHO, should be based on group discussions, problem solving, and case studies.

In the last round of the study more than one respondent insisted on changing the name of the course to "Medical Ethics" or "Islamic Principles and Ethics in Medicine." The reason is that some topics are not directly related to ethics—for example, history of medicine, Prophetic medicine, quarantine and community protection, and women's work in medicine. More topics were suggested by some experts—for example, forbidden medicines and *halal* (legally permissible) and *haram* (legally prohibited) aspects in medicine.

Conclusions and Recommendations

The three rounds of feedback in the study indicated a consensus among the participants on the importance of teaching IME and the feasibility of its being included in the curricula of medical schools in Muslim countries. However, there was no consensus on whether teaching IME would make a difference. This would need to be verified.

The obstacles to teaching IME stated by the respondents are surmountable. There was no consensus on some topics to be taught in IME. This is expected, as some of these are gray areas for which moral reasoning needs to be worked out. Some novel titles were added by participants.

On how to teach IME, participants also provided useful suggestions. One of these is worth highlighting: self-learning, which prepares students to be life learners as more challenging ethical problems are likely to arise in the future. A combination of methods can be utilized in teaching IME. Whatever method is used, the teaching of IME should be longitudinal—that is, over the years of undergraduate education—and should be the responsibility of all medical teachers, each in his/her own specialty. One of the limitations of the current study is that there was no full consensus on all questions addressed.

To make a difference, the teaching of IME should cover not only cognitive but also attitude and skills domains. There is an urgent need to train faculty in IME in most universities in the Muslim world. Training in IME should be reinforced by conducting relevant research, particularly qualitative research, and developing graduate and fellowship programs. Subjects that are pertinent to current problems in the Muslim world should be on the list in IME. Most important of these are human rights and equity in health, from an Islamic perspective.

The preparation of a comprehensive standard textbook of IME, qualitative research, postgraduate degrees in IME, and, if possible, specialized journal(s) in medical ethics are all possible interventions that would enhance IME. One expert suggested testing the value of group discussions versus workshops in teaching IME. The next step in research is to explore "how to learn IME," as suggested by one expert in the last round.

NOTES

1. The hadith is narrated in Muḥammad Nāṣir al-Dīn al-Albānī, *Ṣaḥīḥ al-jāmi' al-ṣaghīr wa-ziyadātuhu* (Damascus: al-Maktab al-Islāmī, 1969).

2. Isḥāq b. 'Alī al-Ruhāwī (d. 931), *Adab al-Ṭabīb* (Riyadh: Markaz al-Malik Fayṣal li-l-Buḥūth wa-l-Dirāsāt al-Islāmiyah, 1992).

3. Razes (Abū Bakr ibn Zakariyya al-Rāzī, d. 925), *Al-Ḥāwī fī l-ṭibb* (Beirut: Dār Iḥyā' al-Turāth al-'Arabī Publishing and Distributing, 2002). Apparently Razes decided to become a physician when he observed the malpractices of some physicians of his time.

4. "Yūsuf ibn Ismā'īl al-Juwaynī, known as Ibn Kutbi or as Ibn Kabīr (fl. 1311), Mā lā yaṣa'u al-Ṭabīb Juhluhu," unpub. manuscript in the Library of the Hunterian Museum, University of Glasgow.

5. Omar H. Kasule, "Jurisprudence of Biotechnology," paper presented at a seminar organized by Kampong Baru Medical Center, Kuala Lumpur, October 2003.

6. As one example of the marginalization of religious and moral values in medical ethics, consider the opinion of a recent article that clinical ethics is not founded in theology but is instead a subdiscipline of medicine, centering on the doctor-patient relationship (M. Siegler, E. D. Pellegrino, and P. A. Singer, "Clinical Medical Ethics," *Journal of Clinical Ethics* 1 [1990]: 5–9). In contrast, Kasule rightly asks in "Jurisprudence of Biotechnology": "If the doctor-patient relationship is the foundation of clinical ethics, how well will it do in the future if the foundation is not solid?"

7. D. Beauchamp, "Life-Style, Public Health and Paternalism," in *Ethical Dilemmas in Health Promotion,* ed. Spiros Doxiadis (Chichester, N.Y.: Wiley, 1987), 69–81. The Qur'an translation is from Muhammad Asad, *The Message of the Qur'an* (Gibraltar: Dar al-Andalus, 1980), 409.

8. See also the preceding essay by Hasan Shanawani and Mohammad Hassan Khalil in this volume.

9. Singer, Pellegrino, and Siegler, "Clinical Ethics Revisited," *BMC Medical Ethics* 2 (2001): 1.

10. Ibid.

11. See, however, the contribution by Hamza Eskandarani in this volume.

12. Siegler and others, "Clinical Medical Ethics"; P. Singer, M. Siegler, and E. D. Pellegrino, "Research in Clinical Ethics," *Journal of Clinical Ethics* 1 (1990): 95–98; E. D. Pellegrino, M. Siegler, and P. Singer, "Teaching Medical Ethics," *Journal of Clinical Ethics* 1 (1990): 175–80; E. D. Pellegrino, M. Siegler, and P. Singer, "Future Directions in Clinical Ethics," *Journal of Clinical Ethics* 2 (1991): 5–9.

13. Theodore Jay Gordon, "The Delphi Method," in *Futures Research Methodology* (New York: American Council for the United Nations University, 1994), 1–30.

14. Harold A. Linstone and Murray Turoff, *The Delphi Method: Techniques and Applications* (Newark: Department of Information Systems at the New Jersey Institute of Technology, 2002), http://www.is.njit.edu/pubs/delphibook/ch1.html.

15. Holly Powell Kennedy, "Enhancing Delphi Research: Methods and Results," *Journal of Advanced Nursing* 45, no. 5 (2005): 504–11.

16. Ibid.

17. The participants were identified through the author's personal knowledge of their interest in the subject, by a literature search, and by recommendations by their institutions. Each of the participants was contacted individually; initially by phone and later personally or by e-mail. The letter sent to them contained a preamble with a description of the study, its objectives, and the time frame for the study. Responses were received by hand, e-mail, and fax.

18. Gordon, "Delphi Method."

19. Kennedy, "Enhancing Delphi Research."

20. Siegler and others, "Clinical Medical Ethics."

21. Kheder Ali al-Zahrani, "Teaching Medical Ethics," in proceedings of the conference on "Medical Ethics in Islam: How Different?," Riyadh, Saudi Arabia, March 2003, 82.

22. Singer and others, "Clinical Ethics Revisited."

23. Ibid.

24. Ibid.

25. Al-Zahrani, "Teaching Medical Ethics," 82.

26. World Health Organization, *Ethics of Medicine and Health* (Arabic), Technical Report Series No. 4 EMRO, WHO EM/ PHP/ 1/ A/ G, Alexandria, Egypt, 1998.

ABDULAZIZ SACHEDINA

Defining the Pedagogical Parameters of Islamic Bioethics

Secular bioethics has only recently begun to take religious perspectives seriously. Religion and medicine courses in some universities across North America have incorporated Christian and Jewish perspectives for some time, but Islamic, Buddhist, and Hindu perspectives are only now gaining recognition. This late inclusion of Islamic perspectives can be partially attributed to the lack of materials in English on Islamic bioethics. Moreover those materials that have been published actually deal with juridical-religious opinions rather than ethical deliberations based on principles and rules as developed in Islamic legal sciences. Here and there in these writings one reads references to the principle of "public interest" (*maslaha*) without any elucidation about its function, either as a principle in legal theory or as a rule of utility or beneficence that promotes the good in ethical decision-making. Instead, there is an abundance of juridical opinions (fatwas) deduced from the revealed texts on issues in biomedicine such as abortion, end-of-life decisions, and more recently, genetic engineering or stem cell research, without any ethical discussion on the rightness or wrongness of the act in its medical scientific and clinical practical settings.

The other major reason for the dearth of Islamic perspectives appears to be a lack of general interest in Islamic ethics among scholars of Islamic studies, in Western universities as well as in the Muslim world. There has been minimal Muslim participation in, for instance, comparative ethics programs in religious studies programs. Islamic theological ethics began to be taken seriously after Hourani's and Fakhry's[1] pioneering studies on the subject drew attention to the richness of the subject and its organic relation to Christian-Hellenistic natural and rational theologies. What passes for Islamic ethics in Muslim countries is mostly Aristotelian ethics and not theological ethics introduced by Hourani's groundbreaking study on the Muʿtazili theologian Qadi ʿAbd al-Jabbar.[2] Aristotelian ethics as taught in the Muslim world deals with development of the virtuous life as part of one's spiritual and moral discipline. Consequently what has been circulating as "Islamic bioethics" has little to say about ethics as a discipline that endeavors to understand the moral reasoning behind ethical decisions.

This is not surprising. Today a majority of Muslims writing on such biomedical issues are physicians who are interested in these issues through their training in the West. It is important to keep in mind that it was in the West that autonomy as an overriding right of a patient found institutional and legal-ethical support. In Islamic communitarian ethics, autonomy is far from being recognized as one of the major bioethical principles. Moreover, in the Muslim world medical practice continues to remain authoritarian and paternalistic, depriving patients and their families of any substantial role in determining the pros and cons of a treatment in critical care, where ethical dilemmas predominate. Hence, although these writers have access to the descriptive contents of religious-legal opinions in their original Arabic or Persian or their translations, they have little or no training in the normative contents of Islamic legal methodology or theological ethics and ethical principles that inform juridical sciences in Islamic jurisprudence. In the absence of essential information about the underlying ethical principles that guide the juridical research in Islamic law, the literature in English that I have examined thus far suffers from sweeping, immature judgments about Islamic positions. In some cases, "Islamic" is used simply to legitimize the ascription of the contents to Islam, with no indication that normative sources of Islamic ethical reflection provide a variety of opinions and resolutions to each ethical dilemma in biomedicine. These articles and studies, although important in their own right, can hardly form the backbone of Islamic bioethics. Instead, this emerging discipline needs to define its epistemic parameters and develop both a methodology and a justificatory mechanics of moral reasoning that explore and open venues for deriving ethical "recommendation (*tawsiyya*)" rather than "judicial opinion (fatwa)" on issues that confront human health and medical research in Muslim societies.

To underscore the importance of the normative sources that validate fresh rulings, Islamic biomedical ethics cannot ignore judicial opinions and the sources that provide their legitimization as being Islamic. Actually judicial opinions function as raw material for further inquiry into moral reasoning that undergirds these rulings. In other words, the fatwa-literature should be investigated for the purpose of exploring and understanding the legal reasoning behind the rulings. Such an investigation could unfold the rational-textual methodology (*al-ijtihad al-shar'i*) and enable the researcher to identify operative principles and rules that Muslim jurists employ in their resolution of new cases.

Figures 1 and 2 emphasize the subtle methodological differences between legal and ethical forms of deliberation and decision-making. The first schematizes the legal methodology for deducing a new legal ruling from authoritative precedent; the second shows the ethical methodology for reaching a reasonable tentative recommendation.

Figure 1. Patterns of legal decision-making

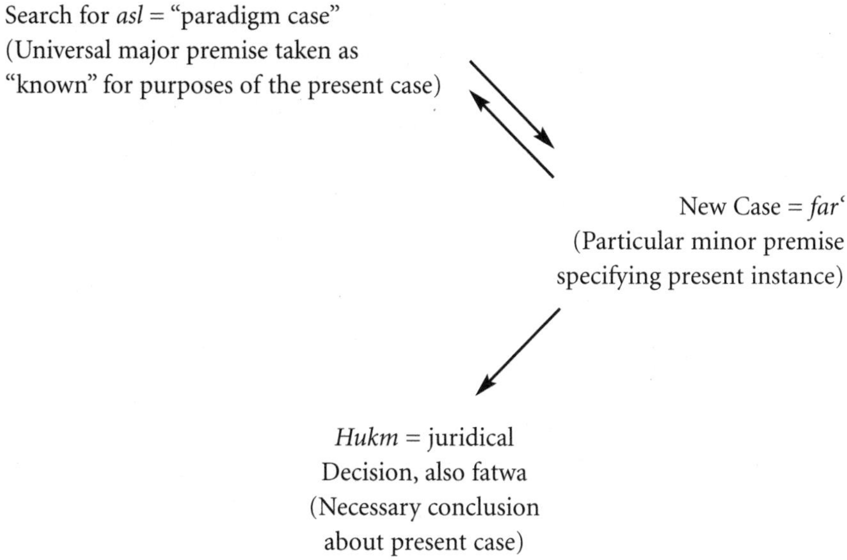

Search for *asl* = "paradigm case"
(Universal major premise taken as "known" for purposes of the present case)
New Case = *far*ʿ
(Particular minor premise specifying present instance)
Hukm = juridical Decision, also fatwa
(Necessary conclusion about present case)

Figure 2. Patterns of ethical decision-making

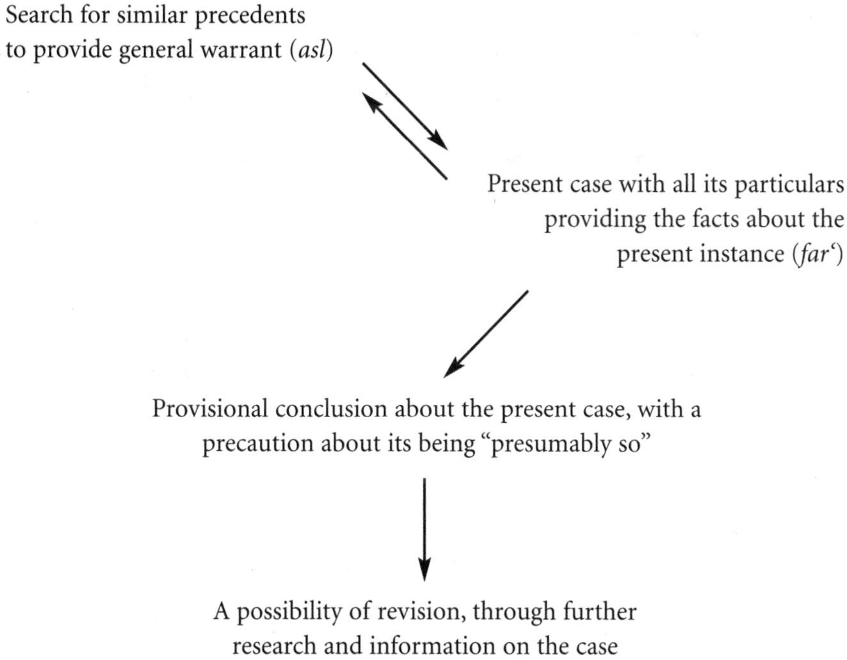

Search for similar precedents to provide general warrant (*asl*)
Present case with all its particulars providing the facts about the present instance (*far*ʿ)
Provisional conclusion about the present case, with a precaution about its being "presumably so"
A possibility of revision, through further research and information on the case

As shown in figures 1 and 2, both legal and ethical deliberations search for a precedent in the normative source (*asl*) to derive a resolution for a new case (known as *nazila* or *far'*). The search for a paradigm case is interactive, in the sense that it moves back and forth from normative to present case. The resolution in the legal case is the fatwa, which carries the authority of being implemented, whereas the resolution in the ethical case is simply to provide a recommendation that could change as the case begins to unfold in its complexity, seeking a justifiable conclusion.

It is important to state that the foundation of Islamic biomedical ethics cannot be laid solely on Islamic legal studies. The scope of Islamic legal studies includes medical jurisprudence (*fiqh al-tabib*), but it does not deal with biomedical ethics as the discipline is defined today. The total absence of any discussion about the moral underpinnings of religious duties in Islamic jurisprudence renders bioethics beyond the scope of Sharia studies. It is for this reason that in teaching Islamic bioethics there is a need to constantly avoid reducing the inquiry to fatwa investigation. There is no question that the presuppositions that underlie legal rulings are ethical in intent, because Muslim jurists make frequent mention of public good and promotion of benefit as justificatory evidence for the rulings that deal with social ethics. These rulings, not unlike ethical judgments that are derived at the end of ethical deliberations, are deduced as a result of meticulous study of the revealed, normative texts that provide principles in the form of paradigm cases. Ethical inquiry, in contrast, does not lead to an enforceable ruling resembling a judicial decision in Islamic law; rather, even when it uses some of the same principles that are used to derive a judicial decision, it strives to achieve clarity about a case at hand so that it can make recommendations about its resolution. This difference between a legal-religious ruling and an ethical resolution is worth keeping in mind when selecting appropriate readings on Islamic biomedical ethics.

Teaching Islamic Bioethics

In reviewing some recently published articles and books[3] on Islamic biomedical issues, one can gauge the spirit of Islamic juridical inquiry; however, it is hard to fathom and extract ethical deliberations that must guide human action in such cases. More important, this literature hardly provides the frame of reference for comparative study between Islamic and, for instance, Jewish or Christian bioethics. At this time Islamic bioethics will have to be taught in a comparative mode since there is a dearth of both teachers and resources to craft a uniquely Islamic bioethics curriculum in any Western university. Further, biomedical education in an Islamic context cannot succeed pedagogically without the inclusion of certain topics. Therefore the following subjects are suggested as a basis for an Islamic biomedical ethics curriculum in the context of Muslim cultures and societies:

Islamic theology and ethics, Islamic moral philosophy, philosophy of legal decision-making in Islam, and history of biomedical ethics in the West. Justification for including the history of bioethics in the West as a required subject is based on my experience in teaching bioethics in Iran, where social and political expectations from health-care institutions as well as professionals are in stark contrast with patient empowerment in the democratic and liberal societies of the West.

Since bioethics is anchored in timeless ethical norms and time-bound experience of living as humans, the subject matter of bioethics is an admixture of ethnocentric cultural context connected to geography, history, language, and ethnic tension of each community. Consequently bioethics intellectually moves from case to norm and from norm to case, in that order.

In addition Islamic bioethics needs to construct a language that is understood across cultures and traditions in order to take advantage of the opportunity to sit in dialogue with other religious or secular bioethics. Religiously based bioethics in other Abrahamic traditions shares certain common methodological features with Islam in the way an ethical dilemma is investigated and in the process of arriving at a resolution. On many occasions, both in teaching and in researching, I have found Jewish legal reasoning in consonance with Islamic legal doctrines. However, without a common bioethical vocabulary, a comparison based on commonality or differentiation between Islam and other Abrahamic traditions is difficult to undertake. Since the natural home for Islamic bioethics is a comparative ethics program within a religious studies department, it is important to emphasize the teaching of Islamic legal and ethical methodology as shown in figures 1 and 2, so that students can identify the moral-legal principles that are operative in justificatory processes employed by Muslim jurists.

In defining the pedagogical ends of Islamic bioethics, there are two related questions that must be answered. The first question deals with the general approach that should be adopted to maximize our understanding of Islamic foundational sources. The second question deals with the way Muslim culture should be interpreted in its assessment of health-care institutions and the overall expectation of the peoples with Muslim religious identity, whether they live in Muslim countries or in the West. In other words, do we need to develop a course that specifically looks at Muslims as distinct peoples with their own specific cultural experience and normative sources, or should we look at the bioethical issues as the byproduct of a universal biomedical technology that is impacting on people's expectations about life and their responses to the moral dilemma that they encounter in their everyday interaction with the world of science and medical advancement?

The other point that needs to be raised in connection with the limited scope of fatwa-literature on the biomedical issues is the fact that such literature often mirrors a particularly Arab or Persian attitude toward health-care issues, concealing the diversity of cultural attitudes toward illness and well-being in Muslim societies. Recent studies in Muslim cultural attitudes toward organ donation reveal the importance of cultural presumptions, including the way religious opinions are sought and ignored, and rarely applied, to resolve practical matters arising from moral considerations connected with conflicting claims, interests, and responsibilities.[4] Anthropological and sociological studies on Muslim attitudes toward new biomedical technology and its impact on human relationship (which is the heart of communal ethics in Islam) further corroborate my observation that in teaching about Islamic bioethics one needs to go beyond the fatwa-literature to do justice to bioethical issues by probing into highly controversial ethical dimensions of the cases in their clinical and cultural settings.

Who Should Teach?

Essentially, in the absence of any academic curriculum to train teachers of bioethics in the Islamic countries, it is impossible to determine what qualifications should be sought for those who teach the subject, whether in the context of Muslim or non-Muslim societies. While some Muslims have received their training in bioethics programs at Western universities, they lack cultural legitimacy to speak with the same authenticity in Muslim societies. The culturally specific bioethics that speaks to the social-political and cultural conditions prevalent in the West could hardly benefit these candidates preparing to teach in the Muslim world if they do not receive, at least, foundational training in normative and practical resources of their own tradition and culture. This situation makes the task of teaching Islamic bioethics in the West both challenging and exciting, as I have discovered in workshops that I led in Tehran under the auspices of Behishti University of Medical Sciences and UNESCO in 2007.

These workshops, which were conducted with the participation of seminary-trained religious scholars, provided me a rare opportunity to determine the distinguishing boundaries, separating Islamic legal from ethical studies, for Muslim jurists. In addition I also determined the substance of the courses, keeping in mind both the global and local aspects of bioethical discourse to allow for full Muslim participation in reaching ethical resolutions to the problems that have arisen since the advent of modern biomedical technology in health-care institutions. The distinction between ethical and juridical enquiry that I have introduced in Iran continues to be debated among the jurists. In response to the need to develop textbooks to teach theological ethics in the modern context, a major project of translating fundamental texts dealing with Christian and secular ethics and moral development is under way. The specific aim of this project is to develop moral reasoning within the social and political contexts of Muslim professions, including medical practice. Secular bioethics that has been thus far imported from the West (through the translations of Western studies and the pioneering articles and reports of Muslim physicians returning from abroad) cannot meet the challenges that face health-care institutions in the Muslim world if that training does not include culturally sensitive norms and rules to resolve moral problems facing the medical profession and patient care.

Practical Aspects of Teaching

An Islamic biomedical course should provide discussion of the ways in which ethical norms interact with cultural realities to produce a specific response to a moral dilemma. As such, such a course should respond to the following questions:

Are norms derived only from Revelation, or are they extracted from cases that function as the source for the derivation of the norm?
What is the significance of locating norms in history and culture?
How do we assess human experience as a key element in intuitive reasoning?
How do we assess culture as a source of moral presuppositions?
What does it mean to consider ethics as a source of moral choices in various social/political/economic contexts?

The role that intuitive reasoning plays in providing practical resolution cannot be overlooked. This practical dimension reflecting various moral facets of a case by considering conflicting claims, interests, and responsibilities is totally absent in the fatwa-literature.

Consequently the course should begin with the sources of ethical norms in Islam and situate the ethical epistemology both in revealed texts and intuitive reasoning. Introducing the students to reading the Qur'an and the Tradition (Sunna) in the context of biomedicine can be approached in two ways: 1) by taking up a case and moving through the normative sources inductively to find appropriate citations and interpretations that lead to plausible resolution(s); or 2) by going directly to the juridical methodology to indicate the deductive process that is in place among Muslim jurists to provide a response to the new case. This approach enables students to enter the field of Islamic ethics through the legal theory (*usul al-fiqh*) that is well developed in the juridical studies.

Both inductive and deductive reasoning in resolving an ethical dilemma provides the most direct experience with the ways in which normative sources are appropriated and then applied to resolve a moral dilemma. Also at this stage, a brief history of Islamic theological ethics is essential to dispel any monolithic understanding of the way that divine command ethics of the majority Sunni theologians interacts with deontological and teleological ethics of Shiite theologians. Hourani's classification of Islamic ethics into "subjective theism" (also known as "divine command ethics" in which good or evil is determined by reference to the scripture) and "objective rationalism" (also known as deontological ethics, that is, good or evil is objectively present in the act itself) is pedagogically useful in categorizing Islamic bioethics as a subfield of Islamic theological ethics.[5] This general understanding of moral epistemology is fundamental to appreciating the categorization of human action in Islamic ethics (required/necessary, recommended/good, forbidden/evil) with sometimes similar and at other times different signification of the categorization system in Islamic jurisprudence. Moreover it serves as a comparative aspect for the study of bioethics founded on different religious or cultural traditions.

Following a delineation of the juridical-ethical scope of the Islamic tradition and an explanation of the method of deriving legal-ethical decisions, Islamic bioethical principles and rules as developed and explicated in jurisprudence may be introduced. The principles and rules function as a bridge between revealed text and reason, correlating the conclusion as a normatively validated resolution. Islamic ethics requires the principles to be extracted from normative sources recognized by the community as "Islamic," and justification and legitimization are dependent on moral principles and rules established in Islamic legal theory. It is important to note that intuitive reasoning is an essential methodological process to resolve ethical dilemmas in biomedical ethics.

Through my seminary training in the legal theory and legal reasoning behind judicial rulings, I have determined specifically Islamic principles and rules that are part of the justificatory process expressly stated in some major biomedical decisions (for example, the permissibility of abortion when the mother's life is in danger) given by both Sunni and the Shiite jurists. Although some of the principles evoked in the legitimization of an ethical resolution share moral validation with secular bioethics (such as promoting beneficence and preventing maleficence), Islamic bioethics has depended largely on the principle of "no harm and no harassment" (*la darar wa-la dirar*) to resolve the majority of ethically problematic issues. A large number of articles on new issues in Arabic and Persian resort to the "no harm" principle for justificatory purposes, but several other principles are also regularly used, such as public interest (*maslaha*), necessity (*darura*), protection against distress and constriction (*'usr wa haraj*), and necessity to avert probable harm (*daf'al-darar al-muhtamal*).

Seminar on Islamic Biomedical Ethics: A Model Syllabus

A syllabus on Islamic biomedical ethics (which I developed over the last decade of teaching in the context of a theology, ethics, and culture subfield within the discipline of religious studies) can serve as a summary. I have sometimes taught bioethics under a seminar on Islamic law, ethics, and society and at other times under Islamic theology and ethics, but basically, I have followed the approach in the course outline below. In addition, in teaching the course to the teachers of bioethics, both clerics and physicians, in recent months in Behishti Medical Sciences University in Tehran, under a teaching-fellowship program that aims to develop conceptual and practical clarity in clinical ethics, I observed that the distinction between *fiqh*-studies and bioethics has assumed epistemic importance among Muslim jurists. It is gratifying to note that both Muslim physicians and Muslim jurists have taken up theological ethics as foundational to explore Islamic moral philosophy as it pertains to biomedical research and practice. This is just the beginning of Islamic bioethics, which must come to terms with the presuppositions of Western secular bioethics, namely, democratic politics and individual autonomy in determining one's rights to accept or reject a particular treatment or in consenting to become a subject of highly intrusive medical research. Without patient empowerment in the Muslim world, Islamic biomedical ethics will continue to remain a marginal discipline in medical programs across Muslim societies.

The Course

How do Muslims solve their ethical problems in biomedicine? Are there any distinctive theories or principles in Islamic ethics that Muslims apply in deriving moral judgments in bioethics? The seminar will undertake to discuss the development of a new subfield in Islamic legal and ethical studies. Although there is a long history of legal theoretical studies among Muslim legal scholars, there is a movement within the study of social ethics and its various applications in research and biomedical ethics to define its methodology as well as application in the growing awareness of the ethical issues that confront both medical and legal professionals in the Muslim world. The emergence of a specifically Islamic approach to the resolution of ethical problems in health-care ethics indicates both casuistry and principle-based ethical deliberations and rulings. The seminar will outline the moral reasoning that Muslims have developed to provide ethical guidelines in various areas of ethical problematics in research as well as clinical settings. It will, furthermore, relate these ethical principles to the moral experiences of contemporary Muslims living under different circumstances to examine the role of human experience/intuitive reasoning in deriving ethical decisions. The core of the seminar will be devoted to understanding the way culture provides the moral presuppositions, and ethics the formal normative framework, for Muslim moral choices. There is in every culture an admixture of the ethnocentric, bound to a particular geography, history, language, and ethnic strain; and the universal, which is common to all humans as humans. The course will highlight the interaction between particular and universal in resolving ethical problems in biomedicine. Selected readings in theological ethics, legal methodology, and application and a growing literature on the new rulings in bioethics will provide students of Islam and comparative ethics an opportunity to understand the underpinnings of Islamic theology and legal-ethical methodology that guide public health and medical research in Muslim countries around the world.

The Format

The seminar will be conducted in the interactive format, whereby each week students will prepare short presentations based on the readings for that week as a team (one preparing a short summary, the other critiquing the reading, and so on) in such a way that each participant will have three opportunities to present different aspects of the class materials. To encourage debate and discussion, from time to time, the class will be presented with bioethical cases to resolve the moral dilemma facing all those related to the case.

Requirements

Reading materials to prepare for class presentation and discussion will include the following:

Abdel Rahim Omran, *Family Planning in the Legacy of Islam*
Munawar Ahmad Anees, *Islam and Biological Futures: Ethics, Gender and Technology*
Aziz Sheikh and Abul Rashid Gatrad, *Caring for Muslim Patients*
Mohammad Hashim Kamali, *Principles of Islamic Jurisprudence*
Fazlur Rahman, *Health and Medicine in the Islamic Tradition*
Majid Fakhry, *Ethical Theories in Islam*
Selected articles

The seminar will also include regular presentation of short papers in class and a final paper on a selected topic (fifteen to twenty-five pages).

Seminar Subjects

The subjects under discussion will include the following:

General discussion about Islamic tradition and its ethical presuppositions: normative sources and their applications in deriving legal-ethical decisions
Theological differentiations: the makings of Islamic ethical traditions
Understanding human suffering and illness as a form of divinely ordained test
Legal and ethical categories: necessary, good, forbidden, neutral in formulation of religious-moral values
Ethical-legal methodology: moral reasoning
Principles and rules in Islamic ethics: the role of reason and its relation to Revelation-based ethics
Beginning of life, family planning, and related biomedical issues
Sexuality in Muslim culture and its impact on biomedical practice
Cultural and ethical issues related to AIDS and other epidemics
Death and dying in Muslim culture: euthanasia, physician-assisted suicide
Organ donation and transplant: who owns the human body?

Genetic engineering, genetic testing, and gene therapy
The future of biomedical ethics in the Muslim world: the role of Organization of the Islamic Conference

NOTES

1. George F. Hourani, *Reason and Tradition in Islamic Ethics* (Cambridge: Cambridge University Press, 1985); Majid Fakhry, *Ethical Theories in Islam* (Leiden: Brill, 1991).

2. George F. Hourani, *Islamic Rationalism: The Ethics of Abd al-Jabbar* (Oxford: Clarendon Press, 1971).

3. In her recently published work *Islamic Medical Ethics in the Twentieth Century,* Vardit Rispler-Chaim analyzes fatwa literature and claims that there are no specifically Islamic principles that undergird the legal-religious decisions among Muslim jurists. Some articles on abortion also follow the same kind of legalistic analysis of the biomedical issues.

4. See, for examples, the essay by Sherine Hamdy and that by Debra Budiani and Othman Shibly in this volume.

5. Hourani, *Reason and Tradition in Islamic Ethics,* 17, introduces the latter distinction in deontological norms.

MARCIA C. INHORN

Conclusion

This volume reflects the growing attention in the new millennium to Islam as the religion of approximately 1.3 billion people worldwide. That the health, illness, and healing of that population may be inflected by Islamic values and norms is a subject of considerable importance, but it is one that has been inadequately studied, particularly in comparison to the other monotheistic traditions, Judaism and Christianity, with which Islam shares its Abrahamic past. Thus this book begins to fill an important lacuna, not only in connecting Islam to the Judeo-Christian ethical tradition but also in providing important insights into Islamic medical ethics per se, on both textual and experiential levels.

Perhaps the single most important contribution of this volume is its interdisciplinary impulse: the fact that essays have been solicited from scholars in history, Islamic studies, bioethics, and anthropology. Many of these scholars have called for increasing cross-fertilization of discourses and ideas, in order to overcome the "silo effect" of disciplinary isolationism (see the essay by Hasan Shanawani and Mohammad Hassan Khalil). Nonetheless it is apparent that each discipline has a unique contribution to make to the study of Muslim medical ethics, and it is important to enumerate those contributions.

The historians in this volume have reminded us of the antiquity of medical traditions and treatises in the Muslim world—traditions and treatises that, in fact, predate Islam and that are still expressed today in the medically syncretic healing traditions of Islamic countries such as Morocco, Egypt, Iran, and Indonesia. Furthermore, these historians have shown that a concern for medical ethics, trustworthiness in the doctor-patient relationship, and harm reduction are ancient concerns that have inflected Islamic medical practice for many centuries. Although such discussions of appropriate ethical behavior and *adab* (physicians' "bedside manner") have evolved over time in the Muslim world, these concerns are of ongoing relevance today, as seen in the new focus on patient-centered care and cultural competence in medical training.

The Islamic studies scholars in the volume, including the coeditors, have brought to the forefront the need to carefully examine Islam's textual sources in any analysis of Muslim medical ethics. Nonetheless these sources—be they the Qur'an and hadith, Islamic jurisprudence and legal texts, fatwas issued by leading *'ulama',* or regulatory guidelines issued by bioethics committees in the Muslim countries—must be carefully contextualized historically, geographically, socioculturally, and even politically. Seemingly normative Islamic texts are not neutral; they may be produced through processes of debate and negotiation, and once produced, they may lead to multifarious interpretations and practices.

Indeed the Islamic studies scholars in this volume make it clear that there is no monolithic "Islam" or, for that matter, a singular "Islamic position" on any given medical subject. Islam is characterized by sectarian differences, both within and between the majority Sunni and minority Shiite branches. Within each religious community, *'ulama'* may diverge significantly in their opinions and write conflicting fatwas on medical subjects ranging from abortion to organ transplantation (see the essay by Sherine Hamdy). Similarly, ordinary Muslims may or may not follow the lead of prominent clerics, and they may or may not observe the religion and follow its normative practices (for example, prayer). In addition, on the level of practice, Islam has traditionally been characterized by a rift between more "orthodox" and "popular" or "folk" interpretations of the religion. The latter may involve recourse to Islamic Sufi and maraboutic healers and "saint" veneration at religious pilgrimage sites, neither of which is condoned by more scripturally minded adherents to the religion (see the essay in this volume by Viola Hörbst).

In short there is a need for greater local specificity in the study of Muslim medical ethics in which the false dichotomy between "norms" and "practices" is overcome (as Thomas Eich argues in his essay) and Islam is understood as heterogeneous, varying through space and through time. In order to do this, Islamic essentialisms must be assiduously avoided; yet, essentialization is a rampant problem in the English-language bioethics literature on Islam (see the essay by Shanawani and Khalil).

The bioethicists in this volume, many of them practicing physicians, have focused on the specificities of Islamic bioethics, through their attention to individual case studies, of the kind that come before medical ethics committees in the West. When the bioethical gaze falls on individual patients in communication with physicians and other health-care personnel, the importance of religion and patients' religiosity may be highlighted, as clinicians come to deal with the spiritual world of the Muslim patients in their care. It is here that universalizing, Western-generated bioethical discourses of patient autonomy, beneficence, nonmaleficence, and distributive justice may come into conflict with non-Western, Muslim understandings of bioethical behavior (see the essay by Shabbir Alibhai and Michael Gordon). In the "local moral worlds"[1] of Muslims, patients may deemphasize autonomy in favor of relationality (to family and to God); they may highlight the role of suffering as God's test or punishment; they may abide by the belief in predestination and, hence, forbid the withdrawal of life support; and they may expect medical assertiveness and paternalism in doctor-patient communication.

Thus the Western bioethical emphasis on patient autonomy and the focus on secularism in the clinical encounter may be entirely inappropriate when Western practitioners work with their Muslim clientele, who may be coerced into accepting Western bioethical standards in medical decision-making. This insight on the potential for "bioethical collision" in the Muslim-to-non-Muslim clinic encounter is crucially important, especially given the rapid growth of diasporic Muslim populations in both Europe and the Americas.

Several essays by medical anthropologists in this volume emphasize the importance of capturing the lived experience and local moral worlds of Muslim patients and their physicians through the unique methodology of ethnography. Through ethnographic fieldwork—with its focus on in-depth interviewing, participant observation in clinical settings, and community immersion over several months or years—medical anthropologists come away with a rich, if inherently subjective, understanding of health, illness, healing, and the religious valences of all of these categories as lived, on both a normative level within communities and on the level of individual life histories. Several fine examples of medical ethnography in this volume highlight the ways in which Muslims grappling with issues of health and illness, birth and death look to their religion as an important source of spiritual guidance and solace. However, these essays also highlight the ways in which pragmatic factors—such as a multiparous Muslim woman's desire to stop childbearing, an infertile Muslim man's desire to prove his fertility through polygyny, and a dying Muslim patient's desire to "buy" a kidney from a desperately poor donor—may go against dominant discourses of the religion, including ethical edicts issued through fatwas and other Islamic regulatory bodies.

This study of pragmatics and resistances in the Muslim world, especially their impact on health-related decision-making, is extremely important. Only through understanding real people's pragmatic desires and moral dilemmas can we begin to understand the intersections between religion and other important axes of social life, for example, gender, class, age, race, and nation. As described cogently by Debra Budiani and Othman Shibly in their discussion of organ donation in Egypt, the condemnation of paid donorship across the Muslim world has not prevented exploitative organ trafficking across the region. Thus the next step for Islamic ethicists is to figure out how to operationalize the Islamic prohibition against trafficking and thereby prevent exploitation of the most downtrodden members of Muslim societies. The need for advocacy of the exploited in the spirit of social justice and human rights is only too clear.

This reality encourages reflection on the moral economy of new biomedical technologies such as organ transplantation or assisted reproduction. Clearly such biotechnologies are making their way rapidly across the Muslim world, thereby invoking numerous ethical and legal debates. Even though such technologies may be scientifically deployed and somatically experienced in similar ways across cultural settings, they tend to produce differing moral responses, which may include enthusiastic accommodation, cultural reconfiguration and hybridization, or resistance and rejection based on local sentiments of moral repugnance. Depending on the cultural setting, these technologies have ramifications for personhood, kinship, and family life that can be viewed as either deeply unsettling, profoundly liberating, or more commonly, some patchwork of both. Indeed, new biotechnologies are not received in cultural or moral "vacuums," including in the Muslim world.[2] This is abundantly clear in the specific examples of organ transplantation, abortion and sterilization, assisted reproduction and embryo preservation, and end-of-life technologies (including euthanasia) described in this volume.

The future challenge in the study of Muslim medical ethics is to move beyond these categories of reproduction, human organs, and death and dying. Without denying the importance of these topics, it is nonetheless fair to say that they have become hackneyed as the subjects of Islamic ethics and perhaps bioethics more generally. It is time to broaden the focus to include some of the other pressing but seriously underemphasized issues of moral/ethical concern in the Muslim world. These would include inter alia, the global pandemics of HIV/AIDS, hepatitis C infection, and avian flu, as well as the ethically appropriate handling of Muslim patients; childhood immunization for life-threatening diseases such as polio and local resistances to such vaccination as cloaked in Islamic terms; the epidemic of smoking (including now-fashionable water pipes) and subsequent smoking-related morbidity and mortality, especially among Muslim men but also their family members; genetic problems related to high rates of consanguinity in some Muslim communities; violence of all kinds against Muslim girls and women; and the health effects of war, trauma, and displacement among many populations living in the Muslim world. These are just a few examples; many others could be cited.

To end on a personal note, it is my hope that many more young scholars, working at the intersection of religious studies, anthropology, and medicine, will take up the call to pursue such topics in Muslim medical ethics. The opportunities are manifold, given how little work has actually been done in these areas. Indeed this book is one of the few volumes on Islam and bioethics in the English-language literature. As such, it represents a major contribution to multiple fields of study, and it may be of great practical value to both Muslim and non-Muslim health-care practitioners as they interact with patients in an increasingly multicultural world.

NOTES

1. Arthur Kleinman, *Writing at the Margins: Discourse between Anthropology and Medicine* (Berkeley: University of California Press, 1997).

2. Inhorn, *Local Babies, Global Science.*

GLOSSARY

advance directive (AD) a legally binding statement of preferences for treatment at the end of life

ajal life span; the hour of death appointed by God

akhlāq Aristotelian or virtue ethics; ethics in general

'alaqa blood clot; the second stage of fetal development

'ālim sing. of *'ulamā'*; a religious authority; literally, one who knows

amāna a trust from God; a reference to the human body based on the Qur'an

'aql reason; an authoritative source of law for Shiite Islam (after Qur'an and Sunna)

ART assisted reproductive technology; methods of assisting infertile couples to have children

Ash'arī a school of Islamic theology, very influential in Sunni Islam; founded by Abū ḥasan al-Ash'arī (d. circa 941)

al-Azhar University the leading university in Egypt; pronouncements by the rector of al-Azhar have substantial authority in the Sunni Muslim world

cadaveric donations organs removed from donors after death

casuistry case-based reasoning, as opposed to reasoning from principles

ḍarūra necessity; external mitigating factors

diastole relaxing of the heart muscle; opposite of systole

DNR a do-not-resuscitate order; legally binding statement expressing the will of the patient not to be revived in the case of heart or lung failure

fatwā (pl. *fatāwā*) a nonbinding legal opinion, rendered by a mufti

fiqh jurisprudence; legal discourse; knowledge

fuqahā' jurists; those trained in the discipline of *fiqh*

furū' the application of the law, as opposed to its sources (*uṣūl*)

GCC Gulf Cooperative Council: including Bahrain, Kuwait, Oman, Qatar, Saudi Arabia, the United Arab Emirates, and Yemen

goses in Jewish law, the dying individual; someone on his/her deathbed

ḥadīth a recounting of authoritative sayings or actions; words and deeds of the Prophet Muhammad as collected by his companions

ḥakīm physician; literally, "wise person"

Halacha Jewish religious law; a Hebrew word meaning "the way"

Ḥanafī the most widespread of the four Sunni schools of law, dominant in Turkey, the Eastern Mediterranean, and South Asia

Ḥanbalī the least widespread of the four Sunni schools of law, dominant in the Arabian peninsula

ḥarām forbidden; one of the five values of legal action

ḥurma sanctity of the human body

'Ibāḍī a minor sect of Islam, still found in some areas of North Africa

ICSI Intracytoplasmic Sperm Injection, a treatment for male-factor infertility

IFA Islamic Fiqh Academy, refers to either the Majma' al-fiqhī al-islāmī of the Organization of the Islamic Conference (Jedda) or al-Majma' al-fiqhī al-islāmī of the Muslim World League (Mecca)

iftā' the giving of legal opinions (fatwas) by muftis

ijhāḍ abortion

ijmā' consensus, usually of the scholars; an authoritative source for Islamic law, after Qur'an and Sunna

ijtihād the exhaustive effort of a jurist (*mujtahid*) in investigating and deducing the law in a novel or unprecedented case

imām Sunnism: the leader of prayer or of a congregation; a political leader

Imām Shiism: one of the twelve descendants of the Prophet who led the community; the twelfth Imām remains hidden and will return; Ismā'īlī Shiism: one of forty-nine descendants of the Prophet who lead the community, the current one of which is known as the Aga Khan

IOMS Islamic Organization of Medical Sciences (Kuwait)

IUD intrauterine device, a form of contraceptive

IVF in vitro fertilization, fertilization of the egg outside of the womb

Ja'farī the dominant Shiite school of law, found among the Imāmī (Twelver) Shiites, who made up some 80 percent of Shiites in 2007

jihād a lawful and legitimate war against non-Muslims or, at times, Muslims; any legitimate and just struggle

madhhab school of law; group of scholars sharing a common outlook on sources and their interpretation

makrūh disapproved, reprehensible; one of the five legal categories

Mālikī one of the four Sunni schools of law, dominant in North and West Africa

Mande ethnic groups in Mali, Guinea, Ivory Coast, Senegal, and the Gambia that share related languages and sociopolitical, economic, and religious institutions

maqāṣid al-sharī'a the aims of the Sharia; principles perceived as underlying Islamic law

marabout West African term for a holy man, spiritual adviser, Sufi.

maṣlaḥa the principle of general societal welfare

MEDLINE an exhaustive search engine of medical literature sponsored by the National Medical Library and the National Institutes of Health of the United States, http://medlineplus.gov/

mubāh allowable, indifferent; one of the five legal categories

muḍgha cohesive lump of flesh; the third stage of fetal development

muftī a jurisconsult; authoritative person who renders a legal opinion (fatwa) in response to a query

mujtahid a jurist who performs *ijtihād* or is qualified to perform *ijtihād*

Mu'tazalī a school of Islamic theology, very influential in Shiite Islam

nidation implantation of the fertilized egg in the lining of the uterus

niyya intention

nuṭfa drop of semen; the first stage of the fetus

OIC Organization of the Islamic Conference (Jedda), an intergovernmental organization representing fifty-seven Muslim states

oocytes human egg cells

qāḍī **(pl.** ***quḍāt*****)** a judge in an Islamic legal court

Qur'ān God's revelation to the Prophet Muhammad; the most authoritative document in Islam

Shāfi'ī one of the four Sunni schools of law, dominant in Egypt and Southeast Asia

Sharī'a Islamic law; the correct path of action as determined by God

Shiites, Shī'a a Muslim sect that differs from Sunnis in several ways, especially their veneration of the Prophet's family; Imāmī Shiites are dominant in Iran and Iraq; Ismā'īlīs are found in South Asia and East Africa; Zaydis dominate in Yemen

ṣūfī one concerned with the esoteric side of religious belief; a mystic

Sunna the second authoritative source for Muslims; the correct way of doing things; the Prophet's exemplary action as recorded in hadith

Sunni the majority sect of Muslims, as opposed to Shiite

sūra one of the 114 chapters of the Qur'an

systole the contracting of the heart muscle that produces the pulse; opposite of diastole

tafsīr interpretation, usually of the Qur'an

tawṣiya advice; recommendation made by an ethical committee

'ulamā' religious scholars; literally, the people of knowledge

umma Muslim community; supercedes all other loyalties

uṣūl al-fiqh theoretical literature concerning authoritative sources; literally, roots of jurisprudence

ẓāhirī a historically important school of law, emphasizing literal interpretation of the sources

Zaydī a subgroup of Shiites, found in Yemen

BIBLIOGRAPHY

'Abd al-Razzāq, Ibn Hammām al-Ṣan'ānī. *Al-Muṣannaf.* 12 vols. Beirut: Dār al-Kutub al-'Ilmiyya, 2000.

Abdel Haleem, M. A. S. *The Qur'an.* New York: Oxford University Press, 2004.

Aberth, John. *The Black Death: The Great Mortality of 1348–1350.* Boston: Bedford / St. Martins, 2005.

Abou El Fadl, Khaled. *The Great Theft: Wrestling Islam from the Extremists.* San Francisco: Harper, 2005.

Abouna, George M. "Ethical Issues in Organ and Tissue Transplantation." *Experimental and Clinical Transplantation* 1, no. 2 (2003): 125–40.

———. "Negative Impact of Trading in Human Organs on the Development of Transplantation in the Middle East." *Transplantation Proceedings* 25, no. 3 (1993): 2310–13.

Abouna, George M., and others. "Experience with 130 Consecutive Renal Transplants in the Middle East with Special Reference to Histocompatibility Matching, Antirejection Therapy with Antilymphocyte Globulin (ALG), and Prolonged Preservation of Imported Cadaveric Grafts." *Transplantation Proceedings* 16, no. 4 (1984): 1114–17.

Abū Dāwūd, Sulaimān Ibn al-Ash'ath. *Sunan Abī Dāwūd.* 3 vols. Beirut: Dār al-Kutub al-'Ilmiyya, 1996.

Abu-Lughod, Lila. *Dramas of Nationhood: The Politics of Television in Egypt.* Chicago: University of Chicago Press, 2005.

———. "Zones of Theory in the Anthropology of the Arab World." *Annual Review of Anthropology* 18 (1989): 267–306.

Ad Hoc Committee of the Harvard Medical School. "A Definition of Irreversible Coma: Report of the Ad Hoc Committee of the Harvard Medical School to Examine the Definition of Brain Death." *Journal of the American Medical Association* 205 (August 5, 1968): 337–40.

Afsaruddin, Asma. *Excellence and Precedence: Medieval Islamic Discourse on Legitimate Leadership.* Leiden: Brill, 2002.

Ajlouni, K. M. "Values, Qualifications, Ethics and Legal Standards in Arabic (Islamic) Medicine." *Saudi Medical Journal* 24, no. 8 (2003): 820–26.

Akrami, S. M., Z. Osati, F. Zahedi, and M. Raza. "Brain Death: Recent Ethical and Religious Considerations in Iran." *Transplantation Proceedings* 36, no. 10 (2004): 2883–87.

Aksoy, S. "A Critical Approach to the Current Understanding of Islamic Scholars on Using Cadaver Organs without Prior Permission." *Bioethics* 15, nos. 5–6 (2001): 461–72.

al-Albānī, Muḥammad Nāṣir al-Dīn. *Ṣaḥīḥ al-jāmi' al-ṣaghīr wa-ziyadātuhu.* Damascus: al-Maktab al-Islāmī, 1969.

Alibhai, S. M., and M. Gordon. "Muslim and Jewish Perspectives on Inappropriate Treatment at the End of Life." *Archives of Internal Medicine* 164, no. 8 (2004): 916–17, author reply, 917.

Allbutt, Sir Clifford. *Greek Medicine in Rome.* London: Macmillan, 1921.

Ambers, R. B., and A. M. Babey Brooke. *The Pulse in Occident and Orient.* New York: Santa Barbara Press, 1966.

American Association for the Advancement of Sciences. *Guide to R&D Funding Data: International Comparisons.* Washington, D.C.: American Association for the Advancement of Sciences, 2006.

Anees, Munawar Ahmad. *Islam and Biological Futures: Ethics, Gender and Technology.* London: Mansell, 1989.

Anagnost, A. "A Surfeit of Bodies: Population and the Rationality of the State in Post-Mao China." In *Conceiving the New World Order: The Global Politics of Reproduction,* edited by F. Ginsburg and R. Rapp, 22–41. Berkeley: University of California Press, 1995.

Asad, Muhammad. *The Message of the Qur'an.* Gibraltar: Dar al-Andalus, 1980.

al-Ashqar, 'Umar Sulaymān. "Al-Istifāda min al-ajinna al-mujhaḍa aw al-zā'ida 'an al-ḥājja fī l-tajārib al-'ilmiyya wa-zirā'at al-a'ḍā'." In *Ru'ya Islāmiyya li-zirā'at ba'ḍ al-a'ḍā 'al-bashariya,* edited by 'Abd al-Raḥmān al-'Awaḍī and Khālid Madhkūr, 393–99. Kuwait: al-Munaẓẓama al-Islāmiyya li-l-'Ulūm al-Ṭibbiyya, [1992?].

Asman, O. "Abortion in Islamic Countries—Legal and Religious Aspects." *Medicine and Law* 23, no. 1 (2004): 73–89.

'Aṭiya, Jamāl al-Dīn. *Nahwa taf'īl maqāṣid al-sharī 'a.* Damascus: Dār al-Fikr, 2001.

Avicenna (see also Ibn Sīnā). *The Canon of Medicine.* Edited by L. Bakhtiar. Chicago: Kazi, 1999.

———. *Kitāb al-shifā'.* Cairo: al-Hay'a al-Miṣriyya, 1983.

———. *Liber de Anima.* Louvain: Peters, 1968.

———. *Livre des directives et remarques.* Edited by A. M. Goichon. Paris: Vrin, 1972.

al-'Awaḍī, 'Abd al-Raḥmān, ed. *Al-Injāb fi dau' al-Islām.* Kuwait: al-Munaẓẓama al-Islāmiyya li-l-'Ulūm al-Ṭibbiyya, [1984?].

———. *Ru'ya islāmiyya li-zirā'at ba'ḍ al-a'ḍā'al-bashariya.* Kuwait: al-Munaẓẓama al-Islāmiyya li-l-'Ulūm al-Ṭibbiyya, [1992?].

al-'Awaḍī, 'Abd al-Raḥmān, and Khālid Madhkūr. *Al-Ru'ya al-islāmiyya li-ba'ḍ al-mumārasāt al-ṭibbiyya.* 2nd ed. Kuwait: al-Munaẓẓama al-Islāmiyya li-l-'Ulūm al-Ṭibbiyya, 1995.

———. *Ru'ya islāmiyya li-ba'ḍ al-mushkilāt al-ṭibbiyya al-mu'āṣira.* Kuwait: al-Munaẓẓama al-Islāmiyya li-l-'Ulūm al-Ṭibbiyya, 1999.

Badawi, Z. "The Role of the Church in Developing the Law: An Islamic Response." *Journal of Medical Ethics* 28, no. 4 (2002): 223.

Ballaster, Luis Garcia. "Problem in Diagnosis." In *Galen: Problems and Prospects,* edited by Vivian Nutton, 13–46. London: Wellcome Institute for the History of Medicine, 1981.

Banchoff, Thomas. "Path Dependence and Value-Driven Issues: The Comparative Politics of Stem Cell Research." *World Politics* 57 (January 2005): 200–230.

Banwell, S. S., and J. M. Paxman. "The Search for Meaning: RU 486 and the Law of Abortion." *American Journal of Public Health* 82, no. 10 (1992): 1399–1406.

al-Bār, Muḥammad 'Alī. *Khalq al-insān bayna al-ṭibb wa-l-Qur'ān.* 11th ed. Jedda: al-Dār al-Sa'ūdiyya li-l-Nashr wa-l-Tauzī', 1999.

Barnes, J. "Galen on Logic and Therapy." In *Galen's Method of Healing,* edited by F. Kudlien and R. Durling, 50–101. Leiden: Brill, 1991.

Battin, Margaret P. "Euthanasia: The Fundamental Issues." In *Readings in Health Care Ethics,* edited by Elisabeth Boetzkes and Wilfred J. Waluchow, 363–84. Peterborough, Ont.: Broadview Press, 2002.

Beauchamp, T. L., and J. F. Childress. *Principles of Biomedical Ethics.* Oxford: Oxford University Press, 2001.

Belk, Russell W. "Me and Thee Versus Mine and Thine: How Perceptions of the Body Influence Organ Donation and Transplantation." In *Organ Donation and Transplantation: Psychological and Behavioural Factors,* edited by James Shanteau and Richard Jackson Harris, 139–58. Washington, D.C.: American Psychological Association, 1990.

Benedictow, Ole. *The Black Death 1346–1353: The Complete History.* Rochester, N.Y.: Boydell Press, 2004.

Bercovitch, M., A. Waller, and A. Adunsky. "High Dose Morphine Use in the Hospice Setting: A Database Survey of Patient Characteristics and Effect on Life Expectancy." *Cancer* 86, no. 5 (1999): 871–77.

Berker, F. "Not Contradicting the Religion: Islam Has Been Putting an Emphasis on Family Planning for 14 Centuries." *Integration* 47 (Spring 1996): 4.

Bernard, Marie. "La critique de la notion de nature (*ṭab'*) par le *kalām*." *Studia Islamica* 51 (1980): 59–107.

Bewley, Aisha, trans. *Tafsir al-Qurtubi.* London: Dar al-Taqwa, 2003– .

Bhashti, A. S. "Islamic Attitude towards Abortion and Sterilization." *Birthright* 7, no. 1 (1972): 49–51.

Bledsoe, C., A. Hill, U. d'Alessandro, and P. Langerock. "Constructing Natural Fertility: The Use of Western Contraceptive Technologies in Rural Gambia." *Population and Development Review* 20 (March 1994): 81–113.

Boethius. *Fundamentals of Music.* Edited by C. Palisca. New Haven, Conn.: Yale University Press, 1989.

Bommel, A. van "Medical Ethics from the Muslim Perspective." *Acta Neurochirurgica* (supplement) 74 (1999): 17–27.

Borell, Merriley. "Training the Senses, Training the Mind." In *Medicine and the Five Senses,* edited by William F. Bynum and Roy Porter, 244–321. London: Cambridge, 1993.

Borsch, Stuart J. *The Black Death in Egypt and England: A Comparative Study.* Austin: University of Texas Press, 2005.

Bragason, E. H. *Interviewing through Interpreters.* Newsletter of the Psykologisk Institut, Århus Universitet, Denmark. http://mit.psy.au.dk/ckm/newsletter/nb23/23-egil.htm, accessed October 10, 2004.

Brand, Saskia. *Mediating Means and Fate: A Socio-political Analysis of Fertility and Demographic Change in Bamako, Mali.* Leiden: Brill, 2001.

Brockopp, Jonathan E. "Cultivating a Liberal Islamic Ethics, Building on Islamic Civil Society." *Journal of the Society for Christian Ethics* 27, no. 1 (2007): 23–26.

———. "Islam and Bioethics beyond Abortion and Euthanasia." *Journal of Religious Ethics* 36 (March 2008): 3–12.

———. "Islamic Ethics of Saving Life: A Comparative Perspective." *Medicine and Law* 21, no. 2 (2002): 225–41.

Brockopp, Jonathan E., ed. *Islamic Ethics of Life: Abortion, War, and Euthanasia.* Columbia: University of South Carolina Press, 2003.

Broeckaert, B. "Ethical Issues at the End of Life." In *Palliative Care Nursing: Principles and Evidence for Practice,* edited by S. Payne, J. Seymour, and C. Ingleton. Berkshire: Open University Press, forthcoming.

Broeckaert, B., and the Flemish Palliative Care Federation. *End of Life Decisions—A Conceptual Framework.* Brussels: Federatie Palliatieve Zorg Vlaanderen, 2006.

Broeckaert, B., and J. M. Nuñez Olarte. "Sedation in Palliative Care: Facts and Concepts." In *The Ethics of Palliative Care: European Perspectives,* edited by H. Ten Have and D. Clarke, 166–80. Buckingham: Open University Press, 2002.

Broumand, Behrouz. "Transplantation Activities in Iran." *Experimental and Clinical Transplantation* 3, no. 1 (2005): 333–37.

Browne, E. G. *Arabian Medicine.* Westport, Conn.: Hyperion, 1921.

Browner, Carole H., and Carolyn F. Sargent. "Anthropology and Studies of Human Reproduction." In *Medical Anthropology: A Handbook of Theory and Methods,* edited by Thomas Johnson and Carolyn F. Sargent, 215–29. New York: Greenwood Press, 1990.

Budiani, Debra. "Consequences of Living Kidney Donors in Egypt." Presentation and proceedings of WHO and MESOT meetings, Kuwait, November 26–29, 2006.

———. "Facilitating Organ Transplants in Egypt: An Analysis of Doctors' Discourse." *Body and Society* 13 (2007): 125–49.

al-Bukhārī, Abū ʿAbd Allāh. *Ṣaḥīḥ al-Bukhārī.* 8 vols. Cairo, 1898; 9 vols. Cairo: Dār Maṭābiʿ al-Shaʿb, 1960–67?

Bureau of Statistics and Planning Commission and Macro International Inc. *HIV/AIDS Indicator Survey 2003–4.* Calverton, Md:. Macro International Inc., 2005.

———. *Tanzania: Demographic and Health Survey 1996.* Calverton, Md.: Macro International Inc. and Bureau of Statistics and Planning Commission, 1997.

Bylebyl, Jerome. "Galen and the Non-natural Causes of the Variations of the Pulse." *Bulletin of the History of Medicine* 45 (1971): 482–85.

Caldwell, J. C., and P. Caldwell. "The Fertility Transition in Sub-Saharan Africa." In *Fertility and the Current South African Issues of Poverty, HIV/AIDS and Youth,* 117–23. Cape Town: Human Sciences Research Council, 2002.

Calero Secall, M. Isabel. "El Proceso de Ibn al-Jaṭib." *Al-Qanṭara* 22, no. 2 (2001): 421–61.

Camara, Sory. *Gens de la Parole: Essai sur la condition et le rôle des griots dans la société Malinké.* Paris: Mouton, 1976.

Carlisle, D. "Life-Giving Fatwa." *Nursing Times* 91, no. 29 (1995): 14–15.

Carter, A. "Agency and Fertility: For an Ethnography of Practice." In *Anthropology Theorizes Reproduction: Integrating Practice, Political Economic, and Feminist Perspectives,* edited by S. Greenhalgh, 55–85. Cambridge: Cambridge University Press, 1995.

Clarfield, A. M., M. Gordon, H. Markwell, and S. M. Alibhai. "Ethical Issues in End-of-Life Geriatric Care: The Approach of Three Monotheistic Religions—Judaism, Catholicism, and Islam." *Journal of the American Geriatrics Society* 51, no. 8 (2003): 1149–54.

Cloonan, K., C. Crumley, and S. Kiymaz. "The Historical, Scientific, Cultural, and Economic Aspects of Gender Pre-selection." In *Developmental Biology,* edited by S. F. Gilbert, 7th ed. Sunderland, Mass.: Sinauer, 2003.

Cohen, Lawrence. "The Other Kidney: Biopolitics beyond Recognition." In *Commodifying Bodies,* edited by Nancy Scheper-Hughes and Loïc Wacquant, 9–30. London: Sage, 2002.

Comaroff, John L., and Jean Comaroff. "Of Fallacies and Fetishes: A Rejoinder to Donham." *American Anthropologist* 103, no. 1 (2001): 150–60.

Comerasamy, H., B. Read, C. Francis, and S. Cullings. "The Acceptability and Use of Contraception: A Prospective Study of Somalian Women's Attitudes." *Journal of Obstetrics and Gynaecology* 23, no. 4 (2003): 412–15.

Congourdeau, Marie-Hélène, and Mohamed Melhaoui. "La perception de la peste en pays Chrétien Byzantine et Musulman." *Revue des Études Byzantines* 59 (2001): 95–124.

Conrad, Lawrence. "A Ninth-Century Muslim Scholar's Discussion of Contagion." In *Contagion: Perspectives from Pre-modern Societies,* edited by Lawrence Conrad and Dominik Wujastyk, 163–77. Burlington, Vt.: Ashgate, 2000.

———. "'Umar at Sargh: The Evolution of an Umayyad Tradition on Flight from the Plague." In *Story-Telling in the Framework of Non-fictional Arabic Literature,* edited by Stefan Leder, 488–528. Wiesbaden: Harrassowitz, 1998.

Crotty, M. *The Foundations of Social Research: Meaning and Perspective in the Research Process.* London: Sage, 1998.

Daar, A. S. "Current Practice and the Legal, Ethical and Religious Status of Post Mortem Organ Donation in the Islamic World." In *Organ Replacement Therapy: Ethics, Justice, Commerce,* edited by W. Land and J. B. Dossetor. Berlin: Springer, 1991.

———. "Ethical Issues: A Middle East Perspective." *Transplantation Proceedings* 21, no. 1 (1989): 1402–4.

———. "Money and Organ Procurement: Narratives from the Real World." In *Legal and Social Issues in Organ Transplantation,* edited by Theo Gutmann, A. S. Daar, R. Sells, and W. Land, 298–314. Munich: Pabs Publishers, 2004.

———. "Organ Donation—World Experience: The Middle East." *Transplantation Proceedings* 23, no. 5 (1991): 2505–7.

———. "South Mediterranean, Middle East, and Subcontinent Organ Transplant Activity." *Transplantation Proceedings* 33, nos. 1–2 (2001): 1993–94.

Daar, A. S., and B. al-Khitamy. "Bioethics for Clinicians: 21. Islamic Bioethics." *Canadian Medical Association Journal* 164, no. 1 (2001): 60–63.

Danforth, William H., and William B. Neaves. "Using Words Carefully." *Science* 309 (September 16, 2005): 1816–17.

al-Daqr, Nadā Muḥammad Na'īm. *Mawt al-dimāgh bayna al-ṭibb wa-l-Islām.* Damascus: Dār al-Fikr, 1997.

Dehne, K. L. "Knowledge of, Attitudes towards, and Practices Relating to Child-Spacing Methods in Northern Burkina Faso." *Journal of Health, Population, and Nutrition* 21, no. 1 (2003): 55–66.

DeJong, W. "Abortion and Islam" (in Dutch). *Tijdschrift voor ziekenverpleging* 21, no. 16 (1968): 666.

———. "Islam and Medical Ethics" (in Dutch). *Tijdschrift voor ziekenverpleging* 23, no. 2 (1970): 63–65, and 23, no. 7 (1970): 359–61.

Del Pozo, P. R., and J. J. Fins. "The Globalization of Education in Medical Ethics and Humanities: Evolving Pedagogy at Weill Cornell Medical College in Qatar." *Academic Medicine: Journal of the Association of American Medical Colleges* 80, no. 2 (2005): 135–40.

Dieterlen, Germaine. *Essai sur la religion Bambara.* 2nd ed. Brussels: Editions de l'Université de Bruxelles, 1988.

Dobbelaere, K., M. Elchardus, J. Kerkhofs, L. Voyé, and B. Bawin-Legros. *Verloren zekerheid: De Belgen en hun waarden, overtuigingen en houdingen.* Tielt: Lannoo, 2001.

Dols, Michael. *The Black Death in the Middle East.* Princeton, N.J.: Princeton University Press, 1977.

———. "The Comparative Communal Responses to the Black Death in Muslim and Christian Societies." *Viator* 5 (1974): 269–87.

Dorff, Elliot, and Louis Newman, eds. *Contemporary Jewish Ethics and Morality.* New York: Oxford University Press, 1995.

Doxiadis, Spyros, ed. *Ethical Dilemmas in Health Promotion.* Chichester: Wiley, 1987.

DuBose, E. R., ed. *Religious Beliefs and Health Care Decisions: A Quick Reference to 15 Religious Traditions and Their Application in Health Care.* Chicago: Park Ridge Center for the Study of Health, Faith, and Ethics, 1995.

Dudgeon, Matthew R., and Marcia C. Inhorn. "Men's Influences on Women's Reproductive Health: Medical Anthropological Perspectives." *Social Science and Medicine* 59 (October 2004): 1379–95.

Duffin, J. "The Cardiology of R. T. H. Laennec." *Medical History* 33 (January 1989): 42–71.

Duriez, B., J. R. J. Fontaine, and D. Hutsebaut. "A Further Elaboration of the Post-critical Belief Scale: Evidence for the Existence of Four Different Approaches to Religion in Flanders-Belgium." *Psychologica Belgica* 40, no. 3 (November–December 2000): 153–81.

Dwyer, J. C., and J. Haws. "Is Permanent Contraception Acceptable in Sub-Saharan Africa?" *Studies in Family Planning* 21 (1990): 322–26.

Dyer, S. J., N. Abrahams, N. E. Mokoena, and Z. M. van der Spuy. "'You Are a Man because You Have Children': Experiences, Reproductive Health Knowledge and Treatment-Seeking Behaviour among Men Suffering from Couple Infertility in South Africa." *Human Reproduction* 19, no. 4 (2004): 960–67.

Ebrahim, A. F. *Abortion, Birth Control and Surrogate Parenting: An Islamic Perspective.* [Indianapolis]: American Trust Publications, 1989.

———. "Islamic Ethics and the Implications of Modern Biomedical Technology: An Analysis of Some Issues Pertaining to Reproductive Control, Bioethical Parenting and Abortion." Ph.D. diss., Temple University, 1986.

———. "Islamic Jurisprudence and the End of Human Life." *Medicine and Law* 17, no. 2 (1998): 189–96.

———. "The Living Will (*Wasiyat al-Hayy*): A Study of Its Legality in the Light of Islamic Jurisprudence." *Medicine and Law* 19, no. 1 (2000): 147–60.

———. *Organ Transplantation: Contemporary Islamic Legal and Ethical Perspectives.* Kuala Lumpur: A. S. Noordeen, 1998.

Edelstein, Ludwig. *Ancient Medicine.* Baltimore: Johns Hopkins University Press, 1967.

Eich, Thomas. "The Debate about Human Cloning among Muslim Religious Scholars since 1997." In *Cross-Cultural Issues in Bioethics: The Example of Human Cloning,* edited by Heiner Roetz, 291–310. Amsterdam: Rodopi, 2006.

———. *Islam und Bioethik: Eine kritische Analyse der modernen Diskussion im islamischen Recht.* Wiesbaden: Reichert, 2005.

Eisenberg, V. H., and J. G. Schenker. "The Ethical, Legal and Religious Aspects of Preëmbryo Research." *European Journal of Obstetrics, Gynecology, and Reproductive Biology* 75, no. 1 (1997): 11–24.

Elgood, Cyril. *Medical History of Persia and the Eastern Caliphate.* London: Cambridge, 1951.

Elwan, Omaia. "Empfängnisregelung und Abtreibung im Islam." In *Rechtsvergleichung und Rechtsvereinheitlichung,* edited by Eduard Wahl and Rolf Seick, 439–70. Heidelberg: Winter, 1967.

———. "Das Problem der Empfängnisregelung und Abtreibung: Die herrschende Auffassung des Staates und der religiösen Kreise in islamischen Ländern." *Zeitschrift für vergleichende Rechtswissenschaft* 70 (1968): 25–80.

Engelhardt, H. Tristram. *The Foundations of Bioethics.* New York and Oxford: Oxford University Press, 1996.

Entralgo, Lain. *Doctor and Patient.* New York: Macmillan, 1967.

Ernst, Carl. *Following Muhammad: Rethinking Islam in the Contemporary World.* Chapel Hill: University of North Carolina Press, 2003.

Esack, Farid. "Muslims Engaging the Other and the Humanum." In *Sharing the Book: Religious Perspectives on the Rights and Wrongs of Proselytism,* edited by John Witte Jr. and Richard C. Martin, 118–44. Maryknoll, N.Y.: Orbis Books, 1999.

Eskandarani, H. A. *Assisted Reproduction Technology, "State-of-the-Art."* Rabat: Islamic Educational, Scientific and Cultural Organization (ISESCO), 1996.

Everson, S. *Aristotle on Perception.* Oxford: Clarendon, 1997.

Evrigenis, Ioannis. "Doctrine of the Mean in Aristotle's Ethical and Political Theory." *History of Political Thought* 20 (Autumn 1999): 393–416.

Fahmy, Khaled. "The Anatomy of Justice: Forensic Medicine and Criminal Law in Nineteenth-Century Egypt." *Islamic Law and Society* 6 (June 1999): 224–71.

————. "Women, Medicine and Power." In *Remaking Women: Feminism and Modernity in the Middle East,* edited by Lila Abu-Lughod, 35–72. Princeton, N.J.: Princeton University Press, 1998.

Fakhry, Majid. *Ethical Theories in Islam.* Leiden: Brill, 1991; 2nd expanded ed., 1994.

———. *Islamic Occasionalism.* London: Allen and Unwin, 1958.

Faour, M. "Fertility Policy and Family Planning in Arab Countries." *Studies in Family Planning* 20 (September–October 1989): 254–63.

Farage, Samar. "Galenic Medicine." In *Encyclopedia of Science, Technology and Ethics,* edited by Carl Mitcham, 812–13. New York: Macmillan, 2005.

Farmer, H. G. *History of Arabian Music to the 13th Century.* London: Luzac and Co, 1929.

Fierro, Maribel. "El principio mālikī sadd al-dharā'ī' en el Kitāb al-ḥawādith wa-l-bida' de Abū Bakr al-Turtūshī." *al-Qanṭara* 2 (1981): 69–87.

Flannelly, L. T., K. J. Flannelly, and A. J. Weaver. "Religious and Spiritual Variables in Three Major Oncology Nursing Journals: 1990–1999." *Oncology Nursing Forum* 29, no. 4 (2002): 679–85.

Floyer, John. *The Physician's Pulse-watch: or An Essay to Explain the Old Art of Feeling the Pulse.* London: Sam Smith, 1707.

Fortier, Corinne. "Le lait, le sperme, le dos. Et le sang? Représentations physiologiques de la filiation et de la parenté de lait en islam malékite et dans la société maure de Mauritanie." *Cahiers d'Études Africaines* 40, no. 161 (2001): 97–138.

Foucault, Michel. *The Birth of the Clinic.* New York: Vintage, 1973.

Fox, Renée C., and Judith P. Swazey. *The Courage to Fail: A Social View of Organ Transplants and Dialysis.* Chicago: University of Chicago Press, 1974.

Franklin, Sarah. "Science as Culture, Cultures of Science." *Annual Review of Anthropology* 24 (October 1995): 163–84.

Freed, A. O. "Interviewing through an Interpreter." *Social Work* 33, no. 4 (1988): 315–19.

Galenus, Claudius. *Galen: Selected Writings.* Edited by Peter Singer. London: Oxford, 1997.

———. *Galen Opera Omnia.* 20 vols. Edited by C. G. Kuhn. Leipzig: C. Knoblochii, 1892.

———. *Galen on Medical Experience.* Translated by H. A. R. Gibb. London: Oxford University Press, 1944.

Gallagher, Nancy. *Medicine and Power in Tunisia 1780–1900.* Cambridge: Cambridge University Press, 1983.

Gannon, Kenneth, Lesley Glover, and Paul Abel. "Masculinity, Infertility, Stigma and Media Reports." *Social Science and Medicine* 59, no. 6 (2004): 1169–75.

Gatrad, A. R. "Muslim Customs Surrounding Death, Bereavement, Postmortem Examinations, and Organ Transplants." *British Medical Journal* 309, no. 6953 (1994): 521–23.

Gatrad, A. R., and A. Sheikh. "Medical Ethics and Islam: Principles and Practice." *Archives of Disease in Childhood* 84 (January 2001): 72–75.

———. "Palliative Care for Muslims and Issues before Death." *International Journal of Palliative Nursing* 8, no. 11 (2002): 526–31.

Gatrad, A. R., G. Mynors, P. Hunt, and A. Sheikh. "Patient Choice in Medicine Taking: Religious Sensitivities Must Be Respected." *Archives of Disease in Childhood* 90 (2005): 983–84.

Geschiere, Peter. *Village Communities and the State: Changing Relations among the Maka of South-Eastern Cameroon since the Colonial Conquest.* London: Kegan Paul International, 1983.

Ghanem, Isam. *Islamic Medical Jurisprudence.* London: Probsthain, 1982.

Ghods, Ahad J. "Renal Transplantation in Iran." *Nephrology Dialysis Transplantation* 17, no. 2 (2002): 222–28.

Gladston, Iago. "Diagnosis in Historical Perspective." *Bulletin of the History of Medicine* 9 (April 1941): 367–84.

Glannon, Walter. *Biomedical Ethics.* New York: Oxford University Press, 2005.

Glaser, B. G., and A. L. Strauss. *The Discovery of Grounded Theory: Strategies for Qualitative Research.* New York: Aldine, 1967.

Glock, C. Y., and R. Stark. *Religion and Society in Tension.* Chicago: Rand McNally, 1965.

Goldsand, G., Z. R. Rosenberg, and M. Gordon. "Bioethics for Clinicians: 22. Jewish Bioethics." *Canadian Medical Association Journal* 164, no. 2 (2001): 219–22.

Golmakani, M. M., M. H. Niknam, and K. M. Hedayat. "Transplantation Ethics from the Islamic Point of View." *Medical Science Monitor* 11, no. 4 (2005): RA105–9.

Gordon, Michael, and Shabbir M. H. Alibhai. "Ethics of PEG Tubes—Jewish and Islamic Perspectives." *American Journal of Gastroenterology* 99, no. 6 (2004): 1194.

Gordon, Theodore Jay. "The Delphi Method." In *Futures Research Methodology.* Edited by Jerome Glenn, 1–30. New York: American Council for the United Nations University, 1994.

Goyal, Madhav, Ravindra Mehta, Lawrence Schneiderman, and Ashwini Sehgal. "Economic and Health Consequences of Selling a Kidney in India." *Journal of the American Medical Association* 288, no. 13 (2002): 1589–93.

Gräf, Erwin. "Die Stellungnahme des islamischen Rechts zu Geburtenregelung (tanẓîm al-nasl) und Geburtenbeschränkung (taḥdîd al-nasl)." In *Der Orient in der Forschung,* edited by Wilhelm Hoenerbach, 209–32. Wiesbaden: Harrassowitz, 1967.

Green, J. "Death with Dignity: Islam." *Nursing Times* 85, no. 5 (1989): 56–57.

Greenhall, E., and M. Vessey. "The Prevalence of Subfertility: A Review of the Current Confusion and a Report of Two New Studies." *Fertility and Sterility* 54, no. 6 (1999): 978–83.

Gross, M. L. "Medical Ethics Committees in Israel: Implementing the Israel Patient Rights Act and Terminating Life-Sustaining Treatment." *Israel Medical Association Journal* 3, no. 6 (2001): 461–64.

Grosz-Ngaté, Maria. "Hidden Meanings: Explorations into a Bamanan Construction of Gender." *Ethnology* 28, no. 2 (1989): 167–83.

Grundmann, Johannes. "Scharia, Hirntod und Organtransplantation: Kontext und Wirkung zweier islamischer Rechtsentscheidungen im Nahen und Mittleren Osten." *Orient* 45, no. 1 (2004): 27–46.

Gunby, J., and S. Daya, on behalf of the IVF Directors Group of the Canadian Fertility and Andrology Society. "Assisted Reproductive Technologies (ART) in Canada: 2001 Results from the Canadian ART Register." *Fertility and Sterility* 84 (September 2005): 590–99.

Hadolt, Bernhard, and Monika Lengauer. "Kinder-Machen: Eine ethnographische Untersuchung zur Handhabe von ungewollter Kinderlosigkeit und den Neuen Reproduktionstechnologien durch betroffene Frauen." Ph.D. diss., University of Vienna, 2003.

Hadot, Pierre. *Philosophy as a Way of Life.* London: Blackwell, 1995.

Hall, Rupert. "Studies in the History of the Cardio-vascular System." *Bulletin of the History of Medicine* 34 (1960): 391–413.

Hallaq, Wael. *Authority, Continuity and Change in Islamic Law.* Cambridge: Cambridge University Press, 2001.

———. *A History of Islamic Legal Theories.* Cambridge: Cambridge University Press, 1997.

Hamdy, Sherine. "Our Bodies Belong to God: Islam, Medical Science, and Ethical Reasoning in Egyptian Life." Ph.D. diss., New York University, 2006.

Hankinson, R. J. *Cause and Explanation in Ancient Greek Thought.* Oxford: Clarendon, 1998.

Hanks, G., C. J. C. Roberts, and A. N. Davies. "Principles of Drug Use in Palliative Medicine." In *Oxford Textbook of Palliative Medicine,* 3rd ed., edited by D. Doyle, G. Hanks, N. Cherny, and K. Calman, 213–25. Oxford: Oxford University Press, 2005.

Harris, C. R. S. *The Heart and Cardio-vascular System in Ancient Greek Medicine.* Oxford: Oxford University Press, 1973.

Hasan, K. Z. "Islam and the Four Principles: A Pakistani View." In *Principles of Health Care Ethics,* edited by R. Gillon, 93–103. New York: John Wiley and Sons, 1994.

Ḥasan, Muḥammad Mahjūb Muḥammad. *Muḥammad Mutwallī al-Shaʿrāwī: min al-qarya ilā al-ʿālamiyya.* Cairo: Maktabat al-Turāth al-Islāmī, 1990.

Hatem, Mervat. "The Professionalization of Health and the Control of Women's Bodies as Modern Governmentalities in 19th Century Egypt." In *Women in the Ottoman Empire,* edited by M. Zilfi, 68–80. Leiden: Brill, 1997.

Hathout, Hassan. "Bioethics Developments in Islam." *Bioethics Yearbook* 3 (1993): 133–47.

———. "The Ethics of Genetic Engineering: An Islamic Viewpoint." *Journal of the Islamic Medical Association of North America* 22, no. 3 (1990): 99–101.

———. "Islamic Basis for Biomedical Ethics." In *Transcultural Dimensions in Medical Ethics,* edited by Edmund Pellegrino, Patricia Mazzarella, and Pietro Corsi, 57–72. Frederick, Md.: University Publishing Group, 1992.

Hathout, Hassan, and B. Andrew Lustig. "Bioethical Developments in Islam." In *Theological Developments in Bioethics: 1990–92,* edited by Andrew Lustig, 133–47. Dordrecht: Kluwer, 1993.

Hauptman, Paul J., and Kevin J. O'Connor. "Procurement and Allocation of Solid Organs for Transplantation." *New England Journal of Medicine* 336, no. 6 (1997): 422–31.

Hayward, Clare, and Anna Madill. "The Meanings of Organ Donation: Muslims of Pakistani Origin and White English Nationals Living in Northern England." *Social Science and Medicine* 57, no. 3 (2003): 389–401.

Hedayat, K. M., and R. Pirzadeh. "Issues in Islamic Biomedical Ethics: A Primer for the Pediatrician." *Pediatrics* 108, no. 4 (2001): 965–71.

Heide, A. van der, L. Deliens, and K. Faisst. "End-of-Life Decision-Making in Six European Countries." *Lancet* 362, no. 9381 (2003): 345–50.

Henninger, S. K. *Touches of Sweet Harmony.* Berkeley, Calif.: Huntington Library, 1974.

Hijawi, S. A. A. "Human Infertility: Ethical Implications of Modern Researches in Genetics." In *Proceedings of the Islamic Educational, Scientific and Cultural Organization (ISESCO) Seminar, Doha, Qatar, February 13–15, 1993,* 213–25. Doha, Qatar: ISESCO Publication, 1993.

Hill, T. P. *The Challenges of Aging: Retrieving Spiritual Traditions.* Chicago: Park Ridge Center for the Study of Health, Faith, and Ethics, 1999.

Hogan, D., and B. Biratu. "Social Identity and Community Effects on Contraceptive Use and Intentions in Southern Ethiopia." *Studies in Family Planning* 35, no. 2 (2004): 79–90.

Holford-Stevens, Leofranc. "The Harmonious Pulse." *Classical Quarterly* 43, no. 2 (1993): 475–79.

Hollos, M., and U. Larsen. "From Lineage to Conjugality: The Social Context of Fertility Decisions among the Pare of Northern Tanzania." *Social Science and Medicine* 45 (1997): 361–72.

———. "Marriage and Contraception among the Pare of Northern Tanzania." *Journal of Biosocial Science* 36, no. 3 (2004): 255–78.

———. "Which African Men Promote Smaller Families and Why? Marital Relations and Fertility in a Pare Community in Northern Tanzania." *Social Science and Medicine* 58, no. 9 (2004): 1733–49.

Hoodfar, Homa, and Samad Assadpour. "The Politics of Population Policy in the Islamic Republic of Iran." *Studies in Family Planning* 31, no. 1 (2000): 19–34.

Hörbst, Viola. "Infertility and In-Vitro-Fertilization in Bamako, Mali: Women's Experience, Avenues for Solution and Social Contexts Impacting on Gynecological Consultations." *Curare* 29, no. 1 (2006): 35–46.

Horine, Emmet. "An Epitome of Ancient Pulse Lore." *Bulletin of the History of Medicine* 10 (1941): 209–49.

Hourani, George F. *Reason and Tradition in Islamic Ethics.* Cambridge: Cambridge University Press, 1985.

———. *Islamic Rationalism: The Ethics of Abd al-Jabbar.* Oxford: Clarendon Press, 1971.

Ibn 'Abd al-Barr, Yusuf b. 'Abdallāh. *Al-Tamhīd fī -mā fī l-Muwaṭṭa'-min al-ma'ānī wa-l-asānīd.* 2 vols. Beirut: Dar al-Kutub al-'ilmiya, 1981, 1992.

Ibn 'Ābidīn, Muḥammad Amīn. *Ḥāshiyat Radd al-muhtār 'alā al-durr al-mukhtār.* 8 vols. 3rd ed. Cairo: Maṭba'at Muṣṭafā al-Ḥalabī, 1984.

Ibn Abī Usayba, Aḥmad b. al-Qāsim. *'Uyūn al-anbā' fī -ṭabaqāt al-aṭibbā'.* Beirut: Dār Maktabat al-ḥayāt, 1965.

Ibn al-Khatīb, Muḥammad b. 'Abdallāh. *Al-Iḥāṭa fī akhbār al-Gharnāṭa.* 4 vols.. Cairo: Maktabat al-Khanjī, 2001.

Ibn al-Nadīm. *The Fihrist of Ibn al-Nadīm.* Translated by Bayard Dodge. New York: Columbia University Press, 1985.

Ibn Ḥajar al-'Asqalānī, Aḥmad b. 'Alī. *Badhl al-mā'ūn fī faḍl al-ṭā'ūn.* Edited by Aḥmad 'Iṣā m 'Ābd al-Qādir al-Kātib. Riyadh: Dār al-'Āṣīma, 1990.

———. *Fatḥ al-bārī bi-sharḥ al-Bukhārī.* 13 vols. Cairo: al-Maṭba'a al-Salafiyya, n.d.; 28 vols. Cairo: Maktabat al-Kulliya al-Azhariyya, 1978; 16 vols. Beirut: Dār al-Fikr, 1993.

Ibn Ḥanbal, Aḥmad. *Al-Musnad.* 6 vols. Beirut: Dār al-Fikr, 1993; 20 vols. Cairo: Dār al-Ḥadīth, 1995.

Ibn Isḥāq, Ḥunayn. *Masā'il fī -l-ṭibb.* Cairo: Al Ahram Center, 1980.

Ibn Kathīr, Ismā'īl b. 'Umar. *Tafsīr al-Qur'ān al-'Aẓīm.* Beirut: al-Maktaba al-'Aṣriyya, 1998.

Ibn Māja, Muḥammad b. Yazīd. *Sunan.* 2 vols. [Cairo]: Dār Iḥyā' al-Turāth, 1975.

Ibn Qutayba, 'Abdallāh b. Muslim. *Ta'wīl mukhtalif al-ḥadīth.* Edited by Riḍā Faraj al-Hamāmī. Beirut: al-Maktaba al-'Aṣriyya, 2003.

Ibn Sīnā, Abū 'Alī (see also Avicenna). *Al-Qānūn fī -l-ṭibb.* New Delhi: Jamia Hamdard, 1993.

Ibrahim, Yasir. "The Spirit of Islamic Law and Modern Religious Reform: *Maqāṣid al-sharī'a* in Muḥammad 'Abduh and Rashīd Riḍā's Legal Thought." Ph.D. diss., Princeton University, 2003.

Idrīs, 'Abd al-Fattāḥ Maḥmūd. *Al-Ijhāḍ min manẓūr islāmī.* Cairo: self-published, 1995.

Ilkilic, Ilhan. *Begegnung und Umgang mit muslimischen Patienten: Eine Handreichung für die Gesundheitsberufe.* Tübingen: Interfak. Zentrum für Ethik in den Wissenschaften, Eberhard-Karls-Universität Tübingen, 2003.

Inhorn, Marcia C. *Local Babies, Global Science: Gender, Religion, and In Vitro Fertilization in Egypt.* New York: Routledge, 2003.

———. "Making Muslim Babies: IVF and Gamete Donation in Sunni versus Shi'a Islam." *Culture, Medicine and Psychiatry* 30 (2006): 427–50.

———. *Quest for Conception: Gender, Infertility, and Egyptian Medical Traditions.* Philadelphia: University of Pennsylvania Press, 1994.

———. "Religion and Reproductive Technologies: IVF and Gamete Donation in the Muslim World." *Anthropology News* 46, no. 2 (2005): 14–18.

———. "'The Worms Are Weak': Male Infertility and Patriarchal Paradoxes in Egypt." *Men and Masculinities* 5, no. 3 (2003): 236–56.

Islamic Code of Medical Ethics. Kuwait: First International Conference on Islamic Medicine, Islamic Organization for Medical Sciences, 1981.

'Iyāḍ b. Mūsā. *Ikmāl al-mu'lim bi fawā'id Muslim.* 9 vols. Mansurah: Dar al-Wafa' li-l-Tiba'a wa-l-Nashr, 1998.

Iyilikci, L., and others. "Practices of Anaesthesiologists with Regard to Withholding and Withdrawal of Life Support from the Critically Ill in Turkey." *Acta Anaesthiologica Scandinavica* 48 (April 2004): 457–62.

Izhar, N. "The Unani Traditional Medical System in India: A Case Study in Health Behavior." *Geographica Medica* 19 (1989): 163–85.

Jackson, Sherman A. "The Alchemy of Domination? Some Ash'arite Responses to Mu'tazilite Ethics." *International Journal of Middle East Studies* 31, no. 2 (1999): 185–201.

Jacquart, Danielle, and F. Micheaux, eds. *La medecine arabe et l'occident medieval.* Paris: Maisonneuve, 1990.

Jacquart, Danielle, and G. Troupeau. "La Consultation Médicale de l'observation du malade à la prescription." In *A l'ombre d'Avicenne: La Médecine au temps des Califes,* edited by Jeanne Mouliérac, 77–81. Paris: Institute du Monde Arabe, 1997.

Jam'iyyat al-'ulūm at-ṭibbiyya al-Islāmiyya al-munbathiqa 'an niqābat al-aṭṭibā' al-Urduniyya. *Qadāyā ṭibbiyya mu'āṣira fī ḍau'al-sharī 'a al-Islāmiyya.* Amman, 1995.

Jansen, Jan. "Griot`s Impression Management and Diplomatic Strategies." In *Mande–Manding: Background Reading for Ethnographic Research in the Region South of Bamako (Mali),* edited by Jan Jansen, 131–61. Leiden: Leiden University Press, 2004.

Jeffery, R., and P. Jeffery. *Population, Gender, and Politics: Demographic Change in Rural North India.* Cambridge: Cambridge University Press, 1997.

al-Jeilani, M. "Pain: Points of View of Islamic Theology." *Acta Neurochirugica,* supplement 38 (1987): 132–35.

al-Jīdī, 'Umar. *Al-Tashrī ' al-Islāmī .* Morocco: Manshūrāt 'Akāẓ, 1987.

Johansen, Baber. *Contingency in a Sacred Law: Legal and Ethical Norms in the Muslim* Fiqh. Leiden: Brill, 1999.

———. "Legal Literature and the Problem of Change: The Case of the Land Rent." In *Islam and Public Law: Classical and Contemporary Studies,* edited by Chibli Mallat, 29–47. London: Graham and Trotman, 1993.

Jonsen, Albert R., Mark Siegler, and William J. Winslade. *Clinical Ethics: A Practical Approach to Ethical Decisions in Clinical Medicine.* 5th ed. New York: McGraw-Hill, Medical Publishing Division, 2002.

Jonsen, Albert R., and Stephen Toulmin. *The Abuse of Casuistry: A History of Moral Reasoning.* Berkeley: University of California Press, 1988.

Joralemon, Donald. "Organ Wars: The Battle for Body Parts." *Medical Anthropology Quarterly,* n.s., 9, no. 3 (1995): 335–56.

Kaḥḥāla, 'Umar Riḍā. *Mu'jam al-mu'allifīn.* Beirut: Mu'assasat al-Risāla, 1993.

Kamali, Mohammad Hashim. *Principles of Islamic Jurisprudence.* 2nd ed. Cambridge: Islamic Texts Society, 1991.

Kandela, Peter, "The Stethoscope." *Lancet* 352, no. 9122 (1998): 997.

Kapborg, I., and C. Berterö. "Using an Interpreter in Qualitative Interviews: Does It Threaten Validity?" *Nursing Inquiry* 9, no. 1 (2002): 52–56.

Kapki, B. "Deep Listening: Revealing the Pulse." *Massage and Body Work* (April/May 2002): 22.

Kastenbaum, Robert J. *Death, Society, and Human Experience.* 8th ed. Boston: Pearson Education Inc., 2004.

Kasule, Omar H. "Jurisprudence of Biotechnology." Paper presented at a seminar organized by Kampong Baru Medical Center, Kuala Lumpur, October 26, 2003.

Katz, Marion Holmes. "The Problem of Abortion in Classical Sunni *fiqh.*" In *Islamic Ethics of Life: Abortion, War, and Euthanasia,* edited by Jonathan E. Brockopp, 25–50. Columbia: University of South Carolina Press, 2003.

Kemper, F. H. C. "Religiositeit, etniciteit en welbevinden bij mannen van de eerste generatie Marokkaanse moslimmigranten." Ph.D. diss., Katholieke Universiteit Nijmegen, 1996.

Kennedy, Holly Powell. "Enhancing Delphi Research: Methods and Results." *Journal of Advanced Nursing* 45, no. 5 (2005): 504–11.

Keshavjee, Salmaan. "Bleeding Babies in Badakhshan Symbolism, Materialism, and the Political Economy of Traditional Medicine in Post-Soviet Tajikistan." *Medical Anthropology Quarterly* 20, no. 1 (2006): 72–93.

al-Khader, Abdullah A. "Cadaveric Renal Transplantation in the Kingdom of Saudi Arabia." *Nephrology Dialysis Transplantation* 14, no. 4 (1999): 846–50.

Khan, A. "Islamic Philosophy and Medical Ethics." In *Islamic Perspectives in Medicine,* edited by S. Athar, 103–5. Indianapolis: American Trust Publications, 1993.

al-Khaṭṭābī, Muḥammad al-ʿArabī. *Al-Ṭibb wa-l-aṭibbā' fī -l-Andalus al-islāmiyya.* 2 vols. Beirut: Dār al-Gharb al-Islāmī, 1988.

al-Kīndī, Yaʿqub b. Isḥāq. *al-Falsafa al-ūlā.* Damascus: Dār Maʿād, 1977.

Kingdom of Saudi-Arabia, Ministry of Health. "SCOT Protocol: Directory of the Regulations of Organ Transplantation in the Kingdom of Saudi Arabia." *Saudi Journal of Kidney Diseases and Transplantation* 5, no. 1 (1994): 37–98.

Kleinman, Arthur. "Local Worlds of Suffering: An Interpersonal Focus for Ethnographies of Illness Experience." *Qualitative Health Research* 2, no. 2 (1992): 127–34.

Koyre, A. *From the Closed World to the Infinite Universe.* Baltimore: Johns Hopkins University Press, 1968.

Krawietz, Birgit. "*Ḍarūra* in Modern Islamic Law: The Case of Organ Transplantation." In *Islamic Law: Theory and Practice,* edited by Robert Gleave and Eugenia Kermeli, 185–193. London: I. B. Taurus, 1997.

———. *Die Ḥurma: Schariatrechtlicher Schutz vor Eingriffen in die körperliche Unversehrtheit nach arabischen Fatwas des 20. Jahrhunderts.* Berlin: Duncker and Humblot, 1991.

———. "Ethical Versus Medical Values According to Contemporary Islamic Law." *Recht van de Islam* 16 (1999): 1–26.

Kridli, S. A., and K. Libbus. "Establishing Reliability and Validity of an Instrument Measuring Jordanian Muslim Women's Contraceptive Beliefs." *Health Care for Women International* 23, no. 8 (2002): 870–81.

Kridli, S. A., and S. E. Newton. "Jordanian Married Muslim Women's Intentions to Use Oral Contraceptives." *International Council of Nurses* 52 (2005): 109–14.

Kunin, J. "Should Patients Be Told the Truth about Their Illnesses? Jewish Perspectives." *Israel Medical Association Journal* 4, no. 9 (2002): 737–41.

Kuriyama, Shigehisa. *The Expressiveness of the Body and the Divergence of Greek and Chinese Medicine.* New York: Zone Books, 1999.

Lane, S. D. "Gender and Health: Abortion in Urban Egypt." In *Population, Poverty and Politics in Middle East Cities,* edited by Michael E. Bonine, 208–34. Gainesville: University of Florida Press, 1997.

Lane, S. D., J. M. Jok, and M. T. El-Mouelhy. "Buying Safety: The Economics of Reproductive Risk and Abortion in Egypt." *Social Science and Medicine* 47, no. 8 (1998): 1089–99.

Larijani, B., and F. Zahedi. "Islamic Perspective on Human Cloning and Stem Cell Research." *Transplantation Proceedings* 36, no. 10 (2004): 3188–89.

Lavy, Jean. *Méthode très facile pour developer les secrets de la nature dans le corps humain par l'exploration du Pouls.* Paris, 1821.

Leclerc, Lucien. *Histoire de la medecine arabe.* 2 vols. Paris: Ernest Leroux, 1876.

Leeton, John. "The Early History of IVF in Australia and Its Contribution to the World (1970–1990)." *Australian and New Zealand Journal of Obstetrics and Gynaecology* 44, no. 6 (2004): 495–501.

Leslie, Charles M., ed. *Asian Medical Systems: A Comparative Study.* Berkeley: University of California Press, 1976.

Levey, Martin. "Medical Ethics of Medieval Islam with Special Reference to al-Ruhawi 'Practical Ethics of the Physician.'" *Transactions of the American Philosophical Society* 57 (1967): 1–100.

Liebeskind, C. "Unani Medicine and the Subcontinent." In *Oriental Medicine: An Illustrated Guide to the Asian Arts of Healing,* edited by J. Van Alphen and A. Aris, 39–66. Boston: Shambala, 1996.

Lifton, R. J. *The Nazi Doctors: Medical Killing and the Psychology of Genocide.* New York: Perseus Books, 1988.

Linstone, Harold A., and Murray Turoff. *The Delphi Method: Techniques and Applications.* Newark: Department of Information Systems at the New Jersey Institute of Technology, 2002.

Lloyd, G. E. R. "Theories and Practices of Demonstration in Galen." In *Rationality in Greek Thought,* edited by M. Frede and G. Stryker, 255–77. Oxford: Clarendon, 1996.

Lock, Margaret. "Transcending Mortality: Organ Transplants and the Practice of Contradictions." *Medical Anthropology Quarterly* 9, no. 3 (1995): 390–93.

———. *Twice Dead: Organ Transplants and the Reinvention of Death.* Berkeley: University of California Press, 2002.

Lohlker, R. *Schari'a und Moderne: Diskussionen über Schwangerschaftsabbruch, Versicherung und Zinsen.* Stuttgart: Steiner, 1996.

Loria, A., and P. Arroyo. "Language and Country Preponderance Trends in MEDLINE and Its Causes." *Journal of the Medical Library Association* 93, no. 3 (2005): 381–85.

Lukoff, D., R. Provenzano, F. Lu, and R. Turner. "Religious and Spiritual Case Reports on MEDLINE: A Systematic Analysis of Records from 1980 to 1996." *Alternative Therapies in Health and Medicine* 5, no. 1 (1999): 64–70.

Mahfouz, Naghib. *The History of Medical Education in Egypt.* Cairo: Government Press, 1935.

Mahmood, Saba. *Politics of Piety: The Islamic Revival and the Feminist Subject.* Princeton, N.J.: Princeton University Press, 2005.

Majūsī, ʿAlī Ibn ʿAbbās. *Kāmil al-ṣināʿa fi-l-ṭibb.* Frankfurt am Main: Institute for the History of Arabic-Islamic Science at the Johann Wolfgang Goethe University, 1985.

Mālik b. Anas. *Al-Muwaṭṭaʾ.* Beirut: Dār al-Gharb al-Islāmī, 1994.

al-Maqqarī, Abū l-ʿAbbās Aḥmad b. Muḥammad. *Nafḥ al-ṭīb.* 8 vols. Beirut: Dār Ṣādir, 1988.

Marriott, Edward. *Plague: A Story of Science, Rivalry and the Scourge That Won't Go Away.* New York: Metropolitan Books, 2002.

Masri, M. A., A. Stephan, A. Barbari, S. Rizk, and G. Kamel. "A Comparative Study of HLA Allele Frequency in Lebanese, Arabs, United Arab Emirates and East Indian Populations." *Transplantation Proceedings* 29, no. 7 (1997): 2922–23.

Massignon, Louis. "La Nature dans la pensée islamique." *Eranos Jahrbuch* 14 (1946): 145–48.

Masud, Muhammad Khalid. *Islamic Legal Philosophy: A Study of Abū Isḥāq al-Shāṭibī's Life and Thought.* Islamabad: Islamic Research Institute, 1977. Revised as *Shatibi's Philosophy of Islamic Law.* New Delhi: Kitab Bhaven, 1997.

Masud, Muhammad Khalid, Brinkley Messick, and David Powers, eds. *Islamic Legal Interpretation: Muftis and Their Fatwas.* Cambridge, Mass.: Harvard University Press, 1996.

Mavani, H., trans. *A Guide to Islamic Medical Ethics.* Montreal: Organization for the Advancement of Islamic Knowledge and Humanitarian Services, 1998.

al-Māzarī, Muḥammad b. ʿAlī. *Al-Muʿlim bi-fawāʾid Muslim.* 3 vols. Beirut: Dār al-Gharb al-Islāmī, 1992.

McCarthy, P., G. Chammas, J. Wilimas, F. M. Alaoui, and M. Harif. "Managing Children's Cancer Pain in Morocco." *Journal of Nursing Scholarship* 36, no. 1 (2004): 11–15.

Miller, David, and Sohail Hashmi, eds. *Boundaries and Justice: Diverse Ethical Perspectives.* Princeton, N.J.: Princeton University Press, 2001.

Moazam, F., and A. M. Jafarey. "Pakistan and Biomedical Ethics: Report from a Muslim Country." *Cambridge Quarterly of Healthcare Ethics* 14, no. 3 (2005): 249–55.

Moazam, Farhat. *Bioethics and Organ Transplantation in a Muslim Society: A Study in Culture, Ethnography, and Religion.* Bloomington: Indiana University Press, 2006.

Mobeireek, A. "Religious Conviction and Decisions Near the End of Life." *Archives of Internal Medicine* 164, no. 8 (2004): 916.

Modrak, D. K. *Aristotle's Theory of Perception.* Chicago: University of Chicago Press, 1987.

Momen, Moojan. *An Introduction to Shi'i Islam: The History and Doctrines of Twelve-Shi'ism.* New Haven, Conn.: Yale University Press, 1985.

Moosa, Ebrahim. "Languages of Change in Islamic Law: Redefining Death in Modernity." *Islamic Studies* 38, no. 3 (1999): 305–42.

Moosa, Najma. "A Descriptive Analysis of South African and Islamic Abortion Legislation and Local Muslim Community Responses." *Medicine and Law* 21, no. 2 (2002): 257–79.

Moraux, P. "Galien comme philosophe de la Nature." In *Galen: Problems and Prospects,* edited by V. Nutton, 87–116. London: Wellcome Institute for the History of Medicine, 1981.

al-Mousawi, M., T. Hamed, and H. al-Matouk. "Views of Muslim Scholars on Organ Donation and Brain Death." *Transplantation Proceedings* 29, no. 8 (1997): 3217.

Mueller, M. J. "Ibnulkhatîbs Bericht über die Pest." *Sitzungsberichte der königlich-bayerischen Akademie der Wissenschaften zu München* 2 (1963): 6–8, 18–21. Munich: Christian Kaiser, 1863.

al-Mufīḍ, Muḥammad b. Muḥammad b. al-Nu'man. *Kitab al-Irshad: The Book of Guidance into the Lives of the Twelve Imams.* Translated by I. K. A. Howard. Elmhurst, N.Y.: Tahrike Tarsile Qur'an, 1981.

Murata, Sachiko. *The Tao of Islam.* New York: State University of New York Press, 1992.

Musallam, B. F. *Sex and Society in Islam: Birth Control before the Nineteenth Century.* Cambridge: Cambridge University Press, 1983.

Muslim Ibn ḥajjāj. *ṣaḥīḥ Muslim.* 5 vols. Cairo: Dār al-ḥadīth, 1991; 5 vols. Beirut: Dār Ibn ḥazm, 1995.

"The Muslim Law (Shariah) Council and Organ Transplants." *Accident and Emergency Nursing* 4, no. 2 (1996): 73–75.

Naamane-guessous, S. "Traditional Methods Still Widely Used." *Planned Parenthood Challenges* 1 (1993): 14–16.

Nasr, Seyyed Hossein. *An Introduction to Islamic Cosmological Doctrines.* New York: State University of New York Press, 1993.

———. "The Meaning and Role of Philosophy in Islam." *Studia Islamica* 37 (1973): 57–80.

al-Nawawī, Yaḥyā Ibn Sharaf. *Sharḥ ṣaḥīḥ Muslim.* Beirut: Dār al-Qalam, 1987.

Neuburger, Max. "A Historical Survey of the Concept of Nature from a Medical Viewpoint." *Isis* 35 (1944): 16–38.

Nicolson, M. *The Breaking of the Circle.* New York: Columbia University Press, 1960.

Niebyl, Peter. "The Non Naturals." *Bulletin of the History of Medicine* 45 (1971): 486–92.

Nutton, Vivian. "Galen at the Bedside: Methods of a Medical Detective." In *Medicine and the Five Senses,* edited by Roy Porter and W. F. Bynum, 7–16. London: Cambridge, 1987.

———. "The Reception of Fracastoro's Theory of Contagion: The Seed That Fell among Thorns?" *Osiris,* n.s., 6 (1990): 196–234.

Nyboe Andersen, A., L. Gianaroli, and K. G. Ngren. "Assisted Reproductive Technology in Europe, 2000: Results Generated from European Registers by ESHRE." *Human Reproduction* 19, no. 3 (March 2004): 490–503.

Oates, W. "The Doctrine of the Mean." *Philosophical Review* 45, no. 4 (1936): 382–98.

Obermeyer, C. M. "Reproductive Choice in Islam: Gender and State in Iran and Tunisia." *Studies in Family Planning* 25, no. 1 (1994): 41–51.

Olmsted, H. "The Moral Sense: Aspects of Aristotle's Ethical Theory." *American Journal of Philology* 69, no. 1 (1948): 42–61.

Omran, Abdel Rahim. "Children Rights in Islam from the Qur'an and Sunnah." *Population Sciences* 9 (July 1990): 77–88.

———. *Family Planning in the Legacy of Islam.* London: Routledge, 1992.

———. *Population in the Arab World: Problems and Prospects.* London: Croom Helm, 1980.

Opwis, Felicitas. "*Maṣlaḥa* in Contemporary Islamic Legal Theory." *Islamic Law and Society* 12 (2005): 182–223.

Patterson, S., L. Balducci, and R. Meyer. "The Book of Job: A 2,500-Year-Old Current Guide to the Practice of Oncology; The Nexus of Medicine and Spirituality." *Journal of Cancer Education* 17, no. 4 (2002): 237–40.

Pellegrino, E. *Medicine and Philosophy.* London: Oxford, 1981.

Pellegrino, E. D., M. Siegler, and P. A. Singer. "Future Directions in Clinical Ethics." *Journal of Clinical Ethics* 2, no. 1 (1991): 5–9.

———. "Teaching Clinical Ethics." *Journal of Clinical Ethics* 1, no. 3 (1990): 175–80.

Perler, Dominik, and Ulrich Rudolph. *Occasionalismus: Theorien der Kausalität im arabisch-islamischen und im europäischen Denken.* Göttingen: Vendenhoeck and Ruprecht, 2000.

Philliber, S., and W. Philliber. "Social and Psychological Perspectives on Voluntary Sterilization: A Review." *Studies in Family Planning* 16, no. 1 (1985): 1–29.

Plummer, K. *Symbolic Interactionism.* 2 vols. Aldershot: Elgar, 1991.

Population Reference Bureau. *Family Planning World Wide: 2002 Data Sheet.* Washington, D.C.: Population Reference Bureau, 2002.

Powers, David S. "Kadijustiz oder Qāḍī -Justice? A Paternity Dispute from Fourteenth-Century Morocco." *Islamic Law and Society* 1, no. 3 (1994): 332–66.

Prabhakar, K. S. "Cadaveric and Living Organ Donation: Natural Limitations; Possible Solutions; Singapore Experience." *Annals of Transplantation* 9, no. 1 (2004): 31–33.

al-Qurṭubī, Aḥmad Ibn 'Umar. *Al-Mufhim li-mā ashkala min talkhīṣ kitāb Muslim.* 7 vols. Damascus: Dār Ibn Kathīr, 1996.

al-Rahāwī, Isḥāq b. 'Alī. *Adab al-ṭabīb.* Frankfurt am Main: Institute for the History of Arabic-Islamic Science at the Johann Wolfgang Goethe University, 1985; Riyāḍ: al-Dirāsāt al-Islāmiya and others, 1992; Cairo: Jāmi'at 'Ain Shams, Markaz Buḥuth al-Sharq al-Awsaṭ, 1993.

Rahman, Fazlur. *Avicenna's Psychology.* London: Oxford, 1952.

———. "Functional Interdependence of Law and Theology." In *Theology and Law in Islam,* edited by G. E. Grunebaum, 89–97. Wiesbaden: Otto Harrassowitz, 1971.

———. *Health and Medicine in the Islamic Tradition: Change and Identity.* New York: Crossroad, 1987.

———. *Islam.* Chicago: University of Chicago Press, 1979.

———. "Islam and Medicine: A General Overview." *Perspectives in Biology and Medicine* 27, no. 4 (1984): 585–97.

———. "Law and Ethics in Islam." In *Ethics in Islam,* edited by Richard Hovannisian, 3–15. Malibu, Calif.: Undena, 1985.

Rather, J. "The Six Things Non-natural." *Clio Medica* 3 (November 1968): 337–47.

al-Raysūnī, Aḥmad. *Naẓariyyat al-maqāṣid 'inda al-Imām al-Shāṭibī.* Rabat: Dār al-Amān, 1991.

al-Rāzī, Abū Bakr Muḥammad b. Zakariyya. *Akhlāq al-ṭabīb.* Annotated by A. M. Soubhi. Cairo: Dār al-Turāth, 1977.

———. *Al-ḥāwī fī l-ṭibb.* 21 vols. Hayderabad: Dā'irat al-Ma'ārif al-'Uthmāniyya, 1955; 23 vols. Beirut: Dar al-Kutub al-'Ilmiyya, 2000; 23 vols. Beirut: Dār Iḥyā' al-Turāth al-'Arabī Publishing and Distributing, 2002.

———. *Al-Sīra al-falsafiyya or The Spiritual Physick of Rhazes.* Translated by A. Arberry. London: Luzac and Co., 1950.

Redmond, K. "Barriers to the Effective Management of Pain." *International Journal of Palliative Nursing* 4, no. 6 (1998): 276–83.

Reinhart, A. Kevin. *Before Revelation: The Boundaries of Muslim Moral Thought.* Albany: State University of New York Press, 1995.

———. "Islamic Law as Islamic Ethics." *Journal of Religious Ethics* 11, no. 2 (1983): 186–203.

Reiser, S. Joel. *Medicine and the Reign of Technology.* London: Cambridge, 1968.

Renard, John. "Muslim Ethics: Sources, Interpretations and Challenges." *Muslim World* 69 (July 1979): 163–77.

Reynolds, L. I., and N. J. Herman-Kinney, eds. *Handbook of Symbolic Interactionism.* Walnut Creek, Calif.: Alta Mira, 2003.

Riad, A. "Current Issues and Future Problems of Transplantation in the Middle East: Syria." *Transplantation Proceedings* 33, no. 5 (2001): 2632–33.

Richey, L. A. "'Development,' Gender and Family Planning: Population Politics and the Tanzanian National Population Policy." Ph.D. diss., University of North Carolina at Chapel Hill, 1999.

Rieser, Stanley Joel. "The Science of Diagnosis: Diagnostic Technology." In *Companion Encyclopedia of Medicine,* edited by Roy Porter and William F. Bynum, 826–51. London: Routledge, 1993.

Rises, Walter. "The Structure of Galen's Diagnostic Reasoning." *Bulletin of the New York Academy of Science* 44 (1968): 778–91.

Rispler-Chaim, Vardit. "Contemporary Muftis between Bioethics and Social Reality: Preselection of the Sex of a Fetus as a Paradigm." *Journal of Religious Ethics* 38 (March 2008): 53–76.

———. "Islamic Medical Ethics and the Right to Privacy." Paper presented at the first International Conference on Medical Ethics and Medical Law in Islam, Haifa, Israel, March 19–21, 2001.

———. "Islamic Medical Ethics in the Twentieth Century." *Journal of Medical Ethics* 15, no. 4 (1989): 203–8.

———. *Islamic Medical Ethics in the Twentieth Century.* Leiden: Brill, 1993.

Rizvi, S. S. A., trans. *The Charter of Rights (Risalatu 'l-Huquq).* Vancouver: Vancouver Islamic Educational Foundation, 1989.

Rodriguez del Pozo, P., and J. J. Fins. "Death, Dying and Informatics: Misrepresenting Religion on MedLine." *BMC Medical Ethics* 6 (July 2005): E6.

Rosenau, Henning. "Der Streit um das Klonen und das deutsche Stammzellgesetz." In *Recht und Ethik im Zeitalter der Gentechnik: Deutsche und japanische Beiträge zu Biorecht und Bioethik,* edited by Hans-Ludwig Schreiber and others, 135–68. Göttingen: Vandenhoek and Ruprecht, 2004.

Rosenthal, Franz. "The Physician in Medieval Muslim Society." *Bulletin of the History of Medicine* 52, no. 4 (1979): 475–91.

Ross, H. M. "Islamic Tradition at the End of Life." *Medical-Surgical Nursing* 10, no. 2 (2001): 83–87.

Rowe, P. I., F. H. Cornhaire, T. B. Hargreave, and H. Mellows. *WHO Manual for the Standardized Investigation and Diagnosis of the Infertile Couple.* Cambridge: Press Syndicate of the University of Cambridge, 1993.

al-Ruhāwī, Isḥāq b. ʿAlī. *Adab al-ṭabīb.* Riyadh: Markaz al-Malik Fayṣal li-l-Buḥūth wa-al-Dirāsāt al-Islāmiyah, 1992.

Sachedina, Abdulaziz. "End-of-Life: The Islamic View." *Lancet* 366, no. 9487 (2005): 774–79.

———. "Human Clones: An Islamic View." In *The Human Cloning Debate,* edited by Glenn McGee, 231–44. Berkley, Calif.: Berkeley Hills Books, 1998.

al-Salāmī, Muḥammad al-Mukhtār. *Al-Ṭibb fī ḍawʿ al-īmān.* Beirut: Dār al-Gharb al-Islāmī, 2001.

Saltonstall, Robin. "Healthy Bodies, Social Bodies: Men's and Women's Concepts and Practices of Health in Everyday Life." *Social Science and Medicine* 36, no. 1 (1993): 7–14.

al-Sanūsī, Muḥammad b. Yūsuf. *Les Prolégomènes Théologiques de Senoussi.* Algiers: Imprimerie Orientale Pierre Fontana, 1908.

Sargent, C., and D. Cordell. "Polygamy, Disrupted Reproduction, and the State: Malian Migrants in Paris, France." *Social Science and Medicine* 56, no. 9 (2003): 1961–72.

Sargent, Carolyn F. "Reproductive Strategies and Islamic Discourse: Malian Migrants Negotiate Everyday Life in Paris, France." *Medical Anthropology Quarterly* 20, no. 1 (2006): 31–49.

Sarhill, N., and others. "The Terminally Ill Muslim: Death and Dying from the Muslim Perspective." *American Journal of Hospice and Palliative Care* 18, no. 4 (2001): 251–55.

Schenker, J. G. "Assisted Reproductive Practice: Religious Perspectives." *Reproductive Biomedicine Online* 10, no. 3 (2005): 310–19.

Scheper-Hughes, Nancy. Combined review of Thomas Koch, *Scarce Goods: Justice, Fairness, and Organ Transplantation* (Westport, Conn.: Praeger, 2002); and Margaret Lock, *Twice Dead: Organ Transplants and the Reinvention of Death* (Berkeley: University of California Press, 2002)." *American Anthropologist* 105 (March 2003): 172–74.

———. "The Ends of the Body: Commodity Fetishism and the Traffic in Human Organs." *SAIS Review: A Journal of International Affairs* 22, no. 1 (2000): 61–80.

———. "The Global Traffic of Human Organs." *Current Anthropology* 41, no. 2 (2000): 91–224.

———. "Commodity Fetishism in Organ Trafficking." In *Commodifying Bodies,* edited by Nancy Scheper-Hughes and Loïc Wacquant, 31–62. London: Sage Publications, 2002.

Scheper-Hughes, Nancy, and Loïc Wacquant, eds. *Commodifying Bodies.* London: Sage Publications, 2002.

Schulz, Dorothea E. "God Is Our Resort: "Islamic Revival, Mass-Mediated Religiosity and the Moral Negotiation of Gender Relations in Urban Mali." Unpublished habilitation, Free University of Berlin.

———. "Promises of (Im)mediate Salvation: Islam, Broadcast Media, and the Remaking of Religious Experience in Mali." *American Ethnologist* 33, no. 2 (2006): 210–29.

Schulze, Reinhard. *Islamischer Internationalismus im 20. Jahrhundert: Untersuchungen zur Geschichte der Islamischen Weltliga.* Leiden: Brill, 1990.

Schuster, Sylvie, and Viola Hörbst. "Introduction." *Curare* 29, no. 1 (2006): 5–16.

Serour, G. I. "Islam and the Four Principles." In *Principles of Health Care Ethics,* edited by Raanan Gillon, 75–91. Chichester: John Wiley and Sons, 1994.

———. "Islamic Developments in Bioethics." *Bioethics Yearbook* 5 (1997): 171–88.

Serour, G. I., M. A. Aboulghar, and R. T. Mansour. "Bioethics in Medically Assisted Conception in the Muslim World." *Journal of Assisted Reproduction and Genetics* 12, no. 9 (1995): 559–65.

Serrano Ruano, Delfina. "Los Almorávides y la teología Ashʿarí: Contestación o legitimación de una disciplina marginal?" In *Identidades marginales,* edited by Cristina de la Puente, 461–516. Madrid: Consejo Superior de Investigaciones Científicas, 2003.

———. "Por qué llamaron los Almohades antropomorfistas a los Almorávides?" In *Los almohades: Problemas y perspectives,* edited by Patrice Cressier, Maribel Fierro, and Luis Molina, 2:815–52. Madrid: Consejo Superior de Investigaciones Científicas, 2005.

al-Shaʿrāwī, Muḥammad Mutwallī. *Al-Fatāwā al-kubrā.* 2nd ed. Cairo: Maktabat al-Turāth al-Islāmī, 2002.

Shaheen, F. A. M., M. Z. Souqiyyeh, K. Ramprassad, and M. S. Attar. "Current Issues and Problems of Transplantation in the Middle East: The Arabian Gulf." *Transplantation Proceedings* 33, no. 5 (2001): 2621–22.

Shapin, Steven. "The Philosopher and the Chicken: On the Dietetics of Disembodied Knowledge." In *Science Incarnate: Historical Embodiments of Natural Knowledge,* edited by C. Lawrence and S. Shapin, 21–50. Chicago: University of Chicago Press, 1996.

Sharp, Lesley A. "The Commodification of the Body and Its Parts." *Annual Review of Anthropology* 29 (2000): 287–328.

———. "Commodified Kin: Death, Mourning, and Competing Claims on the Bodies of Organ Donors in the United States." *American Anthropologist* 103, no. 1 (2001): 112–33.

———. "Organ Transplantation as a Transformative Experience: Anthropological Insights into the Restructuring of the Self." *Medical Anthropology Quarterly,* n.s., 9 (1995): 357–89.

al-Shāṭibī, Ibrāhīm b. Mūsā. *Al-Ifādāt wa-l-inshādāt.* Beirut: Mu'assasat al-Rasūl, 1983.

———. *Al-Muwāfaqāt fī uṣūl al-aḥkām.* 4 vols. Beirut: Dār al-Maʿrifa, 1994.

al-Shawkānī, Muḥammad b. ʿAlī. *Kitāb al-fatḥ al-rabbānī min fatāwā al-Imam al-Shawkānī.* 12 vols. Edited by Abū Muṣʿab Muḥammad Ṣubḥī b. Ḥasan Ḥallāq. Ṣanaʿa: Maktabat al-Jīl al-Jadīd, 2002.

Sheehan, Helen, and S. J. Hussain. "Unani Tibb: History, Theory and Contemporary Practice in South Asia." *Annals of the American Academy of Political and Social Science* 583, no. 1 (2002): 122–35.

Sheikh, A. "Death and Dying—A Muslim Perspective." *Journal of the Royal Society of Medicine* 91, no. 3 (1998): 138–40.

Sheikh, Aziz and Abdul Rashid Gatrad, eds. *Caring for Muslim Patients.* Abingdon: Radcliffe Medical Press, 2000.

Sheil, R. "Policy Statement from the Ethics Committee from the Transplantation Society." *Transplantation Society Bulletin* 3 (June 1995): 3.

Shenfield, Françoise. "Semantics and Ethics of Human Embryonic Stem-Cell Research." *Lancet* 365 (June 18, 2005): 2071–73.

Shiloah, Amnon. *The Dimension of Music in Islamic and Jewish Culture.* London: Variorum, 1993.

Sholkamy, Hania. "Conclusion: The Medical Cultures of Egypt." In *Health and Identity in Egypt,* edited by Hania Sholkamy and Farha Ghannam, 111–28. Cairo: American University of Cairo Press, 2004.

Siddiqi, M. Z. "The *unanī ṭibb* (Greek Medicine) in India." *Islamic Culture* 42 (1968): 161–72.

Siddiqui, A. "Ethics in Islam: Key Concepts and Contemporary Challenges." *Journal of Moral Education* 26, no. 4 (1997): 423–31.

Siegel, Rudolph. *Galen's System of Physiology and Medicine.* Basel, N.Y.: S. Karger, 1968.

Siegler, M., E. D. Pellegrino, and P. A. Singer. "Clinical Medical Ethics." *Journal of Clinical Ethics* 1, no. 1 (1990): 5–9.

Sing, Manfred. "Sacred Law Reconsidered: The Similarity of Bioethical Debates in Islamic Contexts and Western Societies." *Journal of Religious Ethics* 36, no. 1 (March 2008): 97–121.

Singer, P. *Practical Ethics.* 2nd ed. Cambridge: Cambridge University Press, 1999.

Singer, P., E. D. Pellegrino, and M. Siegler. "Clinical Ethics Revisited." *BMC Medical Ethics* 2, no. 1 (2001): 1.

Singer, P. A., M. Siegler, and E. D. Pellegrino. "Research in Clinical Ethics." *Journal of Clinical Ethics* 1, no. 2 (1990): 95–98.

Siraisi, Nancy. "The Music of the Pulse in the Writings of Italian Academic Physicians of the 14th/15th Century." *Speculum* 50 (1975): 689–710.

Skovgaard-Petersen, Jakob. *Defining Islam for the Egyptian State: Muftis and Fatwas of the Dār al-Iftā.* Leiden: Brill, 1997.

Sloan, R. P., E. Bagiella, L. VandeCreek, M. Hover, C. Casalone, T. Jinpu Hirsch, Y. Hasan, R. Kreger, and P. Poulos. "Should Physicians Prescribe Religious Activities?" *New England Journal of Medicine* 342, no. 25 (2000): 1913–16.

Smith, Mark A. "Knowing Things Inside Out: The Scientific Revolution from a Medieval Perspective." *American Historical Review* 95, no. 3 (2000): 726–44.

Soares, Benjamin F. *Islam and the Prayer Economy: History and Authority in a Malian Town.* Ann Arbor: University of Michigan Press, 2005.

————. "Islam in Mali in the Neoliberal Era." *African Affairs* 105, no. 41 (2005): 77–95.

————. "Mali—Im Visier der Islamismus-Fahnder." *Informationsprojekt Naher und Mittlerer Osten: Inamo* 41 (2005): 16–18.

Somlsen, F. "Nature as Craftsman in Greek Thought." *Journal of the History of Ideas* 24, no. 4 (1963): 473–96.

Stearns, Justin. "Infectious Ideas: Contagion in Medieval Islamic and Christian Thought." Ph.D. dissertation, Princeton University, 2007.

Steinberg, A. "A Jewish Perspective on the Four Principles." In *Principles of Health Care Ethics,* edited by R. Gillon, 65–73. New York: John Wiley and Sons, 1994.

Strauss, A., and J. Corbin. *Basics of Qualitative Research: Techniques and Procedures for Developing Grounded Theory.* Thousand Oaks, Calif.: Sage, 1998.

Syed, J. "Islamic Views on Organ Donation." *Journal of Transplant Coordination* 8, no. 3 (1998): 157–60.

Tangwa, Godfrey B. "ART and African Sociocultural Practices: Worldview, Belief and Value Systems with Particular Reference to Francophone Africa." In *Current Practices and Controversies in Assisted Reproduction: Report of a Meeting on "Medical, Ethical and*

Social Aspects of Assisted Reproduction" Held at WHO Headquarters in Geneva, Switzerland, 17–21 September 2001, edited by E. Vayena, P. J. Rowe, and D. P. Griffin, 55–59. Geneva: World Health Organization, 2002.

Taylor, A., and P. Braude. "Ethical Issues Related to the Use of Human Gametes and Embryos in Research and Subfertility Treatment." *Biochemist (Bulletin of the Biochemical Society)* 16, no. 2 (1994): 3–8.

Temkin, Oswei. *Galenism: Rise and Decline of a Medical Philosophy.* Ithaca, N.Y.: Cornell University Press, 1973.

Temple, B., and R. Edwards. "Interpreters/Translators and Cross-Language Research: Reflexivity and Border Crossings." *International Journal of Qualitative Methods* 1, no. 2 (2002): 1–22.

Tober, Diane M., Mohammad-Hossein Taghdisi, and Mohammad Jalali. "'Fewer Children, Better Life' or 'As Many as God Wants.'" *Medical Anthropology Quarterly* 20, no. 1 (2006): 50–71.

Tracy, T. *Physiological Theory and the Doctrine of the Mean in Plato and Aristotle.* Chicago: Loyola University Press, 1969.

Tucker, Judith. *In the House of the Law: Gender and Islamic Law in Ottoman Syria and Palestine.* Cairo: American University of Cairo Press, 1998.

Turner, Bryan S. "The Body in Western Society: Social Theory and Its Perspectives." In *Religion and the Body,* edited by S. Coakley, 15–41. Cambridge: Cambridge University Press, 1997.

Twinn, S. "An Exploratory Study Examining the Influence of Translation on the Validity and Reliability of Qualitative Data in Nursing Research." *Journal of Advanced Nursing* 26, no. 2 (1997): 418–23.

Ullmann, M. *Islamic Medicine.* Edinburgh: Edinburgh University Press, 1978.

———. *Die Medizin im Islam.* Leiden: Brill, 1970.

al-Umran, K. U., and others. "Medical Ethics and Tomorrow's Physicians: An Aspect of Coverage in the Formal Curriculum." *Medical Teacher* 28/29 (2006): 182–84.

Van Ess, Josef. *Der Fehltritt des Gelehrten.* Heidelberg: Universitätsverlag C. Winter, 2001.

Vance, R. "The Doctrine of the Pulse—An Analysis of Its Character and Summary of Its Indications." *Cincinnati Lancet* 26 (1878).

Verhey, Allen, and Stephen E. Lammers, eds. *Theological Voices in Medical Ethics.* Grand Rapids, Mich.: William B. Eerdmans, 1993.

Villalón, Leonardo. *Islamic Society and State Power in Senegal.* Cambridge: Cambridge University Press, 1995.

Von Grunebaum, G. E. "Concept and Function of Reason in Islamic Ethics." *Oriens* 15 (1962): 1–17.

al-Wansharīsī, Abū l-ʿAbbās Aḥmad Ibn Yaḥyā. *Al-Miʿyār al-muʿrib.* 13 vols. Rabat: Dār al-Gharb al-Islāmī, 1990.

Wass, Hannelore, ed. *Death Education, Aging, and Health Care.* New York: Hemisphere, 1990.

al-Wazzānī, Abū ʿĪsā Sīdī al-Mahdī. *Al-Miʿyār al-jadīd al-jāmiʿ al-muʿrib ʿan fatāwa al-mutaʾakhkhirīn min ʿulamāʾ al-maghrib.* Edited by ʿUmar b. ʿAttād. Morocco: Wizārat al-Awqāf wa-l-Shuʾūn al-Islāmiyya, 1996.

Whitby, Stanley G. "Nature and Morality." *Ethics* 51, no. 1 (1940): 49–65.

Wolfson, Harry A. "The Internal Sense in Latin, Arabic and Hebrew Philosophical Texts." *Harvard Theological Review* 28, no. 2 (1935): 69–133.

World Health Organization. *Ethics of Medicine and Health (Arabic).* Technical Report Series No. 4 EMRO, WHO-EM/PHP/1/A/G, Alexandria, Egypt, 1998.

Yāsīn, Muḥammad Naīm. "Ḥaqīqat al-janīn wa-ḥukm al-intifā' bihi fī zirā'at al-a'ḍā' wa-l-tajārib al-'ilmiyya [The reality of the embryo and the ruling about making use of it in organ transplantation and scientific experiments]," in *Ru'ya Islāmiyya li-zirā'at ba'ḍ al-a'ḍā' al-bashariya,* edited by 'Abd al-Raḥmān al-'Awaḍī and Khālid Madhkūr, 393–99. Kuwait: al-Munaẓẓama al-Islāmiyya li-l-'Ulūm al-Ṭibbiyya, [1992?].

Younis Shehada, Nahda. "Justice without Drama: Observations from Gaza City Sharī'a Court." In *Gender, Religion and Change in the Middle East: Two Hundred Years of History,* edited by Inger Marie Okkenhaug and Ingvild Flaskerud, 13–28. Oxford: Berg, 2005.

Youssef, N. "The Status and Fertility Patterns of Muslim Women." In *Women in the Muslim World,* edited by Lois Beck. Cambridge, Mass.: Harvard University Press, 1978.

al-Yūsī, al-Ḥasan b. Mas'ūd. *Al-Muḥāḍarāt.* Edited by Muḥammad Ḥajjī. Rabat: Dār al-Maghrib, 1976.

al-Zahrani, Kheder Ali. "Teaching Medical Ethics." In proceedings of the conference on Medical Ethics in Islam: How Different?, Riyadh, Saudi Arabia, March 11–13, 2003.

Zargooshi, Javaad. "Iranian Kidney Donors: Motivations and Relations with Recipients." *Journal of Urology* 165, no. 2 (2001): 386–92.

———. "Quality of Life of Iranian Kidney 'Donors.'" *Journal of Urology* 166, no. 5 (2001): 1790–99.

Zobel, Clemens. "Les genies du Kòma: Identités locales, logiques réligieuses et enjeux socio-politiques dans les monts Manding du Mali." *Cahiers d'Études Africaines* 36, no. 4 (1996): 625–58.

———. *Das Gewicht der Rede: Kulturelle Reinterpretation, Geschichte und Vermittlung bei den Mande Westafrikas.* Frankfurt am Main: Peter Lang, 1997.

Zomeño, Amalía. "Ibn Lubb." In *Biblioteca de al-Andalus,* edited by Jorge Lirola Delgado and José Miguel Puerta Vilchez, 4:24–28. Almería: Fundación Ibn Tuyafl, 2006.

CONTRIBUTORS

SHABBIR M. H. ALIBHAI is an assistant professor in the Departments of Medicine and Health Policy, Management, and Evaluation at the University of Toronto. A practicing physician who works with geriatric patients, he is senior editor of *Geriatrics & Aging*. He has several publications in major health care journals in the area of end-of-life ethics, with particular interests in Islamic and comparative religious bioethics.

HASSAN BELLA is a professor of family and community medicine with the College of Medicine, King Faisal University, in Dammam, Saudi Arabia. A native of the Sudan, he has published widely on medical and ethical topics; he is particularly interested in developing bioethics courses for medical students. Professor Bella also serves as editor in chief of the *Journal of Family & Community Medicine.*

JONATHAN E. BROCKOPP, an associate professor of religious studies and history at Pennsylvania State University, was the organizer of the March 2006 conference "Islam and Bioethics: Concerns, Challenges and Responses." An expert on early Islamic law, he has also published in comparative religions and comparative ethics. He is the editor of *Islamic Ethics of Life: Abortion, War and Euthanasia* (2003) and served as guest editor of a special focus issue on Islam and bioethics for the *Journal of Religious Ethics* (36, no. 1, 2008).

BERT BROECKAERT coordinates the Interdisciplinary Centre for the Study of Religion and Worldview at the Catholic University of Leuven (Belgium). His main research interests are religious diversity in Belgium and Europe, comparative religious ethics, and end-of-life ethics. He was a member of the Belgian National Bioethics Advisory Commission for four years and serves as ethical adviser to the Flemish Palliative Care Federation.

DEBRA BUDIANI is a medical anthropologist and research associate at the University of Pennsylvania's Center for Bioethics. She is also the executive director of the Coalition for Organ-Failure Solutions (COFS), a nonprofit international health and human rights organization committed to combating organ trafficking. With Diane Tober she has edited a special issue of *Body and Society* (13, no. 3, 2007) titled *Islam, Health, and the Body: Science and Religion in the Modern Muslim World.*

THOMAS EICH is an assistant professor in the Oriental Seminar at the Eberhard Karls University in Tübingen, Germany, and served on the international advisory board for the March 2006 conference at Pennsylvania State University. He has published in the fields of Ottoman history and contemporary Muslim medical ethics. He is the author of *Islam und Bioethik: Eine kritische Analyse der modernen Diskussion im islamischen Recht* (2005) and *Moderne Medizin und islamische Ethik: Biowissenschaften in der muslimischen Rechtstradition* (2008), a reader with translations for classroom use.

HAMZA ESKANDARANI is an associate professor of medical biochemistry at King Faisal University, Dammam, Saudi Arabia. In addition to doing research and publishing in the fields of clinical and medical biochemistry, he is actively involved in the field of reproductive medicine, specifically in embryology and the ethical issues of assisted reproductive technology. He is the author of *Assisted Reproduction Technology: "State-of the-Art"* (1996), a manual reference book widely used in the Arab and Islamic world.

SAMAR FARAGE is a senior lecturer in sociology at Pennsylvania State University. She has published and presented several papers in Europe and the United States on the history of Islamic medicine. She is presently working on a translation of al-Razi's monograph on the ethics of the physician.

MICHAEL GORDON is medical program director of palliative care at the Baycrest Geriatric Health Care system in Toronto, where he was also past vice president of medical services and head of the Department of Medicine and Geriatrics. He is a professor of medicine at the University of Toronto and a member of its Joint Centre for Bioethics. He lectures and writes extensively on issues related to aging as well as medical ethics with a special interest in comparative ethics and Jewish medical ethics. His most recent book, coauthored with Bart Mindszenthy, is *Parenting Your Parents: Support Strategies for Meeting the Challenge of Aging in the Family* (2005).

SHERINE HAMDY is Mellon Postdoctoral Fellow in Anthropology and Science, Technology, and Society at Brown University. A medical anthropologist engaged in questions about ethics, cultural conceptions of the body, contemporary Islamic thought, and the globalization of biotechnologies, she is currently preparing a book based on her dissertation research on the organ transplant debate in Egypt.

VIOLA HÖRBST is a lecturer with the Institute for Social Anthropology and African Studies at Ludwig-Maximilians-University of Munich, where she heads the research project "Infertility and In Vitro Fertilization in Bamako, Mali," financed by the German Association for Research (DFG). She has published in the fields of medicine and globalization as well as infertility in Mali. She served as guest editor of a special focus issue on *Reproductive Disruptions: Perspectives on African Contexts* for the journal *Curare* (2006).

MARCIA C. INHORN is director of the Center for Middle Eastern and North African Studies at the University of Michigan. Her research interests in medical anthropology encompass many fields, including globalization and health, gender and health, religion and bioethics, ethnomedicine, and comparative medical systems. She has conducted research on infertility and the new reproductive technologies in Egypt over the past twenty years, and her most recent monograph is *Local Babies, Global Science: Gender, Religion, and In Vitro Fertilization in Egypt* (2003).

IQBAL H. JAFFER is a second-year medical student at the University of Queensland in Brisbane, Australia. He holds an honors degree in religious studies and psychology from McMaster University, where he focused on comparative religious medical ethics.

SUSI KREHBIEL KEEFE is a Ph.D. candidate in the Department of Anthropology, Brown University. Her essay in this volume is based on an article that appeared in *Social Science and Medicine* under the title "'Women Do What They Want': Islam and Permanent Contraception in Northern Tanzania"; it received the fourth annual student prize from the Council on Anthropology and Reproduction.

MOHAMMAD HASSAN KHALIL received his Ph.D. from the University of Michigan and is an assistant professor of religious studies at the University of Illinois. He specializes in Islamic theology and has published articles on Islamic ethics, Western analyses of Islamic theology, contemporary conversion narratives, and hadith studies. He is currently working on a monograph on Islamic soteriology.

ABDULAZIZ SACHEDINA is Francis Ball Professor of Religious Studies at the University of Virginia, Charlottesville. Sachedina, who has studied in India, Iraq, Iran, and Canada, has been conducting research and writing in the field of Islamic law, ethics, and theology for more than two decades. In the last ten years he has concentrated on social, political, and biomedical ethics, and his latest book, *Islamic Biomedical Ethics: Theory and Practice,* is due to be published in 2008.

HASAN SHANAWANI is a physician and clinical investigator at the Henry Ford Hospital and Wayne State University School of Medicine, both in Detroit, Michigan. He is a research fellow for the Institute for Social Policy and Understanding (ISPU), a nonprofit research organization studying the impact of minority health on America. He conducts research on the needs of patients from minority ethnic and religious groups during critical illness and at the end of life. He is an ethics adviser to the Islamic Medical Association of North America and senior adviser to the Association of Muslim Health Professionals, both based in Chicago, Illinois.

OTHMAN SHIBLY is a dentist/periodontist who is associate director at the Center for Dental Studies, the State University of New York at Buffalo. He also holds degrees in Islamic and Arabic studies, with a focus on human rights in Islamic laws. He teaches Islamic medical ethics at the medical school of the State University of New York at Buffalo.

JUSTIN STEARNS is an assistant professor of religion at Middlebury College. He has previously written on Muslim perceptions of Christians in al-Andalus for the journal *al-Qantara* (2004) and is currently investigating how law, theology, and science presented varying models of authority in the early modern Muslim world.

STEF VAN DEN BRANDEN received his Ph.D. in theology from the Catholic University of Leuven. His dissertation included an analysis of "e-fatwas" on end-of-life decision-making, and he currently works as a scientific researcher at the Interdisciplinary Centre for the Study of Religion and World at the Catholic University of Leuven.

QUR'AN CITATIONS

INDEX